economics for
business
decisions

economics for

business

decisions

LEROY H. MANTELL

School of Government and Business Administration
The George Washington University

FRANCIS P. SING

School of Business Administration
Georgetown University

McGRAW-HILL BOOK COMPANY

New York	Kuala Lumpur	Panama
St. Louis	London	Rio de Janeiro
San Francisco	Mexico	Singapore
Düsseldorf	Montreal	Sydney
Johannesburg	New Delhi	Toronto

Library of Congress Cataloging in Publication Data

Mantell, Leroy H
    Economics for business decisions.

    Bibliography: p.
        1.   Microeconomics.   2.   Industrial management.
I.   Sing, Francis P., joint author.   II.   Title.
HB171.5.M273   658.4   74-39179
ISBN 0-07-040053-9

**To my parents,
LHM**

**To the memory of my parents,
FPS**

    234567890DODO798765432

This book was set in Spartan by Progressive Typographers, and
printed and bound by R. R. Donnelley & Sons Co. The designer
was Marsha Cohen; the drawings were done by John Cordes, J.
& R. Technical Services, Inc. The editors were Jack R. Crutchfield
and Sally Mobley. Peter D. Guilmette supervised production.

contents

preface

This is a book in descriptive and normative applied microeconomics to which has been added some material in econometrics, finance, location theory, and, in a broad sense, behavioral theory of management. Except for the first and last chapter, the book is organized in the sequence in which one presumes decisions must be made when contemplating the introduction or addition of a new product.

The landmark work in this area is generally acknowledged to be that of Joel Dean, to whom managerial economics owes a great debt. But the field is as yet without specific delineation. Except for a few thrusts toward making it either a study in practical decision making or in econometrics, the content is largely as defined by Dean.

When Dean was writing, the choices were broader than they now are. But not long after his *Managerial Economics,* the separate studies of managerial analysis, decision and game theory, and linear programming rapidly made their appearance. Subsequently, capital budgeting began to receive considerable treatment as part of a general movement toward becoming more quantitative.

It is, of course, much easier to be critical than to be correct, but it is reasonable to believe that the table of contents should not be limited by a particular author's interests. On the other hand, we were quite reluctant to offer a menu of available quantitative analytical techniques under the title of managerial economics. If, for example, the method of linear programming is relevant, it should be included, we believe, because it is logically derived from earlier economic models. Also, we think that pure subject matter or topical approaches are inferior to an approach oriented to the kinds of problems faced by the businessman. It is this line of reasoning that leads us to include material on location analysis and on the interpretation of information.

The questions to which we address ourselves are: To what kinds of business problems is economics relevant? To what kinds of business decisions is the reasoning method of economics important?

Most of us are aware that much of what passes for competition in the United States is product development competition. Businesses today are more market-oriented than production-oriented. Hence the company economist is called upon to advise in matters involving the introduction of new products. If the introduction of new products is a matter of dominant concern, it seems reasonable to organize a book that deals with the usefulness of economics in business decision making by discussing the series of decisions to be made in introducing a new product.

Much of the criticism of standard economic theory appears to center about the inadequacy of the simple motives and factor interrelationships assumed by conventional price theory to explain specific kinds of organizational behavior. But economics studies the ways in which resources are or can be allocated in meeting human needs. Business decisions fundamentally concern the allocation of organizational resources in meeting business needs. Economic doctrine puts forth theories which, if followed, would insure an optimal allocation and describes that behavior and those characteristics of the factors of production which may limit the ability of the firm to attain an optimum.

Where economics offers generalized models of human and organizational behavior, or operates in a certain world, business benefits more from models which provide answers to specific operational and policy problems in an uncertain world. Managerial economics, as we see it, attempts to provide a kind of working level, applied theory of the firm which will amplify short-run entrepreneurial effort, assuming it to be profit-motivated in order to insure the survival of the firm.

Basically, Dean's approach was to take particular operational and conceptual aspects of the business and discuss them from the point of view of the economist and then take observed business phenomena and point out to theoretical economists some aspects that were inadequately described by current theory. In addition, he reported on attempts at deriving empirical versions of economists' cost and production functions.

Later writers have attempted to provide a more operational flavor by introducing cases and some material on decision theory. The problem of tying together the subject matter oriented approach still remains. The decision-making approach is designed to rectify this problem of discontinuity, but it is questionable that it can so long as a purely topical classification is retained. We hope that the structure and sequence we have chosen will bring about a more integrated result.

Although the title is *Economics for Business Decisions,* the emphasis is decidedly on the first three words. This book is intended to confine itself to the economic aspects of business problem solving and management analysis. It does, in addition, enter into a discussion of the decision and the problems which arise in the process of making a decision, using what are by now conventional probability methods. Included also is a treatment of the limits of economic models. Here the dynamics of the business system is stressed.

Our primary concern is with the use of appropriate economic doctrine or reasoning to assist in the solution of a particular class of business problems. The object is to point out ways in which the economist can help shape business policy by using economic analysis alone or in conjunction with known business methods, statistics, or accounting practice and theory.

We have tried to make this an uncomplicated book. Text material has been continually subjected to the two tests of plain writing and the abilities of upper-division undergraduates. Mathematical material has been held to a minimum, and then placed in appendixes in order to aid readability. Little prior knowledge of economics or mathematics is presumed.

We would like to acknowledge the assistance of the following people who have read portions of the manuscript at various stages in its development, with the clear understanding that we alone are responsible for errors both of omission and commission:

Mr. David S. Meiklejohn, member of the Board of Directors and Financial Vice-president, American Machine and Foundry Company; Mr. Edwin G. Delcher, Financial Vice-president, Black and Decker Manufacturing Company; Mr. Nelson G. Spoth, Vice-present and General Manager, TRW, Inc., Dr. Othmar W. Winkler, Associate Professor of Business Administration, Georgetown University; and Dr. Robert L. Holland, Associate Professor of Management Science, The George Washington University.

The clerical assistance of Miss Della A. Andersen (for countless retypings), Miss Michele Lin, and Miss Shirley Chen is also gratefully acknowledged.

Leroy H. Mantell
Francis P. Sing

chapter 1
introduction

Before the late 1930s, economics was devoted largely to the study of the forces which determine the distribution of what we have come to call national income or national product. The sole phenomenon giving expression to those forces was supply and demand. Price was their sole quantitative measure, and the price system was the sole channel of information.

The model which evolved was the result of a developmental process going back more than 100 years, and it worked somewhat as follows.

The prices of goods produced for sale and the prices of the factors of production were the result of supply and demand interacting in two separate sets of markets. The task of the manager was seen as that of acquiring some quantity of the factors of production to produce as much as he could of a uniform product. Production was to be expanded to the point where costs were equated to revenues obtainable by selling the product at a given price. Factor prices also were given, since they were arrived at by impersonal market forces.

The decision-making process, such as it was, had two parts: First, the enterpreneur, attempting to increase output, was to match increments to total cost against increments to total revenue. When the rising cost of successive production increments just equalled increments to total revenue, he was to stop. Secondly, he was to limit further inputs of factors when they ceased to be worth in extra output what they cost. Inputs were adjusted to minimize cost, and output was adjusted to maximize net profit.

The model of the business firm was taken from David Ricardo's English wheat farmer who had one kind of product and whose production process was basically fairly simple. The newly developed applications of differential calculus were able to take advantage of a production process turning out a uniform product and able to be adjusted for any output level, few inputs, and a given price for the finished product. This meant that the price which the producer could pay for his inputs was determined by their efficiency.[1]

Two assumptions formed the foundation of this model: first, that the people involved made decisions which the economist regarded as rational; and second, that the result of this rational behavior would be to maximize income and minimize expense or cost. As time went on, business firms grew ever larger and the symbolic representation of the firm used by economics came to bear only a superficial resemblance to the real thing. And, although economists were able to develop some useful analytical tools, the business world regarded the model as too abstract and discarded the tools as irrelevant. Economics consequently made few contributions to the field of management.

But there was another reason for rejection of economists' contributions. Economic thinking tended basically to concern economizing. However, over much of the period from 1850 on, external opportunities for profit far exceeded the opportunity for increasing net profit by looking within. Economic models could therefore be open to the charge of irrelevance.

Within the ranks of economists, there were some who had serious reservations about the practical usefulness of their profession. The work of J. M. Keynes revolutionized economic thinking about the relationship of government to the level of economic activity. During the same decade, 1930 to 1940, the work of E. H. Chamberlin and of Joan Robinson changed the thinking about the relationship of the business firm to the important economic variables of price, demand, and supply.

In the first instance, economics had now some very relevant things to say about the general level of business activity and the level of national income. Briefly, these things meant that government could take steps to adjust that level, and if it did not, the economic system would not always be able to adjust by itself. In the second, it meant that the tools of economic analysis could be applied to the individual firm to produce results relevant to the world of business as the businessman knew it.

Where the work of Keynes asserted that man was not a helpless creature in the face of economic forces, Chamberlin and Robinson asserted that the businessman was not powerless to effect changes in price so as to maximize profit. Advertising and the idea of competition through quality changes rather than price changes only gave theoretical stature to acts of practical business strategy.

Consequently, there was created a theoretical environment which encouraged the development of a branch of economic analysis in which the businessman was seen as a decision maker, one who could consciously choose

[1] See Robert Dorfman, *Application of Linear Programming to the Theory of the Firm*, University of California Press, Berkeley, 1951, for further elaboration of the origin of the model.

between alternative prices, marketing strategies, advertising levels, scope of operation, and productive processes. Joining price theory — that part of economics concerned with the behavior of consumers, producers, and markets — there came econometrics to measure the economic variables, mathematics to formulate models of interbusiness behavior, group theory to explain intrabusiness behavior, and managerial accounting to provide the necessary information and record-keeping reformulation.

Although Dean gave the field its name of managerial economics, other writers have taken advantage of the development of operations research to emphasize more the decision-making aspects of the field. They chose to emphasize quantitatively expressed problem formulations and results. When managerial economics handles economic problems, of course, it is based most often in price theory. The field is, however, more than applied price or decision theory. It is an attempt to provide a body of doctrine, analytical tools, and a theory of use to the businessman in the ordinary conduct of his business affairs. These affairs, as we will see, often involve variables whose treatment requires more than conventional microeconomics.

MODELS, THEORY, AND FACTS

Economic analysis requires that we develop a model of a firm. How much detail the models should contain and whether it is necessary for models to describe all the facts precisely in order to be able to draw valid conclusions are still matters of contention among economists.

Abstract models in the sciences are quite familiar to us, and we feel comfortable with them. In the social sciences, however, models convey an air of unreality and it is easy to believe the conclusions suspect — to sense a need for more facts.

The social sciences deal, furthermore, with human behavior, and therefore theorizing can be a risky business. But transformation from the real world is quite legitimate, and the conclusions are not impaired simply because all the "facts" are not there. Of course, the burden of proof must be on the model builder to show that conclusions may indeed be drawn without a one-to-one correspondence with the real world.

Simplifying assumptions, often useful for the analysis of short-run problems, turn out to be inapplicable to long-run behavior. There has been much difficulty, for example, in understanding the proper role of profits as a motivating force in economic theory.[2] The difficulty has arisen because it is evident that many business decisions are made in apparent disregard of the economists' assumption that maximum profits are desirable.

[2] Robert N. Anthony, "The Trouble with Profit Maximization," *Harvard Business Review*, vol. 38, no. 6, pp. 126–134, Nov.–Dec., 1960.

Most times the difficulty is removed when it is seen that this decision rule is not meant to be inflexible. It is rather meant to be interpreted loosely, involving both the short and the long run rather than the short run alone. But this is one of the difficulties with expressing economic concepts in terms of a mathematical structure which (1) requires for a solution that we maximize or minimize something, or (2) calls for determinate solutions.

Another potential source of difficulty is the rationality assumption to which we have already referred. Many things can be considered rational only from a particular point of view or within a particular frame of reference. One can, therefore, understand some of the conclusions economists draw only if one uses the same definition of rational behavior. The decisions one might make and the conclusions one might draw from a given set of business facts would differ, for example, depending on whether an economist's price theory or a behavioral theory of the firm were the frame of reference.

POINTS OF VIEW

The economist originally was interested in the business firm because it employed factors of production, had a function to perform which contributed to the well-being of the nation. Later he was interested because the firm exercised a key role in allocating national income. The economist today plays an important role in the business firm itself, but most often from an external or "macro" point of view. That is to say, the business executive is concerned about future levels of business activity and wants the economist in most instances to use his knowledge of economic and business indicators to forecast future sales. With the emphasis on mergers and combinations, the economist finds much activity also in providing needed analyses of the effects on competition of any proposed activity in this area.

Managerial economics, however, represents an application of economics to the internal decision-making processes of the firm as it makes plans to allocate resources and convert inputs. Future levels of business activity are important, but only as a constraint or limit within which the firm must operate.

One aspect of managerial economics focuses attention on the profitability implications of decisions. Profitability means, of course, maximizing the difference between total cost and total revenue. Managerial economics looks at those decisions which affect this numerical difference. There are several economic concepts which may be brought into play, since they vitally affect a manager's attitude toward short-run profits. They are significant in that they represent a departure from much conventional business thinking or require the use of concepts which differ from those on which business data systems may be based. These economic concepts differ in meaning or implication from those of other disciplines, notably accounting, in dealing with the same topics. The difference is more important than may appear because accounting, traditionally, has been the source of business decision-making information.

THE NOTION OF PRESENT VALUE

First of all, from the revenue point of view, there is the concept that requires that all incomes be discounted to the present, since that is where the decision has to be made. A dollar of income today is worth more than the same dollar scheduled to be obtained in the future. The reason is that were the dollar to be in hand today, it could be invested to earn income which, when added to the original amount, would result in a principal worth more than just that dollar.

If the annual rate of interest, or the productivity of capital, is 5 percent today, a dollar invested today would be worth $1.05 in one year. Conversely, then, a dollar due in one year is worth less than $1.00 today.

A managerial decision concerning the acquisition of an asset which will provide a revenue at some time in the future must take into account this difference based on the productivity of capital. To defer the acquisition of revenue is to postpone the opportunity of investing it in interest-bearing or profit-producing activity. Consequently, revenue to be received in the future must be worth less today. It is worth precisely that amount which, if received today, would, if invested at the prevailing or expected rate of interest, equal the expected future revenue. In other words, if money is worth 5 percent, the present value of $100 to be received two years hence is $90.70 because that amount, if invested at 5 percent compounded annually, would yield $100 in two years.

OPPORTUNITY COST

Strange as it may seem, the notion of opportunity cost is concerned not so much with cost as with revenue. Opportunity cost is unique in that it represents the revenue lost as a result of a decision to adopt one course of action rather than another. The opportunity cost associated with a decision to be self-employed is the return or income which could have been obtained in the highest-paying alternative occupation. The opportunity costs of assets used to produce an item for use within a business is the revenue which could have been earned were the assets used in the best possible way to produce an item for sale.

Opportunity cost is not the kind of cost that accountants record, because, as we have seen, it represents a decrease or change in the total revenue resulting from a particular decision about how assets are to be used or inputs employed. This peculiarity can possibly best be understood by referring once more to the quantity to be maximized in the decision. When viewed from the point of view of the difference between revenue and cost, a decrease in revenue is no different from an increase in cost. Consequently, a decision which will reduce revenue is the same as a decision to incur a cost of equal amount. If we assume that total revenue represents full utilization of assets in employments representing optimal returns, then any reallocation of assets which results in a return less than optimal or less than maximum is the same as incurring some additional cost which serves to diminish net profit.

Opportunity cost is *not* the difference between the revenue of an alternative and the revenue received. In other words, if the revenue forgone by selecting a particular course of action is $10,000 and the net revenue obtained at present is $9,000, the difference does not represent the opportunity cost. The cost is still $10,000 because this is the amount by which total revenue is diminished by the decision to select the alternative other than this. By selecting the alternative, revenue is now increased $9,000 it is true, but this merely represents the revenue side of the transaction. In summary, the opportunity cost is $10,000, the revenue is $9,000, and the net loss on the decision is $1,000; but this amount is not opportunity cost because it is not a cost figure. It is the loss resulting from the decision.

RELEVANCE OF COSTS

Opportunity cost represents one of a number of costs which may be relevant at the time a decision is to be made. Precisely which costs are relevant of course depends on the factors involved. If, for example, the decision concerns the short run only, then the long-run implications may not be relevant. A decision to accept a one-time order for merchandise may hinge only on whether or not the order can cover the variable or out-of-pocket costs incurred in connection with its manufacture and make some contribution to overhead and fixed costs. This is a decision involving the short run; the long-run implications, while they must be considered, may or may not affect the outcome as they would if the business transaction represented a long-term commitment. In the long run, all businesses must cover their fixed costs and overhead. In the short run there is no such requirement.

Of course, we are not here considering the probable reaction of rivals to this breach of normal pricing practice, merely the dollars-and-cents aspect. The point is that fixed costs have arisen in response to earlier decisions, and whether or not we decide to accept an order for merchandise, those costs will be incurred. They are expenses of being in business and have no necessary relevance to output, except in the long run. Provided no increase in fixed expenses is needed and the assets are available, being not otherwise employed so that their opportunity costs are zero, the relevant costs in connection with a new order are the costs that are incurred because of it. They are the costs directly caused by its production — the incremental costs.

Against these incremental costs, we must balance the incremental revenues to be obtained from selling the merchandise. Once again, our attention is directed to the impact of the decision on the difference between costs and revenues. Fixed costs are not altered by a decision to accept or not to accept an order, provided the facilities exist.

THE EQUIMARGINAL PRINCIPLE

One definition of economics is that it is the science of allocating scarce resources among unlimited ends. Business decision making is then highly economic by its nature. Nearly all of it has to do with the allocation of the resources of the firm, either in the present or in the future. In the latter case, we call it planning.

In an economic sense, an optimal decision will maximize the difference between revenue and cost. But if this decision making concerns allocation of resources, there must be some rule to follow which will insure that the distribution is one which results in maximum net revenue. That rule is called the equimarginal principle. Briefly, the rule states that each scarce resource will be allocated among competing ends, so that the incremental return is equal in each use.

If the resource to be allocated is a production input, then it will be allocated so that the output of the firm is a maximum and costs are a minimum. This result will occur when the inputs are distributed so that the value returned from each application of an input is equal in terms of the dollar value of the output obtained. As another author has put it, the delivery boy should be retained so long as he is worthy of his hire.

DIMINISHING RETURNS

At this point there are some concepts which ought to be mentioned but which will not be studied in detail until later in the book. For example, adding more inputs does not always insure an equal or even a proportionate increase in output. The notion of diminishing returns is well enough known so that reference to it here will not be misunderstood. All inputs are subject to diminishing returns beyond a certain point if one input is fixed in amount. If all inputs are allowed to increase, then the returns from their employment may or may not diminish, depending on the nature of the process. Economists believe, however, that at some point or another, marginal or incremental returns will begin to diminish.

The problem posed by balancing incremental or marginal returns when changing input amounts or mixes is essentially one of insuring that no other combination will provide a greater total product. We must consider that all outputs resulting from equal input contributions increase at a decreasing rate. Hence, if we increase the use of one input and hold the usage of others at the same rate as before, the incremental returns from the variable input will diminish.

This diminishing marginal physical productivity of inputs is what causes the problem. Since all inputs are subject to this kind of diminution, we must balance the extent to which each is used against its separate contribution to total output. We get the right balance when we have maximized total output or have the most efficient production process. The decision is made not by considering production efficiency alone, however, but by taking into account the prices or costs of the inputs. We will balance these prices against the benefit achieved from their use.

SOME ADDITIONAL RELATIONSHIPS

Thus far we have discussed the need to discount incomes to the present, the notion of alternative or opportunity cost, the difference in point of view when considering the time period over which decisions are to be made effective, the fact that total costs may not always be involved in a decision but that incremental or marginal costs may be relevant, and finally, the idea that economic inputs to a production process must be allocated so as to equalize the marginal returns in each use.

Another relationship which is important for an understanding of the economic aspects of a business enterprise may be called the *die-away* curve. This kind of relation is often used to illustrate the rate at which sales of a product fall off when there is no advertising or sales promotion. It is assumed that, as time proceeds, some amount or attained level begins to decrease because no attempt is made to maintain or increase the level. Technically this die-away is termed *entropy* and refers to the tendency of things to decompose or deteriorate over time. The rate of deterioration assumed by the die-away curve is generally taken to be the natural logarithm base e raised to the power of some negative constant, multiplied by the time period concerned.[3] The value computed never disappears entirely; it just diminishes at a constant percentage. It approaches zero but never quite gets there.

This kind of relationship is often used to describe the benefit obtained from an asset. An example might be the stream of revenues a motion picture firm may receive from a given stock of films. The revenue decreases at some fixed percentage rate. The life of the asset can be defined as the number of years within which some proportion of the total potential revenue will be received. Sometimes the relationship is used to describe the behavior of consumer response to a product introduced without benefit of continued advertising. With no advertising beyond an original introduction, sales will be lost over time as consumers switch to other products.

A relationship used quite successfully by operations researchers involves

---

[3] e^{-at} is the die-away factor for cases where the rate of decrease is proportional to the size of the thing decreasing. References may be found under the heading Exponential Distribution.

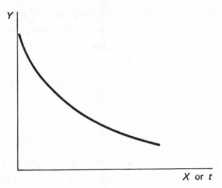

Figure 1-1. The die-away curve

asking, in effect, whether one has to be right or successful all of the time. If warehouse capacity is built so that stock is on hand to meet customer needs, it substantially affects our requirements if we assert that we must always have stock on hand to meet every customer order within forty-eight hours of receipt. If we are willing to meet perhaps 85 percent of those needs within forty-eight hours or are willing to stretch the time period to perhaps seventy-two hours, our requirements would be much less.

The relationship itself is termed the Poisson curve and it works something like this. If L is the expected number of arrivals or occurrences in a period of time, the probability of that number actually taking place is described by a kind of die-away curve similar to that we have described above. This curve attests to the decreasing probability of more than just a few occurrences in a single time period.

The Poisson curve has been used effectively in calculating the size of stocks where the demand for goods is caused by random failures in stocks. It has also been used where the calculated response is a function of the ability of an individual or of an organization to learn or to adapt. Distribution-cost analysts have known about this phenomenon for some time. They have rightly insisted that there is no sense in devoting the same amount of service to all customers, because not all customers are equally profitable or provide the same sales volume. In fact, 20 percent may well account for about 80 percent of the business, while the remaining 80 percent will be responsible for only 20 percent of generated business. Military logistics people speak of "high-value" items. When they do, they are in effect saying that since a small percent of their items account for a large percent of the dollar value of inventory or of shipments, they will concentrate on these. In so doing, they will take care of perhaps 80 percent or some large proportion of the problem and avoid devoting a disproportionate amount of time and expense on a small payoff. In other words, it is better, they

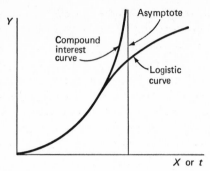

Figure 1-2. The compound interest and the logistic curves

say, to be right 80 percent of the time at a fraction of the cost than 100 percent of the time and raise the cost tremendously. Peter F. Drucker calls this phenomenon the *law of proportionate effect.*

Finally, there is the often used logistic relationship that deals with the life cycle of various organisms or event patterns. The logistic curve, applied by Raymond Pearl, L. J. Reed, S. S. Kuznets, and others in economic and biologic data, was shown by Pearl to describe the growth of insects in an environment with limited resources. The curve is S-shaped, testifying to an initially slow rate of growth but increasing at an increasing rate, followed by a decrease in the rate of growth beyond some point of inflection. Following the decrease in the growth rate, the curve assumes an ultimate stabilization at the top of the S.

If we change the sign of the exponent of the equation for the die-away curve referred to earlier, we will get a compound interest curve with ever-increasing slope, which becomes asymptotic to a vertical. If we then insert a limiting term so that the curve acquires a point of inflection, we have the logistic.[4]

The logistic curve often is used to describe the rate of performance of organizations or the rate at which people learn new methods or techniques. It is useful in estimating the degree to which anticipated costs will be attained. It is also used as a product-life curve, in which sales volume levels are shown against the time period in which the product is introduced and marketed.

PLAN OF THE BOOK

The book is organized around the kinds of problems with which a firm must deal, especially in introducing a new product. We use a procedure somewhat analogous to Du Pont's Venture Analysis shown in Figure 1-3. We begin, how-

[4] See, for example, Harold T. Davis, *The Theory of Econometrics,* The Principia Press, Bloomington, Ind., 1941, pp. 209–239, and Ludwig von Bertalanffy, *General System Theory,* George Braziller, Inc., New York, 1968, pp. 60–63.

ever, with demand forecasting, on the assumption that estimation of a potential demand is more important than any other parameter. We include discussion of the external market environment in which the firm will compete, and demand analysis in which we seek to find a basis for altering the consumer demand for the product and finding a basis for later decisions as to pricing policy. The technical aspects come next and include cost concepts, covering a discussion of those costs which will be relevant to decisions whether or not to produce and in what amounts, and production functions in which the underlying physical characteristics of the business are laid bare. It is these characteristics which form the basis of cost estimates which were discussed above. The method of linear programming is discussed, and its relationship to earlier methods of economic analysis is shown, as well as the way in which production decisions are made. We come to the not too surprising conclusion that a decision that is efficient from a linear programming point of view is efficient also using the older techniques of marginal analysis.

The next section deals with pricing and price discrimination. Pricing decisions determine the prices which will be charged. The effect of the competitive environment and the interaction of pricing decisions and demand estimation is also covered.

Since, in the final analysis, the acceptability of a new product depends on its profitability, the next section deals with profit measurement and control. The various concepts of profit are discussed, together with methods of measure-

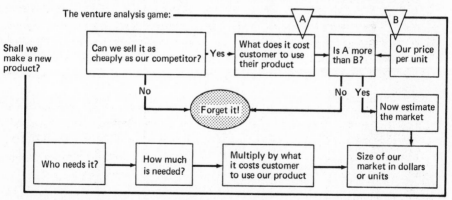

Figure 1-3. Venture analysis. Du Pont has made up a computer program about this model in order to provide answers to questions such as: What will be my share of the market if I raise prices 2¢ a pound? And, if my market share drops 2 percent, what moves can I make with prices, production schedules, and marketing strategies in order to maintain our earnings level? Venture analysis is defined as a "systematic and quantitative discipline for organizing and processing information to guide business decisions." Venture analysis is geared to supply the best possible figures so that each layer of management up to the executive committee can decide where investment dollars can be spent most effectively. The historic role of venture analysis has been to help evaluate the potential of new products until they go commercial. (Source: "Du Pont's Answer Machine," *Business Week*, Dec. 20, 1969, pp. 68–69.)

ment including return on investment. Profit planning and its several methods are taken up, followed by chapters on capital budgeting and the capital expenditure decision. Here we are concerned with questions of expansion or replacement of capital assets and the economic bases for the allocation of capital funds. The present-value concept and uncertainty are incorporated in the discussion, as are comparisons of internal and external rates of return. Since investment decisions often hinge on the impact of certain decisions on the price of the securities of the firm in capital markets, the relationship to the composition of capital is discussed also.

The most significant capital budgeting decision is often a location decision. A new product or expansion of output of a present product often demands that new facilities be built, often at the new location. The next chapter, then, examines something of the economic theory of location and analyzes why firms locate in particular places. Then we take up the relation of location to pricing policy, methods of regional analysis, and the use of particular analytical techniques, including linear programming as it helps determine plant or warehouse location.

The last chapter deals with the decision itself and the way in which decisions are made. The process is discussed in terms of the data environment and the system environment, with particular emphasis on the problem of lags in response. The role of expectations and the evaluation of information are examined, and the need to recognize the policy implications of a problem is stressed. We end with a discussion of the meaning of an effective decision.

Review Questions

1. What basic decision rule did classical economics believe characterized the business process?
2. What behavioral assumptions were basic to the economists' decision model?
3. Why did the economic model not find acceptance among businessmen before 1930?
4. What changes were brought about by J. M. Keynes, E. H. Chamberlin, and Joan Robinson?
5. Christmas savings clubs generally are plans by which banks and similar institutions accept payments to non-interest-bearing accounts. Does the notion of present value alter your opinion about these clubs in any way?
6. What is the opportunity cost of a college education for a returning veteran who will receive $180 per month as a benefit while in school?
7. A retailer is having a clearance sale of inventory at prices as low as cost.

Would it be worth his while to accept a special one-time order for a "big-ticket" item at a price below normal? What costs might be relevant here? Is opportunity cost involved?

8. Why is business decision making economic by its nature?
9. Which economic relationship is involved if we hire a salesman to work on a commission basis?
10. Which economic relationship is involved in a decision to sell nails by the pound? Use gold-plated automobile door handles? Decline to use hand-woven material in men's shirts?

Case 1. University Data Processing

University Data Processing Company is a computer service firm specializing in pay roll processing and similar business services. Founded in 1957 by three computer company salesmen, UDP began operations in a rented loft using cardpunch equipment. Sales reached $1 million in 1963. Five years later revenues were reported in excess of $15 million and for the first nine months of 1969 were reported at $17.5 million. For the years 1967, 1968, and 1969 to date, revenues have gained on the average of 85 percent and internal growth is estimated at 40 percent annually.

QUESTIONS

1. Based on the material given in Chapter 1, what crude estimate might one make of the potential sales volume of this company?
2. What factors might affect the validity of your answer?

Case 2. The Accountant's Valuation Problem

An accountant is faced with the problem of determining the value of a stock of motion picture films in connection with the acquisition of an old-line Hollywood studio. The films have little if any present value for theater showing, but it appears that a trend exists which would make them useful for TV rerun during the late shows and in the summer.

The stock of films is worth $100,000 in immediate rental value for the next thirteen weeks. So far as he has been able to determine, its value for the succeeding thirteen-week period would be about 37 percent of the initial showing period.

QUESTION

1. What estimate should the accountant place on the stock of films, assuming there would be little interest six contract periods beyond the present? (Hint: If tables of e^{-x} are not available, a plot of x, log y should be a straight line.)

Suggested Readings

Chamberlin, Edward: *The Theory of Monopolistic Competition*, Harvard University Press, Cambridge, Mass., 1939, pp. 3–10.

Churchman, C. West, Russell L. Ackoff, and E. Leonard Arnoff: *Introduction to Operations Research*, John Wiley & Sons, Inc., New York, 1957, pp. 157–192.

Friedman, Milton: "The Methodology of Positive Economics," in *Essays in Positive Economics*, The University of Chicago Press, Chicago, 1953, vol. 3.

Galbraith, John Kenneth: "The Language of Economics," *Fortune*, December, 1962, reprinted in Richard E. Mulcahy (ed.), *Readings in Economics from Fortune*, 3d ed., Holt, Rinehart and Winston, Inc., New York, 1967.

Harris, Seymour E.: *John Maynard Keynes*, Charles Scribner's Sons, New York, 1955.

Heilbroner, Robert L.: *The Worldly Philosophers*, Simon & Schuster, Inc., New York, 1953. See chap. IV, The Gloomy World of Parson Malthus and David Ricardo; chap. IX, The Sick World of John Maynard Keynes; and chap. X, The Modern World.

Knight, Frank H.: *On the History and Method of Economics*, The University of Chicago Press, Chicago, 1956, chaps. I and II.

Machlup, Fritz: "Theories of the Firm: Marginalist, Behavioral, Managerial," *The American Economic Review*, vol. 57, no. 1, pp. 1–33, March, 1967.

Marshall, Alfred: *Principles of Economics*, 8th ed., Macmillan & Co., Ltd., London, 1938, book I, book III, chap. V.

McGuire, Joseph W.: *Theories of Business Behavior*, Prentice-Hall, Inc., Englewood Cliffs, N.J., 1964, pp. 1–57.

Miller, David W., and Martin K. Starr: *Executive Decisions and Operations Research*, Prentice-Hall, Inc., Englewood Cliffs, N.J., 1960, chaps. 7 and 8.

Wicksteed, Philip H.: "The Scope and Method of Political Economy," reprinted in *Readings in Price Theory*, Richard D. Irwin, Inc., Homewood, Ill., 1952, pp. 3–26.

part 1
demand
analysis

chapter 2
the external market
environment

In this chapter we will look first at one of a possible number of market environments in which there are many possible sellers and many possible buyers for a uniform product. One by one, we will relax these assumptions until we have examined the whole range of competitive environments in which the firm may be operating.

The external environment in which the firm operates is composed of the parties to whom it desires to sell and rival suppliers desiring to sell to the same parties. If there are large numbers of buyers and sellers, prices will be fixed and beyond the control of any single firm or individual. The fewer the number of sellers, the more control each individual seller can exert over the price. Control over price may be exercised by sellers varying the amounts they wish to offer, in which case we assume the amounts buyers wish to take does not change. Or we may assume that the amount sellers wish to put on the market is constant and that buyers vary the amount they wish to purchase.

In our society, sellers desiring to increase the demand for their product often differentiate it from that of rival suppliers. To the extent to which they are able to attract buyers by qualitative differences in the total product offered, they may achieve a degree of potential control over price. Since they may exercise this control only at the risk of losing customers who do not think the qualitative difference is worth the price increase, it is customary to depict the action as one serving to make the quantity bought vary inversely as price.

In this chapter we will also consider the effect of steps taken to differentiate the product so as to remove it from the effects of price competition. When product differentiation has been successful in establishing the unique qualities of the product, or of the seller, it does not mean that the product has no available substitutes. It merely means that, within given circumstances, many buyers having free choice prefer one to others. Under such conditions, the reaction of rivals becomes important and the chapter will next consider the "kinked" demand curve as a convenient device for explaining this kind of competition.

Many times, rivals will react to price competition by terming it "cutthroat." If the norm is nonprice competition, most firms in the industry will have established a price structure which is internally consistent for each firm and externally consistent considering all other firms and their offerings and prices. For one firm to violate this structure is to upset the rather carefully arranged equilibrium which has been established by the others. As a result, they will tend to regard the move as predatory. In general, economists have, in the past, regarded price competition as the only admissible kind. Businessmen clearly have other views, and we shall next discuss these differences.

The use of price cutting as a tactical weapon to eliminate rivals received much attention during the 1930s. But predatory price cutting may be an inefficient way of securing market dominance. We will next, therefore, take up a recent analysis which concludes that merger and acquisition makes more economic sense.

The earlier assumption that the market environment consisted of many possible sellers and many possible buyers also presumes that sellers are able to sell their entire output without affecting the prevailing price. This is because they are relatively small with respect to the size of the market. Buyers are also presumed to have needs which are not so large individually as to influence the market situation. Under conditions of product differentiation and merger and acquisition, however, and given that not all firms are able to adjust to their environments with equal ease, it is necessary to drop the assumption of equal small firms. We then enter the realm of what is known as market structure or industrial organization.

Finally, as an appendix to this chapter, there is a discussion of two examples of current market structure.

We begin now with price competition, under what is known as conditions of pure and perfect markets.

COMPETITION AMONG MANY SELLERS

Where there are many possible sellers and many possible buyers and a product that has many substitutes, no seller will have the ability to alter price. Hence, prices quoted will tend to be taken as given. Transactions will tend to be at that figure, since no buyer will accept a higher price from any one seller when he can go to another to get the market price, and no seller will care to reduce his price since he can always find a buyer at the prevailing level.

If there is adequate information, so that changes in the availability of

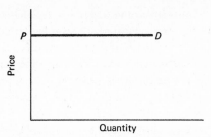

Figure 2-1. Demand curve facing the firm under pure and perfect competition.

supply, prices, and eagerness of buyers are readily known to all, and where also it is possible for firms to enter or to leave the field readily and without penalty, then the price will tend to be uniform and stable. It is likely under some conditions that the price may oscillate more or less about a single value, but this depends on the nature of the system.

The more expensive it is to obtain market information or the greater the penalties associated with the entry of new firms, the more likely it is that different prices will be able to exist in a market for the same product at the same time. With these elements present, market segmentation is likely, as are higher-than-normal profits.

The kind of market described in this section is most likely if the product is homogeneous and uncomplicated. That is to say, any one item may be substituted for any other item, and the consumer can judge its quality for himself. We also assume that he behaves rationally in an economic sense.

The market structure and conditions are characteristic of what is known as pure and perfect competition. The structure is considered to be pure because there are no monopoly elements present. It is perfect because of the absolute availability of market information. The relationship between the market price and the quantity which any single firm may sell at any instant or in the very short run is generally described by means of the chart given in Figure 2-1.

PRODUCT DIFFERENTIATION

Because freedom of entry continually drives revenues closer to costs as more sellers compete for a limited number of buyers, some sellers attempt to assert or build in qualitative differences in their product. Steps include branding for identification, minor advertising, and other sales promotion techniques. These promotional activities attempt to create buyer loyalty to a single producer, so that he is removed from the competitive arena. At the same time, actual product improvement in varying degrees may take place. Product differentiation appears most active, however, where the consumer is unable to detect any difference between the product of the advertiser and those of his competitors. It is most effective when the consumer does not have the technical or scientific means of judging the comparative merits of the products offered to him, or where use of the product is associated in some way with some other aspiration levels the consumer may have. In such instances, maintenance of the price at levels above the competitive level comes to signify a difference in quality which may or may not exist.

The extent of buyer loyalty can be measured by the difference in prices between the differentiated product and others. One way of looking at this kind of price differential is that it is the price of market information not available to the buyer. Because it is a penalty for lack of market information, competition under such circumstances is referred to as imperfect.

The relationship between the price at which the differentiated product is sold and the quantity it is possible to sell at various prices differs from the relationship described as perfect competition because the latter assumes it is impossible for any amounts to be sold unless the price is decreased to a competitive level. Figure 2-2 shows how the demand curve facing the individual firm under pure and perfect competition is changed when the product is differentiated. If we assume other firms enter the field in order to compete, the demand curve D of this producer may fall to D', to indicate that he is selling the same amount but only at the new lower market price brought about by the new competition taking a share of the market.

Assume now one producer is unwilling to agree to the new competitive environment and decides instead to differentiate his product. If he is able to maintain his former price level, it is because he has succeeded in differentiating his offering. However, it is also likely that the amount he is able to sell is somewhat less. This is a plausible conclusion since, had he not differentiated his product, he would have had no sales at all at the old price.

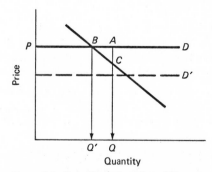

Figure 2-2. The effect of product differentiation on the demand curve.

If he reduces his price to the level of his rivals who do not differentiate their products, then he will sell at least as much as they, but probably more. The relationship between the prices charged by the differentiator and the quantity it is possible for him to sell has been superimposed on the demand curve of the typical pure and perfect competitor. Point B in Figure 2-2 represents the price-quantity relationship which would obtain were he to maintain his price at the cost of a quantity reduction from the original quantity at A. Point C represents the price-quantity relationship were he to reduce his price sufficiently to restore the original volume of sales. Connecting the points, we see that the demand curve facing our imperfect competitor is sloped downward and to the right. Such a downward-sloping curve is characteristic of all forms of monopoly control over a product, whether through product differentiation or actual monopoly.

The stronger the ability of the firm to differentiate its product, the more likely it is that point B in our diagram will move to the right so that the firm has lost fewer customers than before, even though still undersold in price. Should this occur, the line connecting points B and C will be more steep. So we see that the steepness of the demand curve is related to the degree to which the product is differentiated. Conversely, when there is little or no differentiation, the demand curve facing the individual seller tends to be horizontal.

If there is no differentiation, it means that the consumer believes the product of one seller to be no different from that of any other. No competitor will raise his price because no one will follow his lead, and he will not lower his price so long as he believes he can sell his entire output at the market price.

If now we introduce the notion of imperfection into the market, then the seller might have reason to doubt he could sell as much as he wished at the market price. He might in fact believe that he served a rather limited market and that in it there was ample productive capacity. Under these conditions, he might well consider a price reduction in order to increase sales. There is, how-ever, the implicit assumption that his output and that of others in the market are substitutable. If they are not substitutes, our price cutter would not have had to be concerned about the market at all.

If the products are substitutes, a price reduction will be met by price reductions of competitors. If they are not, then quite naturally a price reduction can be made without fear of retaliation. Whether or not the reactions of rivals need to be taken into account depends on the amount of information consumers have as to the degree to which the products are substitutes. Where consumers believe there are no substitutes, the price of a commodity or product may vary widely with little change in the amount demanded. In other words, the demand is said to be inelastic.

When this belief is associated with a single supplier, that supplier is said to have a monopoly. If in fact substitutes exist, but not all consumers believe it to be so, then the monopoly results from successful product differentiation and may be attacked by competitors advancing the idea that their products are substitutes. This process is, of course, monopolistic competition: the competition of monopolists.

While the rivalry of pure competitors revolves around price since all products are complete substitutes for one another, the competition of monopolists, on the other hand, revolves about both product and price.

Sometimes the product is basically incapable of being differentiated from substitutes, as for example where a form of metal ingot or a fuel is involved. In such cases, competition of monopolists is likely to take the form of selling the seller rather than the product. This is especially true where consumer knowledge is adequate, as for example in industrial products where consumers may test the product. Because it is consumer knowledge as to substitutability with other products that causes the seller to take the reactions of rivals into account, where basic industrial goods are concerned, the reactions of rivals may be expected to play an even more important part in competitive action.

THE KINKED DEMAND CURVE

The generally accepted device for explaining price-demand relationships, where the reaction of rivals is more important or as important as the reaction of buyers, is the "kinked" demand curve. Figure 2-3 shows a demand curve D facing a monopolistic competitor where consumer knowledge is adequate but not complete, and hence demand is responsive to changes in price. Since competi-

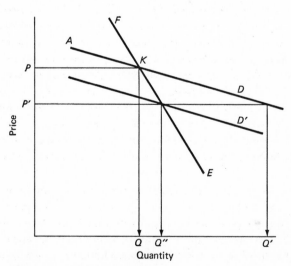

Figure 2-3. The kinked demand curve.

tion does not center on price so much as on the quality of the product or the reputation of the seller, there tends to be a consensus as to price at any one time. This consensus we will denote in Figure 2-3 by P, the going price.

Let us suppose that, for one reason or another, whether a desire to attain a larger share of the market, or simply that management has decided it is necessary to become aggressive, the seller decides to try price competition in an effort to increase Q, the quantity sold, to Q'. Therefore, he reduces his price to P'.

Given the demand curve D facing him, our seller would have every reason to believe that his tactic would be successful in increasing his total revenue ($P \times Q$) to $P'Q'$. His competitors are free to take either of the following actions: increase sales promotional efforts designed to sell the product or the seller, or lower their price to meet his. The more consumers are aware that the products are really substitutes, the more they will tend to buy at the lowest price. Consequently, rival strategy will not exclude the possibility of competing through price. Price competition will therefore tend to occur more often in items which are basically fungible. Retaliation through price cutting is likely where the market is limited or where any one seller can exert a considerable impact on the market. This can occur when the number of monopolistic competitors has been reduced to an identifiable number, that is to say, where there is oligopoly. It is for this reason that price cutting rarely occurs, since if all reduce their prices, then no one benefits.

Figure 2-3 shows a case where the action of all competitors in meeting a price cut has meant that the actual response to a price P' is not the new quantity Q' but the reduced quantity Q''. All rivals of course have had similar reactions, and no one has benefited from the price reduction. The demand curve facing our firm is now at D'. The net result is that prices become once again stable, and competition reverts to product and seller promotion. The quantity each seller has disposed of is greater than before in response to a lower market price generally. Because the actual demand Q'' is less than the presumed Q', the price reduction fails to bring about a more than compensating increase in quantity, and there may possibly even be a decline in revenue. As the reaction occurred because all competitors viewed the products as substitutes, it is incorrect to assume the existence of a new demand curve to the right of the kink, namely KE, more steeply sloped than D, since that would assume less substitutability than before.

If we consider the possibility of our producer raising his price, the kink becomes more evident. He will raise his price if he can ignore substitutes. But this assumes a steep demand curve, possibly KF. Since no one will follow suit, as competitors may believe substitutability to exist, the true curve may well be lower, or KA. In any case, the demand curve has a definite kink and the shape of the curves to either side is affected by the extent of product differentiation, the presence of substitutes, the amount of market information present, and the size and expandability of the market.

OTHER CONCEPTS OF COMPETITION

Obviously the term competition may be given a variety of meanings depending upon the point of view of the person defining it, the nature of the product or service, the structure of the market, and the purpose to be served by the definition. One of the serious gaps in communication between the economist and the businessman has occurred because of differences in their view as to what constitutes competition. Obviously, also, the concept of competition held by the economist, if confined to price competition under conditions of pure and perfect markets, is inadequate to explain product- and seller-oriented promotion. For an adequate explanation, we must turn to the concepts of imperfect and monopolistic competition, which incorporate promotional activity on the part of sellers.

CUTTHROAT COMPETITION

Many businessmen equate price competition with so-called cutthroat competition. If it is remembered that the norm is nonprice competition, then any businessman resorting to price competition is generally facing severe provocation. That is to say, it requires a considerable stimulus for the businessman to reduce prices in order to increase revenues if he is aware of the probable reaction of rivals. In most cases that stimulus is in the nature of unused capacity. It is also possible that decreased costs or the possibility of increasing returns following higher production levels could provide the necessary stimulus. A businessman faced with unused capacity is necessarily operating at higher costs than intended when the firm was designed. The costs are higher because fixed expenses are distributed over less production volume than was intended. If the seller believes that any increase in volume will reduce average costs so that greater total net profit will occur even if a lower price is required to obtain the increase in volume, he may decide to risk the retaliation of rivals. He is, of course, counting on the inability of competitors to produce at average unit costs as low as his.

From the point of view of the competitor, however, the price cutter is a threat because, not being able to lower costs, the price reduction he has been forced to make simply reduces total net profit. Hence he believes his throat is being cut.

In the economists' concept of pure and perfect competition, price warfare of this kind is inadmissible inasmuch as the concept requires not only that the output of each seller be very small in comparison with the whole, but that he be able to sell as much as he wishes at the going price.[1] There are some very special

---

[1] This is provided he can bid successfully for the additional amounts of factors needed to construct additional plant capacity able to produce at present or lower costs.

assumptions regarding costs of operation, market, and capital structure which must be made, however, if one is to draw the conclusion that price warfare would not occur under pure and perfect competition. Since these special assumptions do not apply to the real world, it is somewhat unfair to draw the conclusion, as many do, that pure and perfect competition is desirable as a means of preventing price warfare of this destructive type. It is, after all, one thing to use the concepts of pure and perfect competition as a model which leads to certain conclusions but another to assume that, because the conclusions are desirable, they are applicable. The model has insufficient detail to provide meaningful answers.

Pure competition assumes, for example, that resources flow into and out of industries (however these are defined) in response to changes in consumer demand for the products of the firms comprising the industries. Where resources are easily transferable from one industry to another, the harmful effects of economic dislocation are minimized. Where the capital structure of the firm is such that alternative uses of the assets are few or would bring a lower return elsewhere, a businessman would be likely to reduce prices in an effort to stay in business. This condition is especially true if the ratio of fixed to variable capital is high. A competitor under these conditions, employing more direct or variable costs and less fixed capital, might well feel that he was being subjected to cutthroat competition. Yet this condition is indeed compatible with pure and perfect competition.

Many times the competitor has reason to believe that the purpose of price competition by a rival is to eliminate him. This belief is reinforced if the prices set by the rival are unprofitable from the point of view of the first competitor. It is widely believed that once the competitor has been driven out of business, prices will once more return to former "profitable" levels. Sometimes discriminatory pricing is employed in which rivals set different prices in different areas or markets for the same product.

The notion that price competition is "unfair" arises because members of the industry or market concerned believe they must meet the price reduction or suffer a loss of business. And, if they do reduce prices, then nothing has really been accomplished except that all competitors now operate with reduced profit margins, as we saw when we discussed the kinked demand curve.

Nonprice promotion at the retail level generally means institutional promotion, i.e., advertising the store and its stock selections. At the manufacturer or producer level, on the other hand, nonprice promotion is generally oriented toward the product. When price competition occurs, it generally takes place at the point of sale, which most often is at the retail level. Competitive efforts of producers are rarely price oriented, however, and then only when the retail aspect is relatively unimportant and consumer information is good, as in basic commodities or producers' goods. In the latter case, prices tend to be uni form among producers, and price changes that do occur are usually generated by cost changes rather than by the desire for competitive advantage.

Producers tend toward product emphasis because, in part, these are steps no other producer can readily take. Price changes may invite instant retaliation, but product changes require time for response or imitation.

There is, of course, another reason for the prevalence of nonprice competition. In the long run, the growth of the firm can come only through additional lines or products, whether through innovation or acquisition. Price competition is not an avenue to enterprise growth. There are limits to the amount and assortment of goods a consumer profitably can use. Regardless of the present volume advantage to be secured through price competition, the present product or object of expenditure will inevitably give way to a new or different product to satisfy man's desire for variety. To compete, a producer must be sure that the new product is one produced by him and must continually defend himself against the onslaughts of rivals with substitute products. To be content with price competition in a price-competitive world would imply little innovation and a much slower rate of growth. In an expanding, dynamic economy, producers must concentrate on innovation and product improvement if only to maintain competitive position.[2]

In an economic depression such as that of the 1930s, businessmen battling for survival believe that there is only "so much business to go around." Price reductions would not result in any appreciable increase in the amount demanded since there are during such times so many competing demands for limited or decreasing amounts of money that people would not buy things they could not earlier have afforded. Such a depression also tends to emphasize the aggressive character of nonprice competition. Where price competition is found, it is in the form of rebates and special discounts arranged on an ad hoc basis, rather than as a published or uniform reduction.

EFFECTIVE COMPETITION THROUGH FREEDOM OF ENTRY

The popular notion that the entry of new firms automatically results in competitive behavior which will lead to lower prices is correct if firms presently in the field are earning profits more than are necessary to keep them in business or if the growth of the industry results in those economies of scale we call "external" economies. All too often, however, the entry of another firm simply means that existing business is divided among more competitors, and, far from being lowered, prices are raised or the product is cheapened. Firms operate at less than minimum cost volume, or at least at lower volume than before, thus

[2] See, for example, "Corporations, Where the Game is Growth," *Business Week,* Sept. 30, 1967, pp. 99–120.

bringing about a waste in resource use.[3] The resources represented by the assets of the firm are not being operated so as to produce the output of which they are capable.

Of course, were nonprice competition successful so that the volume of output of one or several competitors were to rise, it might then be possible for them to earn reasonable profits and to begin engaging in price competition. Without a sufficient volume of business, profit margins cannot be reduced for the benefit of consumers. Effective competition requires the active presence of several firms of sufficient size so as to possess economies of scale, with enough financial strength to secure or produce good merchandise at reasonable prices. Adding another firm to a number of marginally operated firms will not create the viable firms necessary for effective competition. Effective competition demands that meaningful alternatives are offered to buyers and sellers.

Effective competition also means, according to Watson, that (1) new firms can freely enter the industry and produce at costs not markedly higher than those of established firms, (2) the firms in the industry are independent, and active rivals and do not engage in collusion, and (3) the number of firms is large enough so that none is dominant.[4]

Actually, what freedom of entry imposes is the threat of potential competition. It may take the form of capital standing by to open competing business firms or, more simply, of the availability of competing merchandise from other markets or foreign countries. The threat of an improved product is also a kind of freedom-of-entry factor serving to keep prices down and quality up.

Where the capital investment needed to enter the field is large, or there are scarce resources needed which are simply not available to a new entrant in the field, or there are rights of franchises which must be acquired and are not available, it is not likely that there will be much freedom of entry.

On the other hand, where freedom of entry is great, capital costs to entrants are low, and there are no special skills needed, it is likely that many will take advantage of this circumstance so that the typical firm will be small and operate at subsistence level. A typical example is the family grocery store; another is the hand laundry. In neither case can the consumer be assured that prices are low, but they are as low as competition can bring them. Buyers do have choices among alternative places of business, and there may be considerable pressure to reduce margins; but prices are still high because the firms are unable to reach a scale of operation which will provide significant economies.

---

[3] It is these wastes to which Chamberlin refers as the wastes of monopolistic competition. This effect could easily be demonstrated but is out of place at this point, for this text.

[4] Donald S. Watson, *Price Theory and Its Uses,* 2d ed., Houghton Mifflin Company, Boston, 1968, p. 266.

PREDATORY COMPETITION

Earlier we referred to "unfair" competition, in which the competitor believes the purpose of price reductions is to eliminate him. This kind of competition is also referred to as "predatory." The standard was given many years ago by Clair Wilcox.[5] "He may cut prices uniformly, deliberately sacrificing present earnings in an effort to obtain future monopoly power and profit. He may discriminate among localities, temporarily cutting his price in one area while he maintains it in others, dropping the fighting brand when it has served its purpose."

Unfortunately there is no way of knowing the intent of the businessman engaging in price competition, and all acts of competition are designed in one way or another to eliminate rivals from the market.

The Standard Oil Case. The most famous of all accounts of predatory price cutting involves the Standard Oil Company in the years before World War I. In the development of antitrust law, this case (1911) is a landmark. Revelations in that prosecution under the Sherman Antitrust Act are reputedly responsible for the singling out of predatory price discrimination to be prohibited under the Clayton Antitrust Act passed in 1914.

Briefly, most accounts hold that the Standard Oil Company of New Jersey used local price cutting in a systematic way, market area by market area, to eliminate rivals and thereby obtain for itself a monopoly position. Whenever rivals attempted to enter and compete, it is alleged, Standard would cut prices in order to discourage them. New analysis casts some doubt that Standard attained its monopoly position through discriminatory price cutting.[6]

Merger and Acquisition versus Price Cutting. Much more simple than price cutting as a means of attaining monopoly power is the merger and acquisition route. Under conditions of freedom of entry, minimal capital requirements, and relatively low technological requirements, there will be competition, but prices will be only as low as the relatively small scale of operation will allow. The oil industry in the years after the Civil War consisted of many small producers. Standard Oil bought out more than 100 refiners yet by 1870 controlled no more than 10 percent of the refining business, as John S. McGee points out.

McGee's argument goes something like this: Competitive firms can generally be bought at the discounted present value of their earnings. That is, they are worth to a purchaser a price which varies as to their prospective earnings, taking into account what money is worth if invested elsewhere. But an investment in a

[5] Clair Wilcox, *Competition and Monopoly in American Industry*, Temporary National Economic Committee, TNEC Monograph no. 21, 1941.

[6] John S. McGee, "Predatory Price Cutting: The Standard Oil (N.J.) Case," *Journal of Law and Economics*, vol. 1, Oct., 1958.

small refinery will not be as profitable as the same investment in a larger firm with monopolistic powers, able to set its own price and achieve some economies of scale. There is, consequently, a gain to the proposed seller who is trading profits for a return on shares of the newly expanding firm, and the new firm can afford to pay more than the assets of the small firm are worth since their worth to the buyer lies in their potential return as part of the monopoly.

But what of the charge that discriminatory prices were used? Clearly, if there are gains to be had from the purchase route, and obviously losses will accrue from price wars, it makes little economic sense to engage in warfare. In addition, the purchase route allows profits to be made at once, while the warfare route requires losses to be sustained first before profits can begin. It is also possible that owners might shut down temporarily waiting for the would-be monopolist to once again raise prices, so that they could resume operation at that time.

It is possible, McGee points out, that what is taken for discrimination between two markets is actually only price decreases in response to increases in supply in the market in which there are alternatives. In any market in which entry takes place, there is the basis for price reduction. Whether or not it will take place depends on the motives of the entrants. If they follow a philosophy of live and let live, then prices will not be lower, although supplies are greater, potentially at least. If the entrants are determined to expand their market share, then prices will be lowered to the new competitive level. The larger firm with the more secure economic base is more likely to survive under such conditions.

Where the assets or personnel of competitors are of use to the expanding firm, then conditions are established under which acquisition or merger will take place. After the removal of the rival through merger or acquisition, prices will return to the levels which obtained before the entry of the expanding firm, and the process may be repeated elsewhere.

Now this procedure is hardly predatory pricing, except when considered from the point of view of the firm facing the new entrant having ambitions to expand. Furthermore, it is difficult to know whether the newly established prices are predatory or merely competitive in response to economic forces. Certainly if the aim is to drive out competition in order to secure a monopoly, the merger and acquisition route is cheaper and more reliable.

MARKET STRUCTURE

Where product differentiation necessitated a modification of older views on theories of competition, disparities in sizes of firms represents an area more or less overlooked in conventional theory. That all firms are small and unable to influence the market price of products they sell is a necessary assumption if supply and demand are assumed to determine price. Since firms were presumed to be small, it was of little concern whether some were larger than others or whether the size distribution of firms was normal or not. When firms became large enough to influence market price, the fact of disparity in size became apparent and the object of considerable study beginning in 1930.

The study was aided principally by the commencement of publication of statistics of income by the Internal Revenue Service of the U.S. Department of the Treasury. For the first time, there were available balance sheet data classified by industry and size of firm. From these data, authors, beginning with Berle and Means in 1932, have drawn varying but generally pessimistic conclusions concerning the rapid growth of large companies and resultant industrial concentration.[7]

In 1931, 49.6 percent of the assets of all manufacturing corporations was held by the largest 139 firms. In 1947 this figure was 45 percent. Of the 1,141 largest corporations in 1960, 492 had sales in excess of $100 million each and aggregated sales volume of $788 billion. In the same year, the remainder of the 1,141 companies, each with sales of less than $100 million, accounted for sales of $15.2 billion. All corporations in that year filed income tax returns showing sales of $849 billion. Two percent of the firms reporting accounted for 40 percent of the total sales volume. And so the story goes.

Industrial concentration was thought to come from the waves of corporate mergers that from time to time have swept the economy. Lintner and Butters have shown, however, that the 1940 to 1947 merger movement, to cite one, had little or no effect on concentration.[8] In the following year, M. A. Adelman found no continuing growth in concentration, but rather a surprising stability, with the share of manufacturing assets held by the largest manufacturing firms remaining at about 44.7 percent between 1931 and 1960. The membership of the top group may alter somewhat, he reported, but it appears that there has been greater stability in position since 1929 than before, with less change taking place in the identities of large firms.[9] Mermelstein finds that there was a clear tendency, through 1964, for the largest corporations to maintain their relative positions in recent years than formerly, and the rate of change in relative position has slowed down.[10]

---

[7] Adolphe A. Berle and Gardiner C. Means, *The Modern Corporation and Private Property,* The Macmillan Company, New York, 1932. See also Joe S. Bain, *Industrial Organization,* John Wiley & Sons, Inc., New York, 1959.

[8] John V. Lintner and John K. Butters, "Effects of Mergers on Industrial Concentration," *Review of Econonics and Statistics,* Nov., 1950. See also Murray F. Foss and Betty C. Churchill, "The Size Distribution of the Post-war Business Population," *Survey of Current Business,* vol. 30, no. 5, pp. 12–20, May, 1950.

[9] M. A. Adelman, "The Measurement of Industrial Concentration," *Review of Economics and Statistics,* Nov., 1951.

[10] David Mermelstein, "Large Industrial Corporations and Asset Shares," *The American Economic Review,* vol. 59, no. 4, part I, p. 531, Sept. 1969.

The Federal Trade Commission, however, is not as sanguine. In its *Economic Report on Corporate Mergers* in 1969 in connection with Senate hearings on economic concentration, it reported that by the end of 1968, the 100 largest industrial corporations controlled a share of all manufacturing assets greater than that held by the 200 largest corporations in 1950. Further, it noted that the 200 largest corporations in 1968 controlled a share of assets equal to that held by the 1,000 largest corporations in 1941 and equal to more than 60 percent of total assets of all corporations. It lay the blame for the increasing concentration at the feet of the current merger movement which began to accelerate in 1966.[11]

As others have pointed out, the United States is committed to the idea of perfect competition among many small sellers, each too small to affect the price, but the facts of the case are that distributions of firms depict concentration. In fact, concentration appears to be a way of life not only in the external environment of firms on the selling side but on the buying side as well. Concentration is found also among consumers.

The estimated growth rate of the top 200 businesses exceeds that of all business taken together. Since World War II, gross national product has multiplied more than four times—from $208.5 billion in 1946 to approximately $940 billion in 1969. Corporations as a whole have exceeded that growth rate, and the larger corporations have grown a great deal more rapidly.

Although product differentiation, merger, and acquisition are generally blamed for the present disparity in growth rates, thus leading to industrial concentration, it is not altogether unlikely that there would have been concentration without these aspects of modern competitive existence.

Even in agriculture, ordinarily considered to be a competitive field closely approximating pure competition, there is concentration. In 1959, 25 percent of farms operated commercially had sales of less than $5,000 each, while another 17.6 percent had sales between $5,000 and $10,000. When you add the further fact that 34.7 percent of the total are considered as part-time businesses with sales annually of less than $2,500, the one-fifth of the total remaining that may be considered successful can only represent a badly skewed distribution.

Concentration as it affects personal income has been noted and discussed as a scientific and ethical problem for many years. What is rejected by many is the notion that there is something inevitable about concentration in the rewards our economic system gives to those rendering it a service. If, however, economic growth is possible only if an organism can learn to adapt itself to its environment, then societal concentration is evidence that adaptive ability is not possessed by all members to an equal degree.

---

[11] *Hearings before the Senate Subcommittee on Antitrust and Monopoly of the Committee on the Judiciary*, 91st Cong., 1st Sess., part 8A (app. to part 8). Staff Report of the Federal Trade Commission, *Economic Report on Corporate Mergers*, U.S. Government Printing Office, 1969.

The external environment would of course show some degree of sales volume concentration even if adaptive ability were, as some believe it is, normally distributed. The result simply would be that there would be a clustering of firms at the average sales size level and less at the lower extreme. The requirements for pure competition might still easily be violated. But there is ample evidence that where a characteristic or function must be learned and is not an attribute given by nature, skewness is quite natural.[12]

It may well be that there are two basic patterns of growth. One may have to do with the ability simply to drive onward along accustomed channels. The other may come from the belief that a company must be market oriented. In the latter case, the motive force is provided by a belief that a market exists for a given product and that the task of management is to develop it.

One thing appears certain: Growth involves risks and continual product-line expansion. At the same time, depending on the nature of the products and the stage of development of the industry or industries involved, the structure of industry may assume varying forms. In order to illustrate the concepts of competition which have been referred to thus far, the appendix contains two case histories of industrial organization.

SUMMARY

In this chapter, we have taken the notion of pure and perfect competition, which has for so long served economists as a model and analytical engine from which they drew conclusions of wide applicability to the economy, and, little by little, modified it so as to make it more responsive to the needs of the managerial economist. Price versus nonprice competition was discussed, the nature of the kinked demand curve as a convenient method of illustrating competition when the reaction of rivals must be taken into account was reviewed, and finally some aspects of industrial organization and business concentration were examined. The inevitability of product rather than price competition among producers in many lines of business was seen.

Appendix. Current Market Structures

In order further to illustrate the concepts of competition referred to in this chapter, the cement and the grocery manufacturing industries have been chosen. The cement industry is an example of moderate concentration and an undifferentiated product, now in the process of becoming vertically integrated.

---

[12] See for further information, Leroy H. Mantell, "On Laws of Special Abilities and the Production of Scientific Literature," *American Documentation*, vol. 17, no. 1, p. 8, Jan., 1966.

The grocery manufacturing industry exemplifies high degrees of concentration with highly differentiated products and a program of planned product innovation. Two subclassifications of the industry also are discussed: breakfast cereals, and crackers and cookies.

THE CEMENT INDUSTRY[13]

Cement production is a capital intensive, highly technological process. Cement is a homogeneous product made to rigid specifications and, as with industrial chemicals, the product of one plant is no different from that of another. Because of low value and bulk, and the widespread availability of raw materials used to make it, cement is not shipped long distances as a rule. In 1964, 90 percent of all cement was used within a radius of 160 miles of point of production. Seventy percent of all cement shipments were intrastate.

When a situation of this kind occurs, although the product is homogeneous and there is complete consumer knowledge, effective competition is unlikely, because only very few plants can compete in any one market on an economic basis. For effective competition, plant sizes would have to be smaller or shipping costs would have to be eliminated as a factor in pricing in order to permit the entry of distant plants.

Nationally, a relatively small number of firms account for a major part of national production and shipments. Four producers accounted for half or more of the shipments in or into forty-five states of the continental United States in 1964 out of the forty-nine firms doing business.

It is customary to use concentration ratios to depict the degree of concentration in an industry. These ratios refer to the proportion of the capacity or sales volume controlled or enjoyed by the four and eight largest producers, respectively. In 1964 the four largest firms accounted for 29.2 percent of total industry productive capacity. The eight largest accounted for 50.2 percent, with the remainder distributed over forty-one firms.

Another way of looking at this kind of data is to rank the number of firms in volume size classes, beginning with the smallest and ascending to the largest firms. Using this format, we see that thirty-one firms, or 63 percent of the industry, comprised less than 10-million-barrel capacity firms, while only one had a capacity exceeding 40 million, and two between 30 and 40 million barrels. Over 80 percent of the plants in existence in 1964 had capacities between 1 and 4 million barrels.

In 1952, Bain[14] reported that cement company executives were of the

---

[13] Material in this section is based on *Economic Report on Mergers and Vertical Integration in the Cement Industry*, Staff Report to the Federal Trade Commission, Government Printing Office, April, 1966. All references are to this report unless specifically stated otherwise.

[14] Joe S. Bain, *Barriers to New Competition*, Harvard University Press, Cambridge, Mass., 1956, p. 230.

opinion that an efficient size for a single plant was between 2 and 2½ million barrels. It appeared, in 1966, that there were economies of scale possible in plant sizes of 5 million barrels or more. Until the 1950s, differences in plant size were basically caused by increases in the number of kilns (burning chambers used to process raw materials) so that a 2-million-barrel plant and a 10-million-barrel plant were not technologically different, the latter being merely five of the former, except for overhead facilities.

In recent years, it is reported that larger kilns have been emphasized, and they have resulted in a variety of cost-saving possibilities, especially in fuel usage, while improving control of quality through automated methods.

There does not appear to be any evidence of economies of multiplant operation based on studies covering the years 1911 to 1964. Fluctuations in profitability were, however, greater from year to year for single-plant companies than for larger firms more geographically diversified. Such larger firms might, therefore, have access to capital on more favorable terms, thus providing some degree of size advantage.

Other sources of multiplant economies, apart from capital costs, are not apparent. As an undifferentiated product, cement is sold to specification. The technology is old and well known, and while some technological advances have been made, they appear to be of an evolutionary rather than revolutionary nature.

Neither access to raw materials nor technology is a barrier to entry of new firms. Equipment and plant design are readily available from equipment and engineering companies. Capital needs for a 1- to 1½-million-barrel plant, the minimum practicable size, reportedly range from between $8 and $14 million. New plants are designed generally with provision for later expansion, and although the initial sizes may be less than 1 million barrels, no finished plant is this small.

With minimum capital needs of $10 million or more, access to capital is critical. According to the Federal Trade Commision, ". . . only four of the thirteen new entrants into the industry can be considered newly established firms (during the period 1960–1965). Two of these . . . were bankrupt before or shortly after completion of their new plants. In both cases the problems encountered centered on access to capital."[15] Where new capacity has been built, it has been through efforts of the bottom twelve firms which, although accounting for only 35 percent of industry capacity, installed over one-half the new capacity built since 1950. This has tended to reduce the size disparity of firms. The growth of the largest cement firms is seen to be much more the result of acquisition activity than the building of new plants, however. The acquisition is both vertical and horizontal.

[15] Op. cit., p. 41.

Aside from the four newly established firms, entry is coming from firms already established in other industries, such as oil-well cementing, mining of nonferrous metals, gas utilities, and construction, or in other lines such as ready-mix concrete and cement manufacturing in foreign countries. It would appear that firms capable of meeting and overcoming capital requirements barriers to entry are those with a successful record in other lines. More likely than not, those applicants for entry are already in some allied fields, such as suppliers of fuel or users of the finished product. This would indicate vertical integration.

Geographic integration also is taking place involving the acquisition of forty plants between 1950 and 1966. Established firms once again have shown this preference for expansion through merger with existing plants. New capacity as a means of obtaining entry into new markets was built in only seven instances.

Cement production, as we have seen, is regional in character. Consequently, any new capacity would have more impact on the potential supply of cement than if the market were national in scope. If we add to this the need for the new capacity to be produced at costs which are competitive, a certain minimum capacity is inferred. Any new entrant will therefore have a significant impact on the regional supply.

In the Northeast, for example, newly built plants must be approximately 4 million barrels in capacity. But this much output would amount to 8 percent of 1964 total shipments. In southern California, an average economical plant size of 5 million barrels will account for 20 percent of shipments to that area.

A potential competitor has then two avenues open to him: first, to build as little capacity as possible in order to minimize the impact on supply and therefore the price structure; and second, to integrate forward so as to insure a market.

Of the thirteen plants built by new entrants during the period 1950 to 1965, ten were relatively small, with initial outputs of between 0.7 and 1.5 million barrels. In a few cases, large plants were built at once, but these had large potential markets made accessible through access to cheap transportation by water; or, as we will note later on, they were able to reduce delivered costs through economies of size even though it meant shipping longer distances.

Cement Distribution. Before World War II, cement was sold primarily to building contractors who manufactured their own concrete or to building-material suppliers who resold it to smaller builders. Since that time, there has emerged the practice of manufacturing ready-mixed concrete, so that instead of making concrete, builders now buy it in a form ready to use. Cement manufacturers have come to see producers of ready-mixed concrete as major customers. In 1964, ready-mixed concrete producers bought 58.8 percent of all cement shipped, while contractors accounted for only 15.1 percent and building-material-dealers, 8.8 percent.

Most concrete manufacturers are small, and in 1964 there were about 4,000 located in and around population centers, with relatively few accounting for significant portions of purchases of cement and concrete output. Large firms differ from small largely in that they operate more plants. Firms shipping 150,000 to 200,000 cubic yards of concrete annually appear to operate twice as many plants and sell nearly four times as much per plant on the average as do firms of less than 50,000 cubic yard volume.

In the large metropolitan markets, the large concrete mixing firms are major outlets for cement manufacturers, and relatively few firms account for the major amount of concrete sold. In Baltimore, the four largest companies account 'or 88 percent of shipments; in Kansas City, 64.6 percent. In the twenty-two major metropolitan areas, in only one instance do the top eight firms account for less than 50 percent of total concrete sales volume. In all, 36 percent of cement consumption by ready-mix firms is accounted for by eighty-one customers of a total of 1,815 reporting to the Federal Trade Commission in 1965.

It is evident, then, that any cement manufacturer desiring to sell any quantity of cement in a metropolitan area would have to compete for the business of a relatively few customers and any attempt by cement firms to merge with ready-mix firms would have the effect of tending to reduce competition.

Vertical Integration in the Industry. Since 1950, forty-eight concrete manufacturers have been acquired by cement manufacturers. About 80 percent of these mergers have taken place since 1960. The number of cement firms with concrete production facilities has increased from two in 1956 to nineteen in 1964. While only 1 percent of ready-mix companies are involved, in 1964 they were responsible for 10 percent of all cement shipments to such firms. In each instance, the company acquired was a substantial factor in a regional market, accounting for between 19 and 45 percent of sales. Consequently, the size of the available market for competitors was diminished. The ready-mix firms formerly bought 35 percent of their needs from the cement manufacturers acquiring them. Presently they report buying 65 percent of their needs, thus displacing 30 percent.

Cement Pricing. Earlier it was pointed out that where basic industrial goods are involved, the generally accepted device for explaining price-demand relationships is the kinked demand curve. Here the reaction of rivals is more important than the reaction of buyers. The kinked curve leads to price stability, but the presence of excess capacity may force price concessions. Since the seller is being sold more than the product, the customer loses no opportunity to apply competitive pressure when it is known excess capacity exists.

From 1950 to 1956, prices of all construction materials increased by 19 percent and cement prices increased by 29 percent, in the presence of utilization rates of 90 percent or more for cement producers. Although prices of construction materials increased in 1959, they then lost half their gain in the next year and remained stable through 1964. Cement prices quoted increased until 1960, remained steady for three years before dropping a little in 1963. Capacity utilization data, however, tell another story.

In 1957, capacity in use dropped from the 91 percent of the year before to 78.2 percent, rising to 80 percent in 1959, dropping then to reach 72 percent by 1962 and rising to 77 percent in 1964. As a result, the Bureau of Labor Statistics index of portland cement prices does not tell a complete story. List price changes take place only after all other price-cutting techniques have been used. There are, for example, discounts for cash, which in the 1950s averaged 10 cents per barrel and by the 1960s had increased to 20 cents. Prompt payment was overlooked at times, and special discounts up to 25 cents were available. Phantom billing was used, in which the cement manufacturer absorbed part of the freight cost by billing as though the shipment were made to a closer point than the actual destination.

Customer Financing. In addition to the tendency of cement manufacturers to buy out large cement customers, there appears also to have been direct financial assistance. This assistance varies from providing direct investment money in order to finance customer expansion to carrying accounts receivable or providing guarantees on loans customers obtain at banks. Carrying of accounts receivable is an important tool for reducing competitive pressure and helping to sell the seller rather than the product.

Profits. With the utilization of capacity hovering in the low 70 percent range, profits have tended to diminish as prices have fallen and costs gone up. Rising costs reflect not only the extra burden of unused capacity (the inability of lower volume to cover overhead at the old rates) but higher distribution costs resulting from increased competitive activity. In an attempt to protect profits and sales volume, forward integration has resulted. It is significant that 80 percent of the recorded acquisitions occurred during periods when excess capacity was rising and profits falling. Areas in which merger activity has been most important have been precisely those in which significant new entry of additional capacity has been noted, as in Texas, Florida, Virginia, and New York.

As markets shrink with the expansion of vertical integration, the risks associated with aggressive competition intensify. As the integration process takes place, the market remaining to the nonintegrated supplier diminishes until the possible benefits from competing may simply not be worth the cost. Since manufacturers serve a number of markets, they are inclined to pursue competitive strategies in those markets in which the probability of success is higher. Hence, they take steps to expand by increasing the number of markets they serve and the resultant forward integration serves to remove much of the available market and reduce the competitive level in what is left.

Captive markets may make it easier to conceal price reductions on cement as processed concrete. Since concrete is generally sold on contract, price discrimination is more possible, since the same prices do not have to apply to all customers. This, of course, makes it difficult for a nonintegrated rival to determine a strategy since any cuts by him will have to be spread to all possible customers and a price reduction to one customer will be followed by similar reductions by all nonintegrated suppliers to the same customer.

Vertical integration may also cause a reduction of competition in the ready-mixed concrete market. If cement manufacturers supply cement to nonintegrated mixed concrete firms, as well as to their own integrated firms, and in the same market, they can raise the price at which they sell both to their own captive firm and to others, but at the same time hold constant the price to builders. This tactic places the nonintegrated firm in a cost-price squeeze. It cannot raise its price without losing customers to the integrated firm and sooner or later leaves the scene.

Reducing the "open" market makes it less likely that new companies will enter the cement manufacturing industry. This is now especially true as the amount of capital and the scale of output required tend to be large, if economical operation is to be attained. The result is to reduce the potential for competition and hence for lowering of prices.

Summary. In this section we have drawn a picture of an industry involving a capital intensive, highly technical process, in which the product is homogeneous and consumer knowledge is excellent. Output has low value and bulk and may readily be made in many geographic locations. There is moderate concentration, and the product is undifferentiated. The industry is in the process of becoming vertically integrated and already exhibits the skewness characteristic of size distributions of many economic phenomena. The growth of the largest cement firms is the result of acquisition, rather than of building of new plants. It has not been possible to bring about any significant product development or manufacturing innovation. New firms tend to expand through building new capacity and do this largely either through efforts of firms in other industries attempting to diversify or of firms in allied fields attempting vertical integration.

Cement companies until recently were aggregations of small plants and, given the nature of the product, prices tended to be stable except where unused capacity was present. The kinked demand curve is generally applicable. With a shrinking open market because of trends toward vertical integration, and the newly developed larger kilns and automated methods increasing the scale at which minimum cost output is possible, the transformation to oligopoly seems likely.

GROCERY MANUFACTURING[16]

Grocery manufacturing includes the production and sale of highly processed packaged foods sometimes called "dry" groceries. Typical examples are baby foods, breakfast cereals, candy, canned soups, cocoa, crackers, instant foods, jams, macaroni, and so on. Excluded are items found in the meat, produce, dairy, bakery, and frozen food departments of most food stores, as well as canned and dried fruits and vegtables.

For the first time, a large part of the consuming public has, since World War II, become sufficiently affluent as to be able to afford substantially larger amounts of money for convenience and variety. This is a trend that began years ago with the introduction of packaged and canned foods, but which received a considerable impetus with improved processing methods. The use of convenience foods is also related to increases in both the level of family income and the amount of activity outside the home. As a result, grocery manufacturers have had to change their traditional ways of looking at their markets. Style and many other basically nonessential factors are more important than price. Consumers will gladly trade money for time and convenience as alternative uses appear for their time. Continual change and consumer credit have both acted as an incentive to buy and made buying possible.

Major grocery manufacturers are large and have varied and extensive lines of products. With minor exceptions, every grocery manufacturer surveyed by the National Commission on Food Marketing had, in 1963, more than one plant producing food products and produced two or more products in at least one or more of their plants. Most companies competed in seven different product categories, with the largest having entrants in seventeen and the next two largest in sixteen product categories.

Most manufacturers distribute their products nationally but prefer to locate their plants close to major markets in order to obtain economies in distribution, according to the National Commission. There appear to be insufficient economies of scale to warrant the development of the very large plants characteristic of the automobile industry, yet the technology requires that the entire process be carried on at one place.

Market Concentration and Competitive Behavior. Markets for individual products are highly concentrated, with the largest four producers generally

---

[16] Material in this section is based on *Studies of Organization and Competition in Grocery Manufacturing,* Technical Study No. 6, National Commission on Food Marketing, Government Printing Office, June, 1966. All references are to this report unless specifically stated otherwise.

selling more than 50 percent of the sales volume of any single product on the market. Twenty percent of the brands account for 75 percent of the sales volume of dry groceries.[17] The core of the entire grocery industry appears to consist of dominant, large, well-financed firms.

Large grocery manufacturers differ from most food processors in that they are marketing agents as much as they are manufacturers. They look upon the marketing process as an integral part of their overall effort.

Expenditures on advertising are high and growing but are considered only part of the marketing plan. Producers use sales promotion, retailer allowances, and personal selling, depending on the nature of the problem. Generally, advertising is most important when products are newly introduced, less important thereafter.

Short-term variations in published prices are deemphasized as a rule, and prices do not fluctuate widely as market conditions change. There is, however, a good deal of changeability in wholesale and retail prices resulting from sales promotional devices such as "cents-off" deals and free coupons. Manufacturers also grant price and bonus case allowances to wholesalers, and these have the effect of reducing retail prices.

Grocery manufacturers prefer not to engage in price competition, but instead emphasize quality and other forms of nonprice competition. With the markets highly concentrated, competition is highly oligopolistic, with only a few major producers competing in any given sector. "Each large seller carefully watches the actions of close competitors, and generally reacts to any significant change in price, quality or selling effort."[18] This is, of course, typical of oligopolistic behavior, to which we have already referred. Oligopolists tend to shun price competition because they believe that competitors will follow any price cut, and therefore no individual producer's market will increase sufficiently to warrant a reduction. This conclusion is especially true of breakfast cereals, where demand is not particularly responsive to reductions in price, in any event.

Since price cutting is not profitable, there is a good deal of product differentiation, which tends to insulate brands or products from competition. When products are not yet sufficiently differentiated, sales promotion is used.[19] Lower ranking firms are more likely to use promotional efforts directed at retailers than are leaders who have, by advertising and other means, established their brands or products.

[17] "How Manufacturers' Brands Dominate in Dry Groceries," *Supermarket Merchandising*, March, 1966, p. 43.
[18] National Commission on Food Marketing, *op. cit.*, p. 16.
[19] Examples of such promotion are retailer assistance, cents-off deals, premiums, etc.

Mergers and Acquisitions. Grocery manufacturers, during the period 1964 to 1965, showed evidence of expansion and diversification of their activities. They grew through internal development, but also often purchased smaller companies in an effort to broaden product lines. Acquired companies often showed rapid growth after merger.

Major food manufacturers with ample financial resources find it less expensive and time consuming to buy a brand name and production facilities and staff, than to go about developing them initially. Procter & Gamble entered cake mixes by acquiring Duncan Hines; Thomas Lipton entered salad dressings by acquiring Wishbone brand. Campbell Soups acquired V-8 vegetable juice, C. A. Swanson and Sons (frozen dinners), and Pepperidge Farms, Inc. (baked goods), between 1948 and 1965, finding the acquisition of these lines an easier route than the development of new brands and products, technical and production facilities, staffs, and distribution channels. But 50 percent of Campbell's sales increase during the period 1954 to 1964 was a result of previously existing lines and newly developed items—in other words, to internal growth. When Campbell bought Swanson in 1955, it manufactured only three kinds of frozen dinners. By 1966, Campbell had expanded the line to include twenty-five different dinners.

Ideally, the major firms try to find a small company with potential for growth. The General Foods purchase of Four Seasons, Inc., in 1954 amounted to the acquisition of a brand name and concept.

Underlying these growth gradients is the desire of some companies to diversify product lines away from items likely to suffer from possible price competition. Many large manufacturers of grocery lines feel there are advantages to increasing size. Sometimes complementary products, such as those produced by Pepsi-Cola and Frito-Lay point to the desirability to merger. Not only are the products compatible, but there are benefits to be had from pooled financial resources, broader scope of operations, shared advertising, and the like. Another reason for diversifying is to provide a hedge against future changes in consumer demand. Where the products are convenience oriented or based on consumer taste, a shift in demand can be dramatic and costly to the unalert.

There are some economies of scale accruing to the smaller firm being acquired. Frequently small and undercapitalized, the acquired firm is often able to get needed financing for expansion, the advice of professionals, and the use of research and development facilities. It may also be able to get quantity discounts in purchasing ingredients, containers, advertising, and supplies. During the early years of merger history, the most significant changes appear to be in the infusion of capital into the acquired firm and the availability and use of management advice.

Expansion through New Products. Probably the most startling evidence of the proliferation of new products is contained in a statement by the president of a food chain to the National Commission on Food Marketing that his buyers had to consider between 4,000 and 5,000 new items each year. This statement acquires heightened significance when it is realized that each supermarket carries only 8,500 items in the grocery department and 6,500 items in all other departments. Of the items considered, perhaps 1,000 are accepted. Needless to say, many others are either dropped or curtailed.

The rationale for new product development is given as the following:

1. Affords an opportunity to take advantage of the demand for convenience foods. The housewife today desires food prewashed, precooked, premixed, or prepeeled.
2. Makes it possible to segment markets into social, economic, or racial groups to create special appeals.
3. Offers means of countering product competition from other firms. There is emphasis on making constant changes, often superficial, to appear to housewives looking for variety.
4. Provides a means of broadening product lines to use company distribution channels more completely.
5. Replaces a product which has been on the market for some time without change.

The pace of new product development and its cost constitute a considerable barrier to entry of new firms. It does not mean that the small local or regional manufacturer cannot compete on a limited basis, but that competition nationally may well be out of the question.

The process of developing a new product, testing it, trying it out in test markets, and finally achieving full distribution takes, on the average, thirty-seven months, with cold cereals taking fifty-five months, and cake mixes twenty-nine months. Of an initial group of seventy-eight items submitted for product testing, Buzzell and Nourse report a failure rate of 37 percent, while of eighty-four submitted to test marketing, 32 percent failed to make the grade.[20]

On the average, it costs $68,000 for research and development and $26,000 for marketing research per product to introduce a new processed food. The figures for cold cereal products are approximately twice that much. In addition, there are capital investments to be made.

Marketing costs are reported as 57 percent of sales for the first year and 37 percent of sales in the second year. Only 30 percent of the products studied

[20] R. D. Buzzell and R. E. M. Nourse, *Product Innovation, the Product Life Cycle, and Competitive Behavior in Selected Food Processing Industries, 1947–1964*, A. D. Little, Inc., Cambridge, Mass., 1966, p. 85.

by Buzzell and Nourse broke even in the first year of introduction. By the end of the third year, 61 percent, and by the fourth, 73 percent had met costs. Of the 124 products studied during the period 1954 to 1964, thirty-seven did not make full market distribution, and eleven were discontinued, even though full distribution had been attained.

These results clearly show that product innovation is costly and problematic and define the businessman's concept of competition.

Market Concentration in Breakfast Cereals, Crackers, and Cookies. Entry into the cold cereal industry is difficult, as we have seen. The declining demand for hot cereals makes that field unattractive for entry. A small number of small, one-product firms manage to compete successfully in this field. By contrast, entry into the cracker and cookie industry is easy. Cost of entry is estimated as no more than $200,000 for crackers and probably less than $150,000 for cookies.

The size of distribution of establishments in the two fields reflects the merger and acquisition activity in the cereal field and the difficulty of entry there, and the relatively easier entry in the cracker and cookie market. The proportion of firms with less than 100 employees, producing cereal preparations in 1947, is reported as 75 percent, while in 1963, although the proportion of the total is down slightly, the reduction in the total number of firms from sixty-four to forty-eight is entirely at the expense of this size class. Establishments reported as producing cookies and crackers having less than 100 employees are 68 percent of the total in 1947 and 76 percent in 1963. The total number increased from 326 to 356, with thirty of the forty-nine reported in the smallest size class.

In major metropolitan markets, the largest four breakfast cereal companies were responsible for about 86 percent of all sales of breakfast cereals in 1965 (Los Angeles, Seattle, Pittsburgh, and Boston). Nationally, the top four firms accounted for between 89.3 percent and 92 percent of the quantity in pounds of ready-to-serve breakfast cereal during the 1954 to 1964 decade. By comparison, the top four companies selling cookies and crackers, in 1964, accounted for only 59 percent of sales, according to the National Commission on Food Marketing.

Integration in Breakfast Cereals, Crackers, and Cookies. Except for a limited amount of backward vertical integration, there is little evidence of activity of this kind in the breakfast cereal industry. Although most manufacturers operate their own oat, corn, or wheat flour mills, these appear to reflect their historical backgrounds. There has been no current activity in this direction.

What backward integration has taken place is limited to ownership of packaging materials plants. The six largest cereal manufacturers supplied 45 percent of their active packaging needs during 1964. In the cracker and cookie industry, there is little integration, except in some instances where major manu-facturers have their own flour mills and a few their own container plants or cer-tain pieces of equipment.

Integration by retailers, however, to include cookie and cracker manu-facture is significant, and involves the larger chains such as A & P, Safeway, and the like. Output in 1963 amounted to about 4 percent of the industry total. Smaller retailers do not attempt to produce their own because of the many com-panies willing and able to provide private label merchandise.

Probably because of the smaller number of firms in the breakfast cereal field, the Federal Trade Commission and the Department of Justice have been vigilant in antitrust activity. Consequently, there have been only a limited number of acquisitions of cereal companies by other cereal companies. Much of the merger activity has involved the so-called "conglomerate" firms, such as the Quaker Oats Company. During the period 1942 to 1962, this firm acquired inter-ests in pet food, flour and feed, meat processing, flour mixes, grain, chile and tamales, and biscuits. The cold cereal business is dominated by conglomerates, while the hot cereal producers are smaller and more specialized.

In the cracker and cookie industry, merger and acquisition activity has been extensive. Indeed, the major firms in the industry are themselves the prod-uct of merger. The major conglomerates are also interested in acquiring medium-sized cracker and cookie bakers. The future may well see some of the marketing methods developed in cereals applied to crackers, cookies, and simi-lar items.

Major producers of cereals and crackers have indicated that one of the principal reasons for seeking to diversify is that it is a good way to become larger. Size has a number of benefits, as we have seen, among which are mar-keting efficiencies and the ability to finance research and development. Whether size provides economies of scale is another matter.

Effects of Size. Data provided by the Bureau of the Census for the National Commission on Food Marketing reveal that smaller establishments producing breakfast cereals are considerably more efficient than the larger plants. Pos-sibly as a result of this awareness, there has been since 1947 some trend toward the smaller-size plant. The value of shipments per establishment increased 4.7 times during the period 1947 to 1963, for smaller plants of the 20 to 249 employee size, while for the larger, over-250 employee category, shipments increased only 2.7 times. The extent of the productivity and cost differential is shown in Table 2-1.

In the production of crackers and cookies, on the other hand, during the period 1954 to 1963, there appeared to be definite economies of scale. In spite of this fact, value of shipments increased per establishment more for the smaller-size plant than the larger. On the other hand, as we have seen, there was an

TABLE 2-1. LABOR PRODUCTIVITY BY SIZE OF
ESTABLISHMENT—BREAKFAST CEREALS, 1947 AND 1963

| | Establishment Size in Year | | | |
| | 1947 | | 1963 | |
Item	20–99	100 and over	20–99	100 and over
Value of shipments per worker in production	$28,494	$30,143	$93,360	$63,490
Value added per production worker	12,207	13,848	45,925	38,134
Pounds per man-hour shipped	76	62	151	81

Source: Bureau of the Census, as reported in Studies of Organization and Competition in Grocery Manufacturing, p. 113.

increase in the number of plants in the under-100 size and the increase may possibly reflect underutilization of newly established firms. In 1963, shipments per man-hour of employment for establishments having less than 100 employees were $13.19. Establishments of the 100 to 249 employee size reported an increase to $14.23, while the next two classes, 250 to 499 and over 500, reported $15.50 and $18.66, respectively.

Although smaller breakfast cereal establishments are more efficient in production than are the larger ones, there are compensating efficiencies in distribution which make larger firms more profitable than smaller firms. As Table 2-2 shows, net income before federal income tax for the largest four firms is three times that of all others except the top eight firms.

There is also evidence that the profitability advantage of larger firms has increased since 1947. There, growth has been consistent with larger profit percentages applied to larger sales volumes. Increasing dollar profits served to fuel additional product proliferation and merger activity.

Net profits before taxes as a percent of sales rose from 8.8 percent in

TABLE 2-2. COSTS AND PROFITS AS PERCENT OF SALES
IN THE BREAKFAST CEREAL INDUSTRY, 1964, BY SIZE OF COMPANY

| | Size of Firm—Sales Volume | | |
Statement Item	Largest Four	Next Four	Other
Total manufacturing cost and expense	52.6%	53.2%	47.5%
Total selling expense	28.0	34.1	40.0
Total administrative and general expense	4.2	4.5	7.5
Total expense	84.8%	91.8%	95.0%
Net income before tax	15.6%	8.2%	5.0%

Source: National Commission on Food Marketing, op. cit., pp. 206–207.

1947 to 14.8 percent in 1964, for firms whose assets were in the over-$5-million class. By comparison, firms in the $0.5- to $5-million-dollar class were able to reach a maximum of 6.6 percent in 1950 and by 1964 earned only 5.3 percent. Smaller firms either operated at a loss or had nominal profits.

In cookies and crackers, economies of scale alluded to above were reinforced by economies in selling and in general and administrative expenses, so that the largest four companies appeared on the average in 1964 to be 2½ times as profitable than the smallest. Net income before taxes for the largest four firms averaged 10.1 percent, while the smaller firms reported in the vicinity of 2.8 to 3.6 percent.

Price Behavior. Prices in the breakfast cereal industry and in the cracker and cookie industry are, of course, administered. Which is to say, they are set by the firms in question and are not determined by a market. Both industries are oligopolistic, the cereal industry more so than the cracker and cookie. Cereal producers believe the demand for their product is not responsive to price reduction to a significant degree, and therefore they do not compete on a price basis. In the cracker and cookie business, where capital requirements are less stringent, there are a number of small fringe firms which attempt to compete on a price basis, and there is in general less concentration. The major manufacturers do not attempt to compete through price changes, however. The largest, National Biscuit Company, has attempted strong product differentiation for many years. The following tabulation (Table 2-3) shows the extent to which, in 1964, it had been successful in insulating itself from price competition.

TABLE 2-3. COMPARISON OF 1964 WHOLESALE PRICES OF SELECTED CRACKER AND COOKIE PRODUCTS OF NATIONAL BISCUIT COMPANY WITH SIMILAR PRODUCTS OF COMPETING FIRMS

Item	Number of Brands Reporting Prices		
	Higher	Identical	Lower
1	1	2	3
2	1	—	3
3	—	—	6
4	1	—	3
5	1	—	7

Source: National Commission on Food Marketing, op. cit., p. 182.

In breakfast cereals, while competition takes the form of new product development and advertising effort, there is implicit price competition in that package sizes are adjusted without altering the price structure. This of course has the same ultimate effect as price changes but is more subtle and does not have the immediate effect of retaliation by rivals. In fact, considerable price difference can exist for different brands of the same kind of product at the same time, as Table 2-4 indicates.

TABLE 2-4. WHOLESALE PRICES OF SELECTED BREAKFAST CEREALS, 1964

Producer	Item	Package Size (oz.)	Price*
General Mills	Country Corn Flakes with Rice	11½	$5.80
	Two similar brands	12	5.60
Quaker Oats	Quaker Muffetts Shredded Wheat	8	.43 lb
	Next higher brand	15¼	.31 lb
	Lowest brand	12	.29 lb
General Mills	Bran Flakes with Raisin	9¾	7.00
	Two similar brands	10	5.39
Kellogg	Froot Loops	7	.59 lb
General Mills	Lucky Charms	7	.59 lb
	Next higher brand	8	.52 lb
	Three lowest	var.	.44 lb
Quaker Oats	Puffed Rice	4	4.30
Purity Mills	Popeye Puffed Rice	6	3.80
National Biscuit	Cream of Wheat	14	.24 lb
Pillsbury	Farina†	13½	.18 lb

* Price is per case, unless otherwise stated.
† Personal observations of one of the authors indicates that this discrepancy in the price of farina had been corrected by 1967.
Source: National Commission on Food Marketing, op. cit., pp. 172–173.

The price leader in the ready-to-serve breakfast cereal industry is Kellogg, although the leadership is not as effective as formerly because of the extent of market segmentation. In other words, where a producer is able to differentiate his product sufficiently, he can ignore the reactions of rivals, and hence he no longer need be guided by the prices set by a dominant firm. According to the Commission on Food Marketing, he will then look to the general pattern of prices in the industry and raise or lower prices according to the general trend. Where products have close substitutes, as in corn flakes, Kellogg is reputedly the price leader.

CONCLUSION

The competition of the real world is infinitely more complex than the models used by economists. Where the economists' model requires, for the most part, that the businessman make only quantity or price and quantity decisions, the real world demands more complex decision making, involving asset uses and resource commitment.

Competition involves processes of product selection, promotion, and pricing. Most firms make more than one product for a number of reasons, but the fact that they do imposes a barrier to the entry of a single-product firm wishing to produce one of the products.

The barrier, first of all, is a cost barrier. It costs a multiple-product firm less to make and sell a new product than it would cost a new company set up to produce only that product. The cost savings are not exclusively in production, unless there are facilities which may be converted. The savings are in the availability of management and in the talent needed to launch a new product. Cost savings are present also in the availability of distribution and promotional capacities, and in many instances these outweigh the manufacturing cost differences. Sometimes the multiple-product firm can take advantage of the fact that products use common raw materials or other inputs.

A firm producing more than one product benefits also from firm name and exposure. Product proliferation is a response to the desire of the consumer for something new. At the same time, there is a degree of lack of information, so that a familiar producer's name provides a degree of reassurance to the consumer. If, for instance, the consumer is going to switch from corn flakes to wheat puffs, the producer would rather have the switch take place to his brand of wheat puffs than another.

Conventionally, multiple-product lines arise from the desire to even out fluctuations in business activity or to compensate for seasonal effects. This is still one important reason for the rise of the conglomerate, but it fails to account for the savings that arise from shared overhead services, which a small and independent firm could not acquire except at much higher cost.

Review Questions

1. What are the reasons for product differentiation and, according to Chapter 2, when will it be most effective? What is the effect on the demand curve facing the individual competitor?
2. How does monopolistic competition differ from pure competition?
3. In what kinds of markets would one expect to find a kinked demand curve facing a seller? What is the significance of the kinked demand curve?
4. How do you account for the difference between the economist's notion of competition and the businessman's version? Why do some businessmen believe price competition to be unfair?
5. Differentiate between pure and perfect competition.
6. What assumptions concerning the nature of the business environment underlie business tendencies toward nonprice competition?
7. What are the prerequisites for effective competition? Where does freedom of entry fit? How about scale of operation?
8. Evaluate the merit of merger and acquisition versus price cutting as a strategy or tactic.

9. Since the advent of industrial concentration, some have advocated the dismemberment of large corporations to prevent monopoly. What do you think of this approach?
10. How do you account for the presence of a kinked demand curve in the cement industry?

Case 1. Scott's Department Store

Professor Jim Carson walked briskly through the busy luncheon crowds on "F" Street to an appointment with Marty Rosen, merchandise manager of Scott's Department Store. Marty had a problem, and, as he had stated over the telephone the night before, if his friend from college days, Jim Carson, didn't have an answer, he, Marty, would be submerged in one of the greatest overstocks in Scott's history.

The Board of Directors of Scott's in 1965 had concurred in Rosen's estimate that the answer to leveling or declining sales in many departments was to upgrade merchandise lines. Indeed, many members of the board aspired to move the store into the "prestige" class, now occuped solely by Evans Department Store, some seven blocks away. Scott's location was at the opposite end of town, in an area which had seen better times and was here and there becoming converted to business use. There were two other large stores on the same street as Scott's and a number of smaller stores. The clientele was drawn largely from office employees and those who arrived by bus. Scott's had recently built a parking garage, so that it was not as dependent as were the others on public transportation facilities.

After greeting his old friend, Marty got right to the point. "Look," he said, "I have $200,000 in furs inventory and this is the middle of February!" Jim got the point. Selling mink and seven-stripe beaver furs was part of Scott's upgrading program. But in that city, George Washington's birthday normally signaled the end of the winter season, and after the end of February, the only possible way to dispose of the overstock was a drastic markdown or a summer sale event. The first would mean a loss, and the second, idle capital in inventory, as well as possible style obsolescence.

Marty showed Jim advertising copy headed "February Fur Bargain." Some fur prices he noted were as much as 50 percent below sale prices he had seen earlier at specialty fur shops in town.

QUESTIONS

1. To what do you attribute the lack of appeal of Scott's fur department?
2. Can you think of similar instances in other merchandise lines?

3. What do you think of Rosen's strategy?
4. According to *Business Week* (Jan. 20, 1968), a former head of merchandising has boasted that Sears, Roebuck was the leading seller of mink and diamonds, with the top for each line at $2,500 and $6,500, respectively. What did Sears, Roebuck accomplish that Scott's has apparently not accomplished?
5. What might the demand curve for fur coats facing Scott's Department Store look like?

Case 2. Steel Industry Structure

In August, 1967, the press reported that steel makers had raised steel plate prices $4 per ton, or about 3 percent. Steel officials cited rising material and labor costs, and hinted then that more price boosts were in the offing.

Price increases were signaled by a move on the part of Bethlehem Steel Corp., and by midweek after the announcement, other major producers had followed.

Since January, nine months earlier, steel producers had boosted prices on products covering more than 25 percent of their product mix. Prices of most tubular products, which total about 1 percent of industry shipment, and of tinplate, $6\frac{1}{2}$ percent of the industry output, were increased 2.7 percent on the average.

Import competition traditionally has followed price rises in domestic steel, but steel executives asserted that with costs rising, they had no real choice. Imports in 1967 were up by 13 percent of the year before. One major appliance maker began to order foreign steel sheet for the first time, placing an order of 10,000 tons. Total steel shipments for the first several months of 1967 were 48.6 million tons, compared with an industry-wide figure of 53.2 million the year before.

In January, 1970, after a history of regular annual increases, Armco Steel Corporation boosted prices on a variety of steel sheets by $4 to $6 a ton. This announcement followed by three days a Bethlehem Steel Corporation announcement that it would raise prices on structural steel shapes by $7 a ton. By midweek, Bethlehem had gained support for its structural steel increases from United States Steel Corporation and Kaiser Steel Corporation, while Inland Steel Company concurred by posting price increases in line with Armco. Bethlehem had chosen to increase its prices for structural steel at a time when the heavy construction market was expected to show some strength. The demand for sheet steel for autos and appliances was not strong, however, and Armco's move puzzled some economists.

A year later, in January, 1971, Bethlehem announced a price increase of up to 12.5 percent on structural steel. The President of the United States, concerned about inflation, warned that he might encourage more foreign imports if the rest of domestic industry followed Bethlehem's example. Several days later, United States Steel, the nation's largest steel producer, announced it planned to increase prices for three kinds of construction steel by an average of 6.8 percent, and the following day, Kaiser announced increases of $10 per ton for standard structural shapes and 20 percent more, or $12 per ton, on carbon steel plates.

The President announced he was gratified that United States Steel had limited its increases in recognition of the inflationary problem facing the nation. The following day, a radio account stated that Bethlehem had elected to reduce its price increase to 6 percent.

QUESTIONS

1. What can we say about the nature of the market structure for structural steel?
2. Is price competition in steel possible?
3. Is product differentiation possible in steel?
4. How effective was the President's threat to lower import quotas for steel?

Case 3. The Computer Software Industry

The business of designing the computer programs and information systems required to give electronic computers directions on how to perform their work is generally characterized by a large number of relatively small and not too well financed firms. These firms generally have 100 to 150 employees. Many rely on government contracts for their livelihood, although there is no question that the great 1970 drought has caused the demise of those relying exclusively on government largesse.

For surviving firms like International Information Systems, the year 1970 was a year in which one could be pleased to survive. The following year, experts predicted, would see mergers among survivors in order to stay viable in the face of declining cash balances.

International Information Systems was one of many small computer software firms riding the wave of prosperity that began in 1968. In the last twelve months, IIS has been forced to cut employment back from 100 to 25 and to share quarters with another firm in the same business, away from the downtown area of Washington, D.C. It had trouble with the companies it had acquired during good times to provide a full range of services, resulting in a cash drain that threatened its very existence in the year to follow.

For a few firms, there are opportunities to buy outstanding stock issues at bargain prices. Serendipity Electronics, Inc., was one such which managed to maintain sales volume in 1970, although profits were off slightly. It acquired the operations of a firm formerly employing 150 people in six offices on the West Coast and has a tentative agreement to acquire 80 percent of the outstanding stock of another firm in the Washington, D.C., area. Also, it was fortunate in 1970 to have had a good-sized government contract, which will be extended into 1971 at the same rate, thus assuring good sales volume for that year also.

For some firms, commercial marketing is a new area, in which methods appropriate for large government contracts may not be economical. Some firms are turning to mail order selling.

QUESTIONS

1. What are the prospects for a software firm to be formed via the merger route?
2. Would the software customers benefit if the industry continued to comprise many small firms?
3. If one firm were to achieve dominance, what chances would it have to restrict freedom of entry? Would the chances be greater if computer programs were patentable as an extension of machine design?

Case 4. The Case of the Mellon Company

In 1960, Coal City's Mellon Company participated in a marketing recognition study of suppliers to the building and construction industry. As the newly appointed president recounted to a business journal reporter, "We ranked above one company in the study and it wasn't even in the business."

For many years, the Mellon Company has been known as a Coal City company that sold "smoky, clangy things to other heavy, grey companies," such as coke ovens, bulk coal chemicals, and steel-making plants. Architectural and construction products accounted in 1960 for one-quarter of the Mellon Company sales.

The new president has a marketing orientation, having been advertising manager of one large firm and an agency account executive before that. He believes the future for the company lies in emphasizing end products, rather than in selling materials that go into the making of end products. This belief has recently been reinforced by a charge from the Federal Trade Commission that Mellon's aggressive price competition and contracting arrangements have given the firm a monopoly position in a key compound used in making rubber tires, pharmaceuticals, and other products.

Until quite recently, the company was in the business of selling creosote-treated wood. Its big items were railroad ties and fence posts, sold by the board foot. It also turned out dyestuffs, which it sold to Southern textile mills.

Because customers need chemically treated wood, but don't particularly like smelly and ugly creosote, the firm has been forced to develop a whole range of new products, from color-treated utility poles and fire-retardant wood to laminated structural beams and arches.

The company is presently exploring the possible expansion into disposable cups, soup dishes, and trays, as an outlet for polyester, and a polyester flooring tile, as well as polyethylene bottles, standard building pannels of expandable polystyrene, a design for a marina dock using laminated wood treated with preservative and combined with buoyant, expanded polystyrene to improve flotation, as well as the use of reinforced plastics for piston rings.

QUESTIONS

1. What are the industry structure implications of the Mellon Company plans?
2. What implications are there for marketing and pricing?

Suggested Readings

Adelman, M. A., and P. Adelman: *A Study in Price-cost Behavior and Public Policy,* Harvard Economic Studies, vol. 113, Harvard University Press, Cambridge, Mass., 1959.

Brown Shoe Company v. United States, 370 U.S. 294 (1962).

Caves, Richard: *American Industry: Structure, Conduct, Performance,* Prentice-Hall, Inc., Englewood Cliffs, N.J., 1964.

Clark, J. M.: "Toward a Concept of Workable Competition," *American Economic Review,* vol. 30, pp. 241–256, June, 1940.

Collins, N. R., and Lee E. Preston: *Concentration and Price-cost Margins in Manufacturing Industries,* University of California Press, Berkeley, Calif., 1968.

Cournot, Augustin: *The Mathematical Principles of the Theory of Wealth,* 1838, reprint, Irwin Paperback Classics in Economics, Richard D. Irwin, Inc., Homewood, Ill., 1963.

Dirham, J. B., and A. E. Kahn: *Fair Competition: The Law and the Economics of Antitrust Policy*, Cornell University Press, Ithaca, N.Y., 1954.

Grether, E. T.: "Industrial Organization: Past History and Future Problems," *American Economic Review*, Papers and Proceedings of the 82d Annual Meeting, May, 1970, pp. 83–89.

Kaysen, C.: *United States v. United States Machinery Corp.: An Economic Analysis of an Antitrust Case*, Harvard Economic Studies, vol. 99, Harvard University Press, Cambridge, Mass., 1956.

Mason, E. S.: *Economic Concentration and the Monopoly Problem*, Harvard Economic Studies, vol. 100, Harvard University Press, Cambridge, Mass., 1957.

Robinson, Joan: *The Economics of Imperfect Competition*, 2d ed., Macmillan & Co., Ltd., London, 1969.

Shubik, Martin: "A Curmudgeon's Guide to Microeconomics," *Journal of Economic Literature*, vol. 8, no. 2, pp. 418–425, June, 1970, on oligopoly theory.

Stigler, George J: "The Kinky Oligopoly Demand Curve and Rigid Prices," *The Journal of Political Economy*, vol. 55, pp. 432–449, 1947, reprinted in *Readings in Price Theory*, Richard D. Irwin, Inc., Homewood, Ill., 1952, pp. 410–439.

chapter 3
business forecasting:
scope
and
techniques

Business forecasting has to do with the process of predicting future events and estimating current and past events. With the aid of forecasts, we feel more confident in coping with the risk or uncertainty inherent in future events.[1] By evaluating the accuracy of past estimates, we are able to correct the estimation process, so that past errors are reduced or avoided. We must, therefore, not only determine with some degree of precision what is going on now, but also establish some means of judging what has happened in the past.

While we will be concerned with the methods used to produce reasonable forecasts, these methods are more properly the province of econometrics or applied economics. Here, they are merely a means to an end. The end is the managerial process by which forecast information is used in the administration of the business enterprise.

SIGNIFICANCE OF FORECASTS

Executives at all levels of a business enterprise make forecasts or, at minimum, make assumptions about the future in connection with operating decisions. The production manager requires estimates of sales in order to plan future production levels. The treasurer requires estimates of economic activity and money availability in order to budget for cash needs. The sales manager needs estimates of inventories in the hands of customers in order to plan sales force assignments. The personnel director estimates labor availability in order to advise

---

[1] The distinction between risk and uncertainty was first advanced by Frank Knight. Simply put, when the probability of occurence of an event is known, risk is present; when the probability is not known, then there is uncertainty.

the production manager of the feasibility of running extra shifts. Collectively, all of these estimates operate to cope with the uncertainty surrounding the firm and make possible its functioning.

Forecasts of probable demand for the output of a firm are a link between the uncontrollable external environment in which the firm operates and the controllable internal environment, which is the organization. This link is generally forged by relating fluctuations in sales to some economic variable representative of the external environment. Assuming the economic variable is routinely forecast by government or by private research agencies, the firm may predict its probable sales level by applying the devised relationship. Generally, such relationships are based on a simple regression analysis, with company sales as a dependent variable.

The sales forcast is an assessment of the impact that the firm will be able to make on the external environment. But it is also an interrelationship between the internal and the external elements in that sales of the product will depend not only on the demand for the product but also on the ability of the firm to meet it. Where the demand depends on the availability of consumer income, holdings of liquid assets, and consumer desire to incur debt, as well as on consumer expectations concerning the future, the supply relies on the firm's production capability, its current level of inventory, cash position, and availability of labor.

Automobile manufacturers, for example, want to know how many cars can be sold in future years so that they can plan commitments as to raw materials, including steel, plate glass, tires, upholstery fabric, and a host of minor accessories and parts. No company can or should make commitments of this kind without some estimate of possible future production, because both over- and underproduction can be costly. Overproduction ties up capital in excess inventory and subjects the company to possible capital losses from inventory depreciation and obsolescence. To carry inventory, the company has to pay interest, explicitly or implicitly, and warehousing and insurance expenses. Overproduction also means that the company is subject to the strong likelihood that subsequent production levels will have to be reduced and that this will have an adverse effect on employee morale, in addition to wasting managerial and capital resources because of idleness.

Underproduction costs the company the revenue which could have been earned had the firm produced enough cars to meet the demand. Such a loss of sales has a possible cumulative effect, in the sense that those customers who switch to a competitor's car may not return.

Economic forecasts play a decisive role in long-term corporate planning, such as for capital expenditures for plant and equipment, forming the basis for construction decisions for new and expanded plant. The construction of new production capacity generally requires considerable lead time, during which sites are investigated, plans are drawn, and actual construction takes place. The layout of the plant, the recruitment of the necessary employees, and the acquisition of the needed equipment and materials takes time and a considerable amount of detailed planning. If we consider that in order to produce a 1975 model automobile, plant must be onstream beginning in 1974, staffing and equipping must take place during 1973, and construction in 1972 and 1973, then the planning and site acquisition must have taken place in 1972 at the latest, while financial planning would have to be undertaken at the latest in 1971. Once the plant is built, the company is committed, for better or worse, and must provide maintenance and pay taxes at minimum, even if it decides not to use the facility, until it is disposed of.

Once the firm does decide to build, the economic forecast then forms an indispensable part of the planning which informs the company whether or not the cash flow will be sufficient to handle the new construction, or whether additional financing will be needed.

DEMAND FACTORS

In forecasting the sales of a particular product, there are factors which affect the demand in the short run, and those which affect it in the long run. The demand for a new automobile, for example, is determined to a large extent by the price of the car and the disposable income of the family. But price affects demand at point of sale, while disposable income available for the purchase operates over a longer period. Income expectations and price expectations also have their relevant time periods. In making a forecast of demand and its responsiveness, we are interested not only in the possible changes in demand but also in the period in which the estimate is relevant.

FLOW VERSUS STOCK DEMANDS

When we make a short-run forecast, we are generally considering the potential demand for something as a function of the economic variables affecting its consumption. Price, disposable income, and expectations as to price and income are generally most important. But if the product is durable in some way, or if a lead time is needed within which to change the rate of output, then the demand relationships are altered.

Let us consider first the demand for a consumer good or a good which is used up shortly after its acquisition. The demand for such a good may be considered as the demand for a flow of goods and services and the variables, price and income, will alter the rate at which the goods are supplied to meet the demand. Consumer durables, on the other hand, render their service over time. The purchase of such a good is a function not only of price and income but also of the useful life of the stock of goods similar in service-rendering capability.

It is therefore necessary in the short run to consider not only the possible uses of such an item, its price and the price of substitutes, and the available disposable income of possible customers, but also the size of the stock of items or substitutes presently in the hands of customers, the age of that stock, and its probable service life. The longer the "run," the less the stock will exercise an influence on our calculations.

NEW VERSUS ESTABLISHED PRODUCTS

In forecasting the demand for a new product, the firm will have to resort to market surveys of consumer need, analysis of sales records of potentially competing products, or analysis of the life cycle of existing products which may be substitutes. If the product is an established one, on the other hand, changes in some key variables such as consumer income or the level of economic activity may provide the required clues. Forecasting, in the latter case, becomes a matter of predicting possible elasticities or responsiveness to key variable changes. The market survey method of predicting new product demand requires that questionnaires be sent to potential customers selected by a random or stratified sampling method.

Sales of a Comparable Product. The sales record of a comparable product may be used as the basis for making an estimate or a prediction of sales of a new product. The problem of forecasting potential sales volume for a wrinkle-free fabric for shirts can be solved by using the annual sales volume of a close substitute, perhaps broadcloth, then calculating the probable market share of the new material, on the assumption that it will replace all or part of the present product. The problem of forecasting, then, has two aspects: first, to forecast the demand for broadcloth, and second, to forecast the market share of the new product.

The Life-cycle Approach. This method is based on the theory, referred to in Chapter 1, that each product goes through a predictable growth pattern following its initial introduction. Application of this method assumes that a product experiences an introductory phase, further development, growth, maturity, stabilization in acceptance, and then decline. The key to using this method is to find a growth pattern in some established product which serves the same market, so as to use its record as a guide. Photocopy machine manufacturers, for example, might possibly have used the growth pattern for computers as a guide in forecasting.

STATISTICAL EVIDENCES OF DEMAND

In analyzing the demand for an established product or a commodity, we attempt to identify and separate out the factors which influence demand responsiveness in different ways. We attempt to isolate those factors such as price change or political events which affect the demand for a product in the very short run. Perhaps a storm, a crop failure, or some other natural or man-made hazard may cause a temporary shortage of the product, and this will be reflected in a price rise. Perhaps the prices of substitutes have risen, thus causing an increase in demand. By plotting the sales of the product against a time scale, we observe the mingled effects of many events and causes. We will not be able to identify all the factors which may cause variation, however, unless we employ the tools of statistical analysis.

If, for example, the demand for a product appears to be influenced mainly by the general level of economic activity, then our forecasting will be concerned almost entirely with methods of predicting the gross national product, or the level of disposable income. We may employ econometric models or systems of simultaneous equations in which the gross national product is a dependent variable. Other models are more concerned with estimating the several components of GNP such as consumption, capital goods spending, or private construction. It may, for example, be more worthwhile to a producer of electrical equipment to have a forecast of the probable level of investment spending than of GNP as a whole.

Product or commodity forecasting generally works from a supplied GNP forecast or a surrogate, such as disposable income or payroll data. It may also be based on a simple trend analysis, employ an econometric model in which product demand is the dependent variable, or use an input-output grid, in which sales are the sum of the anticipated demands of using industries. The aggregated opinions of expert observers, as opinion polls or surveys, also may be used. A recent variation which will be mentioned is termed "Delphi," after the place at which the ancient Greek oracle issued forecasts of things to come.

FORECASTING THE GNP

Forecasting the probable level of the gross national product may employ relatively simple trend analysis, business cycle analysis, or econometric models.

TIME SERIES ANALYSIS

Originally this sort of analysis attempted to discover the nature of economic fluctuations to ascertain if any natural "laws" could be said to govern the level of activity from one period to the next. Time series analysis discovered that there are four different kinds of factors influencing the level of economic activity. These are secular trend, cyclical, seasonal, and random variation.

Trend Effects. Trends, or long-term effects, are like ground swells which lift everything to a higher level and keep them there for appreciable periods. Trend is generally considered to mean long term, and so deals with some basic factors which influence the demand for a product, keeping it moving along in some steady relation to other measures of economic activity. A product that has become part of the fabric of everyday living, and whose consumption is not related to the creation of new markets or uses, may be influenced strongly by population growth and the level of disposable income. We would expect that in such instances the product would exhibit a steady growth, predictable with a fair degree of certainty.

Cyclical Effects. These refer to the interrelationship of the demand for the product with economic factors which are periodic in nature. Let us assume that the product is floor wax. Trend effects would relate floor wax usage to the general level of disposable income and to the fact that as time goes on, more and more people wax their floors and do so with greater frequency. Cyclical effects would have to do with the fact that floor wax may be affected by the number of new houses built and occupied. If housing starts are cyclical in nature, then the demand for floor wax, being a function of the number of new houses occupied, may also have a cyclic feature.

Seasonal Effects. These are somewhat like cyclical effects, but they are more predictable, coming as they do with some degree of certainty at a specified time of the year. At Christmas, it is the custom to do much entertaining, and it might well be that the sales of floor wax would be higher at that time as people clean their homes in preparation. If so, we might well point to a customary increase in demand at this time of the year and term it a seasonal increase.

Random Variation. In making a forecast, the most troublesome problem is to estimate random disturbances. Since their occurrences do not follow any set pattern, nor is there any sign to indicate their impending arrival, we have no way to predict their probable occurrence nor the magnitude of their effects on the results of the forecast. We generally make allowances for this factor in our forecasting models.

Analysis. To analyze the demand for a product, we must consider the part of the demand which is caused by the normal level of sales, usually termed the trend or long-term effect. Next, we consider the cyclical effect and then the seasonal effect. The fluctuations which are residual are usually random, and if we can explain them with reference to known happenings, we are fortunate. Most times we cannot, and we are simply content to show these residuals as unexplained or random.

The influence of cyclical variations also may be felt in the short run, if they happen to coincide with a similar turn in the seasonal. When the sales of automobiles increase in the spring, we generally term this a seasonal effect. But a cyclical revival may occur at that time also, and if these coincide, the automobile industry may well have a banner year. Where seasonals in the auto industry are generally caused by the desire to postpone purchase until the passing of winter, cyclical effects are often related to the aging of existing stocks of cars and the periodic occurrence of heavy buying to renew or replace stocks. This kind of buying may be stimulated in one year by easy money in a credit cycle or by a random occurrence of easy credit coming from other causes. The resultant "bump" in the sales curve may be felt in a cyclic way for a number of years thereafter.

BUSINESS CYCLE INDICATORS

In the field of economic forecasting, the so-called business cycle indicators, pioneered by Wesley C. Mitchell and developed by the National Bureau of Economic Research, play a large part. These indicators can be traced to work done in December, 1937, when Mitchell, together with Arthur F. Burns, conducted a study to find some reliable statistical indicators of cyclical revivals. They studied almost 500 monthly or quarterly economic data series and, from this number, chose twenty-one as the most trustworthy.

To be useful, Mitchell and Burns required that the series be operative under a variety of conditions, lead the cycle by three to six months, sweep smoothly up from each cycle through to the next peak and then smoothly down, be pronounced enough so as to be readily recognized, and finally, be related to general business activity in an obvious way.[2]

The work of Mitchell and Burns was carried forward by Geoffrey H. Moore, who in 1950 published a revised list in a work entitled *Statistical Indicators of Cyclical Revivals and Recessions.* Moore's list retains fourteen of the older series and introduces seven new series. The new series include data on new orders, incorporations, unemployment, income, inventories, bank rates, and installment debt, not available earlier.

Moore also classified his twenty-one indicators into leading, coincident, and lagging, a somewhat different format than before. Further study led Moore and his associates in the National Bureau in 1961 to revise the list and expand it into a set of twenty-six economic series.[3] The set of twenty-six series again is classified into three categories, with twelve leaders, nine coinciders, and five laggers.

In 1966, Moore, in cooperation with Julius Shiskin of the U.S. Bureau of the Census, developed a new list of indicators and an explicit scoring plan to

[2] For a complete statement of their five criteria, see Geoffrey H. Moore, ed., *Business Cycle Indicators,* Princeton University Press, Princeton, N.J., 1961, vol. 1, pp. 165–166.
[3] Geoffrey H. Moore, *Statistical Indicators of Cyclical Revivals and Recessions,* National Bureau of Economic Research, Inc., New York, 1950, p. 68, and, by the same author, *Business Cycle Indicators,* Princeton University Press, Princeton, N.J., 1961, vol. II, pp. 3–63.

help evaluate and select indicators. The plan assigns scores ranging from 0 to 100 to each economic series, depending upon their economic significance, statistical adequacy, historical conformity to business cycles, cyclical timing record, smoothness, and promptness of publication. Admittedly arbitrary, the scoring is explained by the authors as an attempt to make the criteria for selection explicit, and also to increase the amount of information available to the user to aid in evaluating current behavior.[4] This list contains thirty-six leading series, twenty-five coincident series, eleven lagging, and sixteen not classified, for a total of eighty-eight series, of which seventy-two reflect economic fluctuation in general. A short list of twenty-five is also presented to replace the 1961 list of twenty-six series.

The short list of twenty-five series is made up of the following:

Leading indicators:
1. Average length of work week, production workers, manufacturing (hours)
2. Nonagricultural placements, all industries
3. Index of net business formation
4. New orders for durable goods (dollars)
5. Contracts and orders for new plant and equipment (dollars)
6. New building permits, private housing
7. Change in book value of manufacturing and trade inventories (dollars)
8. Index of industrial materials prices
9. Index of stock prices, 500 common stocks
10. Corporate profits after taxes, quarterly (dollars)
11. Ratio, price to unit labor cost, manufacturing (index)
12. Change in consumer installment debt (dollars)

Coincident indicators:
1. Number of employees on nonagricultural payrolls
2. Total unemployment rate
3. Gross national product in constant dollars
4. Index of industrial production
5. Personal income (dollars)
6. Manufacturing and trade sales (dollars)
7. Sales of retail stores (dollars)

Lagging indicators:
1. Unemployment rate, persons unemployed fifteen weeks or more
2. Business expenditures for new plant and equipment (dollars)
3. Book value of manufacturing and trade inventories (dollars)

[4] *Indicators of Business Expansions and Contractions,* National Bureau of Economic Research, Inc., New York, 1967, p. 3.

4. Labor cost per unit of manufacturing output (index)

5. Commercial and industrial loans outstanding, weekly, large commercial banks (dollars)

6. Bank rates on short-term business loans

To make the indicators useful for business cycle analysis, Moore and Shiskin classify the entire series of seventy-two indicators according to their economic interrelationship and cyclical behavior. Table 3-1 (p. 68) shows the indicators classified in this manner.

The twenty-five series on the "short" list are shown in Figure 3-1. These charts are published monthly by the U.S. Department of Commerce in the *Business Conditions Digest* (formerly called *Business Cycle Development*).[5]

THE DIFFUSION INDEX

The statistical data presented in Figure 3-1 are taken from various sources and are reported monthly or quarterly. Although they represent the most reliable indicators available, they cannot be used individually with any great degree of confidence. One swallow doesn't make a summer, and a drop in durable goods orders similarly may not foretell a change in the economic climate.

In order to narrow the chances of making a wrong prediction based on any individual indicator, and to find out how broad and pervasive a recession or a recovery is, a new method of interpreting the series was developed and is called a *diffusion index*. It is formed by counting the number of indicators that are rising at any one time and taking this as a percentage of the number under observation. For example, if nine out of the twelve leading series turn up during a given period, the diffusion index is 75 percent. On the other hand, if nine turn down, the index is 25 percent.

As defined by Moore, it is called a diffusion index because ". . . it shows how widely or narrowly diffused an expansionary movement is among the indicators."[6]

During business cycle expansion, Moore found that such indexes generally are above 50 percent, and during contractions they are generally below that figure. Almost invariably, the leading diffusion index reaches a maximum and begins to decline before the end of a business cycle expansion. It also reaches a minimum and begins to rise before the end of a business cycle contraction.

Usually the diffusion indexes based on leading indicators shift their position before those based on coincident indicators, and these in turn move before those based on lagging indicators. Moore notes that "although the movement and meaning of each individual series should not be lost sight of, the dif-

[5] Note that the numbering is different, however.
[6] Geoffrey H. Moore, *Business Cycle Indicators*, p. 10.

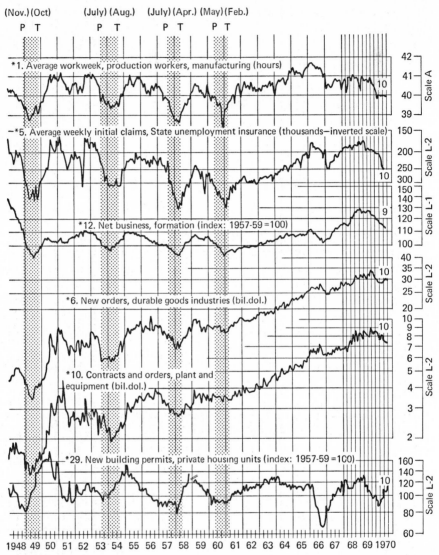

Figure 3-1. Twenty-five cyclical indicators. (Source: *Business Conditions Digest,* U.S. Department of Commerce.)

fusion index provides a convenient summary measure of the scope of cyclical movements in the economy, against which one can compare and analyze the changes in particular indicators."

The working of the diffusion indexes is shown in Figure 3-2.

Diffusion indexes are also constructed on an individual series basis. For instance, a diffusion index for new orders in durable goods may be constructed

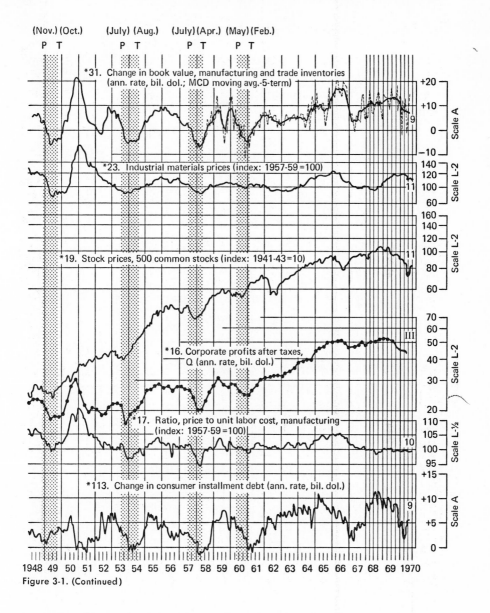

Figure 3-1. (Continued)

by counting the kinds of durable goods industries experiencing an increase in orders and expressing that as a percentage of the total number of kinds of durable goods industries covered. The *Business Conditions Digest* contains diffusion indexes for each individual series.

Diffusion indexes have three limitations which impair their usefulness in forecasting business fluctuations. Two of these are inherent in any business cycle

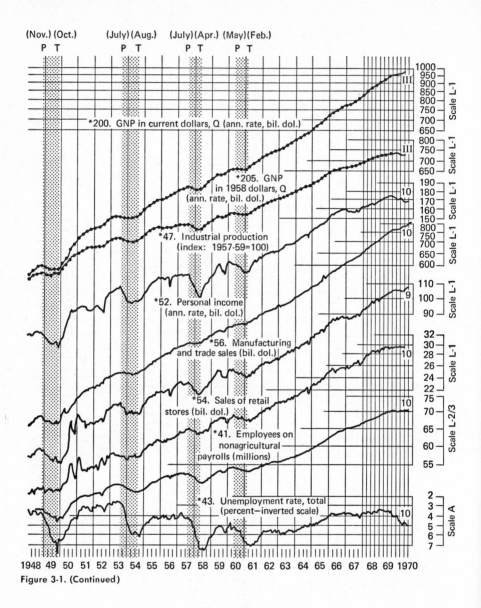

Figure 3-1. (Continued)

indicator. First, they fail to give a clear indication as to the magnitude of the impending change. Second, they are not immune from the effects of random factors which influence their movements. Appropriate only to diffusion indexes is the third limitation, namely, the problem of weight. We cannot say that the decline in new orders for durable goods has the same economic impact as a drop in contracts for new plant and equipment, yet each is weighted equally.

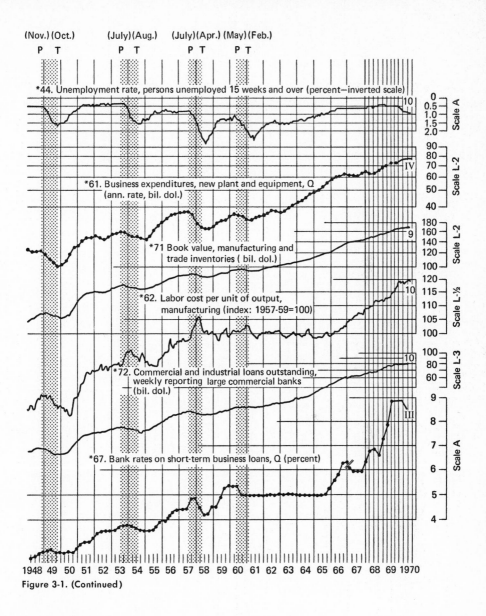

Figure 3-1. (Continued)

ECONOMETRIC MODELS

Econometrics may be defined as a science of economic measurement. It is a combination of economics, statistics, and mathematics. The stuff econometrics is made of is statistical data. An econometrician first formulates a certain hypothesis concerning a given economic phenomenon. He chooses certain vari-

TABLE 3-1. BUSINESS CYCLE INDICATORS

Economic Process Cyclical Timing	1. Employment and Unemployment (14 series)	2. Production, Income, Consumption, and Trade (8 series)	3. Fixed Capital Investment (14 series)	4. Inventories and Inventory Investment (9 series)	5. Prices, Costs, and Profits (10 series)	6. Money and Credit (17 series)
Leading indicators (36 series)	Marginal employment adjustments (5 series)		Formation of business enterprises (2 series) New investment commitments (8 series)	Inventory investment and purchasing (7 series)	Sensitive commodity prices (1 series) Stock prices (1 series) Profits and profit margins (4 series)	Flows of money and credit (6 series) Credit difficulties (2 series)
Roughly coincident indicators (25 series)	Job vacancies (2 series) Comprehensive employment (3 series) Comprehensive unemployment (3 series)	Comprehensive production (3 series) Comprehensive income (2 series) Comprehensive consumption and trade (3 series)	Backlog of investment commitments (2 series)		Comprehensive wholesale prices (2 series)	Bank reserves (1 series) Money market interest rates (4 series)
Lagging indicators (11 series)	Long-duration unemployment (1 series)		Investment expenditures (2 series)	Inventories (2 series)	Unit labor costs (2 series)	Outstanding debt (2 series) Interest rates on business loans and mortgages (2 series)

Source: Geoffrey H. Moore and Julius Shiskin, *Indicators of Business Expansions and Contractions*, National Bureau of Economic Research, Inc., New York, 1967.

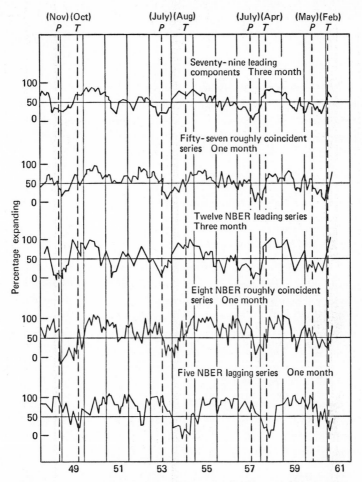

Figure 3-2. Current diffusion indexes, 1948 to 1961: leading, roughly coincident, and lagging series. *Note:* P stands for the peak of the cycle, T for the trough. (Source: Julius Shiskin, *Signals of Recession and Recovery*, National Bureau of Economic Research Inc., New York, 1961, p. 61.)

ables which are interrelated in some manner. As we have seen, the demand for automobiles is related to consumer's disposable income, the age distribution of the stock of existing cars, the price of used cars, the debt-to-income ratio of consumers, and possibly other factors. Through his training in economic analysis, the econometrician is able to arrange these variables in such a manner as to show the functional relationship of the demand for automobiles to the other factors. After the hypothesis is formulated, the econometrician uses his knowledge of mathematics and statistics to construct a model which will explain the "causes" of the economic phenomena under investigation. His last step is to select the statistical data and test the validity of the model.

A SIMPLE MODEL

The simplest econometric model is one which consists of one dependent and one independent variable, plus a random disturbance factor, the so-called *stochastic variable*. For example, if we let Y represent sales of baby food, and hypothesize that it is a function of the baby population X and of a stochastic or random variable u, then we have an econometric model which appears simply as

$$Y = f(x) + u$$

And if we can assume that the relationship is linear, then the equation can be written as

$$Y = a + bx + u$$

The equation means that changes in the baby population will affect changes in the sales of baby food. Since this is a positive relationship, sales of baby food will go up as the baby population increases. How large is the latter's impact on the former will depend on the value of the coefficient b. The term u is introduced here to account for the deviation of the forecast from the actual result.[7]

A MORE COMPLEX MODEL

Econometric models generally contain two basic kinds of equations: behavioral and definitional. One definitional equation states that the level of gross national product is determined by the sum of consumption, investment, and government spending or

$$Y = C + I + G$$

Such an equation simply shows the economic interrelation among the variables but does not show what determines the level of each component. For that, we need behavioral equations such as

$$C = a + bP_{-1} + cW_1 + dW_2 + u_c$$

which states that the level of consumption is determined by last year's profits, this year's wage level paid by private industry and wages paid by government, and a random disturbance factor u.

---

[7] If we knew all the factors at work and had all the necessary data, and if we could account for all randomness in human response, and lastly, if we could eliminate all errors in observation, it might be unnecessary to have such a stochastic variable. See J. Johnston, *Econometric Methods*, McGraw-Hill Book Company, New York, 1963, pp. 5–6.

Lawrence R. Klein formulates six algebraic equations to describe the functioning of the American economy during the years 1921 to 1941.[8] The behavioral equations are:

$$C = a + bP + cP_{-1} + d(W_1 + W_2) + u_c$$
$$I = a + bP + cP_{-1} - dK_{-1} + u_I$$
$$W_1 = a + bX + cX_{-1} + d(t - 1931) + u_w$$

The first is a consumption function, which expresses consumption in terms of profits in the current year P, in the preceding year P_{-1}, wages paid by private industry W_1, government wages W_2, and the disturbance factor u_c. The statistical findings show that the actual consumption function is

$$C = 16.78 + .02P + .23P_{-1} + .80(W_1 + W_2) + u_c$$

and tells us that consumption is affected more by changes in wages than profits. The message is of course contained in the various coefficients or weights. Notice also that last year's profits are more important than this year's profits in determining the level of current consumption.

The investment function describes total net investment I in relation to profits P in the current year, last year's profits P_{-1}, capital stock in the preceding year K_{-1}, and the appropriate random disturbance factor u_I. The study reveals that total net investment is related positively to profits and negatively to capital stock in the preceding year, as shown by the following equation:

$$I = 17.79 + .23p + .55P_{-1} - .15K_{-1} + u_I$$

In other words, as profits increase, corporations are induced to invest more in plant and equipment. Profits in the preceding year have more influence on this year's capital expenditures than do profits in the current year. On the other hand, if capital stock at the beginning of the year is large, net investment will be lower than otherwise. The reason is that corporations build fewer factories and buy fewer machines in the face of excess capacity in existing plants.

The third equation is the demand for labor function, which represents the amount of wages paid by the private sector of the economy. The demand for labor is seen to be dependent on the total value of private industry output in the current year X, and in the preceding year X_{-1}, plus the number of years since 1931 ($t - t_0$), and the random variable u_w. With the coefficients, the equation reads

$$W_1 = 1.60 + .42X + .16X_{-1} + .13(t - t_0) + u_w$$

It indicates that there has been a secular increase in wages paid since 1931. The

[8] The original equations are contained in his *Economic Fluctuations in the United States, 1921–1941*, John Wiley & Sons, Inc., New York, 1950. The method given here is taken from Henri Theil, *Applied Economic Forecasting*, North-Holland Publishing Company, Amsterdam, 1966, pp. 78–82.

findings also show that private industry output in the current year has more bearing on wages currently being paid than does last year's output.

The second group of three equations is definitional. Each equation will follow directly from the definition of each term. For example, X, or private industry output, is represented as being the sum of expenditures for consumption, investment, and government operations, or

$$X = C + I + G$$

The two remaining equations are

$$P = X - W_1 - T$$
$$K = K_{-1} + I$$

These state (1) that profits P consist of the output of private industry X, less wages W_1 paid by private industry and the industry tax bill T, and (2) that current capital stock level K consists of the total of current investment and last year's capital stock.

This system of six equations contains, then, ten variables. Four are outside the model or exogenous, and six are endogenous or within the model. The exogenous variables are wages paid by government W_2, taxes T, all other government expenditures G, and time t. The endogenous variables are consumption C, the total output of industry X, current wages paid by industry W_1, the level of investment I, the level of capital stock K, and business profits P.

The model in effect asserts that, with the proper set of coefficients, we can determine unique values for the endogenous variables, if we know the exogenous variables, and if estimates are supplied for last year's output of private industry X_{-1}, last year's profits P_{-1}, and the level of capital stock in the previous year K_{-1}.

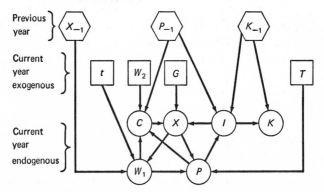

Figure 3-3. Arrow scheme of Klein's model. (Adapted from Henri Theil, *Applied Economic Forecasting*, North-Holland Publishing Company, Amsterdam, 1966, p. 81.)

The way in which the model works is shown in Figure 3-3. Such a set of six equations we term structural, because it defines the structure of the economy. It can be solved in the form given or in a reduced form obtained by expressing each current-year endogenous variable as a function of the lagged and the exogenous variables, a constant, and the random variables. For example, we can solve the consumption function for the system in the following manner, expressing it in terms of lagged and exogenous variables.

$$C = a_0 \qquad \qquad \qquad \text{(constant term)}$$
$$+ a_1 P_{-1} + a_2 K_{-1} + a_3 X_{-1} \qquad \text{(lagged variables)}$$
$$+ a_4 W_2 + a_5 T + a_6 G + a_7 T \qquad \text{(current exogenous variables)}$$
$$+ a_8 u_c + a_9 u_i + a_{10} u_w \qquad \text{(stochastic variables)[9]}$$

FORECASTING PRODUCT DEMAND

Econometric models, as we noted, may have gross national product as either a dependent variable or as an independent variable. In the preceding section, we were essentially assuming that we could use econometric methods to forecast the level of gross national product or of its components. In this section, however, we will assume that income is known and that the dependent variable is the demand for some product or industry output.

CHOW'S MODEL

Chow explains the demand for automobiles by the following general expression:

$$X_t = c\overset{*}{X}_t \,(P, I, u) - kX_{t-1}$$

In this equation, simplified somewhat from the original, Chow states that the demand for automobiles, in time period t, is dependent on $\overset{*}{X}_t$, the desired stock per capita at the end of the year t; P_t, the relative price of automobiles; I_t, the real income per capita; and u_t, the random variable, all for time period t; k, the ratio of the depreciated old stock per capita in the current year to the stock per capita a year earlier; and X_{t-1}, the number of automobiles purchased the year before.

The equation can be written as

$$X_t^1 = (\overset{*}{X}_t^1 - X_{t-1}) + (1 - k)\, X_{t-1}$$

where $\qquad \overset{*}{X}_t = a - bP_t + cI_t + u_t$

[9] Henri Theil cautions that this set may be used if the underlying data are linear, op. cit., p. 82 Since econometric models are essentially a codification of past experience, unexpected changes in the structure and want patterns of the economy can cause complex systems of equations to fail in very spectacular ways. See "Bad Year for Econometrics," Business Week, Dec. 20, 1969, p. 36.

Chow uses twenty-eight annual observations for the period 1921 to 1953, excluding the years 1942 to 1946, and calculates the statistical demand function for the desired stock per capita as

$$\overset{*}{X}_t = 1.1666 - .039544P_t + .020827I_{dt}$$
$$\quad\quad\quad\quad (.004522) \quad\quad (.001749)$$

where $R^2 = .850$ and $s = .738$

He calculates the demand function for the purchase of automobiles per capita as[10]

$$X_t = .07791 - .020127P_t + .011699I_{dt} - .23104X_{t-1}$$
$$\quad\quad\quad\quad (.002648) \quad\quad (.001070) \quad\quad (.04719)$$

where $R^2 = .858$ and $s = .308$

What do these findings mean to United States automobile manufacturers? They mean that increases in the per capita demand for automobiles are related positively (+.011699) to rising real income per capita, but negatively (−.020127) to a higher relative price of cars and also negatively (−.23104) to an increase in the number of cars per capita purchased in the preceding year. Therefore, one may conclude that when real income per capita increases, the demand for automobiles will be higher, assuming no change in the other variables. On the other hand, if the price of automobiles is raised or previous year's sales were to increase, they would reduce the demand for cars in the present period.

Now the question is, "How good is the model in explaining per capita demand during the period under study?" Answering this question is the job of the coefficient of determination R^2, which has a value of .858. This means that 85.8 times out of 100, changes in the demand for automobiles were explained jointly by changes in the relative price of automobiles, real income per capita, and in the number of cars per capita purchased in the last year. The reliability of the coefficients is indicated by the standard errors of the coefficients, which appear in the parentheses below the coefficients themselves. The smaller the standard error, the more reliable is the coefficient for predictive purposes.

Of the three standard errors shown, only the last is somewhat large in relation to its coefficient, and this means that there is a wider spread among the data measuring the variable X_{t-1}, thus rendering this coefficient less reliable as an indicator of the importance of X_{t-1} in the model.

In order to employ the Chow model for forecasting the demand for automobiles, it would be necessary to have an estimate of the level of disposable

[10] Gregory C. Chow, "Statistical Demand Functions for Automobiles and Their Use in Forecasting," in Arnold C. Harberger (ed.), *The Demand for Durable Goods*, The University of Chicago Press, Chicago, Ill., 1960.

income for the year in question and to know the price of automobiles relative to the price of other things. We would also have to have some idea of the level of all prices in order to convert disposable income into real income.

INPUT-OUTPUT MODELS

The input-output model is sometimes said to have originated with the interindustry analysis contained in the famous *Tableau Economique* of Francois Quesnay, court physician to King Louis XV of France. The *Tableau* was used to show how the national product was distributed among different classes of society. Two centuries later, Professor Wassily W. Leontief modified and expanded the *Tableau* into an input-output model capable of analyzing national income accounts and predicting long-term changes in the national economic structure.[11]

These econometric devices consist of tables of matrices which depict the flow of goods among industries and other components of the economy. They present the supply and demand interrelationship among various sectors in the form of coefficients or rates per dollar of output. Input-output analysis is generally used to estimate the production of each of the constituent industries or sectors, if the final demand changes, but assuming that the structure as given by the table does not change.

Normally, the coefficients are calculated from detailed econometric studies of the inputs and outputs of industries showing the sources of their inputs and the percentage distribution per dollar of product and the destination of their output among all demanders. Coefficients can be computed also from simple census information for a given year; however their validity as a forecasting device beyond one or two years might be open to question.

Table 3-2 contains a simple input-output format where the a's stand for

[11] Almarin Phillips presents Quesnay's *Tableau* in input-output model form in "The *Tableau* as a Simple Leontief Model," *Quarterly Journal of Economics*, vol. 69, pp. 137–144, Feb., 1955. Leontief's work is contained in *Structure of the American Economy, 1919–1939*, 2d ed., Oxford University Press, New York, 1951. The advanced student will want to consult Robert Dorfman, Paul A. Samuelson, and Robert M. Solow, *Linear Programming and Economic Analysis*, McGraw-Hill Book Company, New York, 1958, pp. 204–264.

TABLE 3-2. INPUT-OUTPUT FORMAT

Producer	User 1	User 2 . . .	User m	Final Demand	Total Output
1	a_{11}	$a_{12} \cdots$	a_{1m}	d_1	s_1
2	a_{21}	$a_{22} \cdots$	a_{2m}	d_2	s_2
3	a_{31}	$a_{32} \cdots$	a_{3m}	d_3	s_3
.	.	.	.	.	.
.	.	.	.	.	.
.	.	.	.	.	.
n	a_{n1}	$a_{n2} \cdots$	a_{nm}	d_n	s_n

the dollar amount of the products of the industries shown down the side which are used by the industries shown across the top, the d's stand for the final demand for the products of each of the industries in the stub down the side, and total output consists of the final demand, or demand for consumption purposes, plus demand of industries as inputs to another process.

The coefficients are computed by dividing the a's for each user by the total output of the using firm, so that we obtain a menu or percent distribution of the inputs for each. Since the coefficient is calculated by dividing the a_{ij}'s (or any a) by the total output of the user firm, and we calculate similar percents down each user column, then the producers would compute the distribution of their sales by taking each percentage and calculating across the rows to arrive at the s values.[12]

The Almon Model. This input-output model consists of a matrix of 90 rows and 144 columns, developed by a team of economists at the University of Maryland under the leadership of Clopper Almon, Jr. It has a total of 12,960 entries. Of the 144 column vectors, 90 represent intermediate demands or the a's in Table 3-2. The matrix is consequently capable of producing annual forecasts for 8,100 separate commodity flows between industries.

The row vectors include listings ranging from livestock, crops, forestry, and fishery products to business travel, entertainment, and office supplies. Reading across a row vector, we see a profile of its markets, while looking down a column, we find the industry bill of materials, or its spending on capital investment, or a consumer's shopping list, or a government budget, or the export invoice the nation pays annually. Representative table entries are given in Table 3-3 (pp. 78–79).

Tables are prepared for each year for the period 1963 to 1975. From a series of such tables, one can see the changes in market profiles, variations in consumer spending patterns, and changes in bills of materials. A master table is set up to facilitate comparison of growth trends between industries. The arrangement of the matrix for the master table is the same as shown in Table 3-3, except that the body of the table consists of coefficients rather than absolute values.[13]

How the Model Works. The forecasting aspect of the model consists of two parts. First, there is the structural forecast which describes the technology and functioning of the economy, but not its size. Second, there is the dollar volume forecast.

[12] The interindustry demands related to changes in final demands and the resultant output of the economy call for the use of matrix algebra.
[13] Clopper Almon, Jr., *The American Economy to 1975*, Harper & Row, Publishers, Incorporated, New York, 1966, pp. 8–9.

Structural forecasts are of four kinds:

1. Changes in consumer spending per dollar of incremental income. This is based on an analysis of the spending of families of various incomes, combined with a study of postwar changes in spending, income, and prices.
2. Capital spending required per dollar of sales expansion. This has been approximated from annual capital investment data and the depreciation guidelines of the Treasury Department. First, estimates of the stocks of capital equipment were prepared. The growth of these stocks was compared with the expansion of capacity or output in the same industries, thus producing estimates of the capital equipment required per dollar of expanded sales for each industry.
3. Material requirements per dollar of sales. This factor represents the bill of materials per dollar of sales for each of the ninety industries and was prepared by the Department of Commerce for 1958. In some instances after review by the Almon group, trends were projected.
4. Labor required per dollar of sales. This factor is based on an estimate of labor productivity, projected from trends exhibited over the last ten years.

After completing the structural forecasts, the next step was to calculate the dollar volume forecasts. Here, the team faced the problem of circularity, since basically they were dealing with the circular flow of goods and services. The problem arises because investment is part of final demand, which determines output. Output in turn, however, determines the level of investment. After-tax income determines consumer demand, which leads to outputs, which in turn determine employment levels. In order to make employment match the forecast labor force, the team had to come back to revise their forecasts of after-tax 'ncome.[14]

The sales forecasts were arrived at by a six-step procedure:

1. Project government expenditures, exports, and competitive imports.
2. Pick a trial projection of after-tax income per capita, and, on that basis, calculate consumer expenditures per person on the products of each industry in each year of the forecast. Multiply these estimates by the expected population to arrive at an estimate of personal consumption.
3. Pick a trial projection of industry sales for each year of the forecast period. Deduce from it the amount representing investment and construction spending and inventory accumulation for each industry in each forecast year.
4. Add across the rows of all the final demands to get a total final demand column for each forecast year and work back using the structural forecast of material needs of each industry in each year to obtain industry outputs

---

[14] *Ibid.*, pp. 13–15.

TABLE 3-3. INTERINDUSTRY ACCOUNTS (MILLIONS OF DOLLARS)

	Buyer							
	Intermediate Demands					Equipment Investment		
Seller	Livestock	Meat-packing	Steel	Engines & Turbines	Agriculture	Public Utilities	Steel	Automobiles
1 Livestock		14,000						
14 Meat-packing								
43 Steel				230				
49 Engines & turbines					22	250		
Employment (thousands)	5,000	1,640	1,300	85				

TABLE 3-3. (Cont.)

	Buyer								
	Construction						Ultimate Use		
	Residential	Industrial	Offices	Inventories	Competing Imports	Exports	State, Local Government	Federal Government	Consumption
1 Livestock . . .				100	−260	40	10	2	1,500
14 Meat-packing . . .				300	−100	200	27	25	15,000
43 Steel . . .	60	90	80	200	−700	400		120	20
49 Engines & turbines . . .				20	−30	300	5	230	160

5. When industry sales have been found, they are compared with the assumed sales used in step 3 above. If they do not agree, the newly calculated sales are used as the basis for arriving at the level of net new investment and inventory accumulation, repeating as often as needed to obtain agreement.

6. From the output and labor productivity forecasts, employment in industry is calculated. If total employment agrees with the percentage distribution of the expected labor force for the year in question, the task is completed. If not, a new estimate of after-tax income is used and the procedure reverts to step 2.[15]

In making the forecasts, econometric models are employed. For example, the consumption function is expressed in the following equation:

$$C_t = a + b_1 y_t + b_2 p_t + b_3 t + b_4 \Delta y_t$$

where C_t is the per capita annual consumption of a specific item in year t; y_t is per capita disposable income for the same year; p_t is the price index of that specific good divided by the overall price index; t represents the time period in years; and Δy_t represents the change in per capita disposable income in year t from the preceding year.

Differences and Limitations. There is a basic difference between an econometric model and an input-output model as techniques for forecasting. The input-output model takes all interconnection among various industries in the economy into account. The industry forecasts have to be consistent among themselves, since each is an integral part of a total forecast of the level of product which the economy as a whole can achieve. What is more, each dollar of sales is identified by a kind of double-entry system, involving both the seller and the buyer, and this constitutes a check on individual forecasts.

The input-output model has two advantages, then. In forecasting gross national product, the input-output model is disaggregated, which is to say it shows the relative significance of each component in the overall picture. Second, in forecasting for a particular industry, there is the built-in check for internal consistency imposed by the double-entry system.

To management, this model is a valuable tool. In addition to using it as a check on the accuracy of forecasts obtained by using other techniques, it can provide a level of detail that other methods cannot provide. Input-output tables can be developed at any level of detail, provided the information is available. For example, an input-output table has been developed for the electronics industry in which the inputs are in terms of components and equipment.[16] It is also a widely used technique in interregional economic studies.

---

[15] *Ibid.,* pp. 15–17.
[16] *Business Week,* Jan. 25, 1969, p. 62.

Since the models usually employ econometric methods in arriving at many of the needed coefficients, the limitations of econometric models apply also to input-output methods. Also, in making the dollar volume forecasts, certain assumptions are needed as to the volume of federal expenditures and consumer spending. We have no way of knowing how the United States government and state and municipal funds will be spent in future years. We do not know what will motivate corporate spending. There are some who believe that net new investment is curtailed by falling profit margins and high prices, while others just as sincerely believe that business will spend for new equipment in order to combat falling profit margins and forestall the possibility of having to buy in the future at higher prices. The enactment of certain federal legislation has important consequences for capital investment and consumer spending, and there is no way of forecasting these events.

Structurally, we do not know if the relationship among the variables will continue, except as econometric methods give us a means of forecasting the coefficients. The error in the forecast is built in to the error in using the input-output method.[17]

There is an undoubted advantage, however, in the fact that the models do force economists to spell out their assumptions. From the businessman's point of view, it is easy to evaluate the performance of the forecasters and models or forecasting systems. The models also can provide a basis for simulation studies, which are valuable in analyzing the conditions of the economy under various assumptions. Both econometric and input-output models can be used in simulation studies. There is a general agreement that there is no better tool available to improve forecasting in any detail.

OPINION SAMPLING METHODS

In this section, we take up the use of opinion polls and surveys, including the Delphi method. Polls and surveys are employed to discover the anticipations and intentions of corporations and individuals with regard to planned production, consumption, savings, or investment.

THE OPINION POLL

One of the better known opinion polls is prepared by the Gallup organization. Not so widely known, but possibly more important to businessmen, are a

[17] According to the Almon model, growth of gross national product, 1966 to 1972, will depend more on consumer spending than on capital investment. In 1961 to 1966, capital investment accounted for 18 percent of the growth in GNP, while consumer spending accounted for 62 percent. For the period 1966 to 1972, Almon estimated the growth in GNP to be caused 82 percent by consumer spending and only 4 percent by investment outlays. Also, those industries making materials which are being substituted for presently used inputs will see an above-average growth. Among these are aluminum, rubber, and plastics. *Business Week*, Dec. 17, 1966, p. 101.

number of others, including those listed below:

1. Poll of business plans concerning inventory buildup. This poll is taken by the National Association of Purchasing Managers, Inc. A similar survey is performed periodically by *Fortune* magazine.

   The National Association organizes a Business Survey Committee consisting of 225 purchasing executives of manufacturing companies, selected on an industrial and geographic stratified sample basis. Each month these executives complete an opinion survey questionnaire covering six important economic data series: production, new orders received, commodity prices, inventories, employment, and buying policy. They are asked to evaluate each factor as to whether conditions are better, the same, or worse than, the previous month. The completed questionnaires form the basis for the monthly report which is circulated to all members of the National Association and which in turn forms the basis for a press release.

2. Survey of business plans for new plant and equipment. This survey is conducted by the McGraw-Hill Publications Division. A similar survey is conducted by the National Industrial Conference Board and by the U.S. Department of Commerce in cooperation with the Securities and Exchange Commission.

   The McGraw-Hill poll is taken twice yearly, with the spring survey being the larger and more extensive. The survey consists of two parts: The first covers expenditures on fixed assets, and the second covers plans for research and development expenditure. The survey covers all large corporations and some medium-sized companies in nonfarm industries. In terms of employment, the sample accounts for about 40 percent of all employment. In terms of capital expenditure, probably more than half of all new investment is accounted for.

3. Survey of consumer finance and intentions to buy durable goods. The first of these surveys was undertaken for the Board of Governors of the Federal Reserve System early in 1946 by the Division of Program Surveys of the Bureau of Agricultural Economics of the Department of Agriculture. In the following year, the University of Michigan was asked to take over the work, and it has continued it since.[18]

   Originally, the interviews took place from the first week of January

---

[18] Work is conducted by the Survey Research Center of the Institute for Social Research with financial assistance by business. In recent years the Commerical Credit Company published quarterly a brief report on consumer buying plans based on data collected in the population survey of the U.S. Bureau of the Census. Consumers express the likelihood of their purchasing durables in terms of a scale from 0 to 100. The report contains an estimate based on this scale of the "expected value" of dollar expenditure. This method reportedly is intended to correct for any bias that would result in a systematic difference between prospective and actual spending.

through the first week of March of each year and provided information on financial changes and consumer reactions over a two-year period.

4. In January, 1959, the Federal Reserve Board initated a quarterly survey of consumer intentions to buy selected durable goods such as houses, automobiles, and household appliances. These quarterly surveys are conducted as supplements to the Current Population Survey (quarterly) of the Census Bureau. The objective of the survey is to determine various aspects of consumers' spending plans, including their income, their holdings of liquid and nonliquid assets, their indebtedness, and the psychological factors underlying their behavior and attitude toward acquiring additional durable goods. Since 1963 the Census Bureau has conducted this survey without Federal Reserve System sponsorship.

How Conducted. Opinion surveys are conducted in three different ways, depending on the form of communication used. Respondents can be reached by house call, by telephone, or by mail.

In the house call, a firm can send a team of trained public opinion surveyors to ring doorbells of some designated areas. Before the call, samples are often generally distributed, especially where the product is a new one, and time is allowed for the samples to be used. At other times, the sample is delivered personally and used under supervision. Whether the house call or a telephone method of solicitation is used, team selection is critical, because unskilled interviewers can unconsciously bias the results by suggesting the answers they would like to have.

The mail survey is by far the cheapest method, but has several procedural problems. First, although the sample can be selected with care so that the survey is representative, not all persons return their questionnaires. Much valuable information is either lost or may not be used because of the inability to round out the sample.[19]

The questionnaire has to be designed very carefully since it is used without supervision. Most weak surveys turn out to be defective in questionnaire design and in the design of the experiment so that the needed information cannot be obtained. They may also be weak because the needed information is not correlated with the information the questionnaire can produce.

Limitations. Information obtained through polls represents at best anticipations and intentions, not firm commitments. Some responses are not reliable because they are conjectural or are made without accurately referring to the questions

---

[19] See, for example, W. Edwards Deming, *Some Theory of Sampling*, John Wiley & Sons, Inc., New York, 1950, and, by the same author, *Sample Design in Business Research*, John Wiley & Sons, Inc., New York, 1960.

being asked. Plans are subject to change as the underlying economic conditions change, and therefore the information obtained may not be relevant because there is no way of updating the responses.

DELPHI METHODS

The Delphi method is an attempt to arrive at a consensus in an uncertain area by questioning a group of experts repeatedly until the responses appear to converge along a single line. The participants are provided with the responses to previous questions from others in the group by a coordinator or leader of some sort. Each response by an expert is accompanied by his reasons for the position taken. The leader provides each expert with the responses of the others, including their reasons. Each expert is given the opportunity to react to the information or considerations advanced by the others, but all interchange is anonymous. There is no committee effect in which peer group pressures or a desire to please might alter views. Feedback may result in an expert giving weight to a factor previously not believed significant.

The Delphi study was originally designed to obtain forecasts based on a consensus on pure information. The results are believed to reflect ". . . reasoned, self-aware opinions expressed by experts in the light of opinions of associate experts."[20] The Delphi method has been used successfully at TRW, Inc., the Rand Corporation, and elsewhere, especially in the area of technological forecasting.

SUMMARY

Consumer research polls have become a factor with which to reckon, as companies, banks, and the government all try to determine the shape of the future and the reaction to the past. So long as the future consumer demand for goods is based on *ability* to buy, namely income, and a *willingness* to buy, forecasting will be as much art as science.

In addition to the several forms of opinion sampling, we have shown how business cycle indicators attempt to forecast the precise stage of the business cycle and how both econometric and input-output models are used.

The demand for goods, we may conclude, is a joint function of many variables, such as price, income, and expectations as to future prices and income levels. We have seen also that the nature of the demand function is different for goods which render their services over time and where the useful life of the remaining stock must be taken into account. If demand is simply related to a single measure such as the level of disposable income, as is true of retail sales, for example, no great problem is presented. Forecasting the demand for new

---

[20] John C. Chambers, Satinder K. Mullick, and David A. Goodman, "Catalytic Agent for Effective Planning," *Harvard Business Review*, vol. 49, no. 1, p. 112, Jan.–Feb., 1971.

automobiles is, on the other hand, a much more complicated procedure, in which even experts disagree as to the proper selection of relevant variables. In short, the major forecasting problem is to select the variables to which the demand for our product is sensitive. Having done this, we can separate out those variables over which we have control from those which are beyond our control. In nearly all such cases, we will be dealing with total industry demand.

In the next chapter, we will discuss methods of forecasting our share of this total, leaving for Chapters 5 and 6 the discussion of the economic aspects of demand analysis and a more detailed discussion of the various factors influencing demand elasticity.

Review Questions

1. Why is it important in forecasting demand to distinguish between durable and nondurable goods?
2. How reliable are the results obtained through opinion polls?
3. Of the three types of opinion polls discussed in this chapter, which might have more relevance to the capital or producer's goods industries? Why?
4. Why did the National Bureau of Economic Research classify the business cycle indicators into three categories?
5. Can you explain why durable goods orders and changes in inventories are classified as leading indicators?
6. Can you explain why the book value of manufacturing and trade inventories is classified as a lagging indicator?
7. What is the role of econometrics in forecasting?
8. Distinguish between endogenous and exogenous variables in an econometric model.
9. What are the characteristic features of an input-output model? What does such a model try to accomplish?
10. What is the difference between an econometric and an input-output model? How are they related?

Case 1. The John J. Johnson Manufacturing Company

The John J. Johnson Manufacturing Company makes medium and small electric motors for a wide variety of uses, including motors for home appliances and machinery for industrial uses such as lathes and grinding machines.

EXHIBIT 1A. BUSINESS CYCLE INDICATORS — LEADING INDICATORS

Year & Month	(1) Average Workweek of Production Workers, Manufacturing (hours)	(2) Nonagricultural Placements, All Industries (thousands)	(3) Index of Net Business Formation (1957–1959 = 100)	(4) Value of Manufacturers' New Orders, Durable Goods Industries (billion dollars)	(5) Contracts and Orders for Plant and Equipment (billion dollars)	(6) Index of New Private Housing Units Authorized by Local Building Permits (1957–1959 = 100)
1968						
January	40.2	478	113.5	26.84	6.50	97.2
February	40.7	471	114.7	26.81	6.51	120.0
March	40.8	481	113.8	28.00	6.67	121.4
April	40.1	487	112.8	27.37	6.20	113.7
May	40.9	475	112.7	27.17	6.62	106.9
June	40.9	486	114.5	26.70	7.20	107.0
July	40.9	520	119.0	26.92	6.96	107.7
August	40.7	477	119.1	27.33	7.85	107.8
September	41.0	478	121.2	28.38	7.20	116.4
October	40.9	466	123.9	30.28	8.18	115.2
November	40.8	454	123.4	29.32	7.29	119.1
December	40.8	443	125.3	29.38	7.79	122.3
1969						
January	40.6	448	125.2	29.68	7.98	127.2
February	40.1	459	125.8	30.48	7.84	123.4
March	40.9	431	123.2	29.70	7.50	118.7
April	40.8	452	123.9	30.94	8.26	125.5
May	40.7	427	123.1	30.00	8.01	110.6
June	40.7	460	123.6	29.17	7.85	112.0
July	40.6	438	124.6	31.06	7.81	102.6
August	40.6	425	124.2	31.46	7.65	104.0
September	40.7	421	123.1	31.99	8.39	100.4
October	40.5	405	123.2	31.44	7.90	98.9
November	40.5	401	121.7	31.05	7.99	99.5
December	40.7	376	122.3	30.21	8.38	103.5
1970						
January	40.3	387	121.9	29.05	8.86	84.6
February	39.9	361	121.7	29.37	8.58	95.0
March	40.2	357	117.1	28.86	7.61	91.8
April	40.0	349	116.0	28.45	8.17	105.5
May	39.9	338	113.9	29.98	7.57	110.4
June	39.8	329	112.8	30.03	7.64	109.1
July	40.1	318	112.7	31.40	7.87	106.5
August	39.9	(NA)	(NA)	30.37	7.58	112.1
September						

(7) Change in Book Value of Manufacturing & Trade Inventories, Total (annual rate, billion dollars)	(8) Index of Industrial Materials Prices (u) (1957–1959 = 100)	(9) Index of Stock Prices, 500 Common Stocks (1941–1943 = 10	(10) Corporate Profits after Taxes (annual rate, billion dollars)	(11) Ratio, Price to Unit Labor Cost Index, Manufacturing (1957–1959 = 100)	(12) Net Change in Consumer Installment Debt (annual rate, billion dollars)
+ 4.0	99.8	95.04		99.8	+ 4.79
+ 8.5	99.5	90.75	47.9	99.7	+ 8.83
+ 4.1	100.1	89.09		100.0	+ 7.46
+15.9	98.3	95.67		100.0	+ 7.69
+15.9	96.1	97.87	49.7	99.5	+ 8.78
+ 8.5	95.6	100.53		99.8	+ 8.59
+ 6.4	94.4	100.30		99.8	+10.28
+10.2	94.8	98.11	50.0	98.3	+11.21
+ 9.9	96.1	101.34		98.1	+ 8.58
+16.4	97.5	103.76		98.5	+11.36
+ 9.8	100.3	105.40	51.6	91.8	+10.01
+11.2	100.0	106.48		98.7	+ 9.30
+ 3.9	99.2	102.40		99.2	+ 7.69
+15.0	100.2	101.46	52.2	100.2	+ 9.58
+12.8	100.0	99.30		100.0	+ 7.75
+12.9	99.6	101.26		99.6	+ 9.12
+13.5	100.0	104.62	51.8	100.0	+10.15
+ 7.9	100.0	99.14		100.0	+ 9.54
+16.4	112.4	94.71		99.8	+ 7.46
+12.3	115.0	94.18	47.9	99.0	+ 7.20
+12.9	117.4	94.51		98.9	+ 8.38
+18.2	115.6	95.52		98.5	+ 8.03
+ 8.7	115.6	96.21	47.1	98.0	+ 7.44
+13.6	117.2	91.11		97.1	+ 4.98
− 3.5	119.4	90.31		97.6	+ 4.56
+11.7	120.0	87.16	44.6	98.2	+ 5.02
+ 5.9	119.2	88.65		98.0	+ 2.38
+11.1	118.7	85.95		98.5	+ 3.55
− 0.1	118.0	76.06	43.9	97.9	+ 4.98
+ 5.1	115.3	75.59		97.8	+ 5.29
+14.5	112.8	75.72		98.3	+ 5.32
(NA)	111.6	77.92		98.1	(NA)
	111.1	82.13			

EXHIBIT 1B. BUSINESS CYCLE INDICATORS — COINCIDENT INDICATORS

Year & Month	(1) Number of Employees on Nonagricultural Payrolls, Establishment Surveys (thousands)	2. Unemployment Rate, Total (percent)	(3) Gross National Product in 1958 Dollars (annual rate billion dollars)
1968			
January	66,720	3.6	
February	67,165	3.7	693.3
March	67,286	3.7	
April	67,466	3.5	
May	67,550	3.6	705.8
June	67,816	3.7	
July	67,945	3.7	
August	68,088	3.5	712.8
September	68,195	3.6	
October	68,427	3.6	
November	68.664	3.4	718.5
December	68,875	3.3	
1969			
January	69,199	3.3	
February	69,487	3.3	723.1
March	69,710	3.4	
April	69,789	3.5	
May	70,013	3.5	726.7
June	70,300	3.4	
July	70,400	3.5	
August	70,497	3.5	730.9
September	70,567	3.8	
October	70,836	3.8	
November	70,808	3.5	729.2
December	70,842	3.5	
1970			
January	70,992	3.9	
February	71,135	4.2	723.8
March	71,256	4.4	
April	71,163	4.8	
May	70,852	5.0	724.9
June	70,603	4.7	
July			
August			
September			

Index of Industrial Production (1957–1959 = 100)	(5) Personal Income (annual rate, billion hollars)	(6) Manufacturing and Trade Sales (million dollars)	(7) Sales of Retail Stores (million dollars)
161.2	656.3	93,184	27,043
162.0	664.6	93,758	27,449
163.0	671.9	94,463	27,996
162.5	674.2	94,552	27,791
164.2	680.2	96,069	28,158
165.8	685.9	97,423	28,320
166.0	691.0	98,368	28,674
164.6	696.1	97,083	28,760
165.1	701.1	98,549	28,316
166.0	706.2	99,675	28,697
167.5	711.5	100,142	28,806
168.7	716.0	98,671	28,347
169.1	718.7	100,137	28,989
170.1	723.9	101,390	29,289
171.4	730.7	101,510	28,916
171.7	735.3	102,352	29,442
172.5	740.0	103,232	29,386
173.7	746.1	104,127	29,371
174.6	752.7	104,201	29,090
174.3	758.5	104,644	29,346
173.9	763.1	105,903	29,259
173.1	766.7	106,907	29,620
171.4	770.6	105,666	29,471
171.1	774.3	104,758	29,419
170.4	777.8	104,961	29,570
170.5	781.5	106,139	29,980
171.1	787.6	105,218	29,801
170.2	806.0	104,779	30,536
169.0	799.7	106,731	30,502
168.8	798.2	107,702	30,518
169.2	803.3	108,205	30,739
169.0	807.4	(NA)	(NA)

EXHIBIT 1C. BUSINESS CYCLE INDICATORS—LAGGING INDICATORS

Year & Month	(1) Unemployment Rate, Persons Unemployed 15 Weeks and Over (percent)	(2) Business Expenditures on New Plant and Equipment, Total (annual rate, billion dollars)	(3) Manufacturing and Trade Inventories, Book Value (billion dollars)
1968			
January	0.6		144.03
February	0.6	64.75	144.74
March	0.6		145.08
April	0.5		146.40
May	0.5	62.60	147.73
June	0.5		148.44
July	0.6		148.97
August	0.5	63.20	149.82
September	0.5		150.65
October	0.5		152.02
November	0.4	65.90	152.83
December	0.4		153.76
1969			
January	0.4		154.09
February	0.4	68.90	155.34
March	0.4		156.40
April	0.5		157.48
May	0.5	70.20	158.60
June	0.5		159.26
July	0.5		160.63
August	0.6	77.84	161.66
September	0.5		162.73
October	0.4		164.25
November	0.5	77.84	164.97
December	0.5		166.11
1970			
January	0.5		165.82
February	0.6	78.22	166.79
March	0.7		167.28
April	0.7		168.21
May	0.7	80.22	168.20
June	0.8		168.62
July	0.9		169.83
August	0.9	81.05	(NA)
September			
October			
November		82.24	

(4) Index of Labor Cost per Unit of Output, Manufacturing (1957–1959 = 100)	(5) Commercial and Industrial Loans Outstanding, Weekly Reporting Large Commercial Banks (million dollars)	(6) Bank Rates on Short-term Business Loans, 35 Cities (percent)
108.3	65,363	
109.0	65,734	6.36
108.9	66,063	
109.1	67,446	
109.7	67,306	6.84
109.6	67,702	
109.9	68,178	
111.4	68,695	6.89
112.0	69,225	
111.7	70,264	
111.6	71,536	6.61
112.0	72,346	
112.2	73,410	
111.5	74,698	7.32
112.2	74,674	
112.9	76,659	
112.8	77,176	7.86
113.2	77,008	
113.7	76,860	
114.7	77,746	8.82
115.2	78,254	
116.4	78,513	
117.3	78,537	8.83
118.7	80,764	
119.0	78,506	
118.5	78,811	8.86
119.0	78,150	
118.7	78,126	
119.6	78,069	8.49
120.0	78,068	
120.0	78,535	
120.3	80,342	

Sales of the company, which amounted to $250 million in the last fiscal year, have mainly been cyclical. Its products are closely tied to housing construction and to expenditures for plant and equipment. In order to coordinate its production program more closely with sales, the company has been interested in the possibility of employing an economist. Assume that you have taken such a job and that your first assignment is to prepare both short- and long-range forecasts. It is September 1, 1970, and you have decided to use the business cycle indicators as the basis for preparing a short-range forecast. You also begin work on an econometric model for long-range forecasting.

With the most recent business cycle indicators available (Exhibits 1A, 1B, 1C), what conclusions might you reach with respect to business conditions for the second half of 1970 and for the year 1971. Verify your result with the actual events to see how well you can forecast with the aid of the indicators.

Set up an econometric model which you think will best describe the functional relationship between the activity of the John J. Johnson Company and other economic variables. (If you cannot set one up yourself, find an existing model which you believe will serve your purpose.) Try your hand at backcasting, and compare results against the following historical data. All sales are in millions.

Year	Sales
1950	$274
1951	300
1952	258
1953	274
1954	230
1955	296
1956	278
1957	254
1958	208
1959	246
1960	232
1961	216

Currently, sales are averaging about $250 million yearly.

Case 2. Amalgamated Washing Machines

During a management review on February 1, 1968, John Doe, comptroller of Amalgamated Washing Machines, expressed concern about the increasing out-of-stock conditions. He felt that this endangered customer good will and might eventually cause a loss in market share. Moreover, the emergence of new and stiffer competition was posing a real threat to the market position of Amalgamated's new line of automatic washers. Something had to be done before next year's line went into production.

At the review, Joe Smith, vice-president for sales, promised a forecast for 1969's washing machines. As the resident economic analyst and statistician, you have been asked to develop this forecast. Based on prior analysis, you have established that Amalgamated's market share has run a consistent 17 percent of total United States sales over the past fifteen years.

Below is an eleven-year history of personal consumption expenditures for furniture and household equipment (in billions), personal consumption expenditures (total United States in billions), household durables price index (1957–1958 = 100), and total United States sales of washers (in thousands).

Year	Personal Consumption Expenditures—Furniture & Household Equipment (in billions)	Total U.S. Personal Consumption Expenditures (in billions)	Household Durables Price Index	Sale of Washers (in thousands)
1958	$17.1	$290.1	100.3	$3,840.7
1959	18.9	311.2	100.2	4,029.6
1960	18.9	325.2	100.1	3,425.3
1961	19.3	335.2	98.9	3,441.7
1962	20.5	355.1	98.8	3,710.2
1963	22.2	375.0	98.5	3,980.9
1964	25.0	401.2	98.4	4,218.9
1965	26.9	432.8	96.9	4,385.7
1966	29.8	465.5	98.8	4,446.5
1967	31.4	492.2	98.2	4,376.0
1968	34.3	533.7	101.2	4,517.9

QUESTIONS

1. From these figures derive a forecast for 1969 and 1970. Make the model as complex or as simple as you feel necessary. Be prepared to justify your model.

2. Compare your forecast of next year's sales to actual sales in 1969 in *Business Statistics — 1970*.

Note: Case 2 was prepared by Larry V. Moore under the supervision of Francis P. Sing. Mr. Moore is a graduate student at Georgetown University.

Case 3. Utility Load Forecasting

Utility executives, according to an article appearing in a recent issue of *Business Week*, have become accustomed to thinking what not so long ago would have been unthinkable, namely that power blackouts in the fall and winter are as likely as power brownouts in the summer. The problem was accentuated in early February, 1971, when a twenty-block strip of midtown Manhattan was blacked out completely.

Since 1965, major utilities in the Northeast have failed to predict future peak loads. Planners have relied on evenly declining trends for annual percentage increases in electricity consumption peak loads. For the period 1966 to 1967, their forecasts, if anything, were conservative, as the rate of actual growth fell to less than one-half the forecast rate. By the following year, however, they gasped at an actual rate more than double forecast. For the Philadelphia Electric Company, the deficit in 1968 was almost 300,000 kilowatts between actual and forecast peak load after a surplus of 113,000 the year before. Long Island Lighting had been running an increasing deficit, which in 1968 was three times that two years before and was increasing at an annual rate of 30,000 kilowatts.

The theme of the 1964 National Power Survey issued by the FPC was that most of the nation's utilities would have considerable excess capacity, and it saw the key to increased demand in reduced rates. It recommended that utilities could avoid ambitious building projects by using power pools to direct capacity from systems with temporary excesses to those temporarily short of capacity. In this way, power reserves might be reduced from 25 percent to less than 15 percent.

The three basic determinants of power demand, according to utility planners were:

1. A belief that the 6 percent rate of peak load growth would not continue
2. That they would therefore have to sell electricity through rate cutting and promotions, such as bonuses for installing electric appliances
3. That the regional system of interconnections would reduce the need for large capital investment by making it possible to lower power reserves

Not only did the industry underestimate demand, it also overestimated supply resulting from a lack of integrated planning and an inability to upgrade the system's capacity. Excess reserves from the Midwest, for example, cannot be sent to New York, because transmission lines in Ohio and Pennsylvania cannot carry the extra power. Also, each utility, while believing it would draw on the pooled system's full capacity, failed to consider that everyone else might also be tapping the supply.

Until now, the main elements going into the utility forecasts have been new building data, weather conditions, air-conditioning additions, future subway growth plans, and rough estimates of per capita electrical use. Planners are inclined to dismiss aggregate figures on economic conditions, population statistics, and consumer purchases data, but would like to have this kind of information on the local level.

In New York, Consolidated Edison's market has been changing rapidly as high-rise, centrally conditioned buildings create a single-climate year. Utilities normally operate on a seasonal peak basis, running all available capacity in the summer and repairing units in the winter months. Forecasting did not correctly judge the higher power needs of commercial buildings. Their forecasts are based on F. W. Dodge permit and construction award figures which report mainly new construction but not modernization and renovation. Nearly all older buildings had to modernize from 1968 on or lose tenants to newer buildings in the building boom, which began in that year.

In December, 1969, the FPC, reviewing Consolidated Edison's performance and future forecasts, asked that it review its load forecasting methods so as to remove what appeared to be a chronic tendency toward underestimation.

QUESTIONS

1. What factors does it appear were overlooked in the 1964 National Power Survey?
2. How did the electric utilities in 1965 propose to lower costs?
3. How might Consolidated Edison improve its forecasting methods through the use of (a) econometric methods, (b) input-output analyses, (c) Delphi, or (d) consumer expenditure expectation surveys.

Case 4. The Devlin Electronics Corporation

On the first of October, 1970, Steve Devlin, president of Devlin Electronics, was preparing a production schedule for next year's desk calculators. The duration of the production run was scheduled from January 1 through May 31. For the remainder of the year, electronic components for a new missile system would be manufactured. Inasmuch as Devlin Electronics and its competitors would be marketing a revolutionary new desk calculator in 1972, all inventory remaining at the end of the year would be virtually a total loss.

Keeping this in mind, Steve Devlin had his assistant draw up a sales forecast to govern how much would be produced. The forecast indicated sales of 1,500 desk calculators in 1971. It was felt that consumers would not be influenced by 1972 models in their purchases of 1971 models.

The variable cost of manufacturing the calculator was $560.00. Cost to the distributor was $900.00.

While the forecast of 1,500 desk calculators seemed reasonable, Steve did some further checking. On a separate sheet (not shown), Steve computed the ratios of demand to forecast to give him a picture of his staff's forecasting ability. The following table shows a record of forecasts versus sales for the past seven years:

Year	Forecast	Sales
1963	500	450
1964	600	630
1965	660	575
1966	740	700
1967	875	900
1968	975	1150
1969	1300	1275

QUESTION

1. From the data given, how many desk calculators should Devlin Electronics produce in 1971?

Note: Case 4 was prepared by Larry V. Moore under the supervision of Francis P. Sing. Mr. Moore is a graduate student at Georgetown University.

Suggested Reading

Almon, Jr., Clopper: *The American Economy to 1975*, Harper & Row, Publishers, Incorporated, New York, 1966.

Butler, William F., and Robert A. Kavesh: *How Business Economists Forecast*, Prentice-Hall, Inc., Englewood Cliffs, N.J., 1966.

Harberger, Arnold C.: *The Demand for Durable Goods*, The University of Chicago Press, Chicago, 1960.

Lewis, John P.: "Short-term General Business Forecasting: Some Comments on Method," *Journal of Business*, October, 1962, pp. 343–356.

Miernyk, William H.: *The Elements of Input-output Analysis*, Random House, Inc., New York, 1957.

Mo, William Y., and Kung-Lee Wang: *A Quantitative Economic Analysis and Long Run Projection of the Demand for Steel Mill Products*, U.S. Dept. of the Interior, U.S. Government Printing Office, 1970.

North, Harper Q., and Donald L. Pyke: "Probes of the Technological Future," *Harvard Business Review,* May–June, 1969, p. 68 (contains a complete description of the Delphi method).

Okun, Arthur M.: "The Predictive Value of Surveys of Business Intentions," *The American Economic Review, Papers and Proceedings,* vol. 2, no. 3, pp. 218–225, May, 1962.

Tintner, Gerhard: *Econometrics,* John Wiley & Sons, Inc., New York, 1952.

chapter 4
business forecasting:
market
share and
evaluation

Once we have estimated the total size of the market and have arrived at satisfactory methods of estimating the future market potential, there comes the job of translating these national data into specifics. Meaningful market measurement, after all, requires that the characteristics of possible users be known in some detail.

Beyond this point there remain the two steps of determining the actual effect of our selling or market penetration effort and evaluation of forecasting accuracy.

ACQUIRING BASIC MARKET INFORMATION

It may be that we will only divide up the existing demand among more suppliers with the redistribution depending on the degree of product differentiation and price variation. It may be, on the other hand, that we have a product which will appeal to new segments of the market, a potential market as yet not tapped. In this case, we are competing with other possible demands on consumer purchasing power. In offering a new kind of boat, for example, we may be competing with producers of automobiles.

In any event, we must acquire some basic information about our market which goes beyond the rough quantitative estimate to what might be termed a qualitative view. In the last chapter, we discussed ways in which qualitative information often is obtained from consumer panels, a variant of the consumer opinion poll. Here a group of consumers, having a continuing relationship with a testing organization, uses a product and answers a battery of questions concerning it. The testers usually do not know the brand name or the manufacturer's name. Sometimes, on the other hand, groups of employees are used for this purpose, either by the testing organization or by the company. As an alternate, there are some simple statistical methods which will provide more detail on market potential.

MEASUREMENT OF A SPECIFIC MARKET

There are two aspects of detailed market measurement: first, measuring the consumption or use of the product line, and second, estimating the potential of the market.

Available statistics to aid in market measurement are generally of two basic classes: population and income, and industry sales and employment. The first is useful to estimate the size of consumer goods markets, while the latter is of value in measuring the market for industrial goods. These statistics may be used to measure market population and its buying potential.

The manufacturer of a household appliance may for example have an estimate of the total demand for his product in the coming year, but have no way of distributing that demand among geographic areas. Population and income statistics for different areas aid in measuring the size of these specific markets. From population statistics he can obtain the number of households, the rate at which new households are being formed annually, and their geographic location. Questions, such as how often the appliance is replaced, the number of appliances necessary per housing unit, and the average life of the appliance, have to be answered as a rule through the sample survey. Of assistance also might be the quarterly forecasts of *Consumer Buying Prospects,* published by the Commercial Credit Company and based on the survey of consumer buying expectations of the U.S. Bureau of the Census,[1] to which we have earlier referred.

The producer of industrial goods finds that a listing of potential users for his product and their size, in terms of sales or employment, or both, is a good indicator of market potential. A producer of hotel mattresses and bedding would find that a tabulation of hotel and motel businesses in specific geographic areas would be a good guide in defining specific markets. Often, determining the potential extent of use for a product requires a knowledge of the customer's technology. It is in this connection that detailed input-output studies are of value, because they show the extent to which products are used both directly and indirectly.

TWO EXAMPLES OF MARKET MEASUREMENT[2]

The first example shows a method of establishing geographic sales quotas for a household appliance, in this instance a TV set. By multiple regres-

[1] The Bureau publishes the results of its surveys in "Consumer Buying Indicators," Series P-65, in the *Current Population Reports.*

[2] Adapted from *Measuring Markets: A Guide to the Use of Federal and State Statistical Data,* U.S. Department of Commerce, Business and Defense Services Administration, Office of Marketing and Services, U.S. Government Printing Office, 1966.

sion, the relationship of sales of TV sets to population, the number of housing units, consumer income, sales of retail outlets, and the number of TV sets already owned was determined, and appropriate coefficients were found. These coefficients were used as weights in the calculation of a weighted average applicable to a specific area.

For instance, the state of Alabama should account for 1.3 percent of the total sales of TV sets, based on a weighted average percentage calculation in which:

1. Alabama's population as a percent of the United States is weighted as 1
2. The number of housing units as a percent of the United States is weighted as 2
3. Aggregate personal income in Alabama as a percent of United States income is weighted as 3
4. Retail sales of appliance, radio, and TV stores as a percent of United States sales are weighted as 4
5. The percentage of the appliances in use which are located in Alabama is weighted as 5

The sum of the products divided by the sum of the weights (15) is then an index of the proportion of total market which exists in Alabama. In this instance, the data for 1960 are as follows:

Item	Percent of United States	Weight	Product
Population	1.8	1	1.8
Housing units	1.7	2	3.4
Aggregate income	1.2	3	3.6
Retail sales	0.7	4	2.8
TV sets owned	1.5	5	7.5
Sums		15	19.1
Weighted average			1.3

A second example is afforded by a procedure for estimating the total market potential for corrugated and solid fiber boxes in a geographic area. The procedure is based on "end use" of "consumption" statistics by which the use of products by industry groups is determined. The unique aspect in this example is the "consumption per employee" factor to translate national data into local data.

The estimating procedure begins with a tabulation of the value of box shipments by industry group of using industries. It is obtained by applying a percentage distribution of total container shipments to the total value of fiber containers produced in the United States in the year in question. The percentage distribution was obtained from industry sources, while the total value of shipments was obtained from census data. An alternate procedure would have been to use input-output table data which would have shown the value of box use or consumption by industry group.

Paralleling this information, it is necessary to tabulate the employment for each industry group and to calculate then a consumption per employee factor for each industry group. This consumption factor is the means for translating to the local level. For any particular state or county, then, if we have the same industry groups represented as in the percentage distribution for the United States as a whole, the consumption per employee factor may be applied to local employment to arrive at a geographic estimate of the potential market.

For instance, the apparel industry in 1962 accounted for $34,865,000 in fiber box use and employed 1,252,443 persons nationally. Consumption per employee is calculated then at $27. Maricopa County in Arizona lists 1,974 persons employed in the apparel industry. If we multiply this employment figure by $27, we get $53,000 as the estimate of the market potential for fiber boxes in that industry in that county. Repeating for all other represented industries would provide a total county estimate of the size of the market.

The procedure is admittedly simple. However, for a manufacturer of fiber boxes who has no record of selling to the apparel industry in Maricopa County, the information is valuable. Similarly, if sales to the food and kindred products industry group are estimated at $1,845,000, and the company has sales of $184,500 to this industry, or a 10 percent market share, it might well ask why it cannot do as well for all other industries using fiber boxes. If the total market potential is $4,616,000 in Maricopa County, that producing firm ought to be able to sell 10 percent or $461,600 worth of boxes.

THE PROBLEM OF WILLINGNESS TO BUY

Statistical measurement of past performance is becoming an increasingly poor indicator of future demand where consumer goods is concerned. Retail sales no longer bear a significant relationship to the level of disposable income. It is possible that one outcome of raising the level of family income to present heights has been to make spending a function of attitudes and expectations rather than income availability. The level of consumer demand, in other words, has become somewhat less than an automatic function of the level of income but is a function of that and a willingness to buy. This combination of the ability to buy and willingness to buy has been termed, by Katona, Strumpel, and Zahn, consumer's discretionary demand.[3]

One of the first indications that income availability and product demand might not be inseparably linked appeared in 1968, when lowered after-tax in-

---

[3] George Katona, Burkhard Strumpel, and Ernest Zahn, *Aspirations and Affluence*, McGraw-Hill Book Company, New York, 1971.

come did not result in a reduction in total consumer demand. In 1970, the level of federal taxes was lowered, thus resulting in an increase in the level of income available for consumption. Actual consumption remained the same.

Katona and his colleagues believe that as today's consumer grows more affluent and accumulates more "discretionary income" or income over and above that needed for everyday living needs, wishes, attitudes, aspirations, and expectations become increasingly important as the basis for spending prediction. Consequently, they hold, consumer surveys of intentions and sentiments will become increasingly more important than econometric methods.

As regards the individual product, willingness to buy may also be estimated by test marketing. In test marketing, we can analyze various combinations of price, package, and advertising, in order to see how our product performs against competing products. What test area is selected depends on the product and the objectives of the testing program. How this is done is more properly discussed under the heading of marketing or market research. We will assume here that we have a representative test area so that conclusions may be drawn that will apply to the market as a whole without bias and with appropriate levels of confidence. We deal now with the evaluation of the results of sales made in test markets under varying conditions and assume that either by astute detective work or available statistics we are able to obtain information on the volume of sales of competing products so that we have a means of comparing against sales of our own offering. One important kind of information, which may be available only from a test panel and is otherwise difficult to obtain, is the time pattern of purchases made by individual consumers. An approximation may be obtained by survey, but its accuracy is open to some question, as it requires that consumers recall when and in what amounts items were purchased.

Information on market shares obtained from consumer panels relies, of course, rather heavily on our ability to extrapolate from the panel to the test market or to the market area itself.

MARKET PENETRATION ANALYSIS

In addition to market share information, which is current, we are interested in potential market share information. This kind of data is in effect a conclusion from information which we obtain on the success the product has in penetrating a given market area. By penetration we mean the proportion of households or consumers who make an initial purchase and the degree to which that initial purchase is repeated, i.e., the time pattern of purchasing.

William R. King portrays penetration as a function of time, beginning with the introduction of the product into the test area as shown in Figure 4-1. In the diagram, 12 percent of the consuming units have made at least one purchase in the first month, over 8 percent of the total made their initial purchase during the second month, and so on. Now this measure is simply one which gives the

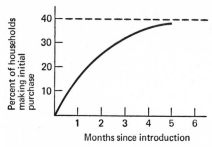

Figure 4-1. Penetration of new product after introduction. (Source: William R. King, *Quantitative Analysis for Marketing Management,* copyright by McGraw-Hill Book Company, New York, 1967, p. 184. Used by permission of the McGraw-Hill Book Company.)

number of consuming units using the product at least once. Since this is insufficient information, we have to add what is termed a *repeat ratio,* which is simply that proportion of the initial purchasers who repeat, or make a second purchase. We may also define a second repeat ratio as that proportion of the first repeaters who repeat for a second time. Naturally, the higher these percentages, the greater the staying power of the product.

Assuming it is possible to obtain such statistics, we have two problems. First, we have the problem of the purchase interval, which will not be the same for all purchasers. Second, we must decide how to account for those who have not had an opportunity to repeat within the specified time period. These problems notwithstanding, certain standards may be evolved by which to judge the success or failure of new product introduction. If, after all, our methods are consistent, we may be able to assert that first repeat ratios of less than some amount have a very high probability of failure or that successful introductions have fairly consistently exhibited other repeat ratio levels. Fourt and Woodlock report successful products have repeat ratios of .5, and a first repeat ratio of less than .15 for packaged groceries implies probable failure.[4] Obviously, most products rely on repeat purchases to stay in the competitive race.

Share of the market also can be compared with market share behavior of products which have been introduced successfully. What are required are market share percentages from month to month of all competing brands. We can then observe the behavior of brands faced with the entry of new rivals. We can also use as a standard the historical market share data for the time periods immediately before test marketing began. We could, for example, calculate an estimated market share somewhere between the best and the worst market share

[4] L. A. Fourt and J. W. Woodlock, "Early Prediction of Market Success for New Grocery Products," *Journal of Marketing,* vol. 25, no. 2, pp. 31–38, Oct., 1960.

performance of competing brands. There is no precedent for the use of the statistical beta distribution for such a calculation, but it appears a likely candidate. Thus, if the market share attainable by the best competing brand is considered as the optimistic figure, the poorest historical showing could be considered as a pessimistic estimate.

Assuming that the personnel concerned could arrive at a likely or probable performance estimate, a statistically probable figure might be arrived at using the formula for the mean of the beta distribution

$$S = \frac{P + 4M + O}{6}$$

where S represents the expected value of the market share, given P the pessimistic estimate, and O the optimistic estimate, with M being the average performance deemed likely by participants.

Changes in market share may be plotted in the form of a kind of limiting curve or sets of curves, against which the performance of the product may be plotted in order to aid in analysis. If we analyze market share changes over the past months by taking first differences in attained percent of the market and select those differences showing the largest increase and the largest decrease in market share from month to month, we can plot the results in the form of bounding curves.[5]

The illustrative data in Tables 4-1 give the required procedure. Table 4-1A shows attained market share percentages for four brands, and Table 4-1B shows first differences representing the month-to-month change in percentage points. Similarly, we might obtain two-month changes in market share.

With this information, we can pick out any periods in which market share changes were reported to be maximum and construct a summary giving the largest increase in market share from month to month, for any two- or three-month period, and so on. We can make up a similar summary for the largest decrease reported. Plotting these data, we have the diagram shown in Figure 4-2.

[5] William R. King, *Quantitative Analysis for Marketing Management*, McGraw-Hill Book Company, New York, 1967, pp. 193–199.

TABLE 4-1A. COMPETITIVE MARKET SHARE DATA

Brand	Percent of Market Held in Month of Survey				
	First	Second	Third	Fourth	Fifth
A	30	25	30	25	20
B	30	40	35	40	30
C	40	35	35	30	10
D	0	0	0	5	20

TABLE 4-1B. MONTH-TO-MONTH
DIFFERENCES IN PERCENT OF
MARKET HELD

	Month First Difference			
Brand	2–1	3–2	4–3	5–4
A	− 5	+5	−5	− 5
B	+10	−5	+5	−10
C	− 5	0	−5	−20
D			+5	+15

If now we superimpose the attained market share data for our product, shifting the axes of the diagram in Figure 4-2, we have the comparison shown as Figure 4-3.

We can enhance the usefulness of the bounding curve diagram by adding curves for changes in market share which encompass varying numbers of changes.

Hence, we might have one set of curves for changes which include at least 50 percent of all changes, 75 percent of all changes, and so on. The former bounding curve would then be that encompassing 100 percent of all changes. There is, of course, no reason why the curves should be limited to three or four months along the horizontal axis. The point of market share calculations for our purposes is to be able to estimate what share of the total market forecast our product will capture. Market share change calculations and the bounding curves give us a basis for estimating probable market penetration and staying power.

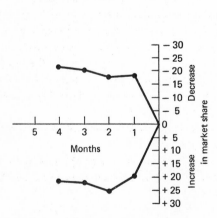

Figure 4-2. Largest increases and decreases in market share of any brand. (Source: William R. King, *Quantitative Analysis for Marketing Management,* copyright by McGraw-Hill Book Company, New York, 1967, p. 194. Used by permission of McGraw-Hill Book Company.)

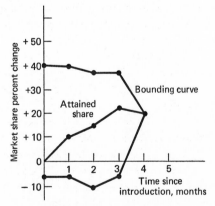

Figure 4-3. Attained market share superimposed on performance record of other brands in the market. (Source: William R. King, *Quantitative Analysis for Marketing Management,* copyright by McGraw-Hill Book Company, New York, 1967, p. 195. Used by permission of McGraw-Hill Book Company.

PREDICTING MARKET PENETRATION

As we are interested in the ultimate penetration level and pattern, a model of average or probable behavior, or some means by which that behavior may be predicted from early information, will be of value. One form of penetration model would appear to possess the property of diminishing returns, in which the cumulative penetration percentage increases in successively smaller increments, until the total penetration becomes asymptotic or levels off and then in all likelihood at some point or other begins to decline.

One form of the penetration model might be an ordinary hyperbolic curve whose equation is

$$Y = \frac{X}{a + bX}$$

and in which Y is asymptotic at $1/b$.

If, from our bounding curve diagram, we conclude that our maximum penetration will be 40 percent, then $Y = .4$ at the asymptote, and from the formula we calculate b as 2.5.

If now we obtain from actual experience a penetration percentage for the first period of perhaps 12 percent, then the a value in the equation can be approximated as

$$Y = \frac{X}{a + 2.5X} = .12, \qquad \text{letting } X \text{ equal } 1, a = 5.083$$

We verify these tentative estimates with data on market penetration for the second period. Assuming actual results are 20.4 percent, our formula gives an approximation of 19.8 percent, and we may want to reconcile the difference. Either the asymptote may be in error, which is to say our product has more potential than we at first assumed because of its greater selling power in the early months, or we may wish to retain the asymptote and merely rework the formula on the assumption that second period results are worth more than first period results.

Setting Y equal to .204, we can recalculate the b value at 1.98 and the new asymptote is .50 instead of our original .40.

Holding the b value constant, which is to assume the original asymptote is valid, we set Y equal to .204 and find a new a value, b remaining at 2.5 and X at 2. The new value comes out as 4.80.

$$.204 = \frac{2}{a + 2.5(2)}$$
$$a = 4.89$$

Using this revised formula, our first month approximation would be .136, as against the actual reading of .12.

For the revised formula, the asymptotic value remaining at .4, the third and fourth month penetration percentages come out to be 24.4 and 27.0, respectively.

Now there are other models which can of course be used. King suggests one in which ". . . increments in penetration for equal time periods are proportional to the remaining 'distance' to the limiting value of penetration."[6] The formula for his model is $rp,1 - r)^{t-1}$, in which r is the penetration limit or asymptote, and p is the constant percent of that limit attained in each time period t. The curve assumes a shape more conventionally associated with the parabola form having the equation $Y = aX^b$.

Again, assuming an asymptote of .4 when X is somewhat large, possibly 10, we can arrive at an a value equal approximately to the first month's performance and the following equation:

$$Y = .12X^{.52}$$

or in logarithmic form,

$$\log Y = \log .12 + .52 \log X$$

With $X = 1$, as in the first time period, $\log Y = \log .12$ and Y of course is equal to .12 or the first month's performance. For the second month, the model estimates Y to be .172. Assuming our actual reading to be .204, we once more have the choice of adjusting the a value, on the assumption that the early readings were too low, or adjusting the exponent, on the assumption that the asymptote is in error.

Letting $Y = .204$, we have a new b value of .76. But this gives us a new asymptote of .691, which, presumably, reason tells us is not likely, at least not in ten periods.

Alternatively, allow Y to equal .204, its actual observed value, b to equal .52, and calculate another a. This turns out to be .142, and when a new asymptote is calculated for this a value, X being 10, we have .471, a not unreasonable result. This means, of course, that the model would overestimate the first month's performance. Which of the two courses to elect is a matter of judgment.

For $X = 3$, the model produces a Y estimate of 25.2 percent, and for $X = 4$, the model produces a Y estimate of 29.3 percent, not too far from the values of 26.3 and 30.4, respectively, produced by the King penetration model.

So much for the newly introduced product. Market share information may, of course, also be calculated for existing products, in which case the model would more likely be some mathematical form other than a simple growth curve. Also, we would have to take into account the amount of advertising and the rela-

[6] *Ibid.*, p. 216.

Beginning with a sales saturation level like the maximum penetration level hypothesized above, we would have to determine the level of advertising and other promotion necessary to maintain the sales and the rate at which sales would decline with decreases in all forms of promotion. Part of the forecasting procedure would then involve applying estimates of sales response to various forms of promotion as well as knowledge of the promotional budget for the coming period.

Another factor to consider is the product life cycle and the stage of that cycle which applies to our product. We have already pointed out that the typical consumer product is believed to have a sales pattern which exhibits growth characteristics exemplified by the exponential curve. This leads to some form of leveling off or cessation of growth. From that time on, various forms of maturation or decline in sales volume may come about, regardless of promotion or advertising, simply because of competitive brand switching and the introduction of new brands.

The strategy behind new product introduction has already been discussed in Chapter 2. The point here is that we are really not going to be able to forecast probable sales volume without detailed information or estimates with which to work. Further discussion of this point would get into Markov analysis of brand switching, for which there are other good sources.[7]

METHODS OF EVALUATING FORECASTS

The consequences of poor forecasting have already been discussed. Inventory overstockages, inventory imbalances, stock obsolescence, and poor production planning with consequent high costs of production are some of the penalties a business must pay for imperfect prediction. For the moment, we are not distinguishing between forecasts and anticipations. The consequences are the same whether, as in the former, we are attempting to predict something over which we have no control, or as in the latter, we have some degree of control, as in planning.

Organizationally, of course, we are speaking of two completely different sets of phenomena. If we have an error in forecasting anticipations, the error can presumably be corrected by adopting better forecasting methods in a technical manner. If, on the other hand, we have an error in planning, then an organizational decision-making process is in question, and while the particular technical methods may be at fault, there may also be the more delicate question of organizational assignment of responsibilities and the human factors involved in convincing someone of the need for a change in planning methods.

To make a plan, an executive will have to prepare preliminary estimates

[7] See, for example, Richard I. Levin and C. A. Kirkpatrick, *Quantitative Approaches to Management,* 2d ed., McGraw-Hill Book Company, New York, 1971.

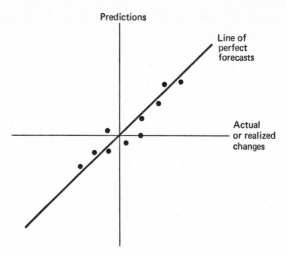

Figure 4-4. Predicted and realized changes. (Source: Henry Theil, *Applied Economic Forecasting,* copyright by North-Holland Publishing Company, Amsterdam, 1966, pp. 21–22.)

of variables over which the organization has no control, as for example the level of national income or of industrial activity. The technical means by which this anticipation is arrived at have been discussed in the preceding chapter. The use or nonuse of these tools, or the incorrect use of these tools, is a managerial problem in decision making and planning, and it is this problem to which we will now devote our attention.

Forecasts must be verifiable to be of value in business planning. In other words, it must be possible to demonstrate, after some period of time, that the forecast was or was not true. Most business forecasts are point predictions or interval predictions which are used to approximate point predictions as the time period becomes more and more removed from the present. Where point predictions are concerned, we have to decide on the degree of forecasting error we are willing to accept because it is practically certain that a point estimate will not be realized. Point predictions should, therefore, be accompanied by a probability statement in order to be regarded as capable of verification. To the extent to which a point prediction is probabilistic, or cannot be asserted with any degree of certainty, it becomes conditional or subject to error and is also therefore an interval prediction, whether we want to have it so or not.

In addition, to be capable of verification, the forecast must be capable of being either true or false, and the concepts used must be well defined. The time or time intervals within which the estimate is made and is to be realized must be defined or else it is not possible to decide whether the prediction has come true or not.[8]

The question we have set out to discuss is how good or how bad a particular set of predictions may be in light of developing conditions. Statistically, we can say that what we would like to do is to minimize the differences between the actual values and the corresponding predicted values. If we use a least-squares technique, then we might have Theil's loss function, which he defines as the weighted sum of squares of the deviations between the actual and the desired values, and we would want to minimize that function.[9]

Forecasts and realizations are often given in terms of predicted and actual percent changes in some quantitative series or another. It is then possible to plot the pairs of data on a set of axes, in which the actual or realized information is plotted against the horizontal axis and the prediction along the vertical axis, as shown in Figure 4-4.

Following Theil, we take this graph with realized changes measured horizontally and rotate it so that the line of perfect forecasts is horizontal. The result is the *prediction-realization diagram,* shown in Figure 4-5.

Notice that any points in a positive or negative quadrant are those in which the error, while present, has at least implied that the prediction and the realization were in the same direction, and that the direction of the change was

---

[8] Henry Theil, *Applied Economic Forecasting,* North-Holland Publishing Company, Amsterdam, 1966, p. 13.
[9] *Ibid.,* p. 16. We will have use for this function in Chapter 5.

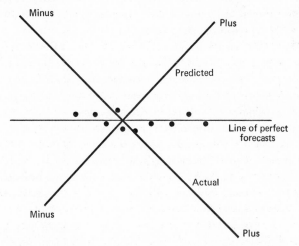

Figure 4-5. Prediction-realization diagram. (Adapted from Henry Theil, *Applied Economic Forecasting,* copyright by North-Holland Publishing Company, Amsterdam, 1966, pp. 21–22.)

accurately predicted. Points lying so that the sign of the predicted value is different from that of the actual, or vice versa, imply that the direction of the change was incorrectly deduced. These are also referred to as turning-point errors, because not only was the absolute value not predicted, but there was a failure to see that the series was going to turn away from the direction of the forecast.

It may also be of interest to see how successive estimates of the future change as the future period comes closer and closer to the present. This change can often be seen when GNP is being estimated based on quarterly performance.

Sometimes it is the case that the actual GNP is being estimated at a time when the date has passed, and as more and more information is made available, the estimate of the actual becomes improved. Whatever the reason, whether estimating the future, or approximating the data on an event which in reality has already taken place, the method of depicting the process of estimation would be the same.

Let us assume we have a firm in which sales forecasts are made by the sales department, as is often the case, where from time to time serious inventory imbalances occur. These imbalances are in or with respect to the various items in the product line, so that shortages take place, and the company is often obliged to interrupt regular production to turn out small lots, or at other times is forced to produce at less than economic lot quantity. Since initial inventory and the production plan are based on yearly sales forecasts, it is possible that (1) the forecast is in error because the data on which it is based turn out to have been incorrect, or (2) the basic data are correct, but the forecast has been incorrectly prepared, or (3) the basic data have been ignored.

We will assume that our company forecasts seven calendar quarters in advance, so that in addition to the quarter in which operations are being conducted, estimates are in hand for the third and fourth quarter of the present year, four quarters of the next year, which might be considered a budget year, and for the first quarter beyond the budget year. We will also assume that we have five items in the sales line, for which seven estimates are made in each quarter, moving out one quarter with each successive estimate.

Let change information be given in terms of natural logarithms, in order to avoid the problem of comparability of percent increases and decreases.[10] Let a_t be the level of some variable in the year t. The observed relative change in an initial estimate of a in year $t - 1$ is then

$$A_t' = \frac{a_t - a_{t-1}}{a_{t-1}}$$

[10] *Ibid.,* p. 47.

TABLE 4-2. PREDICTED AND REALIZED LOG CHANGES IN SALES

Quarter in Which Change Estimated	Actual Quarter						
	1	2	3	4	5	6	7
1	159	257	119	363	159	80	344
2	450	602	225	381	171	97	335
3		583	459	742	0	100	440
4			589	818	−48	196	344
5				825	−80	70	315
6					−65	76	323
7						29	451

Source: Adapted from Theil, op. cit., p. 47.

We will work with the natural logarithm of 1 plus the observed relative change for actual data and 1 plus the predicted relative change for forecasts. In other words, we set

$$A_t = \log(1 + A_t') = \log a_t - \log a_{t-1} = \log \frac{a_t}{a_{t-1}},$$

where log is the natural logarithm. Data are shown in hundreds by multiplying all values by 10,000, thus avoiding decimal points. One set of forecasts is given in Table 4-2, which shows the predicted and realized log changes in sales of an item over a seven-quarter time period.

The figure given for the quarter which is one quarter beyond the actual is considered to be the final real position, amending all prior estimates including that obtained during the quarter in question. For example, using the sixth quarter, we see that the successive forecasts and estimates of the log change over the initial figure are, reading down in Table 4-2,

80, 97, 100, 196, 70, 76, 29.

We take the last figure, 29, as the true value, and note that it was not possible to arrive at this figure until the actual time period had passed. We observe that the original estimate, made in the first quarter, was far too low, since it had to be successively revised upward each quarter. But where the first revision in quarter 1 was a positive change of 80, successive quarters increased it, until by the fourth quarter we were estimating an increase of 196. By the sixth quarter, however, the estimate was down near the original increase, and by the time the quarter had passed and actual data were finally available, the estimate is away from the actual by 29.

Now if we are to obtain information which is of value in improving the estimation process, we must analyze the direction and amplitude of the corrections as well as their timing. We rank the forecasted changes in each quarter in the order in which they approximate the true or seventh value,

4, 5, 6, 7, 2, 3, 1.

The same kind of analysis performed on the remainder of the data shows that first, second, third, and fourth quarters appear to be consistently underestimated until the quarter in which performance actually takes place. For the fifth quarter, the reverse appears to be true, with estimates in excess of the original and incorrect in direction as well as in amount when compared with the actual. What we are pointing out is that the quality of the forecasting is in doubt. Even though the company may proclaim that it forecasts sales seven quarters in advance, in fact its estimates are close to actual results only during the quarter in which they apply.

The first four quarters show a consistent underestimation, followed by gradual increases as the quarter approaches reality. For the fifth quarter (the third quarter of the budget year), for some reason, estimates are initially high, and are followed two quarters later by a reversion to the initial estimate, and then by decreases as the actual quarter approaches.

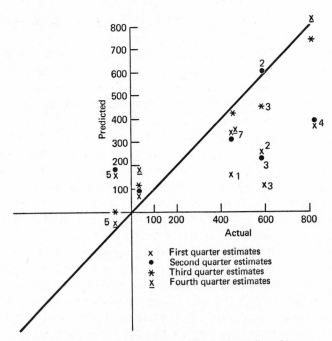

Figure 4-6. Successive changes in estimations of sales. (Adapted from a similar chart appearing in Henry Theil, *Applied Economic Forecasting*, copyright by North-Holland Publishing Company, Amsterdam, 1966, pp. 21–22.

The sixth quarter, which is the last quarter of the budget year, appears to consist of random changes, with increases in estimates being the rule until just six months before the actual, when forecasts revert approximately to the original level, and the actual comes in much lower than any forecast change or correction.

The quality of the initial forecast for the seventh quarter is of course highly suspect and is corrected as soon as the quarter enters the planning picture with the first correction of 344. This correction appears to be fairly consistent for the remainder of the time periods. Figure 4-6 shows graphically the changes in the quality of the estimates over time, for four quarters only.

LIMITATIONS OF BUSINESS FORECASTS

By now Papworth's law must surely be part of the professional humor of the business economist. This law states approximately that if there is a 50 percent probability of an unfavorable event occurring, one can be 95 percent sure it will take place. Coupled with this is the well-known Murphy's law, which states that if a thing can fail, it will. Business planning can find no better description. Business forecasting is an art using scientific method.

RELIABILITY OF DATA

Apart from the operation of the elasticity of expectations, in which one is described as tending to perpetuate the present situation, we have the natural optimism of the salesman, the natural pessimism of the credit manager, and the ingrown biases and value systems of managers all along the line. The data itself, before becoming grist for the mill of the forecaster, may be subject to operations which make it less than reliable. We will have more to say about this in the last chapter.

The likelihood of obsolescence has been pointed out by Winkler, who believes that the forecaster must pay more attention to recent information than to older information because economic data become obsolete and lose their value for describing the economic situation to be forecasted. Data, he says, expire, like certain medicines which to be viable must be fresh. He suggests, therefore, weights for older data should be reduced in proportion to the changes in the underlying economic situation.[11]

A good example of the need for weighting of data is the consumer price index, which is subject to all the ills of any index number, since the components of the index change over time in response to changes in consumer habits and the availability of kinds of goods. Frozen foods replace canned foods, which in turn have replaced fresh foods. Filter cigarettes replace unfiltered long cigarettes, which replace short cigarettes, and so on. Not only do the products change, but the proportion of each purchased by the consumer changes as well. The same

[11] Othmar W. Winkler, "Business Forecasting: The Predictive Value of Statistical Data," *Proceedings of the American Statistical Association*, Business and Economic Statistics Section, 1967, pp. 381–385.

problem holds true for indices of producer's goods. Coefficients of production, or what it takes to produce a given amount of the particular item, change over time, as do the nature of the products themselves and the materials from which they are made.

One last problem arises from the difficulty in obtaining valid price information, especially where list prices are honored more in the breach than in the observance. Discounts are often used instead of price changes, and the nature and extent of the discount given often is a matter of business privacy.

The Wall Street Journal had occasion some time ago to comment on the reliability of some data issued by the federal government.[12] The two kinds of data mentioned were the estimates of construction spending and estimates of inventory. According to the *Journal,* the estimates of construction spending are probably the least reliable economic statistics generated by the federal government, partly at least because of the fact that the construction business is a difficult one in which to survive, and many companies come alive or die on the strength of a single contract. The published data are not based on a direct survey but on estimates of what theoretically should have been accomplished under contracts previously made public.

With regard to inventory data, many firms do not take a physical inventory every month, and in many large companies, there is no uniformity in the way in which inventory is accounted for from plant to plant. If current inventory estimates are in poor condition, consider the fate of the Commerce Department quarterly survey of future inventory, which attempts to measure what will happen to inventory levels.

ERROR OF ESTIMATE

Even if the data the forecaster uses are absolutely accurate, the prediction of future events is still subject to errors of estimation. Our systematic equations may simply be unable to account for all variation in the dependent variable. These unassignable causes or random errors in estimation create a need for another variable in the set of equations, and this variable, as we have seen, is the random or stochastic variable. Its presence in the regression process helps to absorb any error resulting from random causes. In the prediction process, we have two choices. We may set the random variable equal to zero and thus obtain an estimate which is in a sense an average expectation and assumes that no random causes will be operative. Or we can generate a random distribution to provide the required series and supply a value, hoping thereby to improve the estimation.

We have, then, two kinds of errors implied here. One is that error which arises because our independent variables, while they account for much of the variability in the dependent variable, do not account for all of it. Second, we

[12] Richard F. Janssen, "Vital Statistics," *The Wall Street Journal,* Jan. 12, 1966, pp. 1–20.

have changes which come about because there are new forces at work which modify the degree to which variation in the independent variables actually affects the dependent or forecast variable. In other words, the functional relationship between the dependent variable and the independent variables does not remain constant. All economic data are stochastic. The results of a set of estimating equations are not mathematically precise, even though their form might lead one to that conclusion. The final results depend on the actions of people and of economic forces whose tendencies and trends may be seen, but whose governing forces are only imperfectly measured and less than imperfectly forecast.

In general, forecasters are inclined to believe that if they have, by the structure of their estimating equations, taken care of all important systematic relationships, the remaining error is random and a random variable is introduced to take care of it. If the data are not perfect, or the measurement methods are not accurate, and hence the resulting error is not systematic, the random variable may serve to bring about more accuracy in the long run than if it were not used. Period-to-period errors in observations would of course merely serve to lessen the degree of confidence we have in the model.

The extent of possible deviation in estimates is exemplified by the survey of changes in capital expenditures conducted by McGraw-Hill, compared with actual expenditures made over a five-year period, from 1962 to 1966, in which errors as much as 72 percent were observed. The best estimate of increase in capital spending was for 1963, in which the anticipated change turned out to be 60 percent of the actual.[13]

One of the reasons for errors in estimation, apart from the operation of the elasticity of expectations, is that businessmen often must make decisions before there are sufficient data on hand. When more up-to-date information becomes available, they may change their plans, generally after the forecasts have been made and disseminated.

Many businessmen believe that fundamentally one cannot really plan, and the task of the manager is to maintain as many uncommitted and open alternatives as possible, so as to be able to move quickly as conditions develop. Other businessmen complain that the statistics are good, but invariably too late. Business cycle indicators are published one to two months later than desirable for maximum usefulness, and as far as quarterly surveys are concerned, trends are more important than the actual data.

DIFFICULTY IN INTERPRETATION

Interpretation of information is a vital part of the management process. To interpret information is to assess or decide what the information is all about. Another aspect of interpretation has to do with the problem of deducing the

[13] *Business Bulletin*, vol. 48, no. 12, The Cleveland Trust Company, Dec., 1967.

applicability of final results of an analytical process. In 1950 and again in 1956, the diffusion index of twelve leading series of the National Bureau of Economic Research dropped sharply in the early part of the year, after suffering a decline in the preceding year. Was there a severe recession in the offing? Or did we have a cyclical turning point at the bottom of a trough? How, in any case, do you distinguish a turning point from a random disturbance? No one knows for sure.[14]

Despite the considerable progress made in economic forecasting, we still have no adequate explanation for some of the systematic relationships between economic variables. What is more, our economy is too complex to fit neatly into any formula or model or to be accurately depicted by any survey. Moore, in discussing the problem of selecting reliable business cycle indicators, states that ". . . it is impossible, in a set of twenty-one time series, selected for the relatively systematic behavior of the economic processes they represent, to depict all the relationships that contribute importantly to an understanding of the actual cyclical movements of the economy."[15]

Finally, we have feedback effects, about which we will have more to say in the final chapter. These serve to alter the variable being forecast by the mere fact that forecasts are made and acted upon. A case in point has to do with sales and inventory forecasting. If sales are forecast to decline and inventories are forecast to be too large in proportion to sales, business firms will take action to increase sales. Such action may not be within their power. They will also attempt to reduce inventories, which is within their power. But by reducing inventories, they are contributing to additional sales declines over and above those forecast. Responsive forecasting might well consider these reflexive actions in preparing estimates.

SUMMARY

In this chapter, we have explored some simple estimating tools which supplement the macro tools of the econometrician discussed earlier. They help by translating national data into the specific forecasting information needed for business use. The problem posed by affluence and the need, therefore, to test to determine on the spot how well a product will fare, is the subject of a discussion on test

[14] In the fall of 1962, G. H. Moore of the National Bureau of Economic Research almost called the U.S. Department of Commerce to warn of an impending recession. As it turned out, business continued to expand, following a suspicious first half, in 1962 while ten of the fifteen conincident indicators were pointing to a downturn at one time or another. See Alfred L. Malabre, Jr., "Boom's Death Watch, "The Wall Street Journal, Dec. 19, 1966, pp. 1–13.

[15] Geoffrey H. Moore, Business Cycle Indicators, Princeton University Press, Princeton, N.J., 1961, vol. 1, p. 46.

markets and market penetration. Methods of making market share calculations for new products were included. There followed, then, some methods of evaluating forecasts in a systematic manner which involve the use of Theil's prediction-realization diagram. The chapter ended with a brief discussion of the limitations of business forecasts.

Review Questions

1. What is the function of a test market?
2. A firm has 90 percent of the market for a well-established product. It has 60 percent of the market for a newer substitute only recently introduced and to which it is losing customers who formerly used the older product. What might its ultimate share of the market become?
3. A firm has complained of inventory imbalances. What diagnostic tools might be employed and for what reasons?
4. Of what use is the market share curve? How is it constructed?
5. What is meant by market penetration analysis? What is its relation to business forecasting? What kinds of curves, other than that used in the text, might be appropriate?
6. Compare a point and an interval prediction. How is a point prediction affected by the absence of a probability statement?
7. Evaluate the following forecast series against the realized or actual data.

Forecast	Actual	Forecast	Actual
880	875	975	980
950	920	975	975
940	930	1015	995
945	940		

8. What, in your view, is the most important limitation of a business forecast? Why?
9. Comment on the expression "an old price index is worse than none."
10. What is the function of the random variable? How is it estimated? How is it employed in forecasting?

Suggested Readings

Deming, W. Edwards: *Sample Design in Business Research,* John Wiley & Sons, Inc., New York, 1960.

Fourt, L. A., and J. W. Woodlock: "Early Prediction of Market Success for New Grocery Products," *Journal of Marketing,* vol. 25, no. 2, pp. 31–38, Oct., 1960.

Hauser, Philip, and William Leonard (eds.): *Government Statistics for Business Use,* John Wiley & Sons, Inc., New York, 1956.

King, William R.: *Quantitative Analysis for Marketing Management,* McGraw-Hill Book Company, New York, 1967.

Levin, Richard I., and C. A. Kirkpatrick: *Quantitative Approaches to Management,* McGraw-Hill Book Company, New York, 1971.

Morgenstern, Oskar: *On the Accuracy of Economic Observations,* Princeton University Press, Princeton, N.J., 1963.

chapter 5
demand analysis

In previous chapters, we considered the potential size of the market and methods by which we could forecast potential sales volume. We were concerned primarily with the identity of the potential customer, the extent of the probable demand for the product in the long run, and the impact of relevant economic variables. In economic terms, we were concerned with those factors which determine the general eagerness of people to buy a product of the type contemplated.

In this chapter, we are concerned with the reaction of people to our product at a list of possible prices. We will also want to know to what extent the demand for our product is influenced by factors other than price. We will look at the responsiveness of the sales of our product to changes in price, to changes in income, to changes in the demand for other goods, and as a function of the amount of it people already have on hand.

In Chapter 6, we will attempt to bring what we have learned into a procedure for demand forecasting which will look at kinds of goods and the nature of their uses, and note the changes in demand analysis which have to be made, depending on whether the good is a consumer or a producer good, durable or nondurable.

We begin this discussion with the theory of market demand and its basis in the theory of consumer behavior, as contained in standard economic theory.

THE LAW OF DEMAND

It is commonplace to say that firms must produce things that consumers prefer, because consumer purchases are the votes that reelect firms and keep them in office. Since consumers cannot buy everything, and the economy cannot produce everything, there is a continual process of allocation in which limited dollar resources of consumers are divided among the goods and services produced by firms and others. What then determines consumer choice? Basically, the utility or usefulness of a good or service. How much will a consumer buy? It all depends on how strongly he prefers one product to others, how much money he has, how strongly he wants to hold money, how much money he must exchange for each unit of a good or service, and what alternatives there are and at what price.

DEFINING A COMMODITY

Before outlining the main principles of the theory, we must call attention to one of the instances in which economists tend to be somewhat vague. We shall be discussing the demand for a commodity as opposed to the demand for one or more other commodities. Unfortunately, however, the word "commodity" will be used to mean whatever one chooses to have it mean, depending upon the circumstances. The difficulty in defining what is meant by a commodity lies in the level of definition intended or possible. A commodity can be meat, beef, sirloin steak, or hamburger, depending on the level of definition or classification. A commodity can also be defined from the point of view of its intended use, as for example food (not a commodity in the former sense, but something used in feeding), home entertainment (as opposed to radio, television, etc.), light (as opposied to electric light bulbs), and so on. Commodities may also be what are generally known as products, in which case it is generally assumed that some particular firm's output is intended to be represented. Thus, not electric light bulbs, but Sylvania or General Electric light bulbs, are intended.

CONSUMER CHOICE

The nature of the decision process can be seen if we assume that only two commodities are involved and that our consumer or purchaser has only a certain amount of money to spend at the moment. To arrive at any meaningful conclusions, we must assume that our consumer is rational and, given a choice between two things, is willing to express a preference for one over the other.

Second, we will assume that our consumer will perfer more of a commodity to less, which is to say that our commodity has some positive degree of incremental utility so that given the opportunity, he would trade or prefer a unit containing more of the item for one containing less.

Third, we will assume that our consumer's choice is rational if, preferring A to B and B to C, he will also prefer A to C.

Finally, we will assert that there is some amount of A that will compensate for some amount of B, the amounts involved depending on the stocks of A and B already held at the time of the trade.

In conclusion, then, we are stating that the more of A our customer has, the less he will be inclined to accept more of it, and the more eager he would be

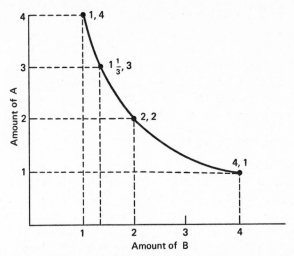

Figure 5-1. A two-commodity world showing possible combinations to which our consumer has no objection.

to obtain B. The more of A he has, the more he will give up to acquire some of B. As his stock of B grows, the less of A he is willing to exchange for equal amounts of B.

There is nothing in the theory which of itself specifies how much of A and how much of B a consumer will hold, except that, for a given level of utility, he will be indifferent so long as he maintains that given level of satisfaction. In Figure 5-1 we represent our consumer in a two-commodity world. The convex (to the axis) curve represents the path of all possible combinations of A and B whose combined utility is the same. Similar curves could be constructed between the present curve and the axes, or to the right of the curve, depending upon whether the combined utility was lesser or greater than the amount of utility represented by the present curve.

Our example is of course symmetrical; the indifference curve shown is a rectangular hyperbola because the amounts of utility and the number of units are the same. If, however, the changes in utility did not parallel the changes in the number of units, then the curve would not be a rectangular hyperbola and, indeed, could be almost any consistent shape. Figure 5-2 illustrates a curve in which the utility amounts are different from the numbers of units.

At X and Y in Figure 5-2, two triangles have been sketched showing the amount of change in quantity of B possessed, associated with a decrease in the amount of A possessed. At triangle X, a decrease in A of one unit is associated with an increase in B of one-quarter unit. At Y, a similar decrease in A is associated with an increase in B of 1½ units. The rate at which our consumer is substituting B for A—that is, giving up A in order to acquire B—is portrayed by these triangles. This rate is termed the marginal rate of substitution and is the

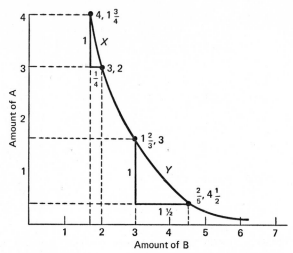

Figure 5-2. A two-commodity world showing a consumer's indifference curve.

number of units of B required to compensate the consumer for the loss of one unit of A. In this example, our consumer is clearly subject to a diminishing marginal rate of substitution as he proceeds down the total utility path.

POOR MAN'S GOODS

We have assumed that our consumer is rational and we have placed a particular meaning on the term rational. We have said that, given a choice, he will exercise that choice and that, normally, he would prefer more of a commodity to less. Now we come to that phenomenon known to economists as *poor man's goods.* It is used to explain why it is that as the standard of life increases beyond a certain point consumers actually begin to demand less of an item than more. The usual example given is that the rich eat less potatoes than do the poor and that if the price of potatoes is increased, normal price-quantity relations will not hold. Instead of buying less, more will be demanded. But this is getting ahead of our story.

In terms of our indifference curve analysis and assuming still that we are in a two-commodity world and that our consumer is now exercising a preference for one commodity over another when his inventory of the latter exceeds a certain point, we have a diagram that looks like Figure 5-3.

Suppose our consumer has five units of Y and is given successively up to four units of X. His total utility will rise to twenty-two as he moves to the right on the diagram. Hence, he is clearly better off for having acquired additional units of X.

Now let us try this exercise vertically, assuming that with an inventory of three units of X, he acquires additional units of Y. It is easy to see that once past five units of Y, his total utility begins to decline, first to nineteen, then to seventeen, and so on, as he increases his stock of Y. If he had four units of X, he would have reached maximum utility with five units of Y and would almost at once have begun to dislike having any more.

Apart from explaining why people have limited needs for some kinds of goods as their income rises, and for this purpose we would of course have to introduce some refinements in our diagram, economists have not done too much with this concept. For the marketing specialist, the concept has a good deal of usefulness. It explains, for instance, why it is best to expand a product line so as to capture various segments of the market where the distinguishing feature of each segment is level of income. It also explains why price lining may be sufficient at times and why at others product differentiation is a virtual necessity. Further, it explains what is implied in the concept of market saturation. But we will explore these concepts in detail later.

At the moment, we are interested in the fact that, for the first time, goods are seen to have a characteristic apart from their quality as a good. The goods satisfy some need which is more than the need to own goods. People want goods for the service they render. The utility arises out of usefulness and is not a mere product of preference for goods as goods. It will, therefore, be perfectly rational for a consumer to buy a higher-priced substitute if the substitute possesses some qualities or can render some service which the lower-priced substitute does not. Price alone, in other words, does not sell a product. The product must possess the correct set of characteristics.

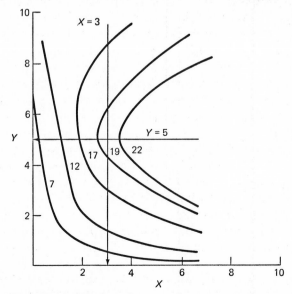

Figure 5-3. Poor man's goods.

Where conventional theory assumes that people want goods because they are goods, a theory advanced recently by Kelvin J. Lancaster is built around the idea that the demand for a product is actually a demand for the services it will render, and these services stem from their characteristics.[1] Since one of these characteristics may be the ability to impart a feeling of uniqueness or distinctiveness, the theory can explain instances in which a consumer will rationally purchase a higher-priced good when a lower-priced good is otherwise a good substitute.

We return now to our two-commodity world and our set of indifference curves to explore further conventional consumer theory.

THEORY OF CONSUMER EQUILIBRIUM

In Figures 5-1 and 5-2, we drew an indifference curve which represented the respective amounts of two commodities whose ownership would provide the same total utility. The curve is convex, slopes downward and to the right in order for an increase in X, compensated for by a decrease in Y, to yield the same total utility. An increase in X, unaccompanied by any change in the quantity of Y, must increase total utility, then, and it would be possible to draw a similar curve or family of curves to the right, or to the left, should we decrease X and hold Y unchanged. Conversely, an increase in Y, unaccompanied by a decrease in X, must increase total utility, and it likewise would be possible to draw the family of curves we have just referred to, holding X constant. Increases in total utility being represented by higher indifference curves, it is possible to stay on the same curve only if increases in X, and Y, respectively, are compensated by respective decreases. This can, of course, only be done if the curves are convex. Convexity also means that the rate of substitution of one commodity for the other is diminishing.

In Figure 5-4 we show, on the same axes used in Figures 5-1 and 5-2, OL representing the amount of X which would be bought if all of a given amount of money were to be spent on that item. OM represents the same point with respect to them Y. If we connect the two points by a line LM, any point would represent a pair of quantities which could be bought out of the stipulated amount of money. The slope of the line LM indicates the ratio of the prices of the two commodities and also the proportions in which each will be bought in order to stay within the budget. Notice it says nothing about which combination will be purchased.

Usually an indifference curve will intersect the line LM. This intersection does not indicate a point of equilibrium, however, because by moving along LM in one direction or another, the consumer can get to a higher curve which gives

---

[1] For a complete explanation, see either "Change and Innovation in the Technology of Consumption," *American Economic Review*, vol. 56, no. 2, pp. 14–23, May, 1966, or "A New Approach to Consumer Theory," *Journal of Political Economy*, vol. 74, no. 2, pp. 132–157 (Apr., 1966).

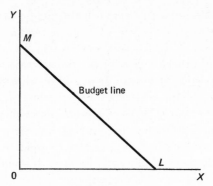

Figure 5-4. Budget line.

him greater total utility. When *LM* is tangent to an indifference curve, or at that point on *LM* in which movement in either direction represents movement toward a lower indifference curve (i.e., a point of intersection as opposed to tangency), total utility is maximized for the amount of the budget available. Tangency represents proportionality between marginal utilities of the goods and the prices at which they are available. The consumer is in equilibrium when the marginal rate of substitution between the two commodities is equal to the ratio of the prices, or else he will substitute one for the other, sliding down the appropriate indifference curve until equality takes place.

We can show increases in income by movements out along each axis reflecting increases in the amount of money available to be spent. If the price ratio remains the same while income or budget increases, we will have a set of lines, out from the origin, parallel to the original budget or price line. But notice that if we should suppose that the price of the commodity represented on the *X* axis were to decrease, the effect would be the same as though we had assumed an increase in income—the line would move to the right, as illustrated in Figure 5-5.

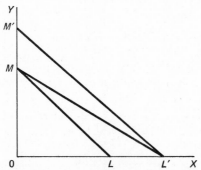

Figure 5-5. Income change and a price change.

The line *LM* represents our original budget line. An increase in our budget would enable us to buy amounts OL' instead of OL, of commodity *X*, or OM' of commodity *Y*, instead of OM, assuming no change in prices of *X* and *Y*.

Now let us assume the price of *X* to decrease, so that the amount of budget available with which we could buy OL of *X* is now sufficient to purchase OL' of *X*. Our new budget line is now *L'M* since, with the original budget, we can still buy no more of *Y* than OM. In other words, the effect of a price reduction is the same as an increase in income, although it would admittedly take a large change in price affecting a major purchase to equal the budget change illustrated in our diagram. The principle, however, is sound. If I am able to save $500 on the purchase of a new automobile, it is as if I had received a measurable increase in income.

Our next illustration shows a family of budget curves tangent to a family of indifference curves. Through the points of tangency in Figure 5-6, a line has been drawn. This line is called the income-consumption curve and it shows the way in which the consumption varies when income increases and prices remain unchanged. There is only one restriction on its shape, and that is that it cannot intersect any particular indifference curve more than once. Therefore these curves generally slope upward and to the right, but many, as does ours, further on move to the left as inferior goods, consumed at lower levels of income, are replaced by goods of higher quality when income increases. The line could, of course, move downward and to the right.

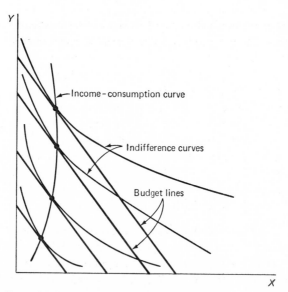

Figure 5-6. Income-consumption curve.

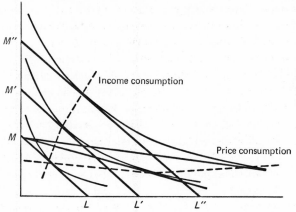

Figure 5-7. Price-consumption curve compared with an income-consumption curve.

If now we assume income to be fixed, we can, as in Figure 5-5, show the effects of a price change. The slopes of the budget lines will vary, depending on whether L is moved and M remains constant, or vice versa. In either case, the path of a line intersecting the tangencies will trace the price-consumption curve as in Figure 5-7.

Notice that as we pass from lower to higher indifference curves, the price-consumption curve lies to the right of the income-consumption curve. We have already seen that a fall in the price of a commodity acts similar to an increase in income. Now we see that a fall in price will also change relative prices so that there is a tendency to substitute the commodity whose price has fallen for others whose price has not fallen as much or at all. The former effect is termed the *income effect of a price change;* the latter, the *substitution effect of a price change.* The total effect on demand is the sum of those two tendencies.

The relative importance of each effect will depend in general on the proportions in which the consumer divides his expenditure between two commodities or between this and other commodities. The income effect is more important if the amount proportionately of income devoted to it is large; the substitution effect is likely to overshadow the income effect if the proportion of income spent on it is small.

DERIVING THE DEMAND CURVE

We pointed out earlier that a demand schedule for a commodity, if plotted, must slope downward and to the right, more being consumed when the price falls, provided of course the good is not an inferior one with a backward curling income-consumption relationship. Now let us see how the demand curve arises from the analytical system we have been using.

Our two commodities, X and Y, in Figure 5-8, are shown in the now-familiar indifference curve system with three budget lines LM, L'M and L''M, each of the lines to the right of LM representing successive price decreases in X. Given points of tangency of the budget lines and the indifference curves, we can find the amounts of X and Y, respectively, that will be purchased as before, by merely moving along the applicable coordinate of the graph. The amounts of X purchased in response to the decreases in price are noted as B and C, A being the original amount purchased before price reduction.

Let us now place an identical quantity scale below the X scale in the indifference diagram and continue the quantity markings A, B, and C down to the new scale. Instead of the quantity of Y, let us now, on the vertical axis, place the price of X. Denoting the prices as 1, 2, and 3, respectively, we can mark on the graph the coordinate points for price and quantity. If we connect these points, we shall of course have a demand curve for X, all other prices remaining constant, and assuming that the system of indifference curves has not also changed.

This demand curve is the representation of what is called the law of demand. The law of demand is simply that the amount demanded will vary inversely as price and, as we see above, is derived from the notion of diminishing marginal utility. Another way of stating the law is that it is a law of marginal demand price. In this form, it indicates simply that the larger the amount of a thing a person has, the less will be the price he will pay for a little more of it.

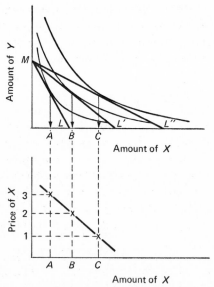

Figure 5-8. Derivation of the demand curve for X.

From this we conclude that the relationship between average revenue, or price, and quantity must be downward sloping.

Since the demand curve is derived from a particular set of indifference curves and budget lines, to which a particular set of prices has been applied, any change in these conditions will alter the demand curve. Any increase, for example, in the purchasing power of money will serve to move the budget lines in their entirety to the right and upward, so that they are tangent to a new set of indifference curves standing for greater amounts of total utility than before. What has happened, of course, is that all prices have dropped, and a given amount of money will buy more units of all commodities. The effect on the demand curve will be to move it to the right, signifying that more will now be purchased at the same list of prices.

Should there be an increase in the amount of money available to be spent, we would have a similar phenomenon, namely, a shift in the demand curve to the right. This shift is now the result of an increased amount of budget available at the same list of prices. We refer to this *shift in the entire demand curve* as a *change in demand*. Such a shift differs in nature from a *change in the quantity of goods demanded* caused by a movement in prices. The latter may be caused by a shift in the supply curve or by direct intervention in the price structure.

The demand curve may shift for reasons other than changes in price or income. It may shift because people's desires and tastes change. Such a change would initially be reflected in changes in the underlying indifference curves and then in the demand curve. A decrease in the intensity of desire for the product will mean that people will be less willing to buy the same amounts as before at the old list of prices. The demand curve will then shift to the left. An increase in the intensity of demand will move the demand curve, on the other hand, to the right.

EFFECT OF SUBSTITUTES AND COMPLEMENTS

Let us now suppose that the price of a good which is a substitute declines. More of that good and less of the original good for which it is a substitute will be purchased. This decrease in demand for the original good will be felt all along the demand curve of the original in varying degrees and will operate to shift the demand curve. Since a substitute is involved, less of our former, more expensive good will be desired at the old list of prices, and hence the curve will move to the left. If the prices of substitutes rise, then of course the demand curve will move to the right.

Where a complementary good is involved, demands move together, so that a rise in the price of a complement will cause, first, a decline in the amount of the complement demanded, and then a decline in the demand for the original good. There is, once again, a shift in the entire demand curve. An example would be a rise in the price of automobiles bringing about a decline, first in the amount of automobiles demanded, then in the demand for automobile tires.

It is not always simple to identify a complementary good since at times goods which are seemingly complementary may upon closer examination be seen to be substitutes. For example, shoe laces are quite obviously complementary to shoes. Should the price of shoes be increased, thereby causing a decrease in the number of pairs of shoes sold, it is possible that no less, and possibly more, laces would be sold. What has happened, of course, is that the existing stock of shoes is being worn more intensively, and therefore laces are needed to make this additional wear possible. A similar example might be cited involving the price of liquor. Should the price of liquor increase, causing a decrease in the amount demanded, it is conceivable that the demand for other ingredients used in making cocktails might increase since, although complements, they are also in a sense substitutes which enable the consumer to compensate for the decrease in the amount of liquor used.

DEMAND ELASTICITY

In this section, we will discuss the parameters of the demand relationship that govern its slope and its shape. We have established that demand is inversely related to price (under most conditions). Now the question is one not of cause and effect but of degree. The amount demanded is not uniformly responsive to changes in price for all prices, and the degree of response is not the same for all goods and commodities and competitive conditions.

One of the factors governing the degree of responsiveness of demand to changes in price is the availability of close substitutes. Earlier, in Chapter 2, it was pointed out that a firm facing competition from close substitutes would have a demand curve facing it that would be more or less horizontal, unless it could succeed in differentiating its product from others. Even though the demand for a product with substitutes is elastic, the demand for the family of products may be quite inelastic. Thus, the demand for brand A of cigarettes may be elastic, but the demand for all brands of cigarettes, in the aggregate, is generally considered to be unresponsive to changes in price over a wide range.

An indication of elasticity to price is provided by the ratio of the percent rise in quantity sold to the percent reduction in price. Since the movements along the price axis and the demand axis are in opposite directions, the coefficient has some properties that are independent of the particular slope of the demand curve. As price diminishes, the ratio of the decrease to the base price will increase. Associated with the price decrease, there should be, for a sloping demand curve, a continually increasing amount demanded. This continual increase means that the ratio of a constant quantity increase to its base—the quantity from which the increase has taken place—must diminish. The resultant ratio, whose denominator—the percent decrease in price—is increasing, and whose numerator— the percent increase in quantity demanded — is decreasing, must result in an elasticity coefficient which approaches zero as price diminishes. Since the elasticity coefficient calculation begins at a very high price and a very small amount demanded, the upper value of the ratio is quite large.

Somewhere along the demand curve, as we move down, the ratio of percent change in the amount that quantity has increased, to a percent change in price associated with it, assumes the value of 1 and this point is termed *unitary elasticity*. Since a price decrease is generally associated with an increase in amount demanded, demand elasticity coefficients are generally assumed to be negative numbers.

Because the scale can affect the calculation of the elasticity coefficient, or the choice of units can affect the slope of the demand curve, it is difficult to make comparisons from one curve to another. Another source of difficulty arises in the selection of the base on which to calculate the percents. One way out of this dilemma is to average the old and the new amounts and use that number as the base for calculating the required percentages.

It might appear that the more toward vertical a demand curve appears, the more inelastic the demand. Actually, while it is true that a perfectly vertical curve or line is perfectly inelastic and a perfectly horizontal line is perfectly elastic, any departure from these limiting conditions results in a straight-line demand curve which is elastic near the top, unitary elastic near the middle, and inelastic from that point downward to the right. The coefficient can be calculated by taking the ratio of the distance from the horizontal axis to any point in question, measured along the demand curve, to the distance from that point, again along the demand curve, to the vertical axis. Figure 5-9 illustrates the various relationships.

We can measure the elasticity of demand to changes in price and calculate the elasticity coefficient in the following manner:

$$\frac{q_2 - q_1}{\frac{1}{2}(q_2 + q_1)} \bigg/ \frac{p_2 - p_1}{\frac{1}{2}(p_2 + p_1)}$$

This formula is called the *arc elasticity coefficient* formula and provides an index of elasticity of demand to price over a range of price measured by the distance from p_1 to p_2. As the distance between the respective p's and q's grows smaller, the formula will change to

$$\frac{\Delta q}{q} \bigg/ \frac{\Delta p}{p}$$

because the p and q values are not so very different from the average of the upper and lower values. This expression can be written as

$$\frac{p}{q} \times \frac{\Delta q}{\Delta p}$$

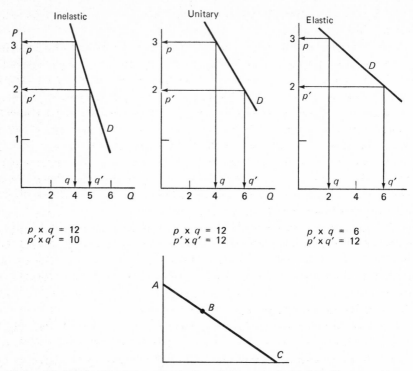

Figure 5-9. Relationship between inelastic, unitary, and elastic demand curves. Note: Decrease in resultant revenue after price change means inelastic demand. No change means unitary elasticity, while an increase means an elastic demand. Elasticity of demand at point B is equal to BC/AB.

and, as Δp and Δq become very small, the expression becomes

$$\frac{p \; dq}{q \; dp}$$

which is the formula for point elasticity. The latter is more applicable to a demand curve when we wish to inquire as to the elasticity of demand at any one point on that curve. An approximation to that value can be obtained by taking the ratio of the lower segment of a tangent at that point to the upper segment, as we described earlier and as shown in Figure 5-10.

Using the "Returns" Curve. In Figure 5-9, we linked elasticity of demand to price, to changes in total revenue. A "returns" curve is another way of plotting total revenue. The maximum point on such a curve is the quantity at which elasticity of demand is unitary.

Figure 5-11 shows the returns curve plotted from the data provided by the demand curve. Where the curve is rising, elasticity is more than 1. Beyond the peak in total returns, elasticity is less than 1, and continues to diminish as the curve falls.

The curve is constructed by first erecting a vertical at $Q = 1$ and marking on it some of the prices corresponding to the quantities in the demand schedule. For example, the demand curve at point A indicates that six items would be sold at a price of $.05. Mark that price on the vertical (indicated as B) and then draw a ray or line from the origin of the graph through B and proceed to a value on the p axis corresponding to total revenue — in this instance $.05 × 6 or $.30. Similar points, connected, provide the total returns graph.

Notice that an increase in price will result in an increase in total revenue only if demand is inelastic to price changes — that is, to the right of the maximum of the total returns curve. Where demand is elastic to changes in price, a price decrease will result in an increase in total returns.

It is important to realize that elasticities are momentary, and it is not possible to say what the price elasticity of demand for a product may be, except at a particular point in time and place and under stated conditions. Nor can we use one particular coefficient on the assumption that it describes the elasticity of demand throughout the length of the curve, because, as we have seen, not only the curvature is involved, but the scale as well.

Sometimes elasticity and slope are confused, especially by the beginning student. The slope of the curve is not the same as elasticity, unless the curve is plotted from the logarithms of the data. The elasticity of q with respect to p is the ratio of relative changes in q and p. If the slope of the line is dp/dq, the elasticity of q with respect to p is $dq/dp × p/q$, as we mentioned in the preceding section. In Figure 5-10, elasticity is given as the ratio of BC to AB, which is the same as $dq/dp × p/q$. In other words, the reciprocal of the slope is used in the computation of the elasticity coefficient.

A way to check for an elasticity coefficient greater than 1 is to estimate the marginal return from a price change. If the increment to total revenue resulting from a change in price is positive, then elasticity of demand is more than 1. This relationship comes about because marginal revenue is 0 where total

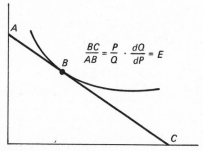

$$\frac{BC}{AB} = \frac{P}{Q} \cdot \frac{dQ}{dP} = E$$

Figure 5-10. Point elasticity.

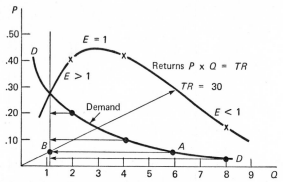

Figure 5-11. Returns curve. (Source: Frederick V. Waugh, *Graphic Analysis: Applications to Agricultural Economics*, Agricultural Handbook No. 326, U.S. Department of Agriculture, Economic Research Service, Washington, D.C., Nov., 1966.)

revenue is a maximum and the demand curve is downward sloping to the right. In Figure 5-12, we see the relationship between the demand curve, total revenue, and marginal revenue.

Notice that the diagram in Figure 5-12 is identical to that of the preceding figure, except that a marginal revenue curve has been inserted. Marginal revenue is simply the rate of change in total revenue. In this diagram, it has been plotted from the data on the following page.

The point at which marginal revenue intersects the quantity axis corresponds to a zero contribution to total revenue, and thereafter, total revenue turns down. Therefore, elasticity of demand goes through the unit position where marginal revenue is 0, and its value is more than 1 where marginal revenue is positive, less than 1 where it is negative.

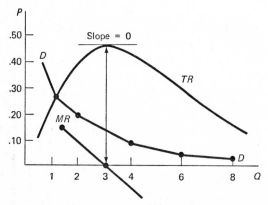

Figure 5-12. Demand, total revenue, and marginal revenue.

Price	Quantity	Total Revenue	Marginal Revenue
.25	1	.25 ⎤	
			.15
.20	2	.40 ⎤	
			0
.10	4	.40 ⎤	
			−.10
.05	6	.30 ⎤	
.02	8	.16	

Income Elasticity of Demand. When we discussed price elasticity of demand, we were concerned with the extent to which increases in the *amount demanded* were associated with reductions in price. Income elasticity of demand, on the other hand, refers to the extent to which there are increases *in demand,* at the same list of prices, caused by increases in income of the demanders. In other words, we are now concerned with the extent to which the demand curve moves to the right when consumer income increases, or in reverse manner, the extent to which the demand curve shifts to the left when consumer income is reduced. Where earlier we assumed that demand was a function of price and held all other variables constant, now we are asserting that demand is a function of income and that price is included among the "all other variables" being held constant.

Income elasticity of demand is defined as the percentage change in quantity sold which would result from a 1 percent change in disposable money income, all other variables being held constant.[2] Elasticity thus computed is generally termed relative elasticity since it is a percentage. Absolute elasticity is also often calculated as a unit response in demand per dollar of additional income. In this instance, the coefficient is of course positive for changes in income since, except for inferior goods, both income and demand change in the same direction.

In Figure 5-8, we saw how the demand curve *is* derived from the indifference curve apparatus, revealing the interdependence of price and the amount demanded. Now in Figure 5-13, we see that the demand curve moves upward and to the right as a result of an increase in income. An increase in income is depicted by a movement of the budget line outward from the origin, reflecting the availability of increased amounts of money to spend. Quite naturally, indifference curves reflecting a higher degree of utility are now tangent, but without change in price levels.

The demand curve *D* is the same demand curve we derived in Figure 5-8. The new demand curve *D'* results from an increase in income which enables our consumer to purchase Y_2X_2 at the same list of prices for Y and X as before. The tangency at the higher indifference curve at point C reflects the new decision,

[2] It is customary to refer to this change as a change in the quantity demanded, but with respect to income and not price.

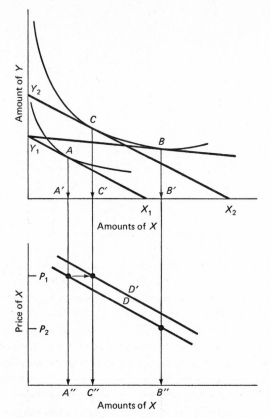

Figure 5-13. A change in demand resulting from an increase in income.

which in turn indicates the shift in the demand curve. Now more will be demanded at the same list of prices because of the rise in income.

The relationship between changes in income and quantity demanded in empirical studies often leads to investigation of the relationship between changes in income and consumption expenditure. The behavior described in Figure 5-14 is generally referred to as Engel's law, from Ernst Engel, the German statistician, who first pointed out that the rate of increase in expenditures for necessaries such as food and clothing tends to fall off with increases in disposable income. Beyond some point, he said, all expenditures increase at a decreasing rate.

The study of the relationship between consumer income and amounts spent on various goods can be approached through budgetary expenditure surveys as conducted by the Bureau of Labor Statistics, the Department of Agriculture's Economic Research Service, and the Survey Research Center of the Uni-

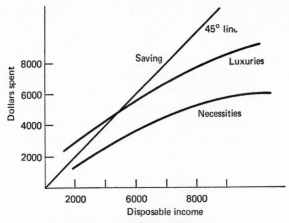

Figure 5-14. Consumption behavior pattern.

versity of Michigan. Surveys of this kind generally consist of reports of family expenditures for different items, classified by the level of income of the respondent. The time period is generally held constant, so that the results then closely approximate the kind of income-expenditure relationship visualized in Figure 5-14.

Another method of studying the relationship between consumption and disposable income is to construct annual reports in the form of consumption schedules. Such a schedule gives annual average income and annual average expenditure for goods for a number of years and indicates the way in which averages move together over time. The result is shown in Figure 5-15

A typical mathematical model derived from income and consumption data for the period 1929 to 1941 is provided by T. Haavelmo. In it, C, consumption, is a function of the level of disposable income Y, both adjusted for price

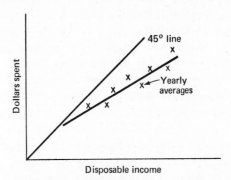

Figure 5-15. General consumption schedule from annual averages.

level changes, in what we have seen from earlier chapters is a typical consumption function form,[3]

$$C = 95.05 + .712Y$$

Thus far, we have examined the relationship between price and the amount demanded, and income and the level of demand. We saw also that the relationship of income to demand is calculated sometimes using the number of units demanded and sometimes in terms of the dollar value of the quantity of demand. In the latter case, of course, since we are estimating changes in consumption in general, demand refers to more than one kind of good.

Cross-elasticity of Demand. The change in quantity demanded as a response to changes in price or in income in the preceding section was expressed numerically as an elasticity coefficient. The coefficient was computed as the ratio of the percent change in quantity to the percent change in price or in income associated with it. But we saw also that the demand for goods could be influenced by the prices of other goods which were substitutes or complements. It should, therefore, not be strange to see that an elasticity coefficient can be calculated which indicates the extent to which the demands for goods are interrelated. This coefficient is termed the coefficient of cross-elasticity of demand.

The expression for cross-elasticity of demand is

$$E_{bp_a} = \frac{\Delta Q_b}{Q_b} \bigg/ \frac{\Delta P_a}{P_a}$$

which means that the elasticity coefficient E is computed as the ratio of the percent change in the quantity of item b demanded to the associated percent change in the price of item a. A fairly obvious instance of substitutes is given by comparing synthetic coffee cream with the real thing. Should the price of cream rise, it would not be unlikely that the demand for the cream substitute would increase. Let the price of some quantity of cream rise 10 percent, say from 25¢ to 27½¢, and it is possible that the usage of the substitute would increase also by 10 percent. The coefficient of cross-elasticity would then be 1. On the other hand, an increase in the price of the substitute would find consumers once more finding cream to their liking, and a new coefficient of cross-elasticity would then have to be calculated to depict the reverse relationship.

There is, of course, no way of knowing what the new coefficient would be without more information, because the reasons for switching from the substitute to the cream might differ from those causing the original switch, and the price levels would also be different, so that the new ratios would differ from the origi-

[3] T. Haavelmo, "Methods of Measuring the Marginal Propensity to Consume," *Journal of the American Statistical Association*, vol. 42, pp. 105ff., March, 1947.

nal 10 percent. We can be sure of one thing, however, and that is that the closer the substitute, the larger the coefficient of cross-elasticity, while if the goods are poor substitutes, their cross-elasticity coefficient would be small.

Sometimes the size of the coefficient is used to determine whether products "belong" to the same industry or represent the same commodity. This criterion is not always a good one where products may be jointly used or jointly produced.

Pipes and tobacco are used together and their coefficient of cross-elasticity will ordinarily be fairly high, but of course with a negative sign. The coefficient of elasticity of complements is ordinarily negative as against a positive coefficient for substitutes.

The cross-elasticity of demand will be less responsive to changes in the price of substitutes if the products share the same production facilities. Suppose, for example, an increase in the price of product A is brought about by increases in raw material costs. The effect on the demand for B, a substitute, should be to increase. But now let us assume that B uses the same plant and facilities as does A. The increase in the demand for B, if it is to be met, will require an increase in the output of B, and this increase can only come about if the output of A is curtailed to make the necessary capacity available. Much now depends on the ability of the plant to produce B in increased amounts as cheaply as before and on the exact relationship between plant capacity and output. If an increase in the supply of B can only come about at increased cost, then it is possible that the price of B also will rise, thus causing a realignment of the entire structure of demand and price.

The variables which have been introduced should now be summarized:

1. Products may be substitutes or complements from the point of view of demand.
2. They may be independently produced or may be joint products.
3. The price changes may come about because the same amount can only be supplied at higher cost while the demand curve is unchanging. If so, there would be a decrease in the amount demanded because of the price increase. Lower costs would result in an increase in the amount demanded.
4. The price changes may originate from an increase or a decrease in demand, without any change in supply conditions.

Suppose, for example, that an increase in price results from an increase in demand. The effect on a substitute which is a joint product will be quite different than if the price increase is caused by increases in costs of materials or other inputs. Examples can be introduced showing the effect on the coefficient of cross-elasticity under each combination of the above conditions, but the student might well do this on his own and allow us to go on to another kind of elasticity, the elasticity of price expectations.

PRICE EXPECTATIONS

One of the defects in the usefulness of the demand curve as an aid in price determination is that it deals with prices as they exist at the exact moment when the schedule is drawn up. But the quantity of an item a businessman or a consumer will buy, when the price is at some level or another, is a short-range planning decision based on the expectation that other prices will remain as they were when the plans were laid. The extent of our demand is based on the degree to which we expect to have use for the commodity or obtain some kind of results from its consumption. In the theory of consumer equilibrium, expectations play little part except insofar as we can presume that one of the parameters of the demand curve is price and another is need, as these are expected to exist at some future time. One of the problems is that the consumer is supposed to want goods simply because they are goods. In production theory, that is not assumed, since goods are desired for their usefulness as inputs to a production process. The demand function or schedule, and hence the list of prices at which various inputs will be demanded, is easily seen to depend upon the list of expected prices at which the output will be sold.

Expected values are usually calculated as the product of the amount expected and the probability of it being received at the end of the relevant time period. It is customary also to take into account that the principal sum would have earned something over the relevant time period, had it been received currently instead of in the future. The earnings rate is most often taken to be the money rate of interest, but may instead be the rate of return on capital employed in similar ventures. Discussion of rates of return will be taken up later, when we discuss the management of capital funds. For our purposes here, an assumed money rate of interest will do. This rate will constitute an opportunity cost involved in making decisions where expectations of future revenues are concerned.

While the relevant interest rate or opportunity cost of money can be calculated with a fair degree of accuracy, the probability aspects are much more general. It is easy to assert that if the probability of getting a sum D of dollars is p, the expected value is the product of the amount and the probability, namely Dp. Calculating p is another matter. There are several alternatives, none of which provides the decision maker with anything more than a relative indication of the true state of affairs.

Statisticians and decision theorists speak of two classes pf probabilities: subjective and objective. By subjective probabilities, they mean estimates based on an individual's best guess as to the future. Objective probability exists when the calculation is made on the basis of some kind of evidence or experience to use as a basis.

A customary example of a probability evident on the basis of experimentation or past experience is the probability of obtaining a head when tossing a coin. If the tossing procedure is fair and not biased, and the coin is a fair coin and not weighted so as to influence the results of the toss, then in the long run, experience tells us, half the time the tosses will produce heads and half the time tails. These are the only alternatives open and they will occur with equal likelihood, since there is no external influence affecting the results. The probability of obtaining a head on any toss is then 50 percent, and the basis for this objective probability is experience, which can be verified by experimentation.

An example of a subjective probability, on the other hand, appears to be present in a recent statement by the chairman of the board of the Diamond International Corporation before the New York Society of Security Analysts. "The $100 million," he was reported as saying, "we are projecting for sales in packaging machinery and automated systems could be on the low side, but we would rather be a little conservative."

Clearly, different men having access to the same information will have differing expectations, depending on the way in which they extrapolate information at their disposal. The chairman appears to have said, in substance, that he assigned a fairly high probability of success to the estimate of $100 million of sales. To find out what other probability estimates might be made, we could, hypothetically of course, ask the chairman how likely it is that sales could be $100 million, or $120 million, $130 million, and so on. If he believes quite strongly that sales of $100 million are very likely, and he is being conservative in his estimate, then he may be able to formulate some estimate of the probability that some other sales level could occur.

The following table indicates the possible sales volume estimates or potential quantities demanded, together with hypothetical probabilities that they will be attained.

Sales Volume	Probability of Attaining at Least That Sales Level
$ 90,000,000	100%
100,000,000	95
110,000,000	90
120,000,000	80
130,000,000	65
140,000,000	50
150,000,000	30
160,000,000	10

Suppose some months have elapsed after the original estimate and that sales have been recorded at an annual rate of $120 million. The original probability, which was more or less subjective, now can be made more objective as we acquire more and more information. It would appear, in fact, quite likely that the former assigned probability of 80 percent must be increased, as it appears more and more likely that $120 million, rather than $100 million, will be sold.

If sales appear to be running at an annual rate below the $100 million mark, on the other hand, then we have to revise our estimates downward. Once more, however, while we have additional information, an important variable is present in the manner in which we interpret that information. If we are customarily optimistic, we may ignore or treat lightly any early results indicating a possible reduction in annual sales, while seizing on any potential increase as supporting our earlier estimates.

What was the basis on which the original estimates were made? Was it simply that the estimate represented a continuation of a past trend? Do we interpret the "conservative" element in the forecast to mean that past trends had been rising, and in order to be reasonably sure of being accurate, the estimator had deflated the figure that would represent a continuation of the past rate of growth? Because demand had been increasing in the past, did he, because he is conservative, produce an estimate which assumed it would decline? There are those who believe that if prices are increasing, they will continue to increase, and if they are falling, they will continue to fall. And then there are those individuals who believe that good things cannot continue, and if prices have been going up, they must now go down.

These personal subjective feelings about demands and prices are rooted in individual value systems and are not, as a rule, subject to scientific investigation and verification.[4] As a rule, however, the more consistent a past behavior pattern or experience, the more likely we are to believe the pattern will continue. This proposition is the basis for the formation of objective probability discussed above. Hence, if prices are increasing, we are more likely to think they will continue to increase. If they are stable, we believe they will continue to be stable. And if they are declining, most of us are inclined to believe further declines are in the offing.

When an increase in the current price is expected to result in a proportional increase in the future price, J. R. Hicks defines the situation as one in which the coefficient of elasticity of expectations is unitary. That is to say, the coefficient measures the ratio of the percent rise in expected future prices to the

---

[4] They do, however, provide a good source of periodical literature. See, for example, Donald H. Woods, "Improving Estimates That Involve Uncertainty," *Harvard Business Review*, July–Aug., 1966, pp. 91–98.

percent rise in its current price. As with other such coefficients, if a current rise in prices is believed to augur a larger than proportionate rise in future prices, the coefficient less than 1, while a rise in price leading to the expectation that price leading to the expectation of a smaller increase in the future gives us a coefficient less than 1, while a rise in price leading to the expectation that prices will fall will give us a negative coefficient.[5]

If some prices currently being paid rise as a result of higher manufac turing costs, and if the elasticity of expectations is greater than 1, the demand curve will shift to the right as buyers show increased eagerness to buy at the prevailing list of prices. They will be anticipating a further price increase in the future arising out of higher costs. If, on the other hand, the elasticity of price expectations is low, a rise in supply prices will merely diminish the amount demanded and cause a further decrease in the quantity sold as the demand curve shifts to the left. Buyers will in this case be waiting for prices to come down before resuming buying at the usual rate.

The demand curve represents, then, not only the amounts that buyers say they will take at a certain list of prices, but the amounts they will buy because of their anticipations of future prices. The effect on the demand curve depends on the extent to which the products they buy in the future can be substituted for purchases today. In other words, the effect on today's demand curve is a function of the degree to which consumption can be postponed or shifted to a future time period.

If you believe that the price of a commodity you use will rise in the future, you will, if at all possible, substitute over time, buying more in the present to take the place of buying in the future. Hence, the expectation of higher prices in the future will cause the demand curve to shift to the right. It is only possible to increase demand in the present if usage can be increased in the present, or if the product can be stored, or if the scale of production or industrial usage can be increased. We can say, then, that there is a scale effect resulting from an anticipation that future prices will differ from present prices. If we expect that future prices will be higher, we will substitute present lower prices for higher future prices, increasing our rate of consumption or usage in the present and lowering it in the future. In this case, the production of some output, if our item in question is an input to a process, may be accelerated at the expense of other products using the same facilities and available inputs. If the product is not durable and its components or raw materials are not durable, there will be no substitution over time. There may, however, be unused capacity, or it may be possible to increase capacity, in which case outputs will not be substituted but will be simply increased.

[5] J. R. Hicks, *Value and Capital*, 2d ed., Oxford University Press, New York, 1946, p. 205.

Demand curves also are the result of prior expectations about prices and product availability. If in one period a given demand curve may be said to exist which takes into account future price expectations, these expectations may or may not materialize. The demand curve in the next period may differ from that expected for one of several reasons:

1. Buyers did not act in conformity with their expectations.
2. Given correct expectations and consistent plans, buyers made incorrect estimates of the future.
3. Buyers may have subjective probabilities which lead them to under- or overestimate the future, and while the actual prices in the future period were as expected, their confidence in the future was not such as to lead them to act.

SUMMARY

In this chapter we have been concerned with the nature and characteristics of the demand system for goods. We have discussed those aspects of consumer behavior important to an understanding of the forces which collectively result in demand elasticity. We have attempted to show that the consumer is influenced by many factors other than price and income, such as standard of living, the desire for need satisfaction, the prices of substitutes and complements, and expectations concerning all of these variables which may cause substitution over time.

Actual buying behavior is a function of the aspiration or need level of the consumer, his ability to satisfy that need from limited resources, the amount of information at his disposal concerning the class of items from which need satisfaction will arise, and expectations as to the future state of all of these.

Classical economic theory attempts to describe this wide range of phenomena under the price-quantity relationship and a behavior rule, which asserts that a buyer's choice will be guided solely by the amount of the item already on hand and its marginal utility. If people are believed to want goods for the services they render, rather than as goods, then some variation of the poor man's goods phenomenon may be required.

Economists have been reluctant, by and large, to include advertising, product differentiation, and other business tools used to manipulate consumer demand in their considerations, because they assume that business attempts to meet consumer preferences as they are revealed by their choices in a free marketplace. To the extent to which the model fails to take into account product differentiation, it may be unable to serve as a basis for predicting consumer behavior.

Review Questions

1. How might an airline manager make use of the economic theory of consumer choice?
2. In Figure 5-1, is the consumer subject to a diminishing marginal rate of substitution as he substitutes B for A?
3. Define the "rational" consumer in economic theory.
4. "Buying, like any other act," say Howard and Sheth, "is merely a portion of an ongoing stream of acts that together constitute total behavior." What problems does the buyer solve according to the indifference map? According to the poor man's goods version of the indifference map?
5. What is meant by the tangency of an indifference curve with a budget line?
6. What is the significance of the income-consumption curve? The price-consumption curve?
7. What might be the effect on the sale of cameras of an increase in the price of film?
8. Evaluate the significance of a demand curve which has a positive slope somewhere along its length.
9. In the period 1960 to 1961, United States consumers reported their family income, total value of food, and value of food consumed away from home, per capita, as follows:

Family Size	Per Capita Income	Total Food Consumed per Capita	Food Purchased away from Home per Capita
1	$1964	$607	$229
2	2693	526	100
3	2201	447	87
4	1859	392	69
5	1540	348	57

    (a) Do these data confirm or cast doubt on the validity of Engel's law?
    (b) Calculate the income elasticity of demand for food.
10. If it is expected that the price of steel will rise because of a union wage settlement which will have the effect of increasing labor costs, what impact might it have on the demand for steel and on present steel prices?

Case 1. The American Motors Corporation

Roy D. Chapin, Jr., who assumed the post of chief executive officer of the American Motors Corporation on February 25, 1967, took the first of a number of steps toward improving AMC's deteriorating financial position by announcing that the price of the Rambler-American had been cut by $200.

But the company's position, despite subsequent improvements in sales, was, if anything, worse by the end of the first calendar quarter. A loss of $21.6 million was recorded on sales of $144.8 million, increasing the net loss for the six-month period to $30.1 million. Comparable figures for the previous year were $4.2 million.

The response to the price reduction is documented by the following news reports:

FEBRUARY 25, 1967. Market share reported down to 2.9 percent in 1966. Price reduced an average of $200, effective at once.

APRIL 13, 1967. Sales for the period April 1 to 10 were up 7.9 percent from 5,193 to 5,604. Firm's market share up .1 percent. Overall increase for forty days, 140 percent, double the preceding forty-day period.

APRIL 14, 1967. Sales for the second week of April were 6,112.

APRIL 28, 1967. Firm reports switching over additional capacity to double Rambler output to 2,400 per week from recent levels. Production total for April, 8,484 cars.

The Rambler price reduction meant that the series would start at an advertised, delivered price of $1,839, compared with the introduced price at the beginning of the year of $2,073. Nearest competition is the Volkswagen 1500 at $1,639 and the Chevy II at $2,090.

Auto manufacturers reported that in the first quarter of 1967, sales fell overall by more than 20 percent, but that in mid-April, sales topped the same period the year before. This was the second ten-day selling period in which dealers sold more cars than in the same period the previous year. In all, during the first two-thirds of April, deliveries were up 2 percent over 1966.

In June, 1967, the Ford Motor Co. began a three-month test in three western districts to test the reaction to a $300 reduction in the price of the Ford Falcon. Dealers were "encouraged" to bring the price of the $2,150 car down to about $1,850, comparable with the VW. For ninety days, dealers sold 5,093 Falcons, an increase of about 20 percent from the corresponding period of a year before. At the same time, Ford dealers in other parts of the country had a 15 percent drop in Falcon sales. Concurrent with the price reduction, West Coast dealers in July reported a 13 percent increase over a year earlier, while sales elsewhere dropped 17 percent. In August, comparable figures were 29 percent and 24 percent, respectively.

QUESTIONS

1. On the basis of the information provided, calculate possible price elasticities of demand for the Rambler-American and for the Ford Falcon.
2. Do you believe that AMC was wise in reducing the price of the Rambler?
3. Consumer expenditures on durable goods were $69.9 and $70.8 billion in the first and second half of 1966, and rose to $71.0 billion in the first half of 1967. The second half is estimated at $73.2 billion. What course of action would you recommend in September, 1967, for the American Motors Corporation. Would you recommend the same course of action for the Ford Motor Co.?
4. Assuming the following table by Dr. Gregory C. Chow of MIT is appropriate, what appears to be the best decision for the American Motors Corp.?

PERCENTAGE CHANGES IN ANNUAL PURCHASE OF AUTO-MOBILES PER CAPITA AS RELATED TO PERCENTAGE CHANGES IN INCOME PER CAPITA AND TO PERCENTAGE CHANGES IN THE RELATIVE PRICE OF AUTOMOBILES

Percentage Change in Relative Price	Percentage Change in Income (per Capita in Constant Dollars)						
	−8	−6	−4	−2	0	+2	+4
+10	−36	−30	−24	−18	−12	−6	0
+ 5	−30	−24	−18	−12	− 6	0	6
0	−24	−18	−12	− 6	0	6	12
− 5	−18	−12	− 6	0	6	12	18
−10	−12	− 6	0	6	12	18	24
−15	− 6	0	6	12	18	24	30
−20	0	6	12	18	24	30	36

Source: *Report, together with Individual Views, of the Subcommittee on Antitrust and Monopoly of the Committee on the Judiciary,* United States Senate, 85th Cong., 2d Sess., Nov. 1, 1958, pp. 130–140.

Case 2. The Coffee Special Dilemma

Supermarkets regularly advertise special low prices on selected items, but not always on the same items. The object of specials or promotions is to present a desirable mix of products at a list of prices that will attract customers to the store to do all of their shopping. By this means, the store hopes to make up in the sale of normally or even higher-priced goods, the losses or reduced margins on the promotion goods. Ice cream and meats are often used as promotion goods.

A local university student requested permission to observe the response of patrons of one store to price reductions in 1-pound cans of coffee. Over the next six months, he compiled the following data and, as agreed, left a copy with the store manager.

CUSTOMER RESPONSES TO PRICE REDUCTIONS IN POUND-SIZE COFFEE

Product	Regular Price	Increase in Sales over Three-day Period		
		10¢ Reduction	20¢ Reduction	Full Price with Bonus Product
A	98¢	1⅓ ×	none	none
B	88¢	1½ ×	3 ×	2 to 3 ×
C	78¢	2 ×	4 ×	4 ×

Products A and B were nationally advertised brands, while product C was a store or private label coffee. The bonus offer referred to in the right-hand column was either a small package of instant coffee or free trading stamps.

The store owner was happy to receive the information but was not quite sure how to interpret it. For example, he was glad to see that the response to a 20¢ price reduction was as great as four times normal sales, but he remembered also that the important consideration in supermarket pricing is to produce that sales mix which consists of enough items at low prices to bring in traffic with a maximum of higher-priced items to increase profit. Price specials are often followed by the less affluent, who shop by the item. Coffee could be a volume seller, and while the large increase in brand C following a 20¢ price reduction was impressive, he felt certain the problem was not that simple.

QUESTION

1. How would you advise the manager?

Case 3. Gasoline Marketing

The Federal Trade Commission recently issued a *Report on Anticompetitive Practices in the Marketing of Gasoline* (June 30, 1967), which contained the following statement:

> The major prefers not to engage in price competition. The total demand for gasoline is highly inelastic, while the demand for branded gasoline is highly elastic, depending on price. In such a situation, price competition among the leading sellers can only be detrimental to each member of the class. Price reductions would be followed by sellers of equal size and would not be accompanied by compensating

increases in total demand. Accordingly, the major favors various forms of non-price competition, the basic forms being competition for the purchase or lease of preferred service station locations and claims of superior service and product quality. A company's market representation largely dictates its share of the product market and the latter is an important factor in determining whether the company will be the price leader or a price follower within the marketing area. Market share is protected or increased on the basis of product differentiation through national advertising, and other forms of non-price competition, such as credit cards and promotions. Superior product quality and service, rather than price, are stressed through massive expenditures for advertising. Thus, it has been estimated that the industry's twenty largest sellers account for approximately ninety percent of the industry's total advertising expenditure.

Independents seek market share primarily through price appeal. Their competitive strategy is to compensate for the major's usual edge in the number and preferred location of stations within a market, and the major's expenditures for advertising and customer services such as credit cards and touring assistance, through the maintenance of a price differential. The price spread between their brands and those of the majors varies depending on conditions within a particular market. It is whatever the independent believes necessary for effective competition with established brands within the constraints of what the majors will allow.

QUESTIONS

1. Illustrate the demand curves facing (a) the major marketer and (b) the independent.
2. Explain and reconcile the divergent views expressed.

Suggested Readings

Alchian, Armen A.: "The Meaning of Utility Measurement," *American Economic Review*, vol. 17, no. 1, pp. 26–50, March, 1953.

Dean, Joel: *Managerial Economics*, Prentice-Hall, Inc., Englewood Cliffs, N.J., 1951, Chap. 4.

Ferguson, C. E.: *Micro-Economic Theory*, Richard D. Irwin, Inc., Homewood, Ill., 1966, pp. 9–104.

Howard, John A., and Jagdish N. Seth: *The Theory of Buying Behavior*, John Wiley & Sons, Inc., New York, 1970.

Marshall, Alfred: *Principles of Economics*, 8th ed., Macmillan & Co., Ltd., London, 1920, Book III, Chap. 4.

Watson, Donald Stevenson: *Price Theory and Its Uses*, 2d ed., Houghton Mifflin Company, Boston, 1968, pp. 16–132.

chapter 6
empirical demand
functions

In this chapter, we shall try to come to grips with the problem of actually formulating the demand function facing the businessman wishing to introduce a new product.

In Chapter 2, we discussed some of the possible shapes the demand curve might assume, depending upon the nature of potential competition and whether or not the product was similar to others or was differentiated. In Chapters 3 and 4, we took up the relationship between the possible demand for the product and the potential market. We discussed the market in terms of the level of economic activity and the income levels of possible buyers, as well as the range of possible uses the product might have or into which it might fit. We might, for example, have analyzed the demand for refrigerators in terms of the level of income of possible buyers, the age of existing refrigeration devices, and whether or not people own their own homes or rent housing. In other words, we were concerned with whether or not the market potential existed for the product at any price.

Most discussions of demand estimation are, in fact, of this type. Income elasticities of demand are generally far more important in forecasting than are price relationships. How much the consumer will spend next year and whether he will spend it on software or hardware, housing or automobiles, is generally more widely discussed than is his probable response to a 10 percent price reduction. Nevertheless, pricing decisions do have to be made, so that we must be concerned with the nature of the demand curve and the size of the market at each of a number of possible prices.

Since we earlier discussed the theoretical aspects of price elasticity of demand and the factors which determine the shape of the demand curve, we now want to see whether we can go to data and construct a demand function which will have predictive value. We will want to see if the application of statistical methods to economic data can produce evidence of the "laws" of supply and demand.

SOME EARLY ANALYSES

Some of the earliest work in statistical analysis of economic data has to do with demand functions. In the seventeenth century, Gregory King, observing that the price of wheat rose when the harvest was poor, tried to arrive at a numerical estimate of the relationship between changes in the volume of transactions and prices. In 1914, H. L. Moore calculated price elasticities of demand for corn, hay, oats, and potatoes. In 1928, there appeared Henry Schultz's monumental *Statistical Laws of Demand and Supply with Special Application to Sugar*, and, in 1938, his still widely used work, *The Theory and Measurement of Demand*.[1]

Schultz confined his inquiry largely to the demand for sugar, corn, cotton, hay, wheat, buckwheat, rye, barley, oats, and potatoes. He also investigated the extent to which the demands for coffee, sugar, and tea; barley, corn, hay, and oats; and beef, pork, and mutton, to name three groups of substitutes, are interrelated. His demand function for wheat is based on a straightforward statistical least-squares procedure, however, and he does not take possible substitutes into account.

He calculated the price elasticity of demand for wheat at $-.2143$ over the years 1921 to 1934. His estimating equation, although challenged by Gerhard Tintner on other grounds, does attempt to take into account not only the extent to which demand varies as price but also shifts in the demand curve that occur over time and which result either from changes in taste or other variables such as income.[2]

In a more complex analysis, Schultz computes the interrelationship between the demands for beef and pork. He analyzes the consumption of beef and veal as it is affected by (1) the prices of beef, (2) the prices of pork, and (3) income levels. He found that for the years 1922 to 1933, the price elasticity of beef was $-.49$, the cross-elasticity of demand for beef with respect to changes in the price of pork was $+.46$, and the income elasticity of demand for beef was $+.36$.

These results may be interpreted to mean that if the price of beef were to go up 1 percent, the amount of beef demanded would decrease by nearly one-half of 1 percent. If the price of pork were to increase 1 percent, the amount of beef demanded would increase by about one-half of 1 percent. Had incomes increased by 1 percent, then the demand for beef would go up a little more than one-third of 1 percent. In all of the foregoing, we are of course assuming that all

---

[1] Both studies were published by The University of Chicago Press, Chicago.
[2] Gerhard Tintner, *Econometrics*, John Wiley & Sons, Inc., New York, 1952, pp. 38-40.

other things remain unchanged. That is, the response to a change in the price of beef would take place as indicated only if prices, incomes, and tastes remain unaltered, unless otherwise indicated.

The role of the elasticity of price expectations is evident in some results by R. H. Whitman involving the demand for steel. In addition to relating the demand for steel to price and to the level of general economic conditions, he includes the rate of change of price over time. The coefficient of price elasticity of demand turns out to be -1.27, which of course means that a rising price is associated with a decline in the demand for steel. The relation to changes over time is quite pronounced, however, and is much larger than the price-demand coefficient, indicating that if the price of steel is rising, consumers expect the rise to continue and will buy more steel than they would otherwise.[3]

There are many other examples of work which has been done and which cannot be covered adequately in this chapter.[4] We will go on to discuss a few of the methods used, leaving to the appendix of this chapter the actual data and details of demonstration. We will consider the problem of demand curve estimation when there are price changes over time, when there are income changes, and where the interrelationships are more involved because the data are internally related.

PRICE CHANGES OVER TIME

The price of beef cattle is affected by the production of beef, and also by changes in population, consumer tastes, and the general level of prices. One way of arriving at the demand function might be to relate the price of beef cattle to the following factors, using the tools of multiple correlation: the amount produced annually, the general price level, the level of consumer income, and population growth. The production of beef is of course affected by the cost of processing meat. The demand for beef may also be affected by population growth and consumer income and by changes in tastes away from starchy foods to red meat, and vice versa. The effect of these variables would be to shift the demand curve over time. Before the effect of price can be isolated, it is necessary to hold constant any variables which would shift the curve as a whole.

Waugh gives a simple but useful method which relates changes in the price of beef cattle to changes in the production of beef and veal.[5]

---

[3] "The Statistical Law of Demand for a Producer's Good as Illustrated by the Demand for Steel," *Econometrica*, vol. 4, pp. 138–152, 1936.

[4] For an excellent brief summary of work in this field, see Tintner, *op. cit.*, and see Herman Wold, *Demand Analysis*, John Wiley & Sons, Inc., New York, 1953 for methodology.

[5] Frederick V. Waugh, *Graphic Analysis: Applications in Agricultural Economics*, Agriculture Handbook No. 326, U. S. Department of Agriculture, Economic Research Service, Washington, D.C., Nov., 1966, pp. 28–29.

To remove the effect of changes in the general level of prices on the prices of goods, it is customary to deflate the latter by dividing each year's price by the corresponding yearly index of all prices. Changes in population growth can be handled by converting production to a per capita figure. In order to correct for changes in consumer tastes over time, it is possible to fit a time-series trend line to per capita production and to the deflated price series, and then to correlate the resultant deviations from the trend in each series.

Waugh, however, chooses to use a simpler approach, which consists of relating the first differences in price and production, without correcting for price and consumption trends. In Appendix A we fit a regression to data given by Waugh, using a simple method of curve fitting called the method of semiaverages. The regression line does not go through the origin, the point at which no change in production is associated with no change in price. It shows, rather, that were there to be no change in production, there would be an annual increase in price of approximately $1.82 per 100 pounds. This increase can be attributed to increases in income or tastes or both. The slope of the regression line is -3.40, which means that for each increase of 1 billion pounds of beef and veal production, the price of beef cattle has decreased on the average about $3.40 during the years covered by the study.

Having obtained an approximate graph for the data, exactly what is it **we have obtained?** What does the relationship

$$Y = 1.82 - 3.40X$$

really mean? Does it constitute a demand curve in the sense in which we have developed it theoretically? If not, what does the price-demand relationship really look like? We will attempt to answer these questions.

Annual consumption per person rose from approximately 75.3 pounds for the years 1947 to 1949 to 104.9 pounds in 1964, according to the U.S. Department of Agriculture. Prices at retail were fairly even, fluctuating about a range of 66¢ in 1956 to 88¢ in 1951. Purchases of livestock for slaughter, an indication of the supply, went from 206,000 head of cattle in 1950, varied, and ended in 1964 at 719,000 head. There were, in other words, two forces clearly at work.

With national income increasing over the years and changes in consumer tastes tending toward more meat, it is safe to assert that the demand curve for beef was moving to the right and possibly also becoming less price responsive. Meanwhile, in response to the increasing demand, production was increasing from 9.53 billion pounds in 1950 (of both beef and veal) to 18.42 billion pounds in 1964. For prices to remain approximately at the same level, the supply curve also would have to move to the right. The path of points at which demand and supply intersect would trace out price-production relationships approximately as shown in Figure 6-1.

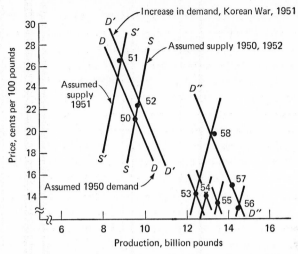

Figure 6-1. Price-production relationship, beef and veal, 1950 to 1958.

It is not possible to deal with more than a few years in a single graph, but the years chosen appear to illustrate the point. In 1950, we assume that demand and supply coincided to produce a market price to farmers as shown by the intersection of *DD* and *SS*, the respective curves. During that year, the Korean War began and set in motion forces which would upset the equilibrium. With the two- to three-year lead time required to produce cattle for market, and some indication in increased eagerness of consumers to buy, we can assume that the demand curve moved to the right to *D'D'*, but that the supply curve quite pos sibly moved far to the left, indicating a producer's expectation of coming short-ages. According to other sources, retail stores had no difficulty in satisfying their needs for meat during 1951, even though prices paid to farmers and by consumers increased. By 1952, production called forth by the high 1951 prices had moved the supply curve back to its 1950 *SS* position from the assumed 1951 *S'S'* position. Prices of meat were still higher than 1950, but this reflected an assumed increase in demand still in effect in 1952.

Beginning with 1953, two years after the high 1951 prices, the supply curve has shifted far to the right, and on our graph in Figure 6-1, there are a series of demand and supply curves drawn so as to intersect at the price-quantity relationships which obtained in 1953, 1954, 1955, and 1956. We may assume that the demand curve shifted to the right, or we may assume a demand curve somewhat flatter, which would possibly pass through all of the points in a single line instead of a more vertical series of curves moving to the right. Since the price elasticity of demand for meat, fish, and poultry as given by Tintner is

—.443 and the income elasticity is +.452, a relatively flat demand curve appears out of the question.[6]

In any event, by 1956, prices had apparently gone so low that some restriction of supply was in order, and by 1957 this had taken place. It might be quite reasonable to imagine the demand curve holding at $D''D''$, with the supply curve shifting back so as to intersect with the demand curve at 1957 and 1958, respectively.

Since the ability to store meat is limited, we generally assume that the amount of meat produced and the amount of meat consumed are the same. How do we know then whether the relationship obtained is really a demand curve? How, in other words, do we identify our relationship?

Tintner provides an analysis in which a demand and a supply curve are derived from the following sets of variables.[7]

$Y_1 =$ quantity of meat, poultry, and fish consumed
$Y_2 =$ price index of meat, poultry, and fish consumed
$Z_1 =$ per capita disposable income
$Z_2 =$ cost of meat processing

By relating the quantity of meat, poultry, and fish consumed, per capita disposable income, and the price index, he derives a demand equation. By relating the quantity consumed, price, and processing costs, he derives a supply equation. It is apparent that relating disposable income to consumption dispenses with demand curve shifts and those changes which might be thought to arise from changes in taste. Residual variations are then related to price.

On the supply side, the same set of prices is related to the same set of consumption data, but now with the intermediation of processing cost data. The assumption here is that if costs increase, a given amount supplied will cost more than before or, to put it another way, an increase in costs will result in a diminution of supply or amount offered and hence consumed. Residuals are then related to price as before.

As a practical matter, Tintner does not believe that this approach is anything more than a beginning, since, among other things, the effects of substitutes and complements are not taken into account.

Our simple two-variable analysis taken from Waugh's work could produce a demand curve if we added incomes as a third variable. In Appendix B, we see how this comes about and whether or not, for practical purposes, we can do any better for forecasting purposes than the curve originally fitted to the difference data in Appendix A.

---

[6] *Op. cit.,* p. 328. Based on 1919 to 1941 data and computed at the means.
[7] *Op. cit.,* p. 169. The time period is 1919 to 1941.

RECOGNIZING A DEMAND CURVE

The estimates of the price change associated with a change in the amount demanded are, of course, another way of expressing the slope of the demand curve fitted to annual price-income-quantity data. Assuming the data are correct, and then that the estimating equations have been correctly derived, and that they explain a significant proportion of the variation in the dependent variable, the resultant relationships may well provide a valid means for estimating the possible effects of a change in price, income, or quantity. But will we have derived a demand curve, and can we estimate price or income elasticities as we have discussed? Obviously from Figure 6-1, the points on which statistical demand curves are based do not always trace out a demand schedule because they are affected by shifts in the entire demand curve. Shifts in the supply curve help to identify the demand curve, and realized annual prices are valid points on the curve, but only if the demand curve is stable.

As we have seen, there are several ways of stabilizing the demand curve. First, we can assume the shifts are caused by changes in income, and remove the effect by first correlating consumption with income. Having done this, we can next relate the unexplained variation in consumption to price. This procedure is followed in Appendix B. Second, we can assume that changes in taste account for shifts in the demand curve. Since these changes reflect alterations in eagerness to buy, and since they take place over time, it is often possible to fit a regression line to a time series, as is also done in the appendix, and relate the unexplained deviations from that relationship to annual prices. Third, we can assume the variations from trend are not completely explained by changes in price, but that there are random shifts in demand which we cannot explain in a systematic way. Under such conditions, a transformation of the data by using successive differences may result in a more consistent demand relationship. This procedure is used in both Appendixes A and B.

By converting the actual data into successive differences, we reduce the intercorrelation among the variables. As will be seen shortly, price is to some extent correlated with income levels, particularly where there are other forces at work in the economic picture. Where there are common causes running through economic variables, they will show common trend and cyclical movements. This tendency was noted in the rise in meat consumption over time and with respect to per capita income. Since per capita income also has risen, it is hard to discriminate between changes in taste owing to changes in the liking for meat and those resulting from commodity substitution made possible by higher incomes.

Multicollinearity, as it is called, does not make it difficult to forecast, but it does make it hard to identify the precise causes of changes in the data.

Statisticians have developed a number of tools to deal with this problem. Using the method of successive differences is one alternative that is particularly useful in connection with the graphic method of curve fitting which we have used. Another useful approach is to combine independent variables in some way into a third or dummy variable and use this combination against a dependent variable or set of variables also in combination. This procedure is termed canonical correlation. F. V. Waugh uses this procedure in dealing with the estimation of demand for beef and for pork, because beef and pork are substitutes, it is not easy to find the effect of price on the consumption of one alone. Waugh combines the price of beef with the price of pork to form a single variable, the consumption of beef and of pork into another, and correlates the resultant series.[8]

INTERRELATION OF PRICE AND INCOME

We have mentioned the fact that it often happens that prices rise as an outgrowth of increases in income. The relationship can become quite complex, and it is difficult many times to determine just what economic forces have been at work and just what curve-fitting methods to use.

For example, variations in the per capita consumption of fruits and vegetables can be related both to prices and to per capita income. As Figure 6-2 indicates, there is a good relationship between prices and per capita consumption for the period 1950 to 1963, and it would not be difficult to visualize a linear demand curve of negative slope. But notice that consumption is also related, but negatively, to disposable income per capita. As income increased, per capita consumption decreased! Prices and disposable income, consequently, show a positive relationship.

The deviations from the line of good fit in Figure 6-2, when plotted annually, produce random fluctuations. Annual consumption per capita also shows a consistently declining trend, with random deviations. One is forced to the conclusion that increases in disposable income are bringing about reductions in the quantity of fresh fruits and vegetables marketed, possibly because of changing food habits accompanying higher incomes. This would be some evidence that the poor man's goods effect was present.[9]

USING DIFFERENCE DATA

In our earlier examples, we attempted to deal with the dynamic aspects of demand analysis by using difference data. That is to say, we related the

[8] See "Regressions between Sets of Variables," *Econometrica*, vol. 10, p. 290, 1942.
[9] Hendrik S. Houthakker and Lester D. Taylor find examples of price-quantity correlation in which the slope turns out to be positive, notably with purchased food and alcoholic beverages. Their solution is to fit a curve to the logarithms of the yearly data. It may be that the results were a by-product of the particular procedure used, however. See *Consumer Demand in the United States, 1929–1970*, Harvard University Press, Cambridge, Mass., 1966, pp. 60–61.

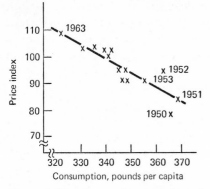

Figure 6-2(a). Price and consumption of fruits and vegetables per capita, 1950 to 1963.

Figure 6-2(b). Disposable income and consumption of fruits and vegetables per capita.

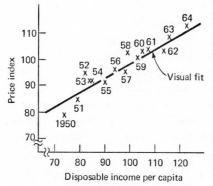

Figure 6-2(c). Prices of fruits and vegetables and per capita disposable income, 1950 to 1963. (Source: National Commission on Food Marketing, *Organization and Competition in the Fruit and Vegetable Industry*, Technical Study No. 4, Washington, D.C., June, 1966.)

demand for a commodity to the change in price over the previous year, or year-to-year changes in quantity produced or consumed were used, instead of the actual demand. Tintner advocates carrying the method of successive differences beyond the first differences in order to reduce random variability. The data are, of course, absolute magnitudes and the graphic method of regression analysis in Appendix B employs a method which relates arithmetic residuals to changes in other variables. In using this method we make the implicit assumption that the effects are additive.

Another way of handling dynamic problems is to convert the data to logarithms. Differences in data then become rates of change or ratios, and we have the added convenience that the coefficients, which in antilogarithmic form become exponents, are the elasticities themselves. Using logarithms, the deviations are not simply added, because adding logarithms results in multiplication, nor subtracted because that would be equivalent to division. Our deviations are then expressed as a ratio or percent of the basic variable, rather than as an amount to be added or subtracted.

Alternatively, it is simple to convert the data to logarithms and then use an arithmetic procedure. Many times economic and sociological data are by their nature curves rather than straight lines. The use of logarithms allows us to deal with the data as though straight lines were appropriate, because rates of change are used and many curves have rates which are substantially uniform. It is a simple exercise to fit a straight line to the logarithms of the data.

SUBSTITUTES AND COMPLEMENTS

Demand is not only a function of price and of income, but as we have seen, may depend upon the price of substitutes or of complementary goods, or upon the intensity of demand for these goods. Butter and margarine are commonly perceived substitute goods, and it is often possible to illustrate the effect of changes in the price of butter on the production of margarine. In order to do this empirically, it is necessary to remove from margarine output the effects of rising levels of disposable per capita income and of changes in the price of margarine. The multicollinearity which causes prices to move with changes in the general price level or with gross national product must of course be removed, and often simple price differencing will accomplish it. There are also more sophisticated tools, which need not concern us here. Wold calculates both the price elasticity of butter, subject to the condition that the price ratio of margarine and butter is held constant, and the cross-elasticity of butter with respect to the price of margarine, the price of butter being held constant.[10] The very strong income and trend effects make it very difficult to isolate the impact of price changes. It may well be that here, as in other instances, the true test of the result will be whether or not the procedure provides useful results. Multicollinearity does not impede the ability to forecast, as we have said. It is nevertheless true that most analyses of the type we have discussed turn out to be more responsive to income changes than to price changes.

THEIL'S *U* STATISTIC

The customary procedure for computing the degree of correspondence between forecast and actual data is the coefficient of correlation, the details of which are available in any elementary text in statistics. Apart from this customary method, one may employ the simpler Theil *U*, which is a statistic that measures

[10] *Op. cit.*, p. 243.

the degree of relationship between a set of forecast data and the actual values. We referred to this statistic in passing in Chapter 4. It is particularly good for our purposes here because it does not require the labor of the least-squares method and may be employed to evaluate any set of consistent forecast information.

The Theil U is given by the formula

$$U = \frac{[(P_i - A_i)^2]^{1/2}}{\sqrt{P_i^2} + \sqrt{A_i^2}}$$

where P is the estimated or calculated value and A is the actual reading. U lies between 0 and 1, with a value of 0 indicating perfect agreement and a value of 1 indicating the complete absence of agreement.[11]

SUMMARY

This chapter has attempted to show some of the methods one might employ in actually constructing a demand function. Also, it has presented a few of the well-known inquiries into statistical derivations of demand functions.

It will be noticed that the relationship between price and amount demanded cannot always be easily identified, especially where income has a strong effect or where there are readily available substitutes.

Although theory consistently places quantity as the independent variable, there may be times, as for example in Figures 6-2(b) and 6-4, when it is convenient to place quantity on the vertical axis. Indeed, some managerial economists hold that it is demand that ought to be expressed as a dependent variable. They prefer to show demand as a function of one or more independent variables, such as income, price, prices of substitutes and complements, or perhaps even of the price of borrowed money needed to finance the purchase. The virtue of this approach is that it indicates quite clearly which variables are under the control of the model builder and which are not.

This approach also is suitable to computerized statistical study which may offer as a convenient by-product a listing of not only the partial correlation coefficients, but also the estimating errors and their significance. Elasticity coefficients also can be simply tabulated so that the impact of all relevant variables is evident, and data can be manipulated or transformed during the regression calculation. Programs allow the user, among other things, to test automatically for serial correlation and to shift dependent and independent variables period by period to test for leads and lags. What is more, computers do not balk if the number of variables gets large.

---

[11] Henri Theil, *Economic Forecasts and Policy*, North-Holland Publishing Company, Amsterdam, 1961, pp. 31–42. See also by the same author, *Applied Economic Forecasting*, North-Holland Publishing Company, Amsterdam, 1966, pp. 26–36.

It should be concluded finally that there is no single coefficient of elasticity, but that we ought really be concerned with the entire demand–independent variable relationship. Then, at any particular place, we can investigate price, income, or cross-elasticities.

Appendix A. Relating Changes in the Price of Beef Cattle to Changes in the Production of Beef and Veal

This appendix uses the method of estimating a price-demand relationship by using first differences of annual data. An estimating equation will be derived by using the method of semiaverages. The result is not as accurate as that obtained by using least squares, but the procedure is faster and more convenient for many purposes. The data are from Frederick V. Waugh's *Graphic Analysis: Applications in Agricultural Economics,* to which we have already referred. Waugh, however, uses a visually fitted line of relationship.

The next step is to plot the first differences data to ascertain whether or not there is any consistency between changes in price and changes in production. The plotted data are shown in Figure 6-3.

The trend or regression line may be inserted in any of several ways, depending on the degree of accuracy desired or the need for more precise statistics for manipulation. For the present, we use the method of semiaverages to give us a quick and fairly accurate fit. The method of semiaverages requires that

TABLE 6-1. PRODUCTION OF BEEF AND VEAL

Year	Price of Beef Cattle to Farmers (dollars per 100 pounds)	Beef and Veal Production (billion pounds)	First Differences	
			Price	Production
1950	23.30	9.53		
1951	28.70	8.84	+5.40	−0.69
1952	24.30	9.65	−4.40	+0.81
1953	16.30	12.41	−8.00	+2.76
1954	16.00	12.96	−0.30	+0.55
1955	15.60	13.57	−0.40	+0.61
1956	14.90	14.46	−0.70	+0.89
1957	17.20	14.20	+2.30	−0.26
1958	21.90	13.33	+4.70	−0.87
1959	22.60	13.58	+1.30	+0.25
1960	20.40	14.73	−2.20	+1.15
1961	20.20	15.30	−0.20	+0.57
1962	21.30	15.30	+1.10	0.00
1963	19.90	16.42	−1.40	+1.12
1964	18.00	18.42	−1.90	+2.00

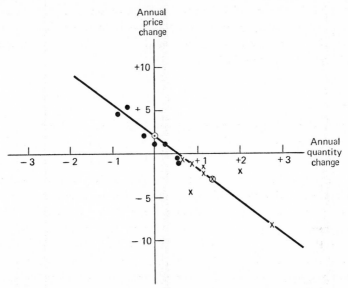

Figure 6-3. Changes in price of beef cattle related to change in production of beef and veal, 1950 to 1964. Note: Dots indicate upper half observations; x indicates lower half.

we array the price-difference data in descending order, carrying with each price difference its associated production difference as shown in Table 6-2.

The regression line does not go through the origin, the point at which no change in production and price occurs jointly, but shows rather that were there no change in production, there would be an annual increase in price of about $1.82 per 100 pounds. The slope of the regression is −3.4, so that the approximate equation for the line is

$$Y = 1.82 - 3.40X$$

where Y is the difference in price from year to year, and X is the associated annual change in production. Naturally, positive changes in price are associated with negative changes in production.

The equation may be calculated following the method of Lipka from the semiaverages in Table 6-2, by dividing the data into two groups of seven observations each as shown, and placing the sum of the residuals in each group equal to zero, so that

$$0 = \Sigma(r - a - bC) \qquad \text{or} \qquad \Sigma r = na + b\Sigma C$$

where n is the number of observations in each group.[12]

[12] Joseph Lipka, *Graphical and Mechanical Computation*, John Wiley & Sons, Inc., New York, 1918, p. 126.

TABLE 6-2. FIRST DIFFERENCES ARRAYED IN DESCENDING PRICE DIFFERENCE ORDER
SHOWING THE COMPUTATION OF SEMIAVERAGES

Price Differences		Production Differences
+ 5.40		−0.69
+ 4.70		−0.87
+ 2.30		−0.26
+ 1.30		+0.25
+ 1.10		0.00
− 0.20		+0.57
− 0.30		+0.55
+14.30	Total	−0.45
+ 2.04	Average	−0.06
− 0.40		+0.61
− 0.70		+0.89
− 1.40		+1.12
− 1.90		+2.00
− 2.20		+1.15
− 4.40		+0.81
− 8.00		+2.76
−19.00	Total	+9.34
− 2.71	Average	+1.33

We have then the following normal equations:

$$+14.30 = 7a - .45b$$
$$-19.00 = 7a + 9.34b$$

Changing the signs of the first equation and adding, we have

$$-33.30 = +9.79b$$
$$-3.40 = b$$

Substituting in the first equation, we have

$$+14.30 = 7a - (.45)(-3.40)$$
$$+1.82 = a$$

And the estimating equation becomes, as above,

$$Y = 1.82 - 3.40b$$

Appendix B. A Three-variable Analysis

In Table 6-3, we show index numbers for per capita income for the period 1950 to 1964, using 1957 to 1959 as a base. By plotting the index

TABLE 6-3. PER CAPITA INCOME, 1950–1964
(1957–1959 = 100)

Year	Index	Year	Index	Year	Index
1950	74.2	1955	85.8	1960	105.0
1951	79.9	1956	94.5	1961	107.6
1952	82.4	1957	97.8	1962	111.7
1953	85.5	1958	99.0	1963	115.2
1954	85.8	1959	103.2	1964	122.0

numbers against the horizontal axis and, from Table 6-1, the annual production of beef and veal on the vertical axis, we obtain the graph shown in Figure 6-4. A straight line is fitted using the method of semiaverages, and the trend values corresponding to each of the per capita incomes is read off. The trend-line equation can be obtained from a pair of estimating equations, using Lipka's procedure as before.

The data are divided into two groups: the first has seven pairs of observations, and the second, eight. Normal equations are written as:

$$81.42 = 7a + 588.1b$$
$$121.28 = 8b + 861.5b$$

from which we obtain $a = -253$ and $b = 3.15$. The estimating equation is then

$$Y = -253 + 3.15X$$

where Y represents annual production, and X is the index of per capita income.

The trend or calculated values are now subtracted from the actual meat production values for each year, and the differences are plotted against the prices of meat contained in Table 6-1.

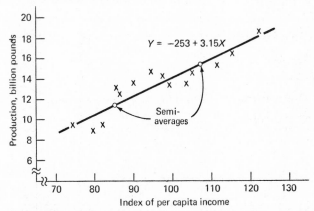

Figure 6-4. Production of beef and veal and per capita disposable income, 1950 to 1964.

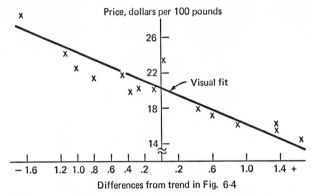

Figure 6-5. Residuals from income production related to prices of meat.

The resultant scatter diagram is shown in Figure 6-5. The sloping relationship indicates that a high price is associated with a negative deviation in which the trend line is above the actual output of meat, while a low price is associated with a positive deviation, which means that more meat is sold than is explained by income changes alone. A price rise of $4 per 100 pounds is sufficient to cause a drop of 1 billion pounds of beef and veal production below the normal calculation, according to this computation.

Since incomes changed in a fairly regular manner over the years in question, it should be possible to fit a simple trend line to time-series data for production, as shown in Figure 6-6, and then to relate the annual prices of meat to deviations from the trend line, much as just done with the production-income data.

Figure 6-7 shows the deviations from trend plotted against annual meat prices, and Figure 6-8 shows the annual differences in the deviations plotted against the annual differences in price. Simple freehand curves are plotted against the observations, or semiaverages are used where shown.

As it stands, Figure 6-8 shows that if there are no changes in price, there

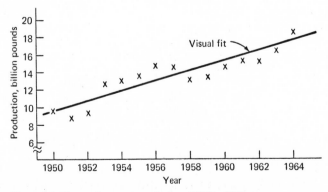

Figure 6-6. Time series: meat production, 1950 to 1964.

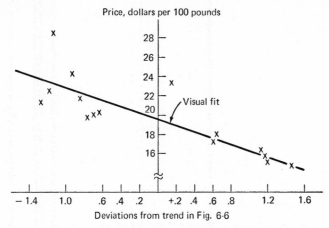

Figure 6-7. Price and deviations from production time-series trend.

will be no deviations from the average annual rate of change in meat production. Given a $2 increase in price, the production of meat will fall below the last deviation from trend by about .8 billion pounds, and given a $2 decrease in price, there will be about the same increase in production. Notice, however, that the curve in Figure 6-8 decreases at the decreasing rate, hence, the price elasticity would increase as the price falls.

In Figure 6-7, where price only is related to the deviations from the production-time trend line, the implication is that a price decrease of $1.20 would result in a positive deviation from trend of .4 billion pounds, where the

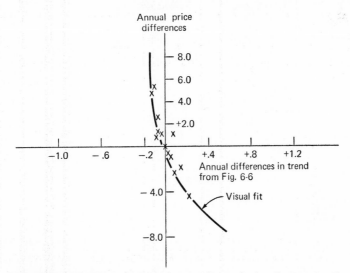

Figure 6-8. Differences in deviations from trend in production of meat, related to annual differences in price of meat.

trend refers to normal annual production. This is a change of $1/3$ billion pounds per dollar of price change in either direction.

Earlier, using Waugh's first difference procedure, but not his fitted curve, we estimated that each increase of 1 billion pounds of beef and veal was associated with a price decrease of $3.40 per hundred pounds. Using the formula above, we obtain a price change of $3.00 per hundred, while if we adjust for income changes, we calculate a change of $4.00 per hundred as the impact of price on output. Waugh calculates $3.825 as the price change associated with a change of 1 billion pounds in the amount demanded.

Review Questions

1. Economists have generally (since the time of Alfred Marshall) placed price on the vertical axis of the price-demand chart. How do you account for this? Criticize from the point of view of the needs of empirical curve fitting.
2. If you were a merchandiser, how would you go about testing to determine the price elasticity of demand for your product?
3. An often-observed phenomenon is an increase in prices during the before-Christmas and before-Easter shopping periods. How do you explain this?
4. What means are available to reduce the effect of intercorrelation among variables?
5. How do you account for the very strong effect of income changes on the demand for goods?
6. What purpose is served by expressing data (a) as per capita, (b) in constant dollars?
7. Derive a demand curve for the following data on United States potato production and wholesale prices as given by the U.S. Department of Agriculture.

Year	Production (million lb)	Price (dollars per hundredweight)	Year	Production (million lb)	Price (dollars per hundredweight)
1951	196	4.12	1958	267	2.32
1952	211	3.58	1959	246	3.52
1953	231	1.92	1960	257	2.58
1954	220	3.20	1961	293	2.34
1955	228	2.99	1962	268	2.52
1956	246	2.61	1963	272	2.71
1957	243	3.42	1964	239	5.16

8. Comment on the reasons for the behavior of a curve drawn to the deviations from the curve fitted in the preceding question.
9. Explain and illustrate the elasticity of price expectations.

10. Relate graphically the following data with data for per capita disposable income (1957 to 1959 = 100) from Appendix B. Fit regression lines and derive estimating equations which explain changes in the amount demanded and changes in demand.

Year	Retail Food Price Index	Per Capita Food Consumption Index	Year	Retail Food Price Index	Per Capita Food Consumption Index
1950	85.8	99.4	1957	97.8	100.2
1951	95.4	97.6	1958	101.9	98.9
1952	97.1	99.5	1959	100.3	101.0
1953	95.6	100.5	1960	101.4	100.5
1954	95.4	100.4	1961	102.6	100.1
1955	94.0	101.1	1962	103.6	100.4
1956	94.7	102.3	1963	105.1	100.8
			1964	106.4	101.8

Case 1. The Demand for Butter and Margarine

Below are given data for the years 1950 through 1966 on the prices and demands for butter and margarine.

EXHIBIT 1. RETAIL PRICES AND PER CAPITA CONSUMPTION FOR MARGARINE AND BUTTER, 1950–1966

Year	Retail Food Price Index 1957–1959 = 100		Per Capita Consumption (pounds)	
	Margarine	Butter	Margarine	Butter
1950	104.8	96.7	6.1	10.7
1951	117.4	108.5	6.6	9.6
1952	99.9	113.3	7.9	8.6
1953	100.4	105.3	8.1	8.5
1954	101.3	96.5	8.5	8.9
1955	98.2	95.4	8.2	9.0
1956	99.0	96.7	8.2	8.7
1957	102.7	99.6	8.6	8.3
1958	100.8	99.5	9.0	8.3
1959	96.3	101.0	9.2	7.9
1960	92.9	100.5	9.4	7.5
1961	99.0	102.6	9.4	7.4
1962	98.4	101.1	9.3	7.3
1963	95.4	101.0	9.6	6.9
1964	95.4	102.0	9.7	6.8
1965	101.9	103.6	9.9	6.4
1966	104.5	112.8	10.5	5.7

QUESTIONS

1. Plot a scatter diagram showing the relationship between changes in the butter price index and deviations from the secular trend in butter consumption.
2. Try to explain variations in butter consumption by changes in the price and consumption of margarine, as well as by changes in butter prices. (Hint: As the price of butter rises relative to margarine, more margarine should be used. Hence, the ratio of the price of butter to that of margarine should vary inversely as the ratio of the consumption of butter to margarine.)
3. Sketch in possible demand curves freehand, or try fitting a regression line using statistical methods.

Case 2. The ABC Food Processing Company

The ABC Food Processing Company historically had been in the business of canning vegetables. In recent years, it had gone into food freezing because it believed frozen foods offered more of a future. Typically, it had advertised its brand of Farm-Sweet canned vegetables in general-line magazines that offered the widest possible circulation. When it began to offer a line of frozen foods, it merely altered its advertising copy to include references to the new line, but made no other changes in what it believed was a fundamentally sound policy.

QUESTIONS

1. If you were the marketing manager of the ABC Food Processing Company, how would you go about reviewing the advertising policy of the firm?
2. What questions would you raise? (Hint: See data in *Expenditure Patterns of the American Family*, National Industrial Conference Board, and *Survey of Consumer Expenditures*, Bureau of Labor Statistics, 1960–1961.)

Suggested Reading

Baumol, William J.: *Economic Theory and Operations Analysis,* 2d ed., Prentice-Hall, Inc., Englewood Cliffs, N.J., 1965, pp. 210–249.

Dean, Joel: *Managerial Economics,* Prentice-Hall, Inc., Englewood Cliffs, N.J., 1951, pp. 177–246.

Salzman, Lawrence: *Computerized Economic Analysis*, McGraw-Hill Book Company, New York, 1968.

Spencer, Milton H.: *Managerial Economics*, 3d ed., Richard D. Irwin, Inc., Homewood, Ill., 1968, chap. 5.

Wold, Herman: *Demand Analysis*, John Wiley & Sons, Inc., New York, 1953.

Working, E. J.: "What do Statistical 'Demand Curves' Show?" *The Quarterly Journal of Economics*, vol. 41, pp. 212–235, 1927, reprinted in *Readings in Price Theory*, Richard D. Irwin, Inc., Homewood, Ill., 1952, pp. 97–115.

part 2
cost
analysis

chapter 7
the basis of
cost

When we set aside discussions of business forecasting and demand analysis and enter upon an analysis of costs and their basis in the conditions under which production takes place, we are in the realm of internal forecasting where the elements involved are somewhat more controllable. Of the five organizational goals covered in this book, two only have so far been discussed and these are sales and market share, neither of which is controllable. The remainder are **production, inventory, and profit.** But the level of production is a function of the level of sales and of desired inventory levels. The latter in turn depends on the characteristics of the production and organizational system of which the firm is part and on the performance goals established by management. Which performance goal will be selected and which inventory level is appropriate depends to a large degree on the costs and expenses involved. In turn, the cost elements in the decision depend on how costs are defined and their definitions depend largely on the concepts of cost which are employed.

COSTS, OUTLAYS, AND EXPENSES

Logic dictates two ways in which one may go about the process of exploring this field. One way which is often used is to begin with production as the underlying physical process and proceed to discuss costs as the reflection of this process. The other, which we have chosen, takes first the elements in the decision-making process beginning with the concepts underlying the definition of cost. It then analyzes cost behavior, with no preconceived idea or explicit statement as to the components of cost except in a gross sense, but with emphasis on cost level–production level–factor price relationships and the ways in which costs and performance goals are interrelated. This discussion sets the stage for the further discussion of production functions and decision making in Chapter 8.

In what follows, we still retain the assumption that the firm aims to maximize its profit. We retain this assumption because, as was pointed out in Chapter 1, managerial economics is concerned with ways in which the difference between revenue and cost may be maximized. It is particularly necessary at this point because production decisions are based on an analysis of the relative profitability of alternative plans. Even if the ultimate decision which is made is one which would not result in a maximum profit, it is still desirable to be aware of the relative profitability so that the opportunity costs of each decision are known.

IMPORTANCE OF THE CONCEPT OF THE FIRM

The way in which we interpret cost and expense depends largely on how we view the business firm. If, as in accounting, we regard the business firm as possessing assets for the purpose of employing them in the production of goods and services, then we will interpret the notion of cost and expense accordingly. Expense will refer to firm-centered liabilities incurred and expenditures made in order to operate the enterprise and maintain the assets. Cost will refer to those elements of expense which have a direct bearing on the production process and which can therefore be allocated to units of production. It is the nature of the relationship between the firm and the production process that is important. The relation is inherent in the allocation process which, in the form of costs, assigns asset values and purchased input expense to output.

The point of view of the economist is quite different. His concern with the firm has always been as a social device that exists to allocate resources. The firm does this job of allocating best if it operates in a competitive environment, so that the prices and costs which arise are not only the lowest possible, but accurately reflect needs and productivities. If the economist studies the firm, it is only because he is interested in the process by which inputs are decided upon and the direction in which inputs, outputs, and prices will move if there is a change in the environment, factor availability, or productivity. The firm as an organization possessing assets and liabilities does not exist. The firm as a processor of inputs is the significant relation. What the economist wants to know is what happens when there is a change in any of the parameters.

It is, therefore, not strange that the only costs in which the economist is interested are those costs which are relevant to changes in operating conditions and which, therefore, change the value of output. Outlays incurred in the past are only relevant if they bring about lowered costs in the present. To the accountant, past expenses are allocable to present output and represent a factor in decision making, most generally because a financial commitment has been made and it is important that assets be conserved. But to the economist, money outlays that affect assets or liabilities are of little concern, except if they reduce current expense or cost, or additionally, if they give rise to opportunity cost. This last would occur if the outlays could have been used in alternative ways with greater returns.

Part of the problem in differentiating between accountants' and economists' versions of cost appears to arise out of careless word usage. The terms cost and expense are often intermixed, and many times it is difficult to know whether either is meant, or whether an outlay or expenditure is really involved and neither a cost nor an expense. Sometimes it is found that the writer is really alluding to the value of an asset recently acquired, as in the "cost of a truck."

So as to be certain in our minds, we will define an *expense* as the acquisition of goods and services by the firm for use in some connection with its operation. We will not be concerned with the legal aspects of the transaction, i.e., whether an asset is given in exchange or a liability is incurred. An expense becomes a *cost* when it may be allocated to an end product. A cost is therefore related to the volume of production and not to the firm as an enterprise, as is true of an expense. Expenses are distributed according to the calendar—over periods of time.

An *outlay* or *expenditure* has nothing to do with the operation of the firm. If it did, it would be an expense or a cost. It is a transaction in a commercial and legal sense and does not pertain either to the firm as an enterprise or to the productive process which is taking place. In other words, an outlay is a balance sheet transaction.

An *asset* is generally acquired for the purpose of facilitating the operation of the firm as an enterprise or as an element in the production process. It is acquired at some price, and this price is popularly termed a cost. It is not a cost in the sense in which the term has been defined above. It only enters the stream of costs when it is allocated to the production process, assuming it has been acquired for that purpose. Economists are not concerned with asset acquisition, nor asset prices, except insofar as the expenditure implies a reduced cost of production or a change in the fixed versus variable capital goods structure of the firm, which in turn affects the shape of the cost functions.

The remainder of the problem in differentiating accounting and economic usage stems from differences in outlook. Since to the accountant, the firm is a collection of assets and liabilities, all expenditures must ultimately be recovered from operations, and the only proper method of viewing cost is as fully allocated. Because the economist looks at relevant costs as those which pertain to changes in operating conditions, he is concerned only with incremental costs. That is to say, he is interested in the change in total cost which comes about because of a decision to adopt a particular course of action involving output or resource use. We include, of course, in this definition of cost the benefits forgone because of any choices which might have been made in connection with that decision or which arise out of it as a consequence. This latter cost is opportunity cost, which we have already discussed in Chapter 1.

In its strictest sense, both economists and accountants would agree that costs refer to the value of goods and services used in the production of a given amount of a commodity or end item. The accountant, because he is interested primarily, although not exclusively, in reporting accurately on the distribution and value of assets, will value goods and services used up in terms of the assets given up by the firm when the inputs were acquired. The economist refers to these as the business costs of a firm. They include not only the total money expenses reported by the record-keeping process, but also costs which have been allocated and costs which have been calculated, such as those arising out of depreciation and depletion expense.

In addition to these accounting or business costs, the economist adds the opportunity cost of the capital employed in the business. Sometimes this added cost is termed "normal" profit, by which we mean that return just sufficient to induce the businessman to leave his capital in that business and not invest it somewhere else. The reason that the economist adds the opportunity cost of capital to accounting or business costs is that he is primarily concerned with that view of the firm as the user of inputs to supply outputs. That is, he wants a full and complete calculation of what it takes to induce the production or supply of the produced item. What it takes is called the supply price of the producer's output.

If our producer incurs costs which exceed the demand price (to differentiate from supply price), then, assuming pure and perfect competition, he will go out of business, because he can earn more on his investment in alternative uses. If his demand price goes below factor cost, he can no longer attract sufficient quantities of the factors of production at prices others are willing to pay. Further development of this point depends on the distinction between variable and fixed cost, which will be taken up shortly.

RELEVANT COSTS

Economic theory is generally concerned with large groups of firms under the pressure of vigorous price competition. The model in the theory used in economics is not designed to explain the way in which real firms behave.

> It is designed to explain and predict changes in observed prices (quoted, paid, received) as effects of particular changes in conditions (wage rates, interest rates, import duties, excise taxes, technology, etc.). In this causal connection the firm is

only a theoretical link, a mental construct helping to explain how one gets from the cause to the effect.[1]

For some economic problems, it is necessary that the firm exist to a more concrete degree than for others. Conversely, for some management problems, a completely realistic model of the firm is not needed. For some problems, where the solution lies in the domain of economic theory, we will use only those variables and functions which are needed to provide an answer. Where costs are involved, relevant costs will depend on the problem to be solved. Many variables will not enter our calculations, simply because the problem to be solved does not require them.

On the other hand, we do look at problems of a particular firm, and we are interested, not only in the possible explanations of the effects of a given change but also in their magnitude. In other words, we need more than qualitative judgments having to do with the probable direction of a change; we need precise numerical results. We must concern ourselves with the real world of the firm and inquire as to specific magnitudes and exact amounts. But this does not mean that we need a high degree of correspondence between the firm in real life and our decision-making process. There are many elements of organizational behavior which are necessary to a description of the way in which a particular firm operates which would not be necessary to discuss economic aspects of relevant behavior.

Relevant costs depend not only on the problem to be solved, but more specifically on the components of the problem. Bearing in mind that we are concerned with the effects of a change or a decision, one of the problem components is time. Time affects the relevance of costs, in that costs become more variable the longer the time period. In the immediate present, all costs are fixed and must be assumed unchangeable. As the time period lengthens within which the decision works itself out, some costs which are fixed become variable, until in the very long run there are no fixed costs at all.

Within any specific time period, there will be some costs which are sunk, which cannot be affected by any current decision, and some costs which are not. We generally refer to those costs which can be changed as *incremental*, since they are a function of the specific decision. An incremental cost which is affected by an output decision is often referred to as a marginal cost when it is expressed as the increment to total cost associated with an increase of one unit in output.

Costs requiring no sacrifice are often used to illustrate the difference in concept between an accountant's and an economist's version of cost. If a resource has no alternative use, an economist would place its value at zero,

---

[1] Fritz Machlup, "Theories of the Firm; Marginalist, Behavioral, Managerial," *American Economic Review,* vol. 57, no. 1, p. 9, March, 1967. See also William J. Baumol, *Economic Theory and Operations Analysis,* 2d ed., Prentice-Hall, Inc., Englewood Cliffs, N.J., 1965.

regardless of the purchase price. The accountant many times is apparently not permitted to assume that any good is a free good. So the relevance of any factor cost to a decision would hinge, from our point of view, on the value of the next alternative use. This is the opportunity given up by any decision to employ the resource elsewhere.

The opportunity concept of cost is often difficult to grasp, except when it is couched in personal terms, where there are not likely to be any conventions or practices which have been learned. The student who has a choice of studying for an examination or working at overtime rates for extra pay must balance the probable results of using his time for additional study against the extra money. It might be that no amount of extra money could persuade him to devote his time to work, because the study time sacrificed had too high a value to him. On the other hand, if his time had no other use, even less than straight-time wages might induce him to work. The housewife who is offered the chance to work part time is quite familiar with opportunity cost as a basis for decision making, especially if she has to hire a sitter, housekeeper, or maid to do the housework she will then not be able to do.

Once again, the usefulness of a factor, hence its alternative cost, depends on the time period involved. The longer the time period, the more likely it is that there will be some opportunity cost because of the additional opportunities for profitable employment revealed as time passes. On the other hand, it may be that a long time period will bring about a diminution of the opportunity cost, especially if obsolescence or deterioration is possible.

Sometimes the relevance of costs hinges on whether or not one can escape the incurring of certain costs if the decision is made to do something or take some action or other. Some fixed costs, for example, can be avoided if a plant is shut down. Others can only be avoided if the company is liquidated or the plant facilities sold, so that period costs are no longer incurred. Some costs may not be avoided because their origin lies in assets which are not only unusable, but unsalable as well. Still others may be regarded as fixed, in an accounting sense, but discretionary in that management may set the level as it wishes. Advertising and sales promotion charges are examples of this kind of cost. Once these charges are set, they are invariant with respect to the level of production. If contracts are involved, the charges may be invariant also as regards stated time periods over which the contracts run. The level of expense may, of course, be altered within these constraints at the pleasure of management.

Compare these expenses to those costs or expenses which flow from the acquisition of equipment or assets. Rescheduling aside, depreciation charges may not be altered or changed unless the asset is sold. The opportunity cost associated with an asset is a function of its profitability or usefulness in alternative occupations. The opportunity cost of an advertising campaign is most generally limited to the return on the investment in alternative uses. The latter is more flexible and wide ranging.

The relevance of costs may be determined by examination of the structure of the production process in which they are incurred. Some costs are common to more than one product; others may be clearly identified as variable with the output of only one product. Still other costs are not only common, but joint, in that they arise out of the production of products whose proportions may not be altered. Remembering that we are discussing costs — expenses which are allocated to output — it may be seen that given a quantity of expense, the allocation to products which share in that resource, is dependent upon the proportion in which the products use the resource and the proportion in which the products are produced. If these proportions are fixed, we have an instance of joint costs and/or joint products.

SHORT-RUN COST ANALYSIS

When we come to analyze factor cost, in a competitive environment, accountants and economists speak much the same language. That they do is because, in a competitive market, prices of goods offered for sale tend to be based on the use to which they can be put which offers the highest return. That is to say, market price and opportunity cost come closer together. If the market is truly competitive, it is likely that they will be identical. Nevertheless, to the accountant, a cost is still an allocated expense which must be reimbursed. To the economist, the cost is simply a resistance which must be overcome in order to bring about the intended conversion of inputs into outputs.

The total cost of any output is the value of all the inputs used in its production. Costs therefore will rise or fall as the ratio of outputs to inputs changes. Such changes may come about as a result of changes in the efficiency of the conversion process, or because the prices of the inputs change.

Average cost is the cost per unit of output needed to overcome the resistance of alternative uses or returns. Sometimes, as we have noted, the extent of the resistance is measured by the prices of the factors used. Internally, where we are attempting to decide upon proper allocation to more than one output, the resistance is generally measured in terms of the usefulness or marginal productivity of the resource in each use. We will discuss this further when we take up the subject of the production function.

Average cost is a function of (1) the organic composition of the firm, and (2) the level of output, prices of inputs being given. The organic composition of the firm refers to the distribution of resources among varying kinds of assets having different degrees of liquidity, or time spans over which they yield services.[2] The cost function will exhibit behavior which differs depending on differences in the organic composition of the capital or asset structure. Let us begin the analysis with a firm whose average cost is everywhere the same for some fixed output total.

Following Boulding, we will present a set of cost curves or relationships beginning with a single product converted directly from money, a variable cost completely consumed in the conversion process, in a single time period.[3] If we are producing the single product at a cost of $2 each, a money stock of $1,000 would allow the production of 500 items. The curve in Figure 7-1(a) is a production opportunity curve, since we are free to stop at any point along the curve and would then have the amounts of money and product indicated on each scale, assuming money stock to read from the origin outward on the vertical axis and production volume from the origin outward on the horizontal scale. If the scale on the vertical axis is calibrated in the reverse, not as budget left over, but as money stock expended, then the curve is actually a total cost curve.

---

[2] The term "organic composition" is somewhat dated, stemming as it does from Karl Marx, but it seems useful in describing the wide range of possible combinations of variable and fixed costs that may exist in a manufacturing or commercial firm.

[3] Kenneth E. Boulding, *Economic Analysis*, 4th ed., Harper & Row, Publishers, Incorporated, New York, 1966, vol. 1, pp. 375–382.

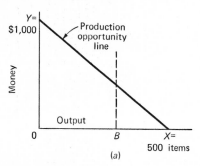

Figure 7-1(a).

Figure 7-1(b).

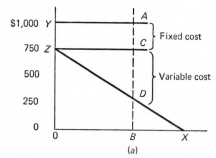

Figure 7-2(a).

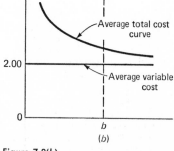

Figure 7-2(b).

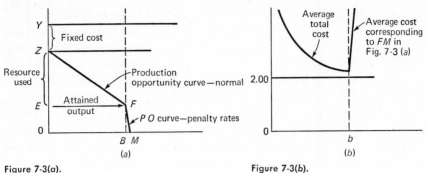

Figure 7-3(a).

Figure 7-3(b).

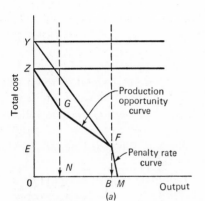

Figure 7-4(a).

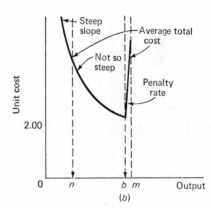

Figure 7-4(b).

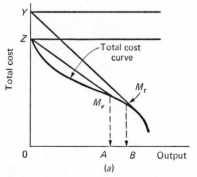

Figure 7-5(a).

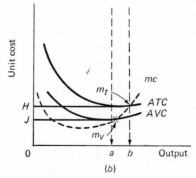

Figure 7-5(b).

Figures 7-1 to 7-5. A set of cost curves. (Source: *Economic Analysis*, 4th ed., vol. I: Microeconomics, by Kenneth E. Boulding: after Figure 77, "Production Opportunity and Cost Curves," Harper & Row, Publishers, Incorporated, 1966.)

The average total cost is the total cost divided by the output volume. Since our average cost is presumed to be constant, the graph is a straight line at $2 per item, as shown in Figure 7-1(b). Notice that so long as we assume that Money exchanges directly for output in the same ratio, the average cost function is horizontal. When as in Figure 7-2(a), the ration between output and total cost changes, the average will also change. And this is precisely what happens when we introduce the assumption that, in addition to a cost which varies directly as output, we have a fixed cost which is incurred in the same amount, regardless of the volume of output. Expenses, such as building depreciation, machinery depreciation, building maintenance, salaries of office help, and the like, continue, regardless of the volume of output, and require deductions from the asset total even if there is no production at all. The total fixed cost is, in other words, defined as the total cost at an output level of zero. Figure 7-2(a) shows the production opportunity boundary made up of fixed and variable cost components.

At output OB, total cost consists of total fixed cost AC and the total variable cost CD. Total variable cost is of course that part of the total which varies as output and consists of raw material inputs, direct labor, and so on. The production opportunity boundary is now defined as YZX. Assuming average variable cost to be the same, namely $2, the average cost function becomes more curved the closer one gets to the point of zero production. This shows the influence of fixed or period costs and is demonstrated in Table 7-1.

In practice, variable costs remain proportionate to total output up to a point at which engineered total plant capacity is reached. Any attempt to increase output beyond rated plant capacity generally results in a sharp

TABLE 7-1. COST SCHEDULES

Output (units)	Total Cost (dollars)	Average Total Cost (dollars)	Fixed Cost (dollars)	Average Fixed Cost (dollars)	Average Variable Cost (dollars)	Money Stock (dollars)	Product Stock (units)
0	100	Inf.	100	Inf.	2.00	900	0
50	200	4.00	100	2.00	2.00	800	50
100	300	3.00	100	1.00	2.00	700	100
150	400	2.67	100	0.67	2.00	600	150
200	500	2.50	100	0.50	2.00	500	200
250	600	2.40	100	0.40	2.00	400	250
300	700	2.33	100	0.33	2.00	300	300
350	800	2.29	100	0.29	2.00	200	350
400	900	2.25	100	0.25	2.00	100	400
450	1000	2.22	100	0.22	2.00	0	450
500	1100	2.20	100	0.20	2.00	−100	500

Source: Kenneth E. Boulding, Economic Analysis, 4th ed., vol. I: Microeconomics, Table 35. Cost Schedules: Fixed Cost, Constant Average Variable Cost, Harper & Row, Publishers, Incorporated, New York, 1966.

increase in variable costs as management tries to use variable inputs to compensate for the nonavailability of fixed inputs. Various assumptions might be made as to the behavior of costs. Figure 7-3 is drawn on the assumption that direct or variable costs increase when maximum plant capacity is reached and that fixed costs remain the same.

In Figure 7-3(a), OB represents rated plant capacity which can be attained at resource use of ZE, EO remaining. The production opportunity curve is drawn from Y through Z to F. With further resources available, management decides to apply additional variable inputs at penalty rates, resulting in much less than proportionate returns. Notice the change in slope to FM and the sharp increase in the variable cost curve from output OB or ob in Figure 7-3(b).

When the plant operates at very low production levels from O to N, variable inputs are not considered to be as efficient as they are when output is somewhat higher, perhaps between N and B. This efficiency reduction is remedied at higher outputs because of the additional specialization permitted and the possibility of specialized increases in staff. Average costs under these conditions are depicted as high at first, then falling as output increases, and finally rising as fixed plant and overhead begin to become inadequate to support additional activity. The resultant diagrams are shown in Figure 7-4.

The final set of drawings, Figure 7-5, shows the most general case, in which all inputs and outputs are continuously variable. Our production-opportunity curve is now labeled as a total cost curve. On the curve of total cost, Figure 7-5(a) the slope of the line drawn from Z to M_v is the average variable cost, and the slope of the line from Y to M_t is the average total cost.

When the total cost curve meets the average variable cost, in Figure 7-5(b), the curved marked marginal cost intersects the average variable cost curve at its minimum, unit cost J. Similarly, the average total cost is a minimum at a cost of H per unit where the slope of the total cost curve at M_t is equal to the average total cost, and that is the slope of the line drawn from Y to M_t. This marginal cost is the rate of change of total cost.

The difference between the model of the firm exhibited in Figures 7-1 and 7-2, on the one hand, and those of the remaining figures lies in the fact that there is some capacity or output level at which costs rise out of proportion to the increases in production. This is why the marginal cost is seen to rise as we try to bring about production beyond the design limits of the plant or fixed resource.

The significance of the marginal cost curve lies also in the fact that it represents the price of increasing output. Assuming that a firm wishes to cover its variable costs at all times, but may on occasion handle business which does not cover all its fixed costs, the relationship between the volume of output and the cost of producing that output is described by a line from the origin in Figure 7-5(b) to point J on the vertical axis, and then running to point m^v and then along the marginal cost curve m_c. In the long run, the price of production is a similar curve, except that it rises on the vertical axis to point *H* and then to the average total cost curve before rising on the marginal cost curve.

We are, of course, assuming that the size of the plant remains the same and that the only variables are inputs of labor, materials, and required services. Basically, we are assuming that costs which are fixed stay that way. If you assume a modular plant or changes in kinds of machinery, to name two possibilities, it would be necessary to assume changes in the cost curves. In order to present as simple a model as possible, we have hypothesized that plant characteristics remain unchanged as output varies. The marginal cost curve above the average variable or average total cost curves refers to changes in total cost arising out of the operation of a given plant. How descriptive this hypothesis is of a given situation depends among other things on the time needed to make changes in plant configuration.

By the term "short run," economists generally mean that length of time within which no changes in configuration can be made. But they also infer something more, and that is that the available supply of the remaining factors of production is unchanged. One of the reasons why the variable cost curve turns up is that labor becomes more difficult to obtain or must be hired at higher rates of pay. If one of the prices of increasing production is a night shift, then premium rates must be paid to labor, and this will serve to cause the average variable cost curve to rise.

As we extend the length of time within which changes in plant configuration and factor usage may be made, the less applicable become our notions as to what is fixed and what is variable. Just as in the very short run all expenses might be considered assets and all costs are fixed, just so in the long run all assets are expenses and all costs are variable. The present tendency in the United States toward a guaranteed annual wage for labor may result in changes in the way in which we view different components of cost. If it makes no difference in labor expense whether output is produced or not, we are in effect dealing with labor as though it were a fixed cost. Similarly, modern trends toward multiuse and multipurpose plants imply much less rigidity in costs heretofore considered as quite fixed. More of this shortly.

EMPIRICAL EVIDENCE OF SHORT-RUN COST BEHAVIOR

The model of the firm generally assumed by accountants for cost-control purposes is that represented by Figure 7-2. It is this form which is used in breakeven charts and in standard costing. The model assumes that costs are in roughly two categories, one of which represents fixed costs which are invariant as regards changes in output, and one of which represents those costs which are variable as output changes, but at a constant rate. In other words, most businessmen assume for everyday working purposes that marginal costs are constant. Standard costing is a considerable convenience, because it eliminates the need for much detailed record keeping. Unfortunately, at times we are prone to commit the "fallacy of misplaced concreteness." This fallacy consists in using theoretical constructs as though they were universally applicable in real life. Economists equally are guilty of this fallacy, and are inclined to believe that because their models assume costs to vary in a curvilinear manner, they always do so in real life. Let us see what real life has to offer.

Our first example is that of a firm in the meat-packing industry.[4] Variable costs consist of materials, labor, and variable plant costs, while fixed costs consist of programmed plant costs which include supervision, and fixed plant costs which include depreciation. Figure 7-6 shows the relationship between the output of the hog slaughtering department and the direct slaughtering costs. These costs are principally direct labor and fringe benefits related to them, incidental utilities, and operating supplies.

Notice that for a given speed of the conveyor chain, costs per head describe the kind of U-shaped average variable cost curve discussed earlier. Management attempts to use the slaughtering facilities at their designed optimum level, which means within the range of the normal work week of thirty-six to forty hours, and with engineered gang sizes.

The U shape is caused by varying operating hours for a standard gang until the maximum work week is reached and then incurring overtime rates for hours in excess of forty per week. Until thirty-six hours are worked, the curve

[4] This example and the diagrams have been adapted from Richard H. Bertholdt, "Planning for Profitability in the Meat Industry," *The Price Waterhouse Review,* vol. 12, no. 3, pp. 11–30, Autumn, 1967.

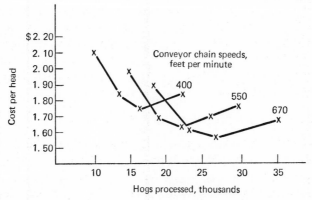

Figure 7-6. Direct costs in meat processing. (Source: Richard H. Bertholdt, "Planning for Profitability in the Meat Industry," *The Price Waterhouse Review,* vol. 12, no. 3, Autumn, 1967, pp. 11–30, by permission.)

slopes downward, just as our average fixed cost curve did in Figure 7-2, because, in effect, labor is a fixed cost at all hours less than thirty-six. From thirty-six to forty hours, average costs drop much less, because although most labor is constant, some expenses begin to rise. Beyond forty hours, overtime payments are incurred. We will have more to say about this example in the next chapter. However, we ought to note that increasing the speed of the conveyor might be considered analogous to using a new process or new plant, in which case we would have a whole new curve. On the other hand, we might consider that altering the speed of the conveyor chain is only one more way in which fixed plant is made to work harder. In that case, the correct variable cost curve might lie along the bottom of the first and the last curves shown, describing a path along the exposed portion of the middle curve.

One way of obtaining empirical cost curves is by obtaining operating information from a number of plants or firms of various sizes. This method has considerable risk, as may be imagined. For one thing, since we are combining different organizations, they cannot be said to represent the same plant merely varying its output level. Of course, if the plants are quite similar as to layout, labor supply, machine types, and other factors, it might be of use to obtain this kind of information for at least an approximation of the kind of cost behavior.

Data are available on retail food store operating costs in which store expense as a percent of sales is related to dollar sales per square foot of floor space. Now again, this is not cost per unit of output, but a similar curve is obtained. By using percent of sales, we compensate for differences in size, and by relating costs to activity per square foot, we again reduce the effects of size of store. A further step in removing discrepancies, which would be introduced because dissimilar units are the basis, is to limit the sample to a specific size range of stores. In Figure 7-7, only stores between 7,000 and 8,000 square feet were included. Other precautions taken are to exclude stores in operation for more than ten years or less than twelve months, and those having an unusual distribution of commodities or product lines, or variations in wage rates.

Since retail stores have no unit output except a dollar of sales, it is not possible to translate the curve in Figure 7-7 into the conventional economist's cost curve. We can, however, perform a reverse operation and show a typical total cost curve in terms of expenses as percent of sales and related to the amount of activity of the firm, size of firm being held constant.

Table 7-2 shows assumed data for an eight-acre farm whose total product increases, in the manner shown, as a result of one variable input, labor. Marginal cost is assumed to be constant for this input, and fixed costs are $160. Since there are diminishing returns, the average and marginal cost of operation of the farm, if plotted, would assume the usual U shape. Let us further assume that average revenue is $20 per ton of output for all amounts produced and sold.

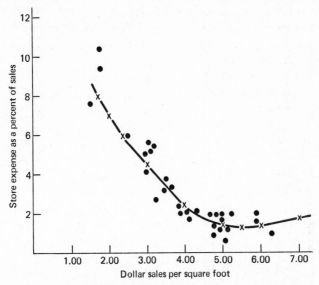

Figure 7-7. Scatter diagram of store expense and sales per square foot.
(Source: National Commission on Food Marketing, *Organization and Competition in Food Retailing*, Technical Study No. 7, U.S. Government Printing Office, June, 1966, p. 141.)

The last two columns of Table 7-2 have been plotted as Figure 7-8, and it is apparent that the J- and U-shaped curves result.

In conventional constructions, the marginal cost curve shows the increment in cost per unit output associated with an increase of one unit in output. In Figure 7-8, there is shown a similar incremental-type curve constructed by plotting the increment in total cost associated with an increment in total sales volume in dollars for each output (sales per acre) level. We have, in other words,

TABLE 7-2. TOTAL COSTS AS A PERCENT OF SALES AND SALES PER UNIT OF SIZE

Total Output	Sales Volume	Total Cost	Cost as Percent of Sales	Sales per Acre
0	0	160	—	0
8	160	180	112	20
24	480	200	45	60
34	680	220	32	85
40	800	240	30	100
42	840	260	31	105
44	880	280	32	110
46	920	300	32.6	115
48	960	320	33.3	120
49	980	340	34.7	122

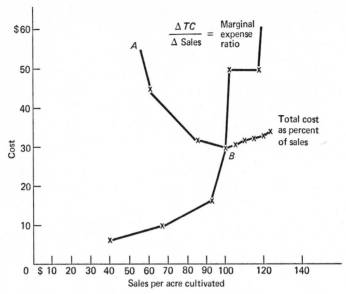

Figure 7-8. Economist's total cost curve and marginal cost curve in terms of sales-expense ratios.

plotted the expense ratio relevant to an increase in sales per unit of capacity. This ratio might be termed the marginal expense ratio.

Assuming our firm is operating at some minimum cost, the price of expanding output beyond that point is given by the marginal expense ratio. In dollar terms, the price of increasing dollar sales from $480 to $680 (see Table 7-2) is the increase in total cost, namely $20, or 50 percent of the sales increment at that level of operations. As curve A, Figure 7-8, shows, at sales volumes up to $100 per acre cultivated, we are selling at ever-decreasing percentage costs. Once we reach the minimum (point B), every 10 percent of increased sales volume begins to require more than 3 percent in added expense, so that when we reach a sales volume of $880, we have incurred 30 percent on the first $800, and 50 percent on the next 10 percent rise, for an average of 32 percent in additional expense. The added sales volume, then, can only be provided at an expense ratio of 50 percent.

Conventionally, graphs and explanations of marginal cost behavior are given in terms of units of output so that marginal cost is explainable as a unit cost. The results, as Table 7-2 indicates, are the same, however. Marginal cost falls, then rises, so that it equals average total cost at a total product of 40, total cost of $240, where sales per acre are $100 and the expense ratio is 30 percent. When total product exceeds 40 units, the increment to total cost goes up to $10, whereas at an output level of 40, average cost is $6 per unit. What these readings mean, then, is that all other things being equal, the price of increasing output beyond the minimum point moves along the marginal cost curve, however that curve is expressed.

Each firm in the community which supplies the same product has a similar curve, so that by adding the relevant amounts, a large single curve may be drawn which describes the amounts all suppliers will offer at varying prices. This large single curve is, in other words, the industry supply curve. Because the curves we have been describing are applicable in the short run only, and the organizational configuration is fixed, the industry supply curve is also a short-run curve. Figure 7-9 shows what such a curve would look like.

Four unit cost levels are identified. At the lowest, Firm I is able to produce at minimum average cost (point a), but Firms II and III are not able to compete. At cost level b, Firm II's minimum average cost is reached, and Firm I is producing at increasing marginal cost. Increasing the cost level to c permits such increases as Firms I and II can squeeze out of plant already nearing capacity. A

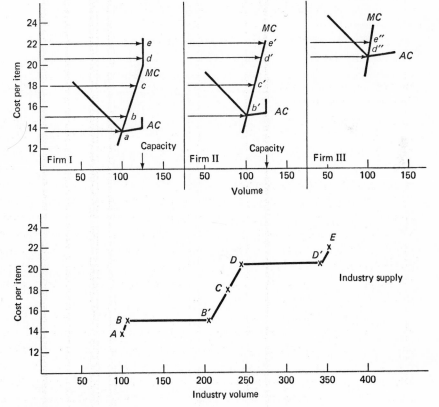

Figure 7-9. An industry supply curve.

further increase in allowable cost to level *d* brings very little increase from Firm I, which is now at capacity, and some increase at marginal cost from Firm II.

The industry supply curve continues to rise sharply from *B'* to *C* to *D*, and finally when level *d* is reached, Firm III's cost minimum is reached and it enters production. When point *D'* is attained on the industry supply curve, further increases in production are available only from Firms II and III. Firm I is at capacity, at e' Firm II is at capacity, and Firm III is operating on its marginal cost curve.

THE BASIS FOR COST CURVES

We have seen how costs vary over a wide range of output or activity levels, but we have not yet explored the reasons why they vary as they do. Of course, we realize that costs are made up of both fixed and variable elements and that some of the variability in unit costs lies in the fact that per unit fixed costs decline as output increases because a fixed amount is apportioned over an increasing number. But variable costs, which are generally considered to be variable with respect to total output, implying a constant rate per unit of output, may also turn up when volume is increased beyond a certain point, as for example in Figures 7-5b and 7-6. In the former diagram, the average variable cost curve actually has a negative slope, a minimum, and then rises, somewhat like the average total cost curve. Most of the decline in average total costs results from the decline in average fixed cost, but there remains the problem of explaining that rise which follows the decline in total and which is the result of increases in variable cost. The question to be answered, then, is why variable costs rise.

There are several terms which might be used to describe the reason for the increase in variable costs. One of the terms which might be used is diminishing returns. Dorfman's term is "bottleneck costs."[5]

To illustrate why costs rise because of bottlenecked operations, Dorfman employs the example of a factory which makes gadgets and a small number of widgets. At small volumes of widget production there is ample capacity, so that a decision to add to the output of widgets poses no real problem. There is ample capacity so that choice of equipment and of work process may be freely made. Labor is available without the payment of overtime rates, and storage space is available for the additional raw materials and goods in process which would be required. The costs associated with increasing the volume of widget production are only the variable costs of production, i.e., labor, materials, supplies, and the fixed costs of added supervision, utilities, factory space changes, and so on. Total costs of production then rise linearly as output increases.

At higher volumes of widget production, it begins to compete with

[5] Robert Dorfman, *The Price System*, Prentice-Hall, Inc., Englewood Cliffs, N.J., 1964, p. 22.

gadgets for the use of machines and facilities. Let us assume that the first evidence of crowding of machines and facilities is in machine scheduling. In order to increase the production of widgets beyond an assumed number—300—room has to be found in the production schedule. That is to say, we must either rearrange the schedule for some machine—drill presses—or reduce the present workload on that work center by cutting back on the output of some other product. Whether or not the drill presses should make widgets or gadgets is a managerial decision. If it is decided to make widgets, the cost of the expanded production ought to reflect the profits lost because some amount of gadgets were not made. In other words, in addition to fixed and variable costs, we must have relevant opportunity costs. If we would make a contribution to profit of $.25 on each gadget, the return on widgets must be at least that much more, or else it is not worthwhile making the change in the schedule.

Supposing that the manager wants to increase the widget schedule by thirty over the available capacity, he will have to find thirty minutes of drill press time, if we assume the press can handle only one per minute. Without exploring the scheduling process in detail, let us assume that the manager decides to curtail the production of gadgets and that gadgets take one-half minute each, so this means a planned reduction of sixty gadgets. Since the profit on a gadget is $.25, the drill press time devoted now to widgets is worth the following:

Setup time	20 minutes	
Production time	330 minutes	
Total	350 minutes	
Labor cost, at 6¢ per minute		$ 21.00
Machine cost, at 50¢ for 30 minutes		15.00
Total drill press cost		$ 36.00
Total drill press cost per widget		.1091

Any other products that are affected by the decision to increase widget production will bring about similar computations. While the profit given up in the first instance was $.25 per item, a further expansion of production requiring another cutback may require that a product be curtailed whose profit contribution is greater. If spigots are the next candidate for reduction, it may be that the profit contribution forgone is $1 per item and that the machine cost turns out to be $.75 per minute. As this process takes place, and assuming that there are no changes in plant configuration, the average cost curve for gadgets will rise. Additionally, not only machine costs will be involved, but there will also be the penalties associated with the use of less efficient machinery and with operation under more crowded plant conditions.

Now let us look at the portion of the cost curve to the left of the minimum. The reason for the curvature in the average variable cost curve to the left of the minimum generally is found in underutilization of plant facilities and labor skills. In other words, the benefits of labor specialization are generally pointed to as the reason that variable cost diminishes relative to output in earlier stages of production. Let us examine this feature more closely.

One of the properties of the organization of work on a large scale is that it is often advantageous to perform it in parallel fashion. That is to say, the various operations which are required to manufacture a product are carried out concurrently, rather than serially. A washing machine, for instance, consists in some models of the agitator, the washing drum, the cabinet, and other major parts.[6] All the parts for any one washing machine are in the process of manufacture at the same time. The advantage of this procedure is that the cycle time per item is reduced, and the total cost is reduced. The cost can be quite high if one machine only is turned out, for the simple reason that there is much unused labor time. If we had a cost system that confined variable cost to that time actually spent on production, the cost would be the same regardless of the level of output until, of course, bottleneck costs were encountered. But we do not define variable costs in that way. We define variable costs as those which vary by design. In other words, we assume that the labor force is planned to provide some volume of output at minimum cost, given the available plant. So if our labor force is actually a fixed expense and we vary only the volume of output, quite naturally labor costs per unit of output will act just as fixed costs per unit of output—they will fall.

The fact is, the larger the volume of production, the more cycle time is reduced, that is, the more the time needed to produce a whole washing machine is lessened. At the same time, the cost function becomes more curved. The more the division of work, the larger must be the volume of work to support it, so that each man on the end of the greatly subdivided work line is busy all the time. The greater the investment in fixed overhead, as for example in automatic factories or automated assembly lines, the larger the planned volume and the greater the difference between average total cost at minimum and at efficient volumes. But is really makes no difference if the overhead is built into plant design or into procedural design, the effect is the same, even though our accounting convention treats it differently.[7]

Apart, then, from questions of efficiency and of choice of materials, costs

---

[6] This illustration and analysis are based on Joseph A. Litterer, *The Analysis of Organizations,* John Wiley & Sons, Inc., New York, 1965, pp. 158–172.

[7] There is another consequence of the subdivision of labor, and that is the penalty associated with the absence of employees. In order to avoid shutting down whole lines, it may be necessary to keep a staff on standby, thus adding to the "variable" cost and raising the left-hand side of the average variable cost curve.

are seen to be a function of the way in which a plant is organized and of available technology. Another way of describing organization and the technological aspects of work is to refer to a process. So what we are saying is that cost levels and cost behavior depend on the choice of the work process, assuming output volume to be unchanged.

At this point, theory has some difficulty coming close to the facts. We cannot allow volume, organization, and technology all to vary; the model becomes too complex. If we allow volume to vary and hold organization and technology constant, we can use the nice continuous cost curve apparatus we have described. But unless we are operating a job shop with work centers, we cannot simply vary the volume of output of one product smoothly from zero to some large number. Output is the product of a number of work centers in parallel, or of assembly lines. A product may be turned out in a number of ways depending on the availability of kinds of inputs, kinds of machines, or the way in which the inputs and the machines are arranged. If we reduce the volume of washing machines, we must use some other process, because using the present process implies a misuse of specialized labor. If we wish to increase the volume of washing machines, we may have to use some other, less specialized process, until we can build up enough volume to create another process of the same kind. The difficulty here, theoretically, is that when we deal with processes, we must assume that a given "chunk" of process with its associated input amounts can provide a given amount of output, regardless of the scale of output. In other words, we assume constant returns to scale.

Both approaches will provide the same answer, however, as we will see.

SUMMARY

In this chapter we described the first of the elements in the decision-making process, namely those which undergird the concept of cost. We saw that the way in which we interpret the notions of cost and of expense is affected by whether we think of the firm as it is related to the production process or as a device for allocating resources. The former point of view will see costs as fully allocated expense; the latter as relevant and incremental and arising out of particular decisions or changes in output levels. The former holds that expenses must be recouped through the sale of output; the latter views costs as arising out of returns possible in alternative uses.

The relation of cost behavior to variations in scale of output was discussed, as were the different concepts of total, average, and marginal cost. Next, several instances of the use of empirical data were given, including an application to retailing, where the output is dollars per square foot of space employed. An industry supply curve was developed from cost curves of individual firms.

Finally, there were discussed some of the reasons why costs vary the way they do. We saw that while the spreading of fixed costs over an increasing number of units of output caused unit costs to decline, at some point variable costs were presumed to rise because of the presence of bottlenecks leading to diminishing returns. As a result, costs were seen as arising from the way in which a plant is organized and out of its technology. In practice, the cost curves of economists can only be used if we do not alter our selection of work process.

Review Questions

1. Differentiate between the accountant's and the economist's version of cost.
2. Differentiate among the terms cost, expense, and expenditure.
3. In what ways or for what reasons are economists interested in asset prices.
4. What are a firm's business costs?
5. Differentiate between incremental and sunk costs.
6. Define opportunity cost.
7. How would you defend the proposition that the costs incurred by a photographic film manufacturer in producing a camera are joint costs?
8. What is the significance of the marginal cost curve?
9. Differentiate between the terms short run and long run as they affect expense classification.
10. What have bottleneck costs to do with rising average variable costs?

Case 1. Carlson's Milling Company

The mill for many years had been a landmark in the small Middle Western town. Mr. Carlson was finding it increasingly difficult, though, to compete with larger firms and had begun to think about upgrading and enlarging his facilities.

The present plant had been in operation for forty years and, although large for its day, its daily capacity, which was rarely reached, was only 350,000 pounds. Furthermore, it was a conventional plant, while newer installations employed either a pneumatic or an air classification system. Also, larger plants sometimes had separate units for hard and soft wheat, an advantage he did not possess.

Mr. Carlson's grandson had just completed a university course in economics and was familiar with cost curves as drawn by economists. From the Western Commission on Food Marketing, he obtained what he thought might be relevant information on plants in the same region and attempted to analyze milling costs in order to advise his grandfather as to the size of an optimum plant. He found out also that an optimum size plant alone might not be the answer, since many firms, in order to increase capacity and flexibility, added smaller units to their facility. Since these smaller units operated at higher cost, true economies of scale would not be reflected in reported cost data.

EXHIBIT 1. COSTS OF OPERATION OF FLOUR MILLING FIRMS*
CLASSIFIED BY DAILY OPERATING SIZE (HUNDRED POUNDS)

Item	400–2,499	2,500–4,999	5,000–7,499	7,500–9,999	10,000–12,499	12,500–15,000
Purchased wheat	$3.76	$3.70	$3.68	$3.61	$3.57	$3.50
Other grains	.15	.11	.03	.05	.00	.15
Purchased flour	.14	.11	.09	.05	.13	.25
Containers	.19	.15	.11	.10	.09	.08
Mill labor	.24	.18	.15	.17	.19	.21
Other mill expense	.04	.03	.03	.02	.03	.04
Power and fuel	.04	.03	.03	.03	.03	.03
Manufacturing overhead	.02	.02	.01	.01	.01	.01
Quality control	.02	.02	.02	.02	.03	.03
Plant depreciation	.05	.04	.04	.04	.03	.03
Insurance	.02	.02	.01	.01	.01	.01
Administrative	.14	.14	.09	.09	.08	.11
Selling expense	.16	.10	.07	.07	.05	.09
Freight out	.24	.38	.32	.33	.62	.30
Taxes	.02	.02	.01	.01	.01	.01
Total	$5.23	5.05	4.69	4.61	4.88	4.85

*The data in this table have been freely adapted from National Commission on Food Marketing, *Organization and Competition in the Milling and Baking Industries*, Technical Study No. 5, U.S. Government Printing Office, June, 1966.

QUESTIONS

1. From the data gathered, prepare curves of total, fixed, variable, and marginal cost.
2. What elements are required to make these curves conform to economic theory?
3. What advice, if any, could you give based on these data?

Case 2. Baking Plant Costs

It was reported by the National Commission on Food Marketing in June, 1966, that it would have required, in 1956, only 261 baking plants, with an average capacity of 800,000 pounds per week, to produce all of the commercial bread which the census reported having been baked in 1963.

Indeed, a number of plants had double this capacity. The trend appears to be toward fewer and larger bread plants, as evidenced by the fact that the number of establishments in 1963 was down by 17 percent from 1958. Capacity utilization of all plants varied from 65 to 86 percent. Some cost information adapted from that reported by the industry is given below. Costs are expressed in dollars per hundred pounds produced.

	Plant Size in Pounds per Week°		
Item	Less than 250,000	25,000 to 500,000	Over 500,000
Ingredients	5.48	5.40	5.37
Total manufacturing labor	2.88	2.68	2.58
Other manufacturing expense	2.18	2.08	2.07
Administrative	1.10	.94	.90
Selling and distribution	4.72	5.03	5.64
Total expense	16.36	16.13	16.56

° Data have been freely adapted.

Although operations such as flour handling have shifted from bag to bulk methods, and dough mixing is more and more on a continuous basis, some installations are reported still to involve conventional batch dough-mixing methods.

As is generally true of many items in the United States, price levels of inputs over the past ten years have been rising, as the following table illustrates.

Category of Labor Input	1965 Price Index of Hourly Wages (1956 = 100)
Bakers	137
Wrappers	140
All direct labor	115
Route salesmen	150
Vehicle maintenance	119
Other sales expense	187

QUESTIONS

1. To what extent are bakers attempting to cope with rising price levels for inputs? How successful do they appear to be?
2. The text refers to the possibility that the correct variable cost curve might lie along the bottom of several short-run cost curves. Can this concept be applied here? What would it mean?

Suggested Reading

Ammer, Dean S.: *Manufacturing Management and Control*, Appleton-Century-Crofts, New York, 1968, pp. 23–51.

Clark, J. M.: *Studies in the Economics of Overhead Costs*, The University of Chicago Press, Chicago, 1923, chaps. 3 and 9.

Dean, Joel: *Managerial Economics*, Prentice-Hall, Inc., Englewood Cliffs, N.J., 1951, pp. 249–324.

Ferguson, C. E.: *Micro-Economic Theory*, Richard D. Irwin, Inc., Homewood, Ill., 1966, pp. 162–184.

Watson, Donald Stevenson: *Price Theory and Its Uses*, 2d ed., Houghton Mifflin Company, Boston, 1968, pp. 189–205.

chapter 8
cost and production
functions

In the previous chapter, we realized that it was necessary to examine the manner in which production takes place in order completely to understand cost behavior. We will approach the subject from two points of view. With the aid of the meat slaughtering example of the previous chapter, we will explore the classical example used in microeconomics, in which there is a single production process and two inputs and it is possible to vary the amounts of the inputs and the outputs, both inputs and outputs varying continuously over some range of values. The example being used is particularly appropriate here because such variation is in fact possible. We will discuss the method by which one decides the appropriate amounts and levels of inputs, if the prices of the inputs are known.

Next we will see what happens when the assumption of a continuous production function is dropped. As is more often true in practice in many lines of production, machines operate at given rates, or not at all. They require certain manning, or they may not operate efficiently. We will modify our example to suit this purpose by assuming that we have found a set of efficient operating points and wish to use these configurations or not use a process or configuration at all. This implies that increases in capacity can only come about by replication or duplication of a given production situation, rather than by changing the number of working hours or the speed of the conveyor. We will see how decisions are made under these conditions and then go on to questions of the long run.

THE CONTINUOUS PRODUCTION FUNCTION

In an ends-means chain of business decision making, the decision to produce something requires a means decision involving the method or process by which production will be carried out. Each process which may be used has associated with it a particular configuration of inputs. Processes may vary in that they use more machinery than labor, in which case they are termed capital intensive. If they use more labor than capital, they are labor intensive.

In the previous chapter, we described the cost behavior of a meat slaughtering firm. The process involves a chain conveyor which might be set to move at different speeds, and to which amounts of labor might be applied over differing numbers of hours per week. Increasing the speed of the conveyor is tantamount to using machinery more intensively. Increasing the number of man-hours per week is equivalent to using labor more intensively.

We can vary the amount of labor hours, keeping machine speed the same; we can vary the speed of the machinery, keeping labor hours constant; or, as will be done later, we can find the most efficient combination of man-hours and machine-hours and increase output by installing replicate layouts, instead of further altering hours or speeds.[1]

Let us begin this exploration by considering a crew working forty hours per week, but at various chain speeds. That is, we are holding labor constant and varying machine usage. The results are relevant to the curves in Figure 7-6 but not directly comparable, since there are costs, other than direct labor, about which we have no information. We will assume the following schedule of input-output relationships to hold at a man-hour figure of forty per week, with gang size constant.

Machine use rate:	225	400	550	670	800	1100
Output (000):	11	16	21	32	45	74

Figure 7-6 has only three curves corresponding to three chain speeds, while we have arbitrarily added one slower speed and two faster speeds, just for illustrative purposes. Such speeds may not be feasible in practice.

We can take any one machine speed, as in Figure 7-6, and allow the man-hour input to vary. For a machine speed of 550 feet per minute, we might have, for example:

Man-hours:	20	30	40	50	60
Output (000):	7	14	21	28	32

In general, we would be interested in obtaining either a given output level from a production situation, or possibly maximizing the output from a given set of inputs. In any case, we would want to see a complete scale of inputs

---

[1] We recognize that altering the speed of the machine implies that manpower is also used more intensively, and extending man-hours implies the use of the machines for the same time period, but we are concerned more with comparing process configurations than we are with exact input productivities and can afford to ignore this point. For our example, manpower productivity changes come about solely from changes in input usage or machine speed as discrete alternatives. The same is true of machine-speed-associated marginal productivity.

and outputs with their associated costs in order to make a decision. By experimenting with various inputs as above, varying man-hours above and below forty for varying chain speeds, and then varying the chain speed to see what output levels we can obtain, we can develop a matrix which we call a *production function* (Table 8-1). It is called a production function because it relates inputs to outputs in a functional way. The output levels are in the body of the table. Another kind of matrix places the output scale along one axis and shows the needed variation in one input in the body of the table.

Notice that the data in the column headed "Machine Use Rate, 550" are identical with the data previously given, and that the schedule of inputs and outputs for a forty-hour week is identical to the line in the middle of the production function. All that we have done is to extend the calculations to all values of machine use rate and man-hours given in Table 8-1.

Assuming our needs for output will be met by a production level of about 16,000 units, we have serveral choices open. First, and proceeding from left to right by machine use rates, we can employ sixty man-hours per week per man and operate the conveyor at the slow rate of 225 feet per minute. If we increase the conveyor speed to 400 feet per minute, we will be able to reduce manpower usage by one-third to forty hours per week per man. A further increase in machine speed to 550 feet per minute will allow a further reduction in manpower, and so on, as indicated.

In Figure 8-1, we have placed man-hours per week on the vertical axis and machine use rates on the horizontal axis. The plotted points represent the inputs needed to turn out 16,000 units. They are connected by a smooth curve, on the theory that if we are able to effect different manpower—machine use rate combinations to attain the same output level, they would form such a continuous line. This line is called an isoquant or line of equal quantity. Similar lines might be drawn for all production amounts.

Let us suppose that labor is $5.60 per man-hour and that machine time rates come to $.000167 per foot per minute including maintenance and depreciation, so that the total machine bill for, let us say, a rate of 550 feet per minute, would be $550 \times .000167$ times the number of minutes in the day or week.

TABLE 8-1. PRODUCTION FUNCTION
(PRODUCTION IN THOUSANDS)

Man-hours per Week per Man	Machine Use Rate					
	225	400	550	670	800	1100
60	16	23	32	46	63	101
50	14	20	28	40	55	88
40	11	16	21	32	45	74
30	7	10	14	22	33	59
20	1	4	7	10	18	43

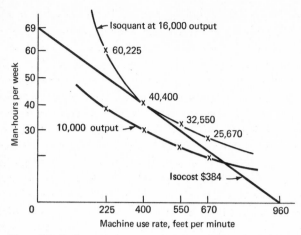

Figure 8-1. Production isoquants at 10,000- and 16,000-unit output.

In order not to complicate this example, we shall assume that machines always are operated forty hours per week, so that the operating cost for a forty-hour week at a use rate of 550 is calculated as 550 × .000167 × 40 × 60 or 550 × $.40 which comes to $220. The corresponding labor bill for a thirty-two-hour week at $5.60 per hour is $179.20, and the total manufacturing cost for the indicated amount of output is the sum of the two, or $399.20.

If we take our assumed labor rate and find the corresponding cost for forty man-hours, and the machine rate for 400 feet per minute, we arrive at $384. Other estimates based on the requirements of the isoquant curve turn out to be greater than this figure. If we then take $384 and find out how much labor alone this would buy, it comes to just under sixty-nine hours. Alternatively, we might purchase a 960-foot-per-minute activity rate on the part of the machinery. Connecting these points, we find the locus of all combinations of inputs whose total cost is exactly $384. We might draw additional lines parallel to this which would represent additional or lesser amounts of money spent on the inputs, provided their prices were the same. Were the price of labor to fall and the price of machine time to rise, the slope of the isocost line would become more steep, and it would be worthwhile to substitute labor for equipment. This would be evident in a shift of the tangency of the isocost line, so that it would be tangent to the left of the present point.

From the foregoing, it is evident how the quantity decision will be made if the object is to maximize production subject to the limitation that total production expenses shall not exceed $384. But let us see how we can be somewhat more explicit.

We have sketched in on Figure 8-1 the isoquant corresponding to an output level of 10,000 units. Naturally, it is everywhere closer to the origin than is the 16,000-unit output isoquant, because it requires fewer inputs. As we can see on the diagram, if we decrease the amount of manpower from sixty man-hours to forty, leaving conveyor speed at 225 feet per minute, we will reduce output from 16,000 units to about 11,000 units, or to a point just above the lower isoquant. The effect of a reduction of twenty man-hours is to lower output by 5,000 units, machine usage being at 225 feet per minute in both cases. The incremental productivity of labor is therefore, over this range, 250 units per man-hour.

Now if we want to increase machine speed from 225 to 400 feet per minute, we see that such an action will take us back to the isoquant we had just left. In other words, we can recoup the lost 5,000 units by adding 400 minus 225, or 175, feet per minute to machine activity. Then the incremental productivity of machine use is 5,000 divided by 175, or a little less than 29 units per foot-minute. If these calculations could be made in terms of the effect of a one-man-hour or 1-foot-per-minute incremental input, we would of course have referred to marginal productivities rather than incremental productivities, but the calculations are otherwise the same.

Moving further to the right, if we subtract an additional ten man-hours, leaving machine usage the same, namely 400 feet per minute, we find ourselves on the 10,000 isoquant. To restore our position on the 16,000 level, we must move to the right to a machine speed of about 630 feet per minute. The incremental (marginal) productivity of labor here is now 500 units per man-hour, an increase over the former level, and the incremental (marginal) productivity of machine use has fallen now to about 21.7 units per foot per minute. So as we reduce labor, machinery staying at the same level, the incremental (marginal) productivity of labor increases; as we add machinery, labor staying the same, the incremental (marginal) productivity of machinery falls.

A curious thing develops at this point. If we average the incremental productivities of labor and of machinery, respectively, we get 375 units per man-hour for labor and 27 units per machine-foot-minute. The ratio of the two is approximately 14:1. The area over which the average is taken has the point (40,   400) on the 16,000 isoquant as its approximate midpoint. This is the point at which the slope of the isocost line is the same as the slope of the curve. It is not really surprising, then, that the ratio of the prices of the inputs should also come out to be 14:1.

This example is intended to illustrate the fact that the economical production level, the point of minimum cost, is not only where the isocost line is tangent to the isoquant, but that it is the place where the ratio of the marginal productivities of the inputs is equal to the ratio of the input prices.

So much then for the production decision where inputs and outputs may be varied continuously. In fact, we know what the efficient points are, because normally we design processes to have certain cost characteristics. If we want to expand output, our decisions are usually among processes and not within a given process. What is necessary is to choose a particular process or combinations of processes, given a list of input prices and process limitations.

DECISIONS BETWEEN PROCESSES

For illustrative purposes, we must now assume that conveyors may be purchased only in four given operating speeds, namely 225, 400, 550, and 670 feet per minute. In order to use a 225-foot-per-minute conveyor, it is necessary to use sixty man-hours of labor per week. Any additional labor is superfluous, unless an additional conveyor unit is purchased. An additional conveyor unit, without the man-hours with which to operate it, is also nonproductive and superfluous. The same statements can be made of the remaining three conveyors whose man-hour needs are, respectively, forty, thirty-two, and twenty-five. Each man-hour–machine combination has an output of 16,000 units. The situation is shown in Figure 8-2.

Except for the fact that we have made it impossible to vary the inputs in a continuous manner, the points described in Figure 8-2 are exactly the same as the corresponding points in Figure 8-1. The same amounts of inputs are used and the same output level is attained. It should therefore not be surprising to see that, if the same kind of isocost line is drawn in Figure 8-2, the same conclusion as to input selection will be reached. The only difference here is that we cannot draw smooth isoquants, so that tangency is possible only at each process corner (viz: A, B, C, D) or, if the isocost line shifts parallel to a line connecting corners, either process or any combination of processes will be acceptable. This last will be indicated by tangency along the whole section of line between two corners.

CHOOSING AMONG OUTPUTS

Production processes do exist which can be analyzed with the aid of the apparatuses described above. Leslie Cookenboo has described one involving oil pipelines.[2] His product is throughput of oil in barrels per day, and the variable input is thousands of horsepower. For a pipe of a given diameter, the use of increasing amounts of pumping horsepower yields a throughput which increases at the decreasing rate. When we increase the size of the pipe, and then use increasing amounts of horsepower, we get the same phenomenon. If pipe and motive power were available in stated combinations only, we would get the process example of the preceding section.

But our example and that of Cookenboo are essentially the same kind of example used originally by David Ricardo in illustrating the phenomenon of diminishing returns. Ricardo had three factors of production: land, labor, and

---

[2] *Crude Oil Pipelines and Competition in the Oil Industry,* Harvard University Press, Cambridge, Mass., 1955. Selections are reprinted in Donald S. Watson (ed.), *Price Theory in Action: A Book of Readings,* Houghton Mifflin Company, Boston, 1965, pp. 79–87.

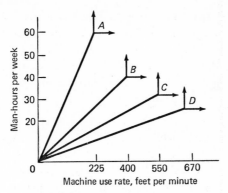

Figure 8-2. Process rays.

capital. The production process might use any proportions of these three factors to produce a single homogeneous commodity. Our example involves the production of a processed animal, Cookenboo uses a gallon of oil pumped, and Ricardo had wheat in mind. Ricardo used this production model to calculate the proportions in which the total income would be distributed between the land-owner and the farmer, assuming that the quantity of land was fixed, but of different classes of fertility.[3] As new capital, in the form of the farmer and his tools, attempts to enter agricultural activity, either land of less and less productivity must be used to expand output or existing land must be worked more intensively. In either instance, the physical product per unit of capital will diminish. Because of this increase in the real cost of production, rents are increased and interest rates come down. The process results in a method of valuation of the factors of production and a basis by which resources can be said to be allocated in a free market. Ricardo's analysis was a study of long-run economic equilibrium, of what he called the "high theme of economic progress." It was not intended to explain entrepreneurial behavior, but that is how it was used over the succeeding years. All that was needed was to transform the English wheat farmer of Ricardo into the entrepreneur of J. B. Say and await the development of the methods of marginal analysis pioneered by Cournot and Senior, and carried forward by Jevons, Menger, and others. The final transformation into a method of analysis of the decision process within the firm was done by Chamberlin, Robinson, and Viner.

There are many who doubt that businessmen make decisions based on marginal analysis, although these procedures are coming more and more into vogue as education in the methods of economic analysis progresses. There are

[3] This discussion of Ricardo and the development of the entrepreneurial model is taken from Robert Dorfman, *Application of Linear Programming to the Theory of the Firm,* University of California Press, Berkeley, 1951.

others who believe that the businessman cannot obtain the kind of information needed to apply marginal analysis. Still others doubt that the necessary preconditions for a determinate solution, as for example the U-shaped average unit cost curve, actually exist in modern production situations. These criticisms, of course, are made of the theory as it applies to the short-run behavior of the businessman and to the entire theory of the firm as an explanation of that behavior.

Dorfman and others have suggested that a more appropriate mechanism to explain production decision making is to be found in the mathematical procedure termed *linear programming.* The procedure is based on the assumption that production processes are modular as in our second example earlier in the chapter, rather than infinitely variable as in the first example. In nonagricultural production, especially where there is the assembly-line use of machinery, we are dealing with whole production systems rather than with several separate inputs which can be adjusted at will. Under such conditions, machinery is likely to be inflexible as regards other inputs, as well as with respect to output. When, as we have said, it has been decided to employ a certain number of machines in a process, all of the other inputs associated with the machinery must be used and in the proper engineered amounts as dictated by the entire system or process. One engineers a module of plant to deliver a given output, and the choice is between turning it on or off or combining it with other such modules to increase output, but not of altering the output levels by altering inputs.

Another more difficult problem arises, from our point of view, and that is that the marginal analysis is difficult to apply when there is more than one output. The diagrams we have used depict two inputs and one output. The diagram is therefore three-dimensional. If you increase the number of inputs, mathematically there is no problem. Of course, it cannot be represented in three dimensions and therefore cannot be drawn. But the conditions for equilibrium are still the same, namely, that the ratio of the prices of the inputs must be equal to the ratio of the marginal productivities. The only difference is that the form changes, so that we speak of the ratio of the price of each input to its marginal productivity. But the output is still a single variable output of homogeneous character. The assumption is that the process is somehow always the same, although the inputs may vary, and that all inputs, although subject to diminishing returns, are nevertheless available in whatever amount is needed. The only limitation lies in the monetary resources of the producing firm, and this is based on the ultimate acceptability of the product produced and sold in the marketplace.

In practice, there are limitations to the availability of inputs such as labor and machine-hours. These can be shown on a conventional isoquant diagram or on the process ray diagram given in Figures 8-1 and 8-2, respectively. The procedure, as it affects both isoquant and process ray, is shown in Figure 8-3.

Here we see that the limit on available labor effectively prohibits the use of process A beyond one module, while B and C may be used to two modules each. The limit on machine time limits the use of process C beyond two modules, and then limits the use of B and A in that order, but that is beyond the diagram. Given the isocost line as drawn, the tangency is at the corner of the isoquant made with process B. As that point is within the labor and machine-hour limits, it is a feasible production decision. If machine-hours become cheap relative to labor hours, so that the isocost line becomes a little more flat, process C might be feasible. If we could somehow alter the characteristics of the processes, so that the intersection between the machine-hour limit and the labor-hour limit were to lie on an isoquant, it would indicate that both of the adjacent processes might be used. If the firm wants to produce as much as possible within the resources available to it, then it might disregard the price ratio of the inputs. It all depends on the particular object one has in mind, namely, whether to produce at the lowest cost, or whether to maximize production subject to resource limitations.

So far, we have confined our discussion to a single output. Suppose that there are limitations on inputs, that the inputs have prices associated with them, and that we have a choice of two outputs, both of which use one or more of the inputs, and further that the outputs have values or prices at which the firm may sell them. In order to represent the method of choosing between two outputs, that is to say, how much of the resources of the firm will be used to produce one output and how much the other, we must alter the nature of the graphic representation. Now, instead of placing the inputs on the axes, we will place the outputs on the axes. We will depict the inputs by using the device earlier used to

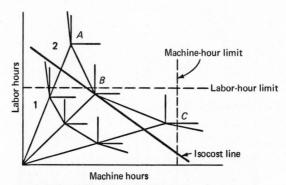

Figure 8-3. Introducing an input limit.

show limitations on inputs and indicate the extent to which each input may be used to produce each output.

Figure 8-4 shows two possible outputs, A and B, for the production of which both labor and machine time are required. There are two differences between the facts of this diagram and the facts of Figure 8-3. First, we now have a choice as to which output we may produce, as well as the amounts of the inputs. Second, we no longer have a choice as to process. That is to say, the technological coefficients of production are now fixed. In other words, we will accept one process which we know uses both inputs and produces both outputs and simply allocate the inputs on the basis of whatever it is we are trying to maximize or minimize. If the prices of the inputs are known, and there is some desirable amount of each output, then we want to minimize total cost of production of a given quantity of each item. We will perform this operation subject to a limitation on the availability of each input and assuming that each input is needed in some fixed amount to produce some unit of output; in other words, the marginal productivity of each input will be fixed.

In Figure 8-4, available machinery will produce sixty-nine units of item A or eighty units of item B, but not both. Labor will turn out sixty units of A or 100 of B, but not both. The maximum output point indicates the amount of A and of B that will use all available imputs and hence provide a maximum total output, provided there are no other constraints. The arrows drawn from the point of maximum output indicate the level of output of each product.

Now let us suppose we wish to find the output which will maximize revenue. It is necessary to introduce the price of each output into the solution procedure. We then will want to find that combination of output which maximizes total revenue and which lies within the technical feasibility of the inputs and their marginal productivities. For example, consider a firm whose output possibility consists of two products, A and B, both of which require the use of

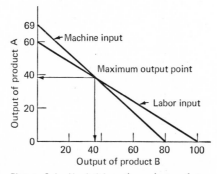

Figure 8-4. Maximizing the volume of two outputs, given two inputs with fixed marginal productivities.

three machines of different kinds, M_1, M_2, and M_3. One unit of A requires machine M_1 be employed for 7.5 hours, machine M_2 for 6.0 hours, and machine M_3 for 3.75 hours. To turn out a unit of B requires 7.5, 12.0, and 15.0 hours, respectively, of each machine. The labor contract stipulates that machinery may work no more than sixty hours per week. The firm may sell as many of each item as it wishes at the going price, and it earns revenue of $1.10 per unit of A and $1.80 per unit of B. It is necessary to determine the level of production of each item which will maximize total revenue.

Total revenue is given by the equation $TR = 1.10x_1 + 1.80x_2$, where x_1 represents the number of units of A and x_2 the number of units of B. It is called the objective function. We will want to find those values of x_1 and x_2 which will give us a maximum TR, within the limits imposed by the total number of hours available for each machine and the number of hours each machine takes to work on each product, which is to say, the process specifications. Remember that we no longer have processes between which to choose. It is assumed that this method of making A's is the most efficient available to us, and the same is true of the B's. All we have now to decide is how many of each we may turn out if it is our aim to maximize our total revenue.

The simplest way to begin appears to be by using Figure 8-5. The number of units of A are measured on the vertical axis and the number of units of B are measured against the horizontal axis. We use a common device for showing limi-

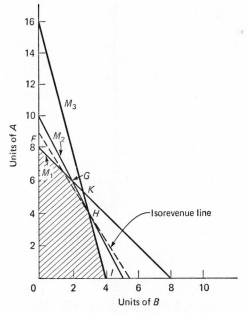

Figure 8-5. Determining the optimum product mix.

tations. We begin with machine M_1, by first marking the number of product A's which may be turned out by that machine in the number of hours available, if it turned out only A's. We do the same for B's, and draw a line from 8 units of A to 8 units of B. We do the same for the other machines, taking care to label each line with the number of the machine.

Each such line states that any point to the left and within the axes represents a feasible combination of inputs with regard to that limit. So it is possible, with regard to machine M_1, to have any combination of A and B products provided A does not exceed 8, and B is the resultant value when A is plotted as some positive number to the left of the limit line.

Notice that some combinations which may be feasible for M_1 may not be so for M_2, for some areas to the right of intersection *I*, while for areas to the left, the reverse is true. As a consequence, taking into account that both products require all three machines, the cross-hatched area bounded by the polygon *OFGHI*, where *O* is the origin, represents the feasible production region.

As the revenue per unit of A is $1.10 and the revenue per unit of B is $1.80, selling 9 of A will provide as much income as selling $5\frac{1}{2}$ of B, and we draw a line from A equals 9 to B equals $5\frac{1}{2}$.[4] Now all we have to do is to move this line to the left or to the right, representing decreases or increases in output, until it intersects a production feasibility region corner farthest to the right, so that the line passes nowhere else within the region. That is, of course, at G, where 6 of A and 2 of B are made.

In order to make use of available M_1 and M_3 resources, Figure 8-5 makes it clear that additional M_2 capacity is required. Assuming no other limitations, M_1 and M_3 will produce $5\frac{1}{3}$ units of A and $2\frac{2}{3}$ units of B. These amounts are represented by the intersection of M_1 and M_3 at point *K*. The question now is, how much M_2 capacity is needed to make full use of M_1 and M_3 resources? To produce $5\frac{1}{3}$ of A and $2\frac{2}{3}$ of B, the output equation for the line M_2 has to be moved out and to the right, parallel to the present line until it passes through point *K*. At that point, we are using 64.02 hours of machine time, or 4.02 hours over the old limit. This usage amount is obtained by multiplying the amounts of A and B by the time factors per item, 6 and 12 hours, respectively.

If we had the opportunity to purchase additional M_2 time, how much would it be worth to us? Clearly it would be worth no more than the increment to total revenue from the sale of the additional output its use would produce. As the additional M_2 time allows us to decrease the output of A by .67 units and increase the output of B by the same amount, the addition to total revenue is equal to $1.80 × .67 less $1.10 × .67 or $.47. The additional machine time is therefore worth exactly $.47, and at any greater cost it is worthwhile to leave

---

[4] The reader will, I hope, excuse the liberty taken in assuming that one may sell a half unit.

M_1 and M_3 unused, because the marginal cost would be greater than the marginal revenue.

Suppose the revenue per unit of B were to be reduced so that it would take 10 units of B to equal the income obtainable by the sale of 8 units of A. The isorevenue line would then run from 8 on the vertical axis to 10 on the horizontal axis, in Figure 8-5. The isorevenue line now would pass through point F, as the only point at which no resource shortage is produced. But this alteration in revenues implies that it is no longer worthwhile to produce output B! Also now, it is quite clear that there is substantial excess capacity in M_3 and some excess in M_2. So we have gone from a situation in which we were *short* of M_2 capacity, so that it was worthwhile renting additional time, to being a seller of M_2 time.

In courses in economic theory, we learn that in this way a freely operating price system allocates the resources of an economy. It would be beyond the scope of this treatment to pursue the subject any further. It is also tempting, but unwise, to pursue the subject of linear programming any further here. The appendix to this chapter contains some mathematical formulations which may be of additional interest.

DIMINISHING RETURNS[5]

Suppose we use the diagramed production function shown partially in Figure 8-1 and extend it by drawing lines of equal production level for each of eight output values. The diagram is based roughly on the data in Table 8-1, which has formed the basis of the discussion in this chapter. The resultant isoquant diagram is shown as Figure 8-6(a). We first draw cross-section lines horizontally at man-hour input levels 30, 40, 50, and 60, and then drop vertical lines through the machine-speed scale to the same scale in Figure 8-6(b). Changing the vertical scale now to read output, we plot the relationship of output to machine speed, man-hour input constant, for the several man-hour input levels shown. Figure 8-6(b), in other words, is based on the rows in Table 8-1. We now want to explore the total output or total product curve developed in Figure 8-6(b).

Beginning at about a chain speed of 400 or less, the total product curves in Figure 8-6(b) appear to be increasing at an increasing rate. This stage is commonly referred to as that of increasing returns, because successive equal increments of input are associated with increasing increments of output. Gradually, as the variable input is increased in amount, its beneficial effects begin to diminish, so that the rate of increase of product growth falls off. It is at this

---

[5] This section and the next employ a technique of shifting axes for which the authors are indebted to Professor Kenneth E. Boulding. See his *Economic Analysis,* 4th ed., Harper & Row, Publishers, Incorporated, New York, 1966, vol. I, pp. 423–435.

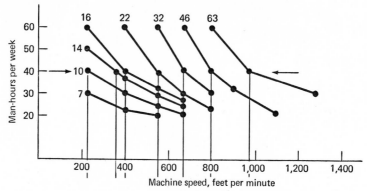

Figure 8-6(a). Isoquant diagram (data in Table 8-1). Output in thousands.

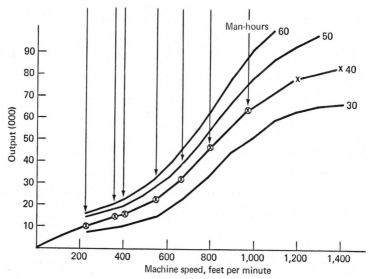

Figure 8-6(b). Output as a function of machine speed. Man-hours input as shown, constant for each individual curve.

stage that we begin to speak of diminishing returns. Reference to Figure 8-7 will further clarify the point.

In Figure 8-7(a), we show the total product curve for a constant input of forty man-hours, previously noted in Figure 8-6(b). But now we have performed a few calculations which will serve to illustrate the phenomenon of increasing and diminishing returns. The particular measure in which we are interested is the rate of change of the total product function, which is to say its first derivative. A simple way of calculating it is, as before, by dividing a change in output by a change in input. So that the curves are more regular, we have shown total prod-

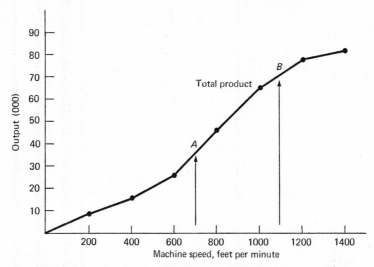

Figure 8-7(a). Output as a function of machine speed. Man-hours constant at forty per week.

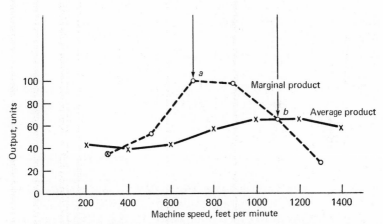

Figure 8-7(b). Average and marginal physical product of machine speed. Man-hours constant at forty per week.

uct for input increments of 200 and calculated the rate of change for each class. An input change from 400 to 600 produces an output change of 10½ (with the aid of forty man-hours of work). Dividing by the input change, since we want to know how much output is associated with a unit change of input, we obtain a figure of 52, which is the incremental or marginal product.[6]

[6] Strictly speaking, one may speak only of a marginal product or marginal anything if there is a continuous function which may be differentiated mathematically. Incremental is the more correct usage here, but the difference, as we indicated earlier, does not appear material.

Another calculation of interest here is the simple average product, which is of course the total output divided by the total input. Both the incremental (marginal) product and the average product curves are drawn in Figure 8-7(b). Notice that the peak of the marginal product curve coincides with the place on the total product curve at which the rate of increase appears to have reached its maximum, which indeed it has. In other words, for values to the right, for inputs greater than 700, the marginal product is diminishing.

Now the average product still increases to the right of this point, which we have marked as A-a on both Figures 8-7(a) and (b), but the rate of increase is decreasing. The average product is a maximum where the marginal product cuts it from above, and from that point on, B-b, where marginal product is less than the average, both the average and the marginal product decline. The total product is still increasing, however!

At what point will it be a maximum? The maximum point is where the marginal return is zero, because so long as any additional input provides a positive increment to output, the marginal return is positive, and the total return still increases.

Assuming that present trends continue and that increasing doses or increments of machine time are increasingly hard to use because of limited man-hour and other inputs, there will come some time when a rate of machine speed will result in a positive decline in output rather than any further increase. At this point, marginal returns or marginal product will be zero, and total product will turn down. The first derivative of the total product curve will be zero, and the function will provide a maximum value for the unknown dependent variable.

RELATION TO COSTS

Earlier, we had assumed that machine time rates were $.000167 per foot per minute and that the cost per hour then came out to $.40, assuming a forty-hour week of operating time. The cost to run 550 feet per minute then would be 550 × $.40 or $220. Assuming that all costs are variable, we can equate variable cost with total cost, and by multiplying all input machine speeds by $.40, we can arrive at a usable total cost for each total output. We might then simply change the scale in Figure 8-7(a) so that machine speeds are replaced by total cost, and the total product curve would then be equal to the total cost curve. Unfortunately, for reasons which will be apparent shortly, and because of convention in such matters, we will have to reverse our axes, so that total output is now on the horizontal axis, and total cost is on the vertical axis. The next step is to prepare the same kinds of marginal and average curves relating to total cost as we did for total product. Now, however, we will be interested in the way in which total cost changes with changes in output. Before, we wanted to know the ways in which output changed with changes in one input. Because it is important that we retain our previous orientation, the axes will be labeled with both the cost and the machine time labels.

Figure 8-8(a) shows total cost as a function of output changes, assuming that cost changes are made up only of variable costs. Points A and B in this diagram are identical with those in Figure 8-7(a), as the curve is the same except

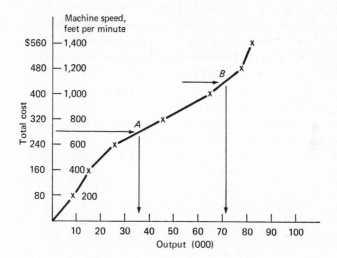

Figure 8-8(a). Total cost as a function of output. Machine inputs shown paralleling cost levels.

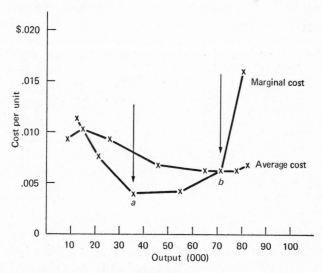

Figure 8-8(b). Average and marginal cost.

for the transposition of the axes. Notice that when we go to Figure 8-8(b), where curves of average and marginal cost are now shown, points A-a and B-b depict places where costs are a minimum. That is to say, A-a is the place at which we have reached the point of diminishing returns as regards cost, and at this point, marginal cost is a minimum and rises thereafter. This corresponds to the same point in the previous diagram, Figure 8-7, where marginal productivity is a maximum. At point B-b, the increase in cost is not at a decreasing rate, but at an increasing rate, and marginal cost rises above the average cost beyond this point. This corresponds to the points in the prior diagram in which marginal product falls below average product. The data on which Figures 8-7 and 8-8 are based are given in Table 8-2.

TABLE 8-2. PRODUCTION AND COST DATA

Variable Input	Output Quantity	Marginal Production	Average Production	Total Cost	Average Cost	Marginal Cost
200	8,500⎱		42	$ 80	$.00941⎱	$.0114
400	15,500⎰	35	39	160	.01032⎰	.0076
600	26,000	52	43	240	.00923	.0040
800	46,000	100	57	320	.00696	.0042
1000	65,000	95	65	400	.00615	.0062
1200	78,000	65	65	480	.00616	.0160
1400	82,000	25	58	560	.00683	

LONG- AND SHORT-RUN COSTS

Thus far, we have discussed production models based on some empirically derived data and shown the basis for short-run cost behavior. Both the linear programming and the conventional continuous functions have been discussed. We want now to return briefly to empirical examples in which it is seen that for many studies of cost behavior, available data will not allow the kinds of constructs we have used. This is especially true under generally used accounting and budgeting methods discussed elsewhere, involving linear cost functions or factors. It turns out that, instead of developing cost curves as we have described them, a different kind of cost-output relation must be developed. Instead of a cost curve depicting the response of output to changes in inputs, at least one factor being fixed, a curve is drawn made up of those points on the former curve which have been discovered by experimentation and research. Let us see how this comes about.

Figure 8-9 shows the estimated processing cost for fluid milk. A unique aspect of this study is that separate curves are available for plants designed especially for butter production and those designed to produce other dairy products as well. In this diagram, the curves are made up of the minimum operating cost points of a number of separate plants. Cobia and Babb have summarized a

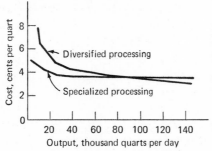

Figure 8-9. Processing costs for fluid milk. (Source: National Commission on Food Marketing, *Organization and Competition in the Dairy Industry*, Technical Study No. 3, U.S. Government Printing Office, June, 1966, p. 297, containing reference to D. W. Cobia and E. M. Babb, *Determining the Optimum Size of Fluid Milk Processing Plant and Sales Area*, Purdue University Agricultural Research Station, Research Bulletin No. 778, May, 1964, pp. 5–9.)

number of studies estimating unit processing costs at various levels of production and capacity utilization.

In general, as the volume of milk processed increases, the unit cost of processing declines, and this relation continues, in theory, up to the limit of the design capacity of the plant. Costs decline fairly rapidly up to 50 percent of capacity, and then more slowly. Large plants have more leeway, since they can vary operations over a wider volume range without significant changes in unit costs, because fixed costs are a smaller proportion of total cost. In other words, a large section of the short-run average cost curve is flat for large plants.

The relationship between the curves in Figure 8-9 and the individual cost curves for the firm developed earlier may be illustrated in the following two diagrams. First, we have, in Figure 8-10, curves for the processing costs for two plants producing butter powder. Next, in Figure 8-11, we have a series of curves for retail food stores, with each curve representing a store of different size.

In Figure 8-10, it is instructive to note that plant 1, at its peak output of 170,000 pounds per day, is able to reduce its costs to $.42 per 100 pounds. Plant 2, at peak output of 360,000 pounds, is able to lower costs to $.35. However, for plant 2 to operate at the same percent capacity as plant 1 is not economical; its costs are then higher by about $.06 per hundredweight. The economies made possible by larger-scale production are evident. But before going further, let us look at Figure 8-11 for retail food stores of various physical size. Here we note that operating efficiency is the same, regardless of size of store, with each curve minimum at about $6 per square foot. The efficiency does

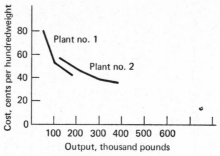

Figure 8-10. Processing costs for two plants manufacturing butter powder. (Source: National Commission on Food Marketing, *Organization and Competition in the Dairy Industry,* Technical Study No. 3, U.S. Government Printing Office, June, 1966, p. 182, containing reference to Lindley E. Juers, *An Economic Analysis of Butter Powder Plants with Particular Reference to the Problem of Joint Costs,* unpublished doctoral dissertation, University of Minnesota, 1957.)

not translate into an equal efficiency in terms of sales, however, where smaller stores are at a disadvantage.

The curves in Figure 8-9 are analogous to the bottom shallow curve marked *B* in Figure 8-11. The curves in Figure 8-10 are analogous to the shorter reverse J-shaped curves in Figure 8-11, which are marked *A*. These last are the kinds of cost curves we derived in the earlier sections of the chapter and which

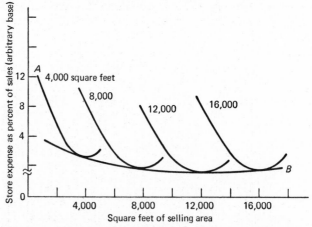

Figure 8-11. Relationship of store expense (as percent of sales) to size of store in square feet. (Source: National Commission on Food Marketing, *Organization and Competition in Food Retailing,* Technical Study No. 7, U.S. Government Printing Office, June, 1966, p. 143.)

we termed average unit cost curves. They are related to the productivity apparatus in the manner shown.

The former—B in Figure 8-11, for example—is the envelope or locus of points of all of the short-run curves derived as in Figure 8-11. Now we are ready to make several points.

First, if one attempts to draw a cost function by obtaining empirical data on cost and output from firms in an industry, the curve describing these data will in all probability look like those in Figure 8-9. That is to say, one will obtain sets of cost and production data for different firms having differing production functions, but operating in the same time period.

Second, such a curve does not describe the relationship of cost to changes in volume for the affected firms, because these kinds of changes follow the smaller, short-run, J-shaped curves of Figures 8-10 and 8-11. The functional differences come about because one firm altering its output level but not its production function (plant remaining the same) is not the same as a firm acquiring another plant or adding to its capacity. When a firm adds to capacity, it either changes its production function, thus acquiring a new short-run cost curve tangent to the long-run curve at a point to the right, or if the production function is the same, then it has added to all inputs in the same proportions as before and does not allow one or more to remain fixed, as is true of the short-run curves.

Third, we can use such a long-run curve for production planning pur poses if it represents the effect on cost of a change in scale of operation

A change in scale comes about when, using Figure 8-6 as reference, both inputs are allowed to vary. The total product curve we then obtain is drawn, not by drawing a horizontal line at one input level and allowing the other input to vary, but by drawing a line from the origin upward and to the right so that increasing output becomes a function of increases in both inputs. We then have a change in scale of operation and the resultant cost curve looks like curve B in Figure 8-11, rather than like curve A. With qualification, economists refer to such a curve as a long-run cost curve or planning curve.

To be a long-run cost curve, such a curve must represent the locus of minimum cost points for the different production levels, where we define minimum very carefully. It does not mean, for instance, that one connects all the lowest points of the short-run curves that fit inside the envelope. It means that, with reference to Figure 8-11, the curve will represent lowest cost alternatives open to a firm in an economic setting in which resources are infinitely divisible and plant size may easily be altered. So, for the 4,000-square-foot store operating at the point in its short-run cost curve where it touches the long-run curve, a move to the right will be to the lowest cost on its curve, but the real cost minimum is in theory below that point on the long-run curve. Hence, a firm which operates to the left of the minimum on the planning curve can never be really functioning at minimum cost because the lowest point on its short-run curve is above the corresponding point on the long-run curve. For each production level at more or less than the long-run minimum, the short-run curve minimum will always lie above the minimum dictated by the long-run curve.

The data obtained by empirical analysis obviously will not be quite the same as the economist's planning curve requirements, because reported cost-production points may represent varying levels on short-run curves, and unless we include information on the proportion of plant capacity used, we will not be able to evaluate it. Second, the economist assumes that movements along the curve are in response to changes in scale and not really to changes in technology, while in practice differences do occur in firms of differing size.

Many times, differences in cost arising out of movements along the long-run curve are confused with differences arising out of movements along the short-run curve. Cost reductions arising out of mass production, for instance, are not evidence that one has in some way invalidated the law of diminishing returns. When a firm engages in mass production, it is moving out along the long-run curve or has changed its production function, so that all inputs may be said to have changed. Hence, what is pointed to are returns to scale and not returns resulting from changes in inputs, one input being unchanged.

In Figure 8-11, the long-run cost curve marked B shows a tendency toward decreasing returns to scale from 12,000 square feet of selling area upward, and increasing returns to 12,000 square feet, when cost is considered as a percentage of sales. Most such curves are drawn in this shallow saucerlike shape, in theory, because of what the economist Alfred Marshall termed "external economies and diseconomies of scale." A new firm getting underway is pioneering in its technology, or new firms are having difficulty in getting established for one reason or another. Sometimes there is not sufficient volume to use certain inputs effectively, or certain processes cannot operate efficiently at low volumes. Over time, however, the firms become established employers for a particular kind of labor, and a market develops for their product. Their technology becomes more known, and labor becomes more accustomed to the kinds of work demanded, so that they become more efficient and, in all, the production process becomes more efficient as the scale of production expands. Beyond some point, the firm must bid for resources from other firms in other lines, and natural resources become more limited. An attempt to build a larger plant means, as we have seen in Chapter 2, that costs do not become lower but in fact rise, because of difficulties in management accruing from mere size limits to the productivity of given processes, and so the curve rises. Another reason lies in the bottleneck costs to which we referred in connection with the analysis of short-run costs.

At what point the long-run cost curve actually rises is open to some debate. Studies of improvements in technology, as for example computers and automated processes, seem to indicate that, in general, in many lines of industry and trade, curves will not turn up. But if these curves do not turn up, then it would appear that the long-run marginal cost curve will remain below the average cost curve for all increases in output. The conclusion is then that any firm that is able to attain a size larger than others in the field will operate at costs which are lower and will thus have a self-perpetuating advantage. Thus, the first firm in the field to attain significant advantages in output levels will attain a competitive advantage which others will not be able to best. Such a condition quite naturally leads to concentration in industry, and, as we have seen, concentration is by no means an unusual outcome.

With regard to the short-run cost curve, theory generally holds that at some point or another, cost will rise, thereby accounting for the U or reverse-J shape of our average unit cost curves and the J shape of our marginal cost curves. Here again, we are in fact on somewhat uncertain ground. Empirical studies indicate that in many cases the short-run average unit cost curve is rather flat over a large part of the production range, because of the particular technology involved.[7] Where this kind of condition exists, as we shall see when we discuss pricing, changes in production volume have no effect on cost levels, and the nice equilibrium mechanisms, assumed by theory to establish the level of production, in many cases do not work.

SUMMARY

In this chapter, we have seen something of the way in which cost behavior is grounded, both in the physical and technical nature of processes and in the way the processes are organized. We have discussed the ways in which output varies with the rate of input and the idea of input substitution to maximize outputs within resource limitations. Also, we have seen how the modern technique of linear programming is based on earlier models of economic theory. Finally, we explored both the ramifications in developing cost curves from empirical data and the concept of the envelope or planning cost curve.

In the appendix, we present a mathematical solution to the product-mix problem, using a linear programming approach known as the method of inspection of the vertices.

Appendix. The Product-mix Problem

The problem illustrated in Figure 8-5 may be dealt with mathematically by a method known as inspection of the vertices.[8]

---

[7] See, for example, Joel Dean, *Managerial Economics*, Prentice-Hall, Inc., Englewood Cliffs, N.J., 1951, chap. 5.

[8] See, for example, Richard I. Levin and C. A. Kirkpatrick, *Quantitative Approaches to Management*, McGraw-Hill Book Company, New York, 1965, chap. 8.

We begin with the following matrix of the number of hours required per item per machine:

	Machines		
Product	M_1	M_2	M_3
A	7.5	6.0	3.75
B	7.5	12.0	15.00

As the maximum work week is 60 hours, and A and B require each machine, we have

$$7.5X_1 + 7.5X_2 \leqslant 60 \qquad (M_1)$$

where X_1 is the number of A's that can be made, X_2 is the number of B's, and no more than 60 hours of running time may be programmed. For the others, we have

$$6X_1 + 12X_2 \leqslant 60 \qquad (M_2)$$
$$3.75X_1 + 15X_2 \leqslant 60 \qquad (M_3)$$

Assuming we are to work the full 60 hours, we can change the inequalities to equalities and solve the resultant set of equations for X_1 and X_2.

Since the feasible region is bounded by the constraint M_1 when A only is produced, we can solve equation M_1 for X_1 by setting X_2 equal to zero.

$$75.X_1 + 7.5(0) = 60$$
$$X_1 = 8$$

We next want to solve M_1 and M_2 for the point at which they have equal X_1 and X_2 values (point G).

$$7.5X_1 + 7.5X_2 = 60 \qquad (M_1)$$
$$6.0X_1 + 12.0X_2 = 60 \qquad (M_2)$$

Solving for X_1 and X_2, we find

$$X_1 = 6$$
$$X_2 = 2$$

Point H is similarly found as the solution of equations M_2 and M_3, and is found to be

$$X_1 = 4$$
$$X_2 = 3$$

Point I is of course defined M_3 when X_1 equals zero and becomes

$$X_1 = 0$$
$$X_2 = 4$$

We now have four sets of feasible product combinations. With constant returns to scale, it will always pay the firm to expand outward from the origin to the limit of one or more inputs. Just which direction we will go depends on our equating the ratio of the marginal revenues to the ratio of the marginal physical products for each process.

To make this comparison, we simply maximize our objective function, which is actually the sum of the products of the marginal revenues and the output quantities. The function here is, of course,

$$TR = 1.10X_1 + 1.80X_2$$

and we substitute each set of X_1 and X_2 values to determine which provides a maximum TR.

For point F we have

$$TR = 1.10(8) + 1.80(0) = \$8.80$$

Similarly for the others

(G)	$1.10(6) + 1.80(2) =$	10.20
(H)	$1.10(4) + 1.80(3) =$	9.80
(I)	$1.10(0) + 1.80(4) =$	7.20

We see that G defines the production quantities having maximum value. At that point, the isorevenue line intersects M_1 and M_2. Assuming no M_2 constraints, M_1 and M_3 will produce $5\frac{1}{3}$ units of A and $2\frac{2}{3}$ units of B.

$$7.5\ X_1 + 7.5X_2 = 60 \qquad (M_1)$$
$$\underline{3.75X_1 + 15.0X_2 = 60 \qquad (M_3)}$$
$$X_1 = 5.33;\ X_2 = 2.67$$

The desired quantity multiplied by the technological coefficients for M_2 yields the following:

$$5.33(6) + 2.67(12) = 64.02,$$

or 4.02 hours in excess of the allowed limit.

The increase in output at prevailing prices is

$$1.10(5.33) + 1.80(2.67) = 10.67$$
$$1.10(6.00) + 1.80(2.00) = \underline{10.20}$$
$$\text{Revenue increase } \$\quad .47$$

Review Questions

1. Comment on the statement, "All well-conceived production operations operate in the region of diminishing returns. . . ."
2. How would you go about deriving a capital-labor substitution curve?
3. Comment on the statement, "There are no capital costs in flying a fully depreciated airplane."

4. Explain what is meant by the term "optimum." How are tradeoffs used to attain optima? Illustrate a constant-benefit tradeoff.
5. What characteristics of modern industry make it difficult to apply the marginal analysis?
6. What assumptions made in linear programming are not made in the marginal analysis?
7. How does linear programming use the concept of opportunity cost in arriving at solutions?
8. If the total cost of production for a product may be approximated by the equation

$$TC = -30,089 + 0.77Q + .70W$$

where TC = total cost, Q = quantity of output, and W = weight of materials used, in pounds.

(a) Sketch the TC, AC, and MC curves of the producing firm, assuming that $Q = W$.
(b) Comment on the possible reasons for the existence of such a relationship between cost and output.
(c) Sketch the probable nature of the isoquant map.
(d) Assuming the diagram to represent a statistically derived curve from data reported by a number of plants, assess its significance.
9. Differentiate between diminishing returns and returns to scale.
10. Compare reasons why the short-run average cost curve and the long-run average cost curve are believed to rise as quantity produced increases.

Case 1. Baking Plant Costs (continued)

In Chapter 7, the text refers to the possibility that the correct variable cost curve might lie along the bottom of several short-run cost curves. In Chapter 8, we discussed the planning curve or envelope.

QUESTION

1. Using the data in Chapter 7, Case 2, apply this concept of the envelope. What are the implications for the industry?

Case 2. A Problem in Isoquants

The following information shows the effect of nitrogen on the production of corn:

Nitrogen Applied (pounds per acre)	Cultivation Labor per Month (man-hours)			
	3	4	5	6
0	70.1	75.1	81.1	86.8
50	71.3	80.5	91.5	97.7
100	72.8	87.3	102.8	109.7
150	74.0	93.0	110.0	115.2
200	75.2	97.0	113.0	120.7

QUESTIONS

1. Construct an isoquant map. *See pg. 216, 8-6 (a)*
2. Construct curves of total, average, and marginal physical productivity for labor.
3. Assuming labor to cost $3 per hour and fertilizer to cost $.05 per pound, draw in an isocost line on the map in question 1 above.
4. Suppose a farmer is currently producing 81.1 bushels per acre using 6 man-hours per acre and no fertilizer. If he wished to reduce his labor input to 5 manhours, approximately how much fertilizer would be required to compensate? At the input prices given, would this be a wise decision? *should be 86.8*
5. Draw in or emphasize the isoquant for 80 bushels per acre on your diagram. Move to the right along the isoquant and periodically calculate the fertilizer marginal substitution rates associated with decreases in man-hours used. Locate the most efficient location on the isoquant given the price ratios of the inputs.

$\Delta N/\Delta L$

Case 3. The Alpha Company

The Alpha Company makes two principal products: the Beta and the Gamma. Both of these products require processing time in three departments as shown below:

Department	Capacity of Departments	Products	
		Beta	Gamma
Fabrication	100	8	1
Painting	50	1	1
Assembly	100	1	4

The factory manager notes that the Beta makes a contribution toward profit (excess of sales price over variable costs) of $100,000, whereas the Gamma makes a per unit profit contribution of $80,000. The

ability to produce either product is limited by the processing capacity in each
department.

QUESTIONS

1. If one produced only Betas, what would be the maximum profit contribution?
2. If the remaining time were used to produce Gammas, what profit would
   result?
3. Solve this problem graphically.
4. Calculate the optimal production quantities which will maximize profit, subject to the capacity constraints.
5. How much idle time is left over? If you were asked to do some extra work
   which would use the remainder of that capacity, what would be a proper expense charge?
6. What is the "value" of an hour of processing in the assembly department? If
   you were offered a device which would increase the capacity of the assembly
   department by fifty hours, would you buy it at a cost of $15,000 per hour?
   $20,000 per hour? (Note: Verify the possible increase in profit contribution
   by recalculating, subject to the revised assembly department constraint.)
   (This case is adapted from John W. Coughlan, *Federal Contributions to
   Operations Research,* Program of Policy Studies in Science and Technology
   (mimeo.), The George Washington University, Washington, D.C., Dec. 5,
   1968.)

Suggested Reading

Dorfman, Robert, Paul A. Samuelson, and Robert M. Solow: *Linear Programming
and Economic Analysis,* McGraw-Hill Book Company, New York, 1958,
pp. 130–203.

Frisch, Ragnar: *Theory of Production,* Rand McNally & Company, Chicago,
1960, chaps. 5 and 6.

Johnson, J.: *Statistical Cost Analysis,* McGraw-Hill Book Company, New York,
1960, chaps. 5 and 6.

Staehle, Hans: "The Measurement of Statistical Cost Functions," *The American
Economic Review,* Vol. 32, pp. 321–333, 1942, reprinted in *Readings in
Price Theory,* Richard D. Irwin, Inc., Homewood, Ill., 1952, pp. 264–279.

Viner, Jacob, "Cost Curves and Supply Curves," *Zeitschrift für Na-
tionalökonomie,* vol. 3, pp. 23–46, 1931, reprinted in *Readings in Price
Theory,* Richard D. Irwin, Inc., Homewood, Ill., 1952, pp. 198–232.

part 3

pricing

chapter 9
pricing policy

Under pure competition, a firm has no control over its price, hence no problem of formulating a policy as to price. The problem of establishing a price policy arises only when a firm has some influence on the demand for its product, and therefore, a certain degree of freedom in setting price. This degree of freedom varies directly with the amount of monopolistic power the firm possesses.

In this chapter, we shall examine pricing policies assuming the firm wishes to maximize anticipated profit.[1] Pricing policy will vary depending on whether one is concerned with a new product or with an established one, as well as on the nature of competitive conditions in each instance.

We have noted, for instance, that a manufactured good has a life cycle similar to that of man. In other words, we can identify the stages of birth, development and growth, maturity, decline, and death. The importance of life cycle to pricing policy lies in the fact that the product may be found to have differing price elasticities of demand at various stages in its life.

Factors responsible for changes in price elasticity throughout its life are (1) novelty, (2) the springing up of substitutes, (3) the length of time needed for demander's consumption patterns to adjust to new products, and (4) the degree of market saturation.

[1] Naturally the decisions which a businessman must make are rarely simple and as clear cut as choosing the most profitable from among several well-defined possibilities. But, "it seems obvious that, if a businessman has the choice of actions leading to two outcomes which are identical in every respect except that one will give a higher profit than the other, we will choose the most profitable one." Karl Henrik Borch, *The Economics of Uncertainty*, Princeton University Press, Princeton, N.J., 1968, p. 167.

In pricing a new product, two commonly used competitive strategies are "skimming" and "penetration," and each calls for a different policy. Depending on the stage of the life cycle and on the price elasticity of demand, either strategy will be elected.

In pricing an established product on the other hand, we may employ incremental cost pricing or full cost pricing. Here competitive conditions assume relatively more importance. When competitive conditions are keen, we may employ an incremental cost policy. When we have some degree of control over our market, we may elect to use full cost as the basis for price. We may also adhere to full cost if the kinked demand curve is descriptive of market conditions. But whether a firm is able to price so that profit is maximized, in a theoretically correct sense, is an open question.

In the first instance, conventional economic theory is an enormous simplification of the real world, as we already pointed out in Chapter 1. The production function itself is a considerable approximation, and because of the vast number of decisions which must be made to insure optimum output, there is a good deal of doubt that the precise output of a production process can be predicted. If it cannot be predicted, then the firm cannot really be sure of the relationship between inputs, outputs, and prices, except in a very general way.

Also it must be observed that the firm itself makes an impact on the environment in which it operates. The prices at which the firm buys or sells cannot be said to be independent of the amounts bought or sold. Perhaps if the firm were to sell less, the price of its product would be higher; perhaps if it were to buy less, its purchase price would be higher or perhaps lower depending on circumstances. In the first instance, the purchase price might be higher if one were thinking merely of discounts for quantity. On the other hand, if the amount bought represents a substantial amount of the market, it might drive the price up.

Undoubtedly also, were we to analyze the actual pricing decisions made by businessmen, we would find that there were other decisions that would have been better, in the sense that they would have yielded more profit. But no one has claimed that businessmen are infallible and the fact that they do not set prices at which profit is maximized may not mean that they did not try.[2]

PRICING OBJECTIVES

In making a pricing decision, the firm has to consider its pricing objectives, the pricing policy it has enunciated in support of these objectives, and its specific pricing procedures.

[2] *Ibid.*

Pricing objectives of a firm may be classified as those designed to:

1. Achieve a given rate of return on invested capital
2. Maintain or improve share of market
3. Differentiate its product or create an image
4. Break into a new market
5. Maintain price stability

RATE OF RETURN

For a given policy, the rate of return on invested capital depends to a large extent on the degree of monopoly power it possesses. Since a firm has the option it may, by a wise combination of make-or-buy decisions, succeed in raising its return on invested capital far above its competitors by producing only those items which it can produce efficiently and contracting from other efficient producers for the remainder.

Each firm generally calculates a target rate of return it expects to earn on its investment in its capital assets. The rates vary among firms within the same industry, partly because of production policy as indicated, and partly because of the superior quality of the product, including its design and style.

Some typical after-tax target rates of return reputedly are: General Motors — 20 percent, Aluminum Company of America — 10 percent, International Harvester Company — 10 percent, United States Steel — 8 percent. Rates of return for manufacturing firms are generally higher than those for public utilities, the latter being regulated by state and, in some cases, federal agencies. Some explanation for differences in rates of return may be found, of course, in simple inertia. A new president taking office may, many times, adopt the same target rate of return as that of his predecessor, simply because he can see no particular benefit in adjusting it.

SHARE OF THE MARKET

To maintain or improve the market share for the firm's product implies pricing a product or products to meet competition. If a firm has a 20 percent share of the market, its sales volume will increase as the market expands, either because of higher consumer income or because more consumers come into the market or both, provided it can maintain its current market share. The market share currently held may already give the firm a favorable rate of return, and if the firm can keep it that way, the earlier objective can be met. For example, for a number of years after World War II General Motors maintained an automobile market share between 46 and 54 percent, even though the firm had not admitted this as one of its goals.[3] Another example is Swift & Co. Kaplan, Dirlam, and Lanzilotti conclude from their study of business pricing that

> the fact that Swift's position in the industry has changed little over the past three censuses of manufacture suggests to the outside observer that overtly or subconsciously the company's activities stem from the objective of remaining a leading factor in the national market. The long-term policy involved in this approach may manifest itself in the company's response to long-term expectations of growth in consumer demand with plans for sharing in that growth. In sum, the mainspring of Swift's pricing policy, if it be said to have one at all, is the maintenance or improvement of its position in the meat industry; and beyond that, the development of specialties that can be differentiated so as to win a market at price levels that will yield a margin above the company's average return.[4]

DIFFERENTIATING THE PRODUCT

To differentiate its product or to create an image of prestige for its product is a common objective of a firm. As indicated in Chapter 2, product differentiation is an essential feature of monopolistic competition, and pricing policy can be used to achieve that goal. For example, the relatively higher prices for jewelry at Tiffany & Co. and the pricing policy for the Continental Mark III by

---

[3] In the 1955 congressional hearings on the factors affecting the stock market, conducted by the Senate Committee on Banking and Currency under the chairmanship of J. W. Fulbright, Harlow H. Curtice, then president of General Motors, was confronted with the question of how large a market share of automobiles General Motors was planning to have. The dialogue went like this:

> The Chairman: . . . The sole question here is, that here was an opportunity to expand your market if you so desired. You had $192 million, you might say, to play with. But you choose to carry all of that in the net profit and to devote none of it to obtaining a wider market to increase your sales. You will admit that the normal procedure is, if you lower prices you will sell more of nearly any article in a competitive market. Is that not true?
> Mr. Curtis: The lower the price the more you sell, if the product you are offering at a lower price has a field.
> The Chairman: . . . Do you really desire to have 60 percent of the market?
> Mr. Curtis: As I pointed out in my brief, we have to keep aggressively competitive in all areas in order to make sure to maintain even our position.
> The Chairman: That is not what I asked you. I asked you if you would like to have 60 percent of the motor car market or not?
> Mr. Curtis: We have no control over the public's approval of the products we offer.
> The Chairman: No, but you can tell me whether or not you would like to, regardless of what it has to do with the public. There is nothing to prevent you from saying yes or no. It is a simple question. Would you like 60 percent?
> Mr. Curtis: I would answer this way: We would hope to continue to be a successful corporation.
> The Chairman: Would you like 55 percent of the total sales?
> Mr. Curtis: We might very well get 55 percent, but it will be very difficult to achieve.
> The Chairman: But it will be against your will and better judgment?
> Mr. Curtis: No.

Stock Market Study, Hearings before the Senate Banking and Currency Committee on Factors Affecting the Buying and Selling of Equity Securities, 84th Cong., 1st Sess., 1955, pp. 830–831.
[4] A. D. H. Kaplan, J. B. Dirlam, and R. F. Lanzilotti, *Pricing in Big Business, A Case Approach,* The Brookings Institution, Washington, 1958, pp. 187–188.

Ford Motor Co. are two well-known examples of using price to create an image of prestige. One peculiar feature of pricing policy to meet this objective is that within a given range the higher the price for a product, the more the customers are willing to buy.[5] Such a phenomenon gives rise to a demand curve which starts out with a positive rather than negative slope, and then bends backward, as indicated in Figure 9-1. When the price of a competing product is lowered, the price of the "prestige" product may have to be reduced also. However, by virtue of product differentiation, a firm can soften or delay the impact on its own prices of price reduction by its competitors. In some cases, particularly where price lining has succeeded in creating a clear difference in product image, the reduction of competitors' prices has no effect whatsoever on the price of the "prestige" product. This same result may occur if the price difference is so great as to remove any notion of substitutability. Normally, of course, the degree of substitutability of one product for another increases as the price differential between the two widens. That is to say, the cross-elasticity between two products becomes greater as price differential becomes wider. For example, Chock-full-O'Nuts coffee in 1969 sold at a premium of $.09 per pound over Maxwell House coffee. It is very doubtful that the price of $.98 a pound for Chock-full-O'Nuts coffee could be maintained if the price of Maxwell House coffee were to be reduced by 20 percent. On the other hand, the price of a Rolls Royce Silver Shadow automobile can still be kept at more than $16,000 even if the price for a Cadillac Eldorado were to be cut by 80 percent, because for those wealthy individuals who might purchase a Rolls Royce, substitution of the lower-priced General Motors car is out of the question.

---

[5] It is quite possible, as we have indicated elsewhere, that this phenomenon is more true of instances in which the consumer has no way of judging quality except by price.

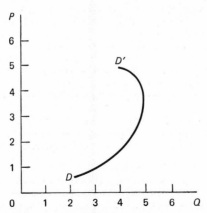

Figure 9-1. Backward-sloping demand curve.

BREAKING INTO A NEW MARKET

For companies wishing to diversify, an important pricing objective relates to breaking into a new market with a present product, or present markets with new products. A firm, in order to survive and prosper, has to develop new products to replace those reaching the maturity stage of their life cycle. The development and exploitation of new products leads to entry into new markets. There are numerous examples in this area and firms such as the General Electric Company and the Radio Corporation of America endeavor to branch out into new territories in order to keep on growing.[6]

PRICE STABILITY

Maintaining price stability as a pricing objective is a corollary of pricing a product in order to obtain a given rate of return on investment. Price stability refers to the absence of any sharp fluctuation in price. In other words, a firm has achieved the objective of maintaining price stability if it can keep the fluctuation within a narrow range, say 5 percent. If a company can maintain the same amount of sales year after year, it can achieve the objective of earning a target rate of return, provided, of course, that it can maintain the stability of prices of its products.[7] Moreover, the maintenance of price stability facilitates corporate planning for production and sales. This is because planning for production requires advance orders and commitments for labor and materials. The estimate of the required inputs and the revenue to be derived from the output can be made more easily if the firm can keep price changes within a narrow range.

It is important to note that maintaining price stability *and* maintaining a

---

[6] See illustrations in Chapter 2. The significance of product replacement is evident from an examination of kinds of items sold in any retail store. There are not many that are more than ten years old.

[7] Generally speaking, to maintain price stability is subordinate to the pricing objective of obtaining a given rate of return on invested capital. There are, however, some companies which put the former objective above the latter. Two examples are cited by Kaplan, Dirlam, and Lanzillotti: United States Steel Corporation and Kennecott Copper Corporation. "Factors considered essential to realization of certain major objectives of the steel industry are, first, stabilization of prices; secondly, protection of steel mill investments in the older, less favorably located centers of production vis-a-vis the more favorable locations of newer producers; and third, enlargement of the competitive market area of each steel plant. The focal point around which these objectives revolve is the United States Steel Corporation, which is generally recognized as the industry's price leader." E. T. Stannard, the late president of Kennecott Copper Corporation, is reported in 1949 as saying that "as he saw it, the instability of copper prices accentuated buying waves by customers and led to overexpansion in the industry on the upturns. When the price of copper skyrocketed, customers lived off their stocks, and demand fell off very sharply." Stannard earlier told the Temporary National Economic Committee (1939) ". . . if we could have uniform business, and let us say the price of copper was 21 cents per pound, it would be a fine thing for the copper industry and a fine thing for the fabricators and the consumers of copper if the price of copper did not fluctuate more than an eighth of a cent per pound per month." *Op. cit.*, pp. 166–176.

given share of the market are not compatible objectives when the firm's competitors begin to revise price either upward or downward. In order to keep a given market share, the firm has to change its price accordingly; otherwise, its market share may be either larger or smaller depending upon the direction the competitors change their prices.

PRICING PROCEDURE

Where pricing policies are the courses top management will take in pricing the firm's products so as to achieve certain preconceived objectives, such as earning a given rate of return or maintaining a given share of the market, pricing procedures may be thought of as the steps taken in setting or adjusting a price. We can distinguish pricing procedure from pricing policy by noting that procedure consists of the formulas or rules used by the firm in setting price. The use of conventional margins between tank wagon and tank car gasoline prices in selling to distributors is one example of the application of pricing procedure. Cyert and March's retail pricing model is another example of routinized pricing. This model shows, for example, that a rule for department store pricing, for some lines in a department studied, is to establish prices that end in .95 and which provide a margin of 40 percent. Pricing procedure then is to divide the cost of the item by .60 and raise or lower the result to the nearest 95-cent figure. Some rules used for testing the applicability of a given price are:

1. Has the competitor reduced his price?
2. Is the customer being given an allowance?
3. Is there a need for a special promotion?
4. Is the merchandise shopworn or soiled?
5. Is the merchandise a postseason return?
6. Was the wholesale price reduced?
7. Is the merchandise substandard?
8. Is the price controlled by the manufacturer?
9. Is this a closeout?

These rules and others were used in the store studied in addition to the more customary procedures relating prices to merchandise turnover. That is to say, merchandise which failed to sell at prevailing prices would of course be subject to markdown, and these rules are in addition to the application of the rules for price adjustment given above.[8]

[8] Richard M. Cyert and James G. March, *A Behavioral Theory of the Firm*, Prentice-Hall, Inc., Englewood Cliffs, N.J., 1963, Chap. 7.

In our discussion of standard cost pricing, we will note that the steps used to arrive at price, such as selecting a standard volume and applying a given markup or margin, are also examples of pricing procedure.

FULL COST PRICING

Earlier we referred to the four different policies a firm may follow. The first of these is full cost pricing, and the procedure most often used to implement this policy is termed "cost-plus" or standard cost pricing. This policy is by far the basic pricing policy because other pricing policies, such as skimming price policy or penetration price policy, evolve about it. Furthermore, it is long term in nature because it is used year-in and year-out, while incremental cost pricing, when employed, generally is for short-run purposes and under particular conditions. Full cost pricing is also known as target rate pricing because one of the components of the full cost is the amount of profit the management hopes to attain. The target rate refers to a desired return on investment calculated by expressing attained profit as a percent of net assets.

Establishing Full Cost Pricing. In establishing a full cost price for its product, a firm begins with an estimate of expected production volume for the fiscal or other suitable time period. The volume estimate is of course based on the procedures discussed in earlier chapters. The next step is to compute the estimated capacity of the firm or plant. The estimated or rated capacity depends on a number of factors such as the particular product mix, expected losses due to quality standards, capability of the work force, and expected down time for maintenance. Many times, rated capacity is affected by the operational procedures used. Certain products are more efficiently produced by job shop procedures; others benefit from more typical assembly line layouts. We also have to consider the extent to which parts of output will be purchased rather than made.

Capacity may be measured in terms of dollars of sales, but without additional information on product mix and price it cannot be compared with preceding time periods. Manpower-hours or machine-hours of input often are used as expressions of capacity, but unless man-hours are matched with machine-hours and all machines can produce all products, it is better to calculate output in terms of product of specific kind and size.

Stigler states that capacity should be defined in terms of the volume of output that can be obtained at a level of unit cost at which long-run and short-run marginal costs are equal. Others contend that capacity is best measured where short-run average cost is a minimum. In any case, we are not concerned with that output which might be obtained at literally prohibitive cost.[9]

The emphasis on the time element in defining capacity results from the fact that theoretically as well as practically a company can continue to expand its plant capacity so long as the demand for the product continues to increase. Therefore, unless time is held constant, there would be no limitation on plant capacity. Suppose for example, an air conditioner manufacturer has only one plant and it can produce 12,000 units of a single uniform product a year, if it operates on an eight-hour shift per day basis. Let us assume further that because of seasonal shutdowns and holidays, the firm operates only nine months out of a year and therefore is capable of producing only 9,000 units of air conditioners on a year-in and year-out basis. In other words, the plant is utilized only up to 75 percent of its capacity.

The next step is to designate this level of output as the standard volume. That is, we define standard volume as the volume of production that the firm is able to achieve on a year-in and year-out basis. This standard volume is set up in order to calculate the average total cost per unit of output which it is expected will be maintained over a number of years. The average total cost is the standard cost, which is defined as the "predetermined cost for each operation, or each unit of finished product . . . intended to represent the value of direct material, direct labor, and manufacturing burden normally required under efficient conditions at normal capacity to process a unit of product."[10]

Standard cost per unit of output is then the total predetermined cost divided by the standard number of units or the number representing standard volume. Actual average total cost may vary from standard for a number of reasons, among which are variation in output, changes in the effectiveness and efficiency of labor, and differences in the quality and cost of materials.

When we add to this standard cost a given amount of markup over cost for profit, we have the full cost price. How much markup will be depends, among other things, on the target rate of return on the investment that management

[9] George J. Stigler, *The Theory of Price*, 3d ed., The Macmillan Company, New York, 1966, p. 157. See also Irving Abromowitz, *Production Management*, The Ronald Press Company, New York, 1967, Chap. 2 and 3, for a discussion of capacity definition.
[10] E. A. Green, *National Association of Cost Accountants Bulletin*, vol. 16, cited in *Accountants' Handbook*, 1944, p. 255. Normal capacity varies with each industry: For example, General Motors Corporation designates 80 percent of its plant capacity as the standard volume, but prior to World War II, it used only 50 percent. United States Steel also designates 80 percent of its plant facility as the normal capacity, while Aluminum Company of America uses only 70 percent of its plant capacity.

hopes to obtain. The following example shows how the calculation is made:

Total fixed cost	$1,000,000
Total variable cost at standard volume	$5,000,000
Total cost at standard volume	$6,000,000
Standard volume of output a year	600,000 units
Standard cost per unit	$10
Total invested capital (long-term)	$6,000,000
Target rate of return after taxes	20 percent
Amount of after-tax profit required	$1,200,000
Profit markup per unit of product	$2
Price (full cost) per unit of product	$12
Total sales based on standard volume	$7,200,000

Annual sales of the firm of course may be higher than the anticipated $7,200,000, and in that case, profit after taxes would be higher than the indicated $1,200,000. In fact, the after-tax profit as a percent of sales will increase faster than sales because, conceptually speaking, units sold in excess of the standard volume bear no fixed cost since all fixed cost has been allocated to the standard volume. On the other hand, if this company's production and sales in a given year fall below the standard volume of 600,000 units, its after-tax profit will decrease at a faster rate than sales because all of the fixed cost has to be absorbed by a smaller number of units of output than the standard volume.[11] Total fixed cost of a firm is presumed to be stable and unchanging as it has been earlier defined, and hence the smaller the number of units produced, the larger the fixed cost per unit.

Advantages of Standard Cost Pricing. The businessman prefers standard cost to average actual cost as a measure of so-called "full" costs because, for one thing, average cost is a historical phenomenon. One knows one's average cost only in the past, while standard cost is the method that a businessman has of forecasting the future. Having used standard costs to forecast, he then relates the actual average experience to the standard and attempts to find out what went wrong either with his operation or with his method of constructing the standard.

Second, businessmen are basically concerned with covering their fixed costs, and the standard cost method insures that all costs are covered. Third, standard cost pricing is used because it allows the firm to make up price lists even before actual production begins. This advantage is especially important

[11] We assume that the sales-to-inventory ratio remains constant, so that the company produces the same amount as it sells in a given time period, and also that the price remains unchanged.

to those firms whose products take a long time to produce, as for example, heavy industrial products or durable household goods.

Standard cost pricing has a fourth advantage in that it eliminates frequent price fluctuation within short periods because standard cost is not affected by output variation. If a firm has to quote a full cost price for its product on an actual volume of production basis, the price may well vary in the short run. Furthermore, continual variation of price may make it difficult to solicit customers' orders in advance.

Stability of price is important in many industries whose products are used by others as raw materials. In negotiating a long-term supply contract, a common occurrence in heavy industry materials, price stability is essential. It may take a long time to finish producing one unit of product, as in shipbuilding or heavy machine tool manufacturing, and it is almost impossible for the producer to quote the price of the output to a prospective customer if the price of input materials is expected to fluctuate greatly.

Standard cost pricing is consistent with target return on investment management procedure.[12] Since standard cost pricing incorporates a given amount of profit required by the target rate of return on investment criterion, if all the units of output based on standard volume production are sold, then, so long as the plant facilities are not changed, profit markup per unit of output is constant. Furthermore, the desired rate of return would be earned on the average if the actual annual production averages standard volume.

Standard cost pricing is of course particularly suitable for industries in which there is price leadership. The leader can either use his own costs or apply a standard costing procedure based on industry maxima which will provide an umbrella for higher-cost producers. Under this situation, there would be uniform pricing in the whole industry. Such a pricing system greatly simplifies the task of the individual businessman, in the way that using a flat-rate manual makes auto repair pricing simple.

Limitations of Full Cost Pricing. Notwithstanding its usefulness, there are some limitations on the use of full cost pricing with which one should be familiar. First, this type of pricing is practically useless for those industries whose products are perishable, where prices of raw materials fluctuate greatly. The meat-packing industry and many farm products are of this type. The price of cattle is very unstable because of the fluctuating supply of cattle, and the carcass price makes up the bulk of the cost of the finished product. Meat is very perishable and

[12] See Otto Eckstein and Gary Fromm, "The Price Equation," *The American Economic Review*, vol. 58, no. 5, Dec., 1968, for an interesting discussion of the relationship between standard cost pricing and the target return investment criterion.

storage is costly and difficult, so setting a standard volume of output on a year-round basis to allocate fixed cost is impractical.

Second, full cost pricing is not flexible enough to meet changes in demand. The price that consumers are willing to pay for a product often bears no close relation to what it cost a given firm to manufacture. This inflexibility also precludes the adoption of a reverse pricing policy for those products whose prices are already given in the markets. For example, International Harvester Company in 1955 reportedly withdrew from refrigerator manufacturing activity partly because prices for different styles of refrigerators were given, and it was necessary for the company to tailor its cost of production and of distribution accordingly if it wanted to break into the appliance market.

To illustrate this point further: A company desiring to produce candy bars has to price its product according to existing price lines, and the problem is to find out whether or not it can produce candy bars of conventional size at the going price. Here, full cost pricing procedures do not work, because we start out with the price of the product and then go back to find the cost of manufacturing and distribution of the product to see whether or not the product can be produced profitably. This kind of pricing policy is referred to as pricing at the market.

Third, full cost pricing is not based upon the concept of relevant cost, and therefore it is frequently not related to the pricing decision at hand. Under certain conditions, it is the incremental cost, not the full cost, which is relevant to the decision the top management has to make. This aspect of pricing decisions will be discussed more fully below.

Lastly, full cost pricing overstates the ability of management to allocate fixed cost precisely. If a firm produces only one product, then this problem does not exist. However, it is rare today to find a firm that produces only one product, and so, in a multiple-product company, the ability to allocate fixed cost appropriately to different product groups is needed in order to make full cost pricing meaningful.

INCREMENTAL OR DIRECT COST PRICING

Of all economic theories which have been used by business executives in their decision making, the incremental concept is most recent. It is, however, proving to be a very powerful tool. The incremental concept, mentioned in Chapter 1, is an extension of the marginal concept. It is like the marginal concept in that both of them deal with the impact of changes in input or output on revenue or cost. It is different from the marginal concept in that it is more flexible and adaptable to various situations including changes in cost as a result of a given decision which does not affect the number of units of output produced. The following three examples will illustrate this point: First, marginal revenue,

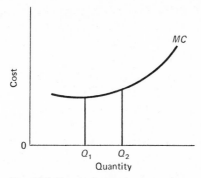

Figure 9-2. Marginal versus incremental cost.

by definition, is the additional revenue received by selling one more unit of the output. It is not difficult to understand this concept, but in the daily operation of a firm it is nearly impossible to measure revenue on a marginal basis, since no firm, with the exception of shipbuilding and perhaps aircraft and some heavy machine manufacturers, sells on a per item basis. On the other hand, a firm will have no trouble measuring revenue on an incremental basis, since all that is required is the increment in total revenue derived from some incremental output. Second, a firm may be operating under increasing marginal cost where inputs are not easily and smoothly related to output, as shown in Figure 9-2. It is troublesome to figure out the marginal cost within the production range of Q_1 to Q_2, because each marginal cost is different from the other. However, it is easy to tell how much the incremental cost will be for the same amount of output, because it is simply the summation of all marginal costs from Q_1 to Q_2. Third, when a firm reduces cost by employing modern and more efficient equipment or production process, the marginal concept is not applicable since there is no change in the number of units produced. The incremental concept is, however, suitable to describe this situation, because the difference in cost before and after the installation of modern equipment is the incremental cost.

Establishing Incremental Cost Pricing. Incremental cost pricing simply means that the price of a product is based upon the incremental cost (or out-of-pocket cost, or direct cost) and not upon the average cost (or fully distributed cost). The difference between the two cost concepts is of course the fixed cost. Incremental cost pricing takes into consideration only the amount of the increase in variable cost. For example, suppose that a firm produces a product with an average cost per unit of $2, which is made up of $1.50 in variable cost and $.50 in allocated fixed overhead cost. Suppose further that the markup is 30 percent, so that we add $.06 more to the price of the product, making it a total of $2.60 per unit. Under incremental cost pricing, the price for the product should be set some-

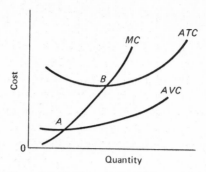

Figure 9-3. Shutdown point and breakeven point.

where between $1.60 to $2.50, depending upon the prevailing market conditions. Any amount of revenue over and above the $1.50 direct cost is a contribution to fixed cost and profit. If the product is priced at $1.80, the contribution is $.30, which is used to meet part of fixed cost and yields no profit. If the earlier volume of business has already covered fixed cost, then the $.30 is all profit.

Point A in Figure 9-3 is the shutdown point, which means that, if the price of the product is below point A, it may pay the firm to shut down its plant. If the price is exactly equal to point A, it makes no difference, except for nonfinancial reasons, whether or not the plant is to be operated.[13] However, if the price is higher than point A but below point B, it is better in the short run for the firm to operate than to shut down, because any revenue in excess of variable cost per unit of output is a contribution to the payment of fixed cost. Point B is of course the breakeven point, and the company will go bankrupt sooner or later if it continues to price its product below that point.

Uses of Incremental Cost Pricing. When and under what conditions does a firm use incremental cost pricing policy? The basic answer is that it is used only for the short run, or on a temporary basis. More specifically, this type of pricing policy is adopted when a firm (1) has unused capacity, (2) has to meet competition, and (3) wants to branch out into new markets. It is easy to understand that unused capacity is a fixed cost to the firm which cannot be avoided even if the firm shuts down the plant, and unused capacity is the most common reason for a

---

[13] Of course, it makes quite a difference if, for instance, the firm wishes to keep its scientists and engineers for future and hopefully profitable operations, or if shutdown costs are substantial. The firm should then continue to produce if the price of the product is just enough to cover the average variable cost, since fixed cost has been incurred, and the shutdown of the plant does not help the situation at all. Furthermore, it is costly to reassemble and train a group of scientists and engineers for future projects.

firm to adopt incremental cost pricing.[14] The best example is the airline industry's policy of allowing young students to pay only half fare when and if there is a vacancy in a departing plane.[15] When a plane takes off with only half of the seats occupied, a passenger paying half fare is worth far more to the airline company than no passenger at all, because the half fare still brings to the airline company some revenue which can be used to pay part of the fixed cost which a departing plane incurs, such as the pilots' salaries, the plane's rental or depreciation, the fuel cost, and the stewardesses' wages. From the viewpoint of marginalism, such a policy is sound, because the marginal cost of carrying one more passenger when the plane is about to take off is so small that the marginal revenue, for all practical purposes, can be considered marginal profit.

The second condition which induces a firm to use incremental cost pricing can be best illustrated by the railroad industry's adoption of this type of pricing policy in the last decade. Prior to the passing of the Transportation Act of 1958, railroad companies were required by the Interstate Commerce Commission to use the so-called fully distributed cost (average cost) to set rates for hauling passengers as well as cargoes. After the act was passed, railroads were permitted to set rates based upon incremental cost (known as the out-of-pocket cost), and the companies immediately seized the opportunity to fight back against the encroachment of the trucking industry into their domain. The famous "paint case" in 1958 was the first concrete result of applying incremental cost pricing to meet competition. Previously, paint was hauled by truck from manufacturing companies to automobile manufacturers. Railroads could not compete against trucking concerns because of the requirement that rates for hauling paint had to be set on the basis of fully distributed cost. In other words, the overhead expense of the line had to be spread over the total tonnage of freight hauled, although it actually cost very little to add a freight car onto an existing train. Now, with out-of-pocket cost pricing, it is far cheaper for railroad companies to haul paint, say from the Du Pont plant in Wilmington, Delaware, to a General Motors plant in Detroit, because the overhead cost of moving the train has already been allocated to existing cargo.

The third situation in which a firm logically can adopt an incremental cost pricing policy is when it wants to break into a new market. There are two ways for a firm to accomplish this: the development of a product better than the one already on the market, or the production of a similar product but with a lower price. Incremental cost pricing policy fits the latter. One good example

---

[14] One of the authors was informed by executives of several well-known corporations that their companies will use incremental cost pricing (they call it direct cost pricing) only when their firms have unused capacities. They do not believe in using this policy under other circumstances.

[15] We mean a *departing* plane and not just a plane because a plane parked on the ground has alternative uses, while a departing plane has no alternative use whatsoever.

here is the Outboard Marine Corporation. For a number of years, the company produced mainly outboard motors, boats, and some lawn mowers. Since the products are highly seasonal, the company found itself burdened with unused capacity during the fall and winter. A couple of years ago, the development of snowmobiles gave the company a break. We have no information as to the company's pricing policy for their line of snow vehicles, but if the company wished to, it could adopt an incremental cost pricing policy. With overhead expenses charged to outboard motors and other products, snowmobiles might be produced at a lower cost than the company's competitors, and so the product might be priced lower.[16]

All three conditions under which a firm can adopt incremental cost pricing involve unused plant capacity. However, even if a firm has no excess capacity, it is still possible to employ an incremental cost pricing policy to meet competition and break into a new market.

One best example is the so-called "loss-leader" item in a price war between competing retail stores. Even though the loss-leader item is actually used as bait to increase sales of those items whose prices have not been reduced, price reduction through incremental cost pricing for a particular item does serve to increase sales and so counterbalance a competitor's attempt to take away the market for the product.

The initial stage of breaking into a new market often involves losses. These losses are mainly the result of large expenditures for research and development and new product starting-up costs. High cost makes high prices for the product inevitable, unless the firm is willing to price the product on an incremental cost basis. High prices, generally speaking, reduce sales of a product, and if there has been a large investment in the development and production of the product, it may not be possible to reach the breakeven point where costs include a full allocation of overhead. On the other hand, if the company prices the product on an incremental cost basis, the lower price may make it possible to sell more of the product. Of course, the alternative does not bring the firm to a full cost breakeven point, but the fully allocated losses may be smaller. By producing more, variable costs may be brought down because of more familiarity with the new product. Also of course, fixed cost per unit of the output declines rapidly. So long as the selling price covers variable cost plus some contribution to fixed cost, incremental cost pricing may be a better way to sell the new product than full cost.[17]

---

[16] Of course, we assume that the cost of producing one unit of snowmobile of the same model is about equal among firms. This means that none of the firms possesses any technological advantage in producing the product.

[17] It is understood, of course, that such a policy is of a temporary nature. As soon as the product has been well accepted, the price can be raised to the level where profit can be realized. Promotional sales are of such a nature.

PRICING POLICY FOR NEW PRODUCTS

The term new products, as used here, refers to those for which there are no close substitutes. To price such new products, a firm may either follow a skimming price policy or a penetration price policy. Basically, both policies require that full cost be covered. The difference between the two is that the former implies a much higher markup so as to skim the cream off the market, while the latter has a much lower markup so as to penetrate the market as broadly as possible. We will explore the meaning of these terms and note that a policy decision requires us to analyze the circumstances under which the product is offered for sale.

SKIMMING PRICE POLICY

The success of a very high initial price (with a very high profit margin) to market a product often is based on the assumption that the demand for a novelty is likely to be inelastic. Novelty creates an image of prestige to the buyers. This is particularly true in the case of consumers' goods. A good example is provided by ballpoint pens. In 1946, a ballpoint pen with the appearance of a Parker 51 fountain pen was sold in southern China for $12, $3 more than the price for a gold-filled Parker 51. This same phenomenon was also seen in the introduction of Polaroid cameras, electric blankets, color televisions, and Hula Hoops. So long as vanity remains a human attribute, skimming pricing has its place in pricing strategy.

Second, in the early stage, a new product has few close substitutes so that cross-elasticity of demand is low. It is true that fountain pens could be a substitute for ballpoint pens, but the need for frequent refilling and the hard point, useful for multiple carbon sets, makes the former no match for the latter. By the same token, a conventional camera can be substituted for a Polaroid camera. However, for one who wants to see his pictures developed and printed quickly, a conventional film process is no match for Polaroid.

Third, markets may be said to be segmented. Introducing a new product at a high price is an effective way to meet the potential demand of a specific upper segment, where the segmentation is based on income. Basically, segmentation of a market is the result of differences in need and income and in price elasticity. A skimming pricing policy recognizes the segmentation of the market and sets an initially high price for a new product, so as to skim the segment least sensitive to price. As the cream or least price-sensitive part of the segment is tapped, the price is set lower to tap the next segment of the market.

The best-known example of skimming is the pricing strategy of Polaroid Corporation. When Polaroid cameras were first introduced, the price tag was so high that only photography enthusiasts and novelty lovers were willing to buy it. The high price remained for a long time, until the company was convinced that the cream from the top segment had already been skimmed. Then the firm brought out a new model with a lower price tag and repeated the process. This strategy has been repeated, until finally the company has brought out a low-priced camera, the Swinger, with the price of $19.95. It was evidently clear to the firm that if cameras at such low prices had been introduced to the market earlier, sales of the higher-priced models would have suffered. As it has turned out, the firm has profited greatly from this pricing strategy.

Fourth, when it is not possible to estimate the price elasticity of demand, a high initial price is safer. During the exploration stage, when the new product is produced in limited quantity, if the product cannot be sold at a high price, the firm may not be willing to manufacture the product, fearing that high costs of initial production and distribution will not be recovered. If the demand turns out to be rather inelastic, a high price will net the company more revenue and profit than a low price. On the other hand, if the demand turns out to be elastic, the company can then lower the price to increase sales. It is much easier to lower the price of a product than to increase it, once the product is out in the market.

Finally, many companies are not willing to finance new products if future earnings are in the distance rather than the immediate present. This is particularly true when there is any doubt as to the duration of the profitability of the new product in the market. Profitability can be threatened when competitive products are introduced or political stability is lacking, as is true in some Latin American countries. The company is naturally anxious to recover its heavy investment in research and development, production, and distribution, including initial sales promotion, when a new product is brought to the market, and to recover it in as short a period as possible. Under the circumstances, the skimming price policy appears indicated for a new product.[18]

When a firm adopts the skimming price policy, it should be prepared to lower the price of the product from time to time or to produce a successively cheaper product in order to keep the product type in the market. The exact time at which to lower the price will depend on (1) the arrival of competing products, (2) saturation of the segment of the market the product is aimed at, and (3) stabilization of production process.

Arrival of competition refers here to the introduction into the market of a product which has the same features as the one already on sale in the market. A conventional camera does not have the same features as those of the Polaroid camera and, therefore, does not compete directly with the Polaroid camera. The arrival of competition in turn depends upon two things: first, the patent protection that a new product enjoys, and second, the rate of return on invested capital that the new product can generate. Of course, the stronger the patent protection, the longer will competition be postponed.

[18] In capital budgeting terminology, what the firm wants is a short payback period for its capital investment.

According to current laws, a firm enjoys patent protection for seven years. For new drugs, the patent protection lasts for seventeen years. However, when any new feature is developed and incorporated into the "old" product, the patent can be extended for another seven years, and this extension possibility helps prevent direct competition, as for example against the Polaroid camera. Second, when the rate of return on invested capital is very high, other companies will try their best to develop a product having the same features as the one enjoying a monopolistic position in the market. Joseph Schumpeter once remarked that, in the long run, monopoly in any industry cannot be maintained. If it were not for patent protection, there probably would be more than one company producing a Polaroid-type camera. It is an open secret that a number of companies here and abroad have been working on a camera and film which are reported to rival Polaroid. One of them, by the name of Kalvar, is reported to have been working on a dry-process photo film which has the same feature as the Polaroid film.[19] In view of the fast spread of scientific and technological knowledge within a country and among industrially advanced nations, it is very doubtful that any company can maintain technological superiority for long.

Once the market position of the new product begins to deteriorate because of expiration of patent protection and the coming of competitors, the firm should immediately lower the price of the product to protect itself from the onslaught of competition or, as we have mentioned, introduce a new lower-priced item.

Saturation of the segment of a market refers to the fact that each consumer in a given segment has already bought one item of product and additional sales are merely for replacement.[20] Once the segment is saturated, the firm should lower the price of the product or introduce a modified product to capture the next segment of the market. For example, the price of cellophane

---

[19] To show how investors anticipated the rate of return Kalvar was supposed to make, the common stock of the company had been bid up to 176½ per share in early 1960s. The price dropped to 10¼ in 1970.

[20] The definition of saturation of a market depends upon the basic consumer unit one is going to use. If we use a household as the basic unit, the saturation of a given segment should be carefully defined. The reason is that as income increases and enough time passes for each household to adjust its living habit or pattern to changes, the concept of saturation expands. Two recent examples suffice to illustrate this point: For a long time, one car for each family was the sales goal of automobile manufacturers in Detroit. As family disposable income increases and surburban living becomes popular (or should we say fashionable), one car for each family becomes inadequate, and so Detroit comes out with a new slogan: two cars in every garage. Previously, when a household bought a new car, it was usually for replacement purpose. When that was the case, automobile builders did not experience any increase in sales. Now, when a household (or family) buys a new car, chances are it is the second car for the enlarged garage, and so sales of automobiles increase. Another well-known example is sales of television sets (black-and-white). The saturation point expands as more and more families buy a second or third television for the house. In earlier days, one television set per family was considered adequate. Now, as most readers experience themselves, the children of a family want to have a separate set for each bedroom in the house.

was reduced year after year during the 1929 to 1946 period, while the prices of its closest substitutes, such as glassine and waxed paper, remained relatively fixed. According to the Du Pont explanation, "each price reduction was intended to open up new uses for cellophane, and to attract new customers who had not used cellophane because of its price."[21]

Stabilization of the production process is the third factor which induces a firm to lower the price of the product. As indicated above, a firm sets a high price for a new product partly because of the high cost of research and development, production, distribution, and sales promotion. To produce a new product often involves production difficulties, either because the manager and workers are not familiar with the new process or because there are some defects in the process of production. As the years go by, defects are removed or rectified, and the manager and workers gain confidence and efficiency in operating the new plant. Consequently, average cost of production declines, thus giving the firm an opportunity to lower the price so as to increase sales of the product. For example, Union Carbide Corporation's triethanolamine, used as an emulsifying agent in cosmetics, floor waxes, and many pharmaceutical products, was first introduced in 1926 at $3 per pound, an exploratory price. Within the year, the price was lowered to $2, as the result of some improvements in production methods. With the tapping of new markets, production expanded and the price was reduced to $.75 two years later. When mass production really got underway in 1929, the carload price was cut down to $.55 per pound. As production continued to expand, the price was reduced further, and by 1939, Union Carbide was selling triethanolamine at the price of $.17 per pound.[22]

PENETRATION PRICE POLICY

Instead of pricing a new product so as to include a high profit margin, a firm may choose to price it with a low profit margin, so that it penetrates the market as deeply as possible. Penetration pricing is used to increase sales at the onset of the introduction of the new product. Du Pont, for example, has stated that its policy for patented and other new products was "to endeavor to increase consumption . . . by aiming at a low profit per unit on a large volume of sales rather than a high margin on a small volume."[23] The pricing policy of Aluminum Company of America is similar. "Alcoa modifies its target pricing according to the nature of the product, the character of demand, the severity of competition, and the peculiarities of the market . . . . New products and those in competition with substitute metals, the company may price promotionally, taking a small margin initially in expectation of building volume and lowering costs; or it may

---

[21] A. D. H. Kaplan, J. B. Dirlam, and R. F. Lanzillotti, *op. cit.*, p. 100.
[22] *Ibid.*, p. 114.
[23] *Ibid.*, p. 152.

set price enough below that of a substitute metal to achieve penetration although in some cases the price may yield less than the target margin for a long period."[24]

In order to use a penetration policy, the price elasticity of demand should be high, so that the lower price will increase sales significantly By increasing the size of production runs, average total cost per unit will decline So even though the price of the product is lower, lower average cost combined with greater volume will eventually improve the profit position, allowing promotional and new product costs to be covered sooner.

A penetration price is advocated if entry of competitors into the market is easy. Without strong patent protection, competitors can easily enter if the profit margin for the product is set high. This is especially true where a large amount of capital and highly sophisticated technology are not required. The introduction of transistors in the early 1950s and the entry en masse into the market by small independent producers in the second half of 1950s affords a good illustration. Practically any electrical engineer, together with several production workers, can start manufacturing transistors, provided several hundred thousand dollars as initial investment can be raised. Since the initial price for transistors was high and profit margin was good, the mass entry into the field was in fact a foregone conclusion. As the competition became fierce and the sharp post-Korean War cutback in defense expenditures occurred, many financially weak companies were forced into bankruptcy. So when the threat of competition is real, a penetration price policy is a better alternative.

The product also ought to be of such a nature that it will be bought and used by many customers and not just by a few. It follows that if a product is unique or a considerable departure from norms, such as for example topless swimming suits for women or Edwardian jackets for men, the demand for which is naturally limited, a skimming price policy, instead of a penetration price policy, is in order.

When a firm uses a penetration price policy, any adjustment in price which has to be made because of the life cycle of the product is relatively small. In other words, since penetration pricing starts out with a low price, subsequent reductions in price will not be great as the product becomes mature. In those instances where the price of a mature product does come down, it is more a result of production efficiency which reduces costs, rather than of the lowering of percent markup for profit.

PRICING POLICY FOR PRODUCT MIX

In discussing pricing policy of a firm, we usually think in terms of a single-product company. But it is rare nowadays for a firm to produce only one product. When

[24] *Ibid.,* p. 31.

we face a multiple-product firm, the pricing problem becomes more complex. In general, products of a firm can be classified as: (1) complementary, such as camera and film, phonograph and records, flashlight and battery; (2) substitutes, such as General Motors' Buick competing against its own Oldsmobile, Philip Morris' Philip Morris versus its own Marlboro, Procter & Gamble's Safeguard soap competing against its own Zest; and (3) independent, such as General Electric's electric light bulbs and jet aircraft engines, Du Pont's nylons and explosives, Bristol Myers' Bufferin and Miss Clairol hair shampoo. Basically, a pricing policy for a multiple-product firm is to set a price for each item so that the overall profit of the firm is optimal. Such a policy does not imply that each product group will produce an equal rate of return on its investment. On the contrary, we sometimes have to price different products to yield different rates of return in order to achieve the optimal profit for the firm. This statement seems to contradict the equimarginal principle, but the contradiction is more apparent than real. This is because, using complementary products as an example, the effort in trying to price each one of them to yield an equal rate of return may actually reduce the overall level of profit. One good example here is in photograph equipment and supplies. We usually buy a few cameras which last a long time. However, we buy a lot of rolls of film during the life of each camera. It is to a company's advantage to price cameras in such a way that almost every person who is interested in taking prictures can afford to buy one. The low markup in profit for the camera can be easily compensated for by the high markup for the film. This is particularly true in the case of Polaroid cameras because of absence of direct competition. At present, the lowest price for a Polaroid camera which can take color film is $29.95, but the full list price for a package of eight-picture color film is $4.49. Over the useful life of a Polaroid camera, one could probably spend hundreds of dollars on color film. Since there is no substitute for Polaroid color film (this is not true in the case of Kodak color film), the overall profit Polaroid Corporation can make on both the camera and film will be much larger than it would have been if the company had tried to price the camera to yield the same rate of return as the color film.

UNIQUE PROBLEMS OF MULTIPLE-PRODUCT FIRMS

In setting a price for each product, a multiple-product firm faces four kinds of problems which a single-product manufacturer does not have: (1) the intensity of competition each product meets in the market; (2) the intensity of competition with which its own products face each other; (3) joint cost allocation; and (4) shifting of economic resources from one product to another in order to achieve the optimal rate of return for the entire firm.

Competition with Other Firms. Since the different products of a multiple-product firm are sold in different markets with a varying degree of intensity of competition, pricing policy for each product has to be adjusted accordingly. As a rule, the degree of intensity of competition determines the percent markup in profit a product is able to earn. When competition is keen, the company normally should price its product comparable to that of its closest competing product, because the cross-elasticity is high. For example, the lowest price 18-inch, black-and-white television set manufactured by Magnavox is priced about the same as that of Motorola, since both companies are known as quality producers. On the other hand, when a firm has a strong monopolistic position in the market, it can price its product higher than those of its competitors'.

General Foods Corporation, for example, prices one of its specialties, Jello, higher than its competitors' similar products because of consumers' strong preference. However, its Maxwell House coffee is priced comparable to Standard Brands' Chase & Sanborn, but lower than Chock-full-O'Nuts coffee. Another example is the way Du Pont priced nylon and rayon. Because the latter was subject to competition while the former was not, the pricing policy for the two products was different. If Du Pont were to price the two products on the same basis it would make much less profit on nylon. On the other hand, it would also earn less profit if the prices were high for both products, but this time the loss would be on rayon, because Du Pont's rayon would be priced out of the market, since there are many other firms producing rayon. So the pricing policy has to be tailored to the need of the market or a segment of the market, and the full cost pricing may not, as explained previously, be considered the universal policy for every product under any conditions.

The following example sums up this analysis: A large, well-known, diversified manufacturing concern has different pricing policies for different products. For its industrial machinery, it uses full cost pricing. For its recreational product, it uses the prevailing market price; that is, it follows the price set by the leader of the field. For some engineering and research projects, it uses a skimming price policy. The management does not believe in adopting an incremental cost pricing policy except when the company has unused capacity. Regardless of the pricing policy a firm uses, the overriding objective is to price each separate product in such a manner as to maximize the firm's profit.

Competition with Firm's Own Products. When a firm produces two or three similar products which serve the same segment of a market, such as General Motors' Buick and Oldsmobile, the pricing policy is to insure that each product will bring in the same percentage of profit in proportion to cost of production and distribution. We do not say the two products should bring in the same amount of profit. On the contrary, if the cost of production and distribution is not the same for the two products, the amount of profit each of the products brings in should also be different. In other words, if a firm uses full cost pricing for both products, the percent markup should be the same in both cases. Otherwise, the firm should abandon the product which yields less and expand the one which yields more in order to increase the firm's overall level of profit. Sometimes, however, this cannot be done, because a given product may have created a clientele which might switch to a competitor's product if the product in question were withdrawn.[25] The long-lasting status of Chesterfield and Philip Morris in cigarette sales, notwithstanding the introduction in recent years of numerous new brands, is a good example.

Allocation of Joint Cost. The third difficulty facing a multiple-product firm is the proper allocation of joint cost among different products groups. From an accountant's point of view, this may not present any problem, because joint cost can be allocated to each product group according to each group's utilization of plant facilities and managerial time and effort. For example, if administrative expenses for a year amount to $20 million and product group A occupies 20 percent of administrative officers' time and office expenses, such as secretaries' salaries, telephone bills, and office supplies, then $4 million should be allocated to product group A.[26] However, there is no neat and clear-cut division of the top management's time and effort, so the problem of proper allocation of joint cost is still with us.

In addition, how can one allocate the additional cost that the expansion of one product group entails? For example, if a firm has to sell bonds to obtain additional funds to expand the production of a given product, the cost of the new financing is not restricted to the interest charges on bonds plus the flotation cost. It includes the impact on the cost of future financing and reflects partly the cost of current borrowing. Supposing that current financing is for product group A and the immediate future financing is for product group B, would the top management allocate part of the cost of future financing to product group A?

Shifting of Economic Resources. When a firm finds out that one product is not producing as high a profit margin as another, it should discontinue the less profitable product and expand the more profitable one assuming, of course, other nonmonetary factors can be quantified. This is because, according to the equimarginal productivity theorem, a firm should shift its economic resources from one product to another until every product (or product group) brings in an equal rate of return on investment. However, there are several constraints which limit the firm's ability to do so. Two of the constraints have already been mentioned; they are the existence of complementary products and of products which

---

[25] More on this point will be taken up later in the discussion of shifting economic resources from one product to another.

[26] A firm may allocate joint cost on various bases, depending upon the norm set by the top management.

have created for themselves a loyal clientele. With regard to the second constraint, the problem facing the top management is to determine whether or not the firm can utilize the resources released by the abandonment of one product to a more profitable venture, bearing in mind that since the product has already fostered valuable goodwill among its customers, it has in effect some advertising value for the firm and is a complementary product in a broader sense. If this is the case, the firm may be unwise to discontinue this particular product.

The third constraint is the desire of a firm to stabilize its revenue and earnings. When the revenue and earnings of a firm fluctuate greatly because of the cyclical nature of its product, it is to the firm's advantage to diversify, either through developing a new product for which the demand is more stable, or by merging with another company which produces a noncyclical product, such as consumers' nondurable goods, even if the newly acquired product may not be as profitable as the former. Vertical integration (merging) in order to insure a steady supply of raw material and thus stabilize earnings also comes under this heading.

PRICE LINING

Price lining refers to the price policy which sets a predetermined pattern or relationship between the price of a product and the quality or the design of the product within a product group. Because of difference in need or price or income elasticity of demand, a firm may offer the same product in various qualities or designs, so as to meet the widest possible demand from customers of various income strata. In retailing, such a pricing policy is often found. Since the manufacturing industry has to supply retailers with products of different quality, it also has to adopt such a pricing policy. For example, men's clothing shops carry suits of the same size in different quality or design and price them accordingly.[27] The same practice is also found in women's dresses. The implication of such a policy to the manufacturers is that, unless a given firm enjoys an indisputable reputation in the field, such as Brooks Brothers in men's clothing and Bergdorf Goodman in women's dresses (both in New York City), the manufacturer's pricing policy has to follow the reverse process of normal pricing procedures. It has to start out with the prices for different grades of the same merchandise offered for sale in the market, then find out how large a profit margin each distributor will get (retailers and wholesalers or jobbers), and finally calculate whether or not it can produce at a cost no greater than the residual part of the market price. This is, as we know, pricing at the market. If the cost of production, excluding the profit margin to the producer, is substantially lower than the

---

[27] One good example here is Hart, Schaffner & Marx, a well-known manufacturer of men's clothing. It produces different grades of suits not only for Wallachs, a reputable New York shop, but also for Robert Hall, a large chainstore catering mainly to customers from the lower-middle income group.

residual part, and problem of pricing is solved.[28] However, if the cost is close to or higher than the residual part of the market price, the questions facing the producer will be (1) whether it is to the firm's advantage to produce a product at less than full cost, (2) whether the firm can reduce the cost of production by changing the design of the product or by substituting one grade of raw material for another, (3) how the wholesale and retail profit margin can be reduced without significantly affecting the sales of the product.

The first problem has been answered already. But the point which should be emphasized here is that incremental cost pricing should be used with caution lest it tend to become a permanent feature of the firm's pricing policy. As to the second problem, the manufacturer should first consult with the retailer as to the salability of a product of new design or new material before he starts mass production. This does not imply that the retailer knows exactly what can be sold and what cannot be sold. It simply means that with the retailer's advice as to the current market trend and with his backing, it will be easier for the manufacturer to dispose of the modified product. Finally, the amount of profit which can be safely reduced from the wholesaler's and retailer's shares depends upon the ability and willingness of both classes of middlemen to find and to switch over to other suppliers who can give them better profit markup for the same kind of product and service, including "free" advertising or sales promotion. In this connection, the degree of competition the producer faces determines, to a great extent, the middleman's ability and willingness to switch.

SUMMARY

In this chapter, we are concerned with how a firm prices its products and the purposes of adopting various pricing policies. We have learned that the pricing policies for a well-established product are somewhat different from those for a new one. For the former, we have standard cost pricing and incremental cost pricing, and for the latter, we have skimming pricing and penetration pricing policies. In addition, we have pricing at the market, product line pricing, and price lining. Depending upon the market conditions, a firm uses a given type of pricing policy to achieve its objectives.

In general, pricing objectives for a firm may be classified into the following categories: to achieve a given rate of return on investment, to maintain or improve shares of the market, to differentiate its product or create an image of superior quality, to break into a new market, and to maintain price stability. Some of these objectives are not compatible with others; that is, while a firm is

[28] Of course, we are now back to the problem of product line pricing and the shifting of economic resources from one product to another in order to achieve the optimal profit level for the firms mentioned in this paragraph.

pursuing one policy, it has to sacrifice another. In the long run, the overriding objective of a firm is to try to maximize profit consistent with the objective of keeping the firm solvent.

Standard cost pricing, which is the most widely used, helps a firm plan for production and sales. Incremental cost pricing, on the other hand, enables a firm to compete for business. Skimming pricing differs from penetration pricing in that the former charges a much higher profit markup than the latter. When a firm produces more than one product, its pricing policy becomes more complicated. In adopting pricing policies for different product lines, a firm should bear in mind the equimarginal principle; that is, each product group should bring in the same percentage of profit with respect to the amount of capital invested in that particular group, with the exception of any two groups which are complementary in nature, such as camera and film. Price lining refers to the setting of a predetermined pattern or relationship between the price of a product and the quality or design of that product within a product group. Because of the difference in need or price or income elasticity of demand, a firm may offer the same product in various qualities or designs so as to meet demands from customers of different income strata.

Review Questions

1. What are the factors which are responsible for changes in price elasticity?
2. What are the pricing objectives which prevail in American corporations?
3. What is the difference between pricing policy and pricing procedure?
4. What is full cost pricing? How is it set up?
5. Why does a firm use full cost pricing policy?
6. What is incremental cost pricing? How is it set up?
7. Under what conditions will a firm use incremental cost pricing?
8. What is skimming price policy? Under what conditions will a firm use this type of pricing policy?
9. What are the symptoms of deterioration of a product's market position?
10. What is penetration price policy? Under what conditions will a firm use this type of pricing policy?
11. What is product line pricing? What type of company will adopt such a policy?
12. What are some unique problems facing a multiple-product firm in pricing its products?
13. What is price lining? What is the difference between this type of pricing policy and product line pricing?

Case 1. The Durawear Company

George Eaton, president of the Durawear Company, is considering setting up a standard cost pricing policy for the company's product. Durawear has been producing men's shirts for fifteen years, with annual sales amounting to around $25 million. Over the years, its products have been sold mainly to the Armed Forces; and the pricing policy has been determined by the contract negotiated with the Army. The contract calls for the delivery of shirts on a fixed price basis. According to this type of contract, the Army allows the company to recover its fixed and variable cost plus a given percent of profit on the total sales. Since the Army's orders account for most of the company's output, and since the profit margin is based not upon the amount of capital invested in the company but upon the sales volume, it has not been practical to set up a standard cost pricing policy for the company's products.

After an extensive discussion as to the desirability of setting up standard cost pricing policy by the members of the executive committee, Mr. Eaton asked John Brown, the company's chief accountant, to prepare a statement showing how much the price per unit of output will be with the target rate of return on investment being set at 20 percent before income tax.

From the company's records, Mr. Brown has found the following information with which he is going to set up a standard cost price for the company's product:

Prime cost per unit:	
Labor	$ 3.00
Raw materials	1.80
Variable overhead expense	800,000
Annual depreciation	1,000,000
Other fixed overhead	
expense	1,000,000
Total invested capital after	
allowance for depreciation	4,000,000

According to the production engineer's report, the full capacity of the two plants owned by the company is 5,000,000 shirts per year. Based upon the past ten years' experience, the company has been able to utilize the plant's capacity only up to 80 percent.

QUESTIONS

1. If you were in Mr. Brown's position, what is the price per unit which you would come up with?
2. What reservations might you have with respect to the data given above?

Case 2. The Lakeside Hotel

Lakeside Hotel, located on the southern tip of Lake George at the junction of Route 9 and Route 9N, about seventy miles north of Albany, the capital of New York State, was built ten years ago at a cost of $5 million. It is a luxury hotel, catering mainly to summer vacationers from higher middle-income families. During the months of June, July, and August, all of its 400 rooms have been fully occupied since its opening in 1960. For the months of May and September, its occupancy rate has been around 70 percent. During the months of April and October, only about half of its rooms have been rented. Because of the policy to shut down completely when the occupancy rate falls below 50 percent, the entire hotel has been closed for the rest of the year.

All rooms in the hotel are equipped with television sets, but they are not air conditioned because of the cool weather in the Adirondack Mountain area. The rates range from $15 to $20 a day for single rooms and $25 to $30 a day for double rooms, depending upon the location of the rooms. The gross annual revenue amounts to around $1,454,000, with a net annual income being $145,400. Since about two-thirds of the annual operating expenses are for overhead, including property tax, the manager of the hotel wonders whether it might be profitable to open the hotel all year and charge only half of the regular rates for the slack season.

QUESTIONS

1. What do you think of the manager's idea to lower the rates by half?
2. Based upon what economic theory can you justify your conclusion?
3. What are the profits of var. occupancy rates

Suggested Reading

Abromowitz, Irving: *Production Management,* The Ronald Press Company, New York, 1967.

Dean, Joel: *Managerial Economics,* Prentice-Hall, Inc., Englewood Cliffs, N.J., 1951.

Eckstein, Otto, and Gary Fromm: "The Price Equation," *The American Economic Review,* vol. 58, no. 5, pp. 1159–1182, Dec., 1968.

Haynes, William W.: *Managerial Economics,* rev. ed., Business Publications, Inc., Austin, Tex., 1969.

Kaplan, A. D. H., J. D. Dirlam, and R. F. Lanzilloti: *Pricing in Big Business,* The Brookings Institution, Washington, 1958.

Mulvihill, Donald F., and Stephen Paranka: *Price Policies and Practices,* John Wiley & Sons, Inc., New York, 1966.

Nemmers, Erwin E.: *Managerial Economics,* John Wiley & Sons, Inc., New York, 1962.

Spencer, Milton H.: *Managerial Economics,* 3d ed., Richard D. Irwin, Inc., Homewood, Ill., 1968.

Stigler, George J.: *The Theory of Price,* 3d ed., The Macmillan Company, New York, 1966.

chapter 10
price
discrimination

During the discussion of the various pricing policies which a firm may adopt, we touched on the subject of price discrimination. Price discrimination to most people is simply the practice of selling the same product (or a substantially similar product) at different prices to different persons. Economists generally prefer to add the qualification that the product must have been produced under the same conditions. The qualification arises because classical economic theory assumes that all profits or returns in excess of cost will be competed away, and if a product is sold at differing prices, and the prices are not based on cost differences, then there is arbitrary and discriminatory pricing.

What we have in mind here is that if a camera sells for $50 in one market or segment of a market, and for $60 in another, and the marginal cost of production does not vary in similar fashion, then price discrimination may be said to be present. The discrimination is made possible because the market can be separated into a number of segments, independent of each other, in which it is possible to speak of separate demand curves for the product, one for each market segment, whose elasticities as to price are different from one another.

A well-known instance of price discrimination is that practiced by theaters or sports arenas which charge different prices for the same seats depending on the time of the day or the day of the week. Invariably, evening prices are considerably higher than daytime prices, and prices for weekend are higher than those during the week. Depending also on the location in the theater or arena, different prices will be charged, although the event is the same for all viewers.

A much-publicized instance of price discrimination is afforded by the drug industry which, as Table 10-1 illustrates, has offered the same drugs at widely differing prices in different cities.

TABLE 10-1. WHAT UNITED STATES CITIES PAY FOR DRUGS

Item (standard strengths)	New York	Atlanta	Miami	Portland, Oregon	San Francisco
Meprobamate	$9.45	$31.20	$10.70	$20.00	$ 9.50
Chloramphenicol	6.73	21.00	15.75	25.50	25.00
Phenazopyridine hydrochloride	4.80	48.00	39.73	No information	
Dextroamphetamine sulfate	.57	22.60	19.43	5.06	1.75

Source: "Drugs, The Price Gap," Newsweek, May 29, 1967, p. 103.

Price discrimination is sometimes made possible through different labeling, in which case the kind of market segmentation is not by locality but by some other classification. Automobile tires manufactured by the same producer show up under one label in a wholly owned retail outlet, a different label in a large retail mail-order house, and other label in a discount auto repair chain specializing in tires and functionally related repairs such as wheel balancing, front end alignment, and brake renewals. In each instance, the market is different, with different elasticities, and different prices are charged to the consumer. Since the product is different in the eyes of the consumer, however, it can be asserted that this is not true discrimination. The consumer is in no position to judge the true merit of the product and must rely on the representations of the seller. It is, therefore, analogous to monopolistic product differentiation.

In this chapter, we will deal with price discrimination in which there is no doubt that the products offered are the same item, and differences in consumer information are not responsible for differences in price. In the sense in which we are defining it, discrimination constitutes the adoption of different prices for different market segments as a simple outgrowth of the demand for the item and the ability of the producer to exploit that demand, generally on the basis of its timing or its place. Because the product is unchanged, we can assume that its marginal production cost is the same for all markets.

SIGNIFICANCE OF PRICE DISCRIMINATION

To a large extent, a successful price policy exemplifies good price discrimination. A good merchandiser is one who is aware of the ways in which to use price discrimination in order to maximize sales and profits. He uses price discrimination in order to obtain a more complete exploitation of the market and hence a better profit level than otherwise might be possible. In the process, he allows the product or service to be made available to many who otherwise would be unable to take advantage of his product or service.

An instance of price discrimination which serves a segment of the market which otherwise would not be able to take advantage of a service is standby and student air transport pricing. By making a lower-priced ticket available for the student or the person on standby, the airlines render a positive service. They serve themselves by selling service that otherwise would go unused at a price which covers out-of-pocket costs and makes some contribution to overhead.

Another such instance is peak-load pricing of public utilities. Public utility loads are notoriously uneven. In order to meet peak demands, capacity must be built. The resources used to build this capacity have opportunity costs. Those requiring the capacity may be charged premium rates equal to the marginal cost of providing it. During off-peak times, however, capacity is available and is at times priced attractively to encourage use. An illustration of this kind of pricing is that presently employed by the telephone companies. Daytime rates exceed those at night and on weekends, to attempt to take advantage and encourage the use of the service, while at the same time making the service available to those who otherwise would not be able to use it. Sometimes lower rates are extended to those who are willing to have their service interrupted or curtailed in the event the utility needs the service for other reasons.

RELATION TO THE EQUIMARGINAL THEORY

The equimarginal theory states that in order to maximize benefit, one allocates resources among competing ends so as to equalize the marginal return in each use. Therefore, if we assume that a product may be sold in a number of separated markets, however separation may be defined, the object of pricing policy will be to set that price which equates marginal revenue in each market.

For example, a company which produces an infrared burglar alarm system, which may be sold in each of two markets, might find that in market A the demand curve has a price elasticity of demand of -3, while in market B, perhaps being hit hard by a crime wave, the elasticity of demand is -1.5. Its pricing practice in each market should reflect this difference in intensity of need. The question is, how?

The equimarginal principal states that the marginal revenue in market A should equal that in market B. There is also a relationship between marginal revenue and price via the notion of elasticity of demand which states that

$$MR = P - \frac{P}{E}$$

If the marginal revenues are to be equal, then we can write

$$P_a - \frac{P_a}{E_a} = P_b - \frac{P_b}{E_b}$$

where the subscripts a and b refer to each market, and E is written as a positive number, even though price elasticity of demand is normally negative.

In market A, a price of $100 will produce a marginal revenue of $67 on the assumption that elasticity is 3. The calculation is

$$MR = P - \frac{P}{E} = 100 - \frac{100}{3} = \$67$$

In market B, however, the elasticity is different, and since we want to equalize the marginal return, we have to set a different price. Setting MR to equal 67 and letting E equal 1.5, we have from the same formula

$$\$67 = P \left(1 - \frac{1}{1.5} \right) = \frac{1}{3} P$$

$$P = \$201$$

The conclusion, then, is that under these restricted conditions, if the price we currently have set in market B is less than $201, it will pay to raise it so that we can maximize net profit.[1] At any lower price, we will be selling more units, but assuming a constant cost per unit, we will be earning less than we could if we raised the price a little and sold fewer units.

If we are allocating a fixed supply of units to both markets, then we would have to consider that reducing the supply of units to market B would require us to increase the supply to market A. We cannot increase the supply to market A unless we lower the price in that market, thereby reducing marginal revenue there. The process of reducing the supply to market B, thus increasing the marginal revenue, and increasing the supply to market A, thus decreasing the marginal revenue, will cease at the point at which the marginal revenues in each market are equal.

RELATION TO MARGINAL COST

The results in the previous section were obtained by an often-used device of holding marginal cost constant. Our first rule was that any given output level should be allocated among markets so as to equalize the marginal revenue in each place. Now to this we will add the necessary condition which we already have seen, that for profits to be a maximum, that level of output must be chosen which equates total marginal revenue obtained from all markets with the marginal cost of production.

In Figure 10-1, marginal cost MC is rising with increases in output, so that the market allocation process is given a constraint it did not have before. The amount to be allocated is assumed to come from current production and is not merely available as assumed earlier. The profit-maximizing level of production

---

[1] Since the formula is based on a particular kind of linear demand curve, elasticities of less than 1 give negative marginal revenue, and elasticities of 1 give 0 marginal revenues. The principle is valid, however, for all elasticities.

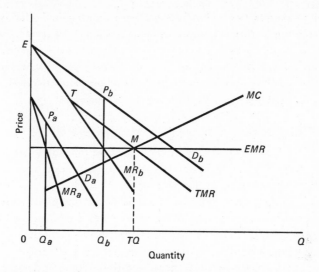

Figure 10-1. Discrimination between markets.

is set by M where the total marginal revenue curve TMR intersects the marginal cost curve MC. TMR consists of the total of MR_a and MR_b and proceeds from E on the vertical axis to T and then through M.

The line of equal marginal revenue or EMR is drawn to the left and right from M, so that it intersects both demand curves D_a and D_b. The price of A which will produce a marginal revenue equal to that of B is P_a, and the corresponding price of B is P_b. The quantity of each which will be allocated is Q_a of A and Q_b of B. The points at which the separate MR curves intersect MC are not significant because they do not represent the marginal cost of the entire output being produced.

If price discrimination is prohibited, the optimal level of output remains at TQ, but as prices will be brought into agreement, profits will necessarily be reduced. The alteration in prices will mean a change in the amounts allocated to each market.

CONDITIONS NECESSARY FOR PRICE DISCRIMINATION

There are several conditions which are conducive to price discrimination, as we have described it.[2]

NONTRANSFERABILITY OF PRODUCTS

First, price discrimination can be employed if it is not possible to transfer a product sold in one market to another, or from one segment of a market to

---

[2] See Joan Robinson, *The Economics of Imperfect Competition*, Macmillan & Co., Ltd., London, 1961, pp. 179–181, for example.

another segment. The best example of this kind of discrimination is where a service has been performed. An operation performed by a surgeon cannot be transferred to another patient, once it has been performed. Similarly, a contract which prevents a purchaser from reselling a product will accomplish legally what is not possible naturally. A brass mill may agree not to resell copper sheets bought for manufacture of its own line of kitchenware.

TRANSPORTATION COST HIGHER THAN PRICE DIFFERENTIALS

Analogously, there may be a geographic separation which, because of transportation cost or tariff, renders resale of a product from one market to another unprofitable, unless the differential is larger than the tariff or the shipping and handling costs. This kind of discrimination can be extended to cover an instance in which a firm with plants in two cities producing the same product under substantially identical conditions nevertheless establishes a price in one city competitive with other local producers, but raises the price in the other city where there are no competitors. The price differential should not exceed the cost of transportation and handling, or else it is presumed that competitors in the first city would ship to the second.[3]

If a firm uses incremental cost pricing for products sold in markets far from the home plant, discrimination may also arise. A firm may sell a product at $10 in its home city and at $9 at a distant city, even though freight costs are $2 per unit. Normally one might assume that the product should sell for $12, if its profit margin is sufficient, so that some profit is made at the lower price or so long as variable and fixed cost and transport costs are covered, even though no profit is made. If the cost structure is based on standard cost and sales in the home territory are enough to cover fixed costs, then any sales over the standard amount might well be at prices from which fixed cost has been deducted. If for instance fixed costs are $3, variable cost is $4, transportation costs are $2, and normal profit is $3, the firm might price its product at $9 for sale at the distant point and cover all remaining costs over fixed cost and gain its normal profit as well. At that price, even though it is lower than the price in the home city, it is not profitable for a purchaser to reship the product from the distant point and compete with the firm on its home ground.

SAME SERVICE FOR VARIOUS TYPES OF PRODUCTS

Price discrimination can be practiced when various groups of customers require the same service for different types of products. Railroads have long charged different rates for shipping different commodities, even though the marginal cost of shipping might not differ from product to product or class to

---

[3] The situation can become somewhat more complicated than given here, especially if the market invasion results in enlargement of the scale of production, thus allowing reduced costs by the competitors.

class. By charging different rates, even though the marginal cost of providing the transportation is the same, the railroads practice discrimination. Such pricing policy is known as the "value of service" policy.[4] The reason why such a policy works is that it is impossible for a shipper to change one commodity into another, say from grain to coal, so as to take advantage of a lower tariff.

There is, of course, another well-known reason, and that is that the costs of transportation are of lesser importance to products of higher value, and higher value products generally can absorb higher freight costs.

PRODUCTS ON SPECIAL ORDER

Price discrimination may be used when products are sold on special order, so that each buyer does not know what prices others pay for a similar product. For example, an aluminum fabricator may charge different prices for making engine blocks for two different automobile manufacturers, or a machine tool builder may quote different prices for two similar machines where the variation in production cost is less than the difference in prices.

Leasing of machinery or other equipment often has been subject to price discrimination. Here the form of discrimination is to base the charge on the volume of machine use when the basis for charging off the value of the machine is obsolescence, which has nothing to do with its activity rate.[5]

PRICE DIFFERENTIALS BASED UPON PRIDE OR IGNORANCE

By appealing to pride or by utilizing ignorance on the part of customers, a firm may practice price discrimination by breaking up a market into different segments having differing price elasticities of demand, in which different prices may be charged. As we pointed out earlier, this begins to take the form of simple product differentiation, in that it includes measures such as labeling, styling, and advertising. These measures alter the bundle of characteristics which the consumer buys, and the price differentials are not then based on differences in time or place.[6]

---

[4] It was termed "third degree" price discrimination by A. C. Pigou. The notion of different forms of price discrimination to express how far a monopolist might go in charging different prices was first employed by Pigou, the great "welfare" economist who identified three degrees of discrimination. The other two, and E. W. Clemens' extension of the third degree, are mentioned later on.
[5] See for example, George J. Stigler's analysis of the use of shoe machinery in *The Theory of Price*, 3d ed., The Macmillan Company, New York, 1966, p. 210.
[6] Early in the development of product differentiation, A. C. Pigou noted that sellers often attempted artificially to create nontransferability among markets through labeling and special marks, ". . . all incidents designed to prevent possible purchasers of the grades that are highly priced relatively to the cost of production from becoming, instead, purchasers of the grades that are sold at a lower rate of profit." *The Economics of Welfare*, 4th ed., Macmillan & Co., Ltd., London, 1960, p. 277. D. S. Watson also includes different prices for branded and unbranded items as a form of price discrimination in his *Price Theory and Its Uses*, 2d ed., Houghton Mifflin Company, Boston, 1968, p. 325.

It should be noted here that this type of price discrimination is similar to the skimming price policy, in that both recognize the existence of different segments of a market and endeavor to make the most profit from sales. However, there is one basic distinction between the two and that is that skimming price policy, as typified by the introduction of penicillin and other antibiotic drugs, sets different prices for an identical product in different time periods. On the other hand, price discrimination based upon pride or ignorance involves selling the same or slightly differentiated products at different prices at the same time.

DEGREES OF PRICE DISCRIMINATION

Price discrimination generally comes in the three models, depending the amount of consumer's surplus the seller is able to extract from the consumer. By consumer's surplus, we mean the area under the demand curve representing total utility obtained, but not paid for, by the consumer. The implication is, of course, that the surplus rightfully belongs to the consumer for having obeyed the law of supply and demand.

Figure 10-2 illustrates the concept as developed by Alfred Marshall, and later used by his pupil Pigou, as the basis for the notion of price discrimination.

FIRST-DEGREE DISCRIMINATION

The demand curve illustrates that at a price of $1, one item would be demanded, that at $.75 two would be taken, at $.50 three would be taken, and at $.25 four would be taken. Since the consumer would have paid $1 for the first, and since by taking four he is saving $.75 on the first item, this is concrete evidence that a surplus has been acquired. Altogether, by buying four at once, the consumer acquires a total value or utility of $.75 above what he pays for on the first, $.50 on the second, and $.25 on the third, while paying exactly the

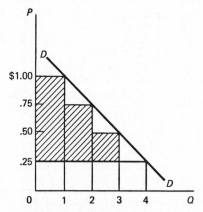

Figure 10-2. Consumer's surplus.

right amount for the fourth. The total consumer surplus may be viewed as the sum of the separate amounts, or $1.50. It is also equal to the shaded area under the demand curve to $P = \$.25$.

The first degree of price discrimination involves pricing so as to take away all of this surplus. Different prices are charged for different units of a product in such a way that the price paid for each unit is exactly equal to the intensity of desire or marginal utility for the product, so that there is no consumer's surplus left to the buyer. A typical example of first-degree discrimination is afforded by the practice of some physicians in setting fees geared to their patient's income.

SECOND-DEGREE DISCRIMINATION

The second degree of price discrimination is similar to the first, except that only part of the consumer's surplus is captured by the seller. The usual example of second-degree discrimination is step or bracket pricing used by public utilities such as electric and gas companies who charge less per unit of product, the greater the volume of consumption. The company prices a given number of units of the product at a certain price for all units from zero to some level of demand. For succeeding demand classes, it progressively reduces the price, as shown in Figure 10-3.

The demander of quantity Q_1 will pay a price P_1 for his entire quantity and obtain a consumer's surplus equal to the shaded triangle below the demand curve at that price. The demander of Q_2, however, although he is given the price reduction rightfully his as the consumer of the increased amount, has his rate reduced to P_2 but only for that portion of his needs above Q_1. According to

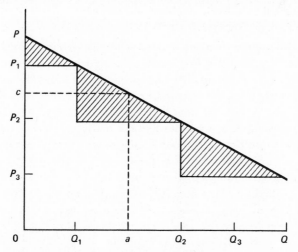

Figure 10-3. Price discrimination of second degree.

demand theory, his consumer's surplus should have been equal to the triangle under the demand curve at P_2. He actually gets only the shaded triangle at that price plus the shaded triangle at price P_1.

In return, one would presume that the utility would argue that the demander of amount a, standing for any amount between Q_1 and Q_2, would receive the excess over Q_1 at price P_2, which is much lower than any price c on the vertical axis, and that in the aggregate there may be no such discrimination.

The Potomac Electric Power Company had the following rate schedule for residential power customers in January, 1970. Such rate schedules are typical.

TABLE 10-2. RATE SCHEDULE FOR ELECTRICITY IN
WASHINGTON, D.C., JANUARY, 1970

Amount Consumed in kwh per Month	Rate per kwh in Cents
First 40	4.20
Next 260	2.23
Next 1,200	1.80
Over 1,500	1.50

Automobile turnpikes evince this kind of discrimination. The toll highway from Fort Pierce to Miami, Florida, is reported to have the following rate structure.[7] The cost of traveling 109 miles from Miami north to Fort Pierce is at the rate of 2.2 cents per mile (including 45 miles of free Interstate Highway). To travel from Fort Pierce north to Wildwood (near Ocala), 156 miles, costs less than 1.6 cents per mile. Concentrating on the Miami area, the cost of traveling the last 11 miles south to the city is 3.33 cents a mile, the last 24 miles south is 2.92 cents per mile, and the last 32 miles south is 2.81 cents per mile.

THIRD-DEGREE DISCRIMINATION

Third-degree discrimination is generally defined as discrimination by class of customer, where a firm breaks up a market into different segments and sells the same product at different prices in each market so as to equate marginal revenue in each market. Discrimination between markets is illustrated in Figure 10-1. We pointed out that in order to practice this kind of discrimination successfully it is necessary that the product or service be incapable of being transferred among markets. Utility pricing affords another example of third-degree discrimination in that different prices are charged for residential, small, and large industrial users. A residential purchaser of power in Washington, D.C., will pay as little as 1.50 cents per kwh for power consumed in excess of 1,500 kwh as compared with 2.75 cents per kwh for industrial customers using the same amount of power up to 2,700 kwh. In fact, the latter still have to

[7] John Penekamp, as reported in *The Miami Herald*, January 28, 1969.

pay 1.80 cents per kwh for power over 3,000 kwh. If the residential consumers could transfer or resell his power purchases to the industrial user, such discrimination could not be enforced. It is also important to note that the rate is sharply reduced for the very large user so that those consuming over 100,000 kwh per month pay only .87 cent per kwh. Because electricity production is subject to declining marginal cost, it is probable that this rate schedule conforms to the underlying cost basis. The high initial rate reflects in all likelihood the higher cost of installing electric service for industrial use, as well as its peak demand nature.

It is interesting to notice that the rate for residential electricity for cooking and heating is lower than that given in Table 10-2. One reason given for this reduction is that the cross-elasticity of demand for electricity for such uses is very high. At higher rates, consumers will switch to alternative methods of heating or cooking. Once more we see attempts to adjust prices in line with demand elasticities in order to equate marginal revenues among customers in different markets.

Third-degree price discrimination may exist wherever there is more than one market. For instance, raw milk is sold in the retail market and for production of cheese and other products in quantities which depend on relative prices in each market. Commodities or products are priced differently for export than they are for domestic markets. Export pricing may be lower because demand is more elastic owing to the competition of locally produced products.

This form of discrimination has been extended to cover the output of more than one product in a single market by Eli W. Clemens.[8] The application assumes that a firm normally has capacity which it is seeking to utilize profitably. It will, therefore, add such additional products to its line as to utilize its productive capacity, until the marginal revenue of the last product added equals marginal cost. The diagram in Figure 10-4 uses somewhat the same method of presentation as does Figure 10-1. The demand curve for the firm's original product is D_1, and it would normally pay to produce quantity Q_1 obtained by the intersection N of the MC curve with MR_1. However the plant has capacity equal to Q_2. Since two separate products are produced with individual demand curves, we must speak of two separate marginal revenue curves. But we have only the single MC which applies to both outputs, since the same plant and processes are being used. We will, then, allocate production capacity so as to equate marginal revenues in each. The output of product 1 is cut back to Q_1' because the marginal revenue from producing product 2 pays more.

The object lesson of this example and of Figure 10-1 is of course that pricing by using uniform markups over cost or uniform percent margins is not

[8] "Price Discrimination and the Multiple-product Firm" Review of Economic Studies, vol. 19, pp. 1–11, 1950–1951.

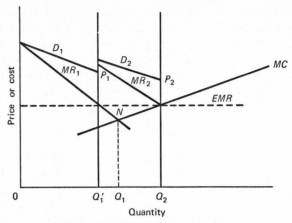

Figure 10-4. Pricing of multiple products.

profit-maximizing behavior. On the other hand, we have not considered the possible reaction of rivals and the cost of finding out, if it can be determined, what the correct marginal revenues and marginal costs may be.

LEGAL ASPECTS OF PRICE DISCRIMINATION

Even though price discrimination may be beneficial to a firm, it is not regarded as such by the federal government. In order to protect financially weaker firms from being attacked by price discrimination exercised by financially stronger companies, the government has passed legislation which attempts to prohibit it. The Robinson-Patman Act of 1936, for example, makes price discrimination illegal if it tends substantially to lessen competition. A prerequisite for finding an illegal price discrimination is a price difference resulting from sales by a seller to two purchasers in the same market of the same product at the same time. Without a finding that there has been a price differential, the courts will not entertain any further legal suit. Although the law states that price discrimination is prohibited where the effect may be to lessen competition or tend to create a monopoly, the finding that one person has been discriminated against must come first, and it is not considered that there is discrimination when products with different marginal costs are sold at the same price.

PERMISSIBILITY OF PRICE DIFFERENTIATION

Allowances may be made in price differentiation on account of differences in grade, quality, or quantity, because of different selling or transportation costs, or when the discrimination is in response to competition.

What kind of cost concept does the federal government use to distinguish permissible discrimination in order to evaluate the cost implications of grade, quality, or quantity, or selling or transportation activity? Normally the basis is some idea of full cost or average unit cost. The concept of average unit cost or full cost is not as clear cut as marginal cost because of the difficulty of allocating common costs over more than one product. From the company's point of view, it is less rigid to define cost in terms of full cost, because of the flexibility it provides in being able to assign common costs to different products depending on the pricing objectives.

THE ROBINSON-PATMAN ACT

The Robinson-Patman Act represented an implicit recognition that, regardless of the fact that two previous attempts had been made to prevent concentration in industrial corporations, small business still was at the mercy of predatory price cutters, who would engage in temporary local price cutting in order to eliminate them and then raise prices to the old level or even higher.[9] It was hoped that by passing this law, it might be possible to maintain and encourage competitive forces in distribution industries. The legislation was believed to be a means of countering the growing number of retail chain stores and their threat to independent shopkeepers, particularly in the drug trade. Chain stores, by virtue of their large financial resources, bought goods in large quantity from manufacturers, thus receiving favorable treatment in the form of quantity discounts, or disguised price concessions in the form of payments in lieu of middlemen's services, or as rebates for advertising conducted by the store on behalf of the product. The discrimination was legal, because prior to the enactment of the Robinson-Patman Act, the Clayton Act had no authority to regulate quantity discounts. Discounts had to be regulated, or else they would be used as a device for circumventing the intent of much of the resale price maintenance effort of the 1930s. At present, the Federal Trade Commission has the authority to fix and establish quantity limits, if it finds that large-volume purchasers are so few as to render price discounts discriminatory or liable to encourage monopoly. Services may not be rendered unless they are available freely to all alike.

Two court cases dealing with price discrimination are given in the appendix to this chapter in order to elaborate on the subject.

SUMMARY

In this chapter we presented a brief discussion of price discrimination — the selling of the same product at different prices to different persons. Some forms of price discrimination such as in utility or entertainment pricing are more or less

---

[9] As pointed out in Merle Fainsod and Lincoln Gordon, *Government and the American Economy*, rev. ed., W. W. Norton & Company, Inc., New York, 1948, p. 493, this concept dies hard. It is a carryover from the robber-baron tactics of the nineteenth century, and as we have indicated in Chapter 2, above, may not ever have been corrected.

taken for granted. Other forms, as in toll turnpikes, occasionally still are news-worthy. Discriminatory low pricing may on the other hand be useful in attracting demand to otherwise unused resources or services or to markets in which consumers otherwise would go without.

The conditions necessary for successful discrimination and the relation to price elasticity of demand are discussed. The conditions were seen to be non-transferability of products, a transportation cost greater than price differentials, specially ordered goods, or consumer preferences or ignorance allowing market segmentation.

Price discrimination varies depending on the extent to which the seller is able to extract consumer's surplus and three types or degrees were identified.

Appendix. Cases in Price Discrimination

ATLAS BUILDING PRODUCTS COMPANY

Appellant v. Diamond Block & Gravel Company, Appellee, U.S. Court of Appeals, Tenth Circuit, August 17, 1959.[10]

Diamond Block & Gravel Company, plaintiff-appellee, is a manufac-turer and seller of cinder concrete building blocks to the building trade in Las Cruces, New Mexico, and the vicinity; that the defendant-appellant, Atlas Build-ing Products Company, manufactures and sells the same products in El Paso, Texas, and the vicinity, where it has a virtual monopoly; and that it also sells those products to the building trade in Las Cruces and the vicinity. Beginning in 1950 and continuing to the filing of this suit, the defendant had systematically sold its products in Las Cruces at prices actually lower than its comparable El Paso sales; that it employed its highest El Paso prices to finance its price war against competitors in New Mexico, including the plaintiff; that such practices constituted price discrimination between different purchasers and the effect of which might be to lessen competition or tend to create a monopoly in commerce in building blocks, or to injure, destroy or prevent competition by the plaintiff with the defendant, and with persons who received the benefit of such discrimi-nations, or with customers of either of them. The suit asked for a triple damage of $200,000.00. The defendant claimed that it lowered its prices in New Mexico to meet competition in good faith. Such action, as we already know, is permitted under the Clayton Act.

Appellant's prevailing prices to dealers and contractors in El Paso during the period in question were 24¢ per standard block, less 10 percent, plus

---

[10] This case is taken, almost verbatim, from the *Federal Reporter*, 2d series, vol. 269, West Publishing Company, Minnesota, 1959, pp. 950–959.

1 1/2¢ delivery charge, or a delivered price of 23.1¢. However, its delivered price in Las Cruces, New Mexico, was 20¢, including a 3¢ haulage charge. The plaintiff's price (starting 1952) for cinder blocks was the same less 10 percent, plus 1 1/2¢ haulage or a net of 23.1¢ delivered price. After the plaintiff failed to meet the 20¢ delivered price continuously, contractors at Las Cruces all bought their cinder blocks from the defendant.

During the prosecution period, the defendant sold $162,000 worth of blocks in the Las Cruces area for prices in excess of 24.1¢, but the evidence showed that during the same period, it sold $603,163 worth of blocks at prices less than 24.1¢ in the same area. The defendant was the largest manufacturer and supplier of cinder concrete blocks in that territory.

Jury at the Federal District Court convicted Atlas Building Products Company for violating the Section II of the Clayton Act. The Court of Appeals upheld the lower court's decision, and the appellant brought the case to the U.S. Supreme Court which in June of 1960 denied the petition. (Atlas Building Products Co., Petitioner v. Diamond Block & Gravel Co., 363 U.S. 843, 4 L. Ed. 2d 1727, 80 S. Ct. 1608)

UTAH PIE COMPANY

Salt Lake City, Utah, plaintiff and three defendants, Continental Baking Company, Carnation Company, and Pet, Inc., all three large nationally known corporations.[11] The suit for treble damages and injunction under sections 4 and 16 of the Clayton Act, 38 Stat. 731, 15 U.S.C. sections 15 and 26 was brought by the plaintiff.[12] The complaint charged a conspiracy under sections 1 and 2 of the Sherman Act, 26 Stat. 209, as amended, 15 U.S.C. sections 1 and 2, and violations by each respondent of section 2(a) of the Clayton Act as amended by the Robinson-Patman Act, 49 Stat. 1526, 15 U.S.C. section 13(a). The issue was price cutting in frozen dessert pies—apple, cherry, boysenberry, peach, pumpkin, and mince. The period covered by the suit was from 1958 through the first eight months of 1961.

Utah Pie Company was a family-owned, small concern in Salt Lake City, and at the time of the litigation employed only eighteen workers, nine of whom were members of the family which controlled the firm. It had been baking regular pies and selling them in Utah and the surrounding states for thirty years by the time it entered the frozen pie business in late 1957. On the other hand, Continental Baking, Carnation, and Pet each entered the field nationally, as well

[11] 87 S. Ct., 1327; 386 U.S. 687; also Louis M. Kohlmeier, "Justices Extend Antitrust Law Regarding Regional Price-cutting by National Firms," *The Wall Street Journal*, April 25, 1967, p. 3.
[12] 15 U.S.C. section 15 provides recovery by the injured party (from the violators of antitrust laws) "threefold the damages by him sustained, and the cost of suit, including a reasonable attorney's fee"; while 15 U.S.C. section 26 provides injunction against private parties from violation of the antitrust laws.

as in the Salt Lake City market, in mid-1950. Sales of the new product rose rapidly with 57,060 dozen frozen pies being sold in the Salt Lake City market in 1958; 111,729 dozen in 1959; 184,569 dozen in 1960; and 266,908 dozen in 1961. Utah Pie's share in that market in those years was 66.5 percent, 34.3 percent, 45.5 percent, and 45.3 percent, respectively.[13] Even though its share of the market declined, Utah Pie's sales of frozen pies increased steadily over the period. Furthermore, its total sales also went up steadily, rising from $238,000 in the fiscal year ending October 31, 1957, to $589,000 in 1961. The operating results for those years showed a loss of $6,461 in 1957; a net income of $7,090 in 1958; $11,897 in 1959; $7,636 in 1960; and $9,216 in 1961. The company's net worth increased from $31,651.98 on October 31, 1957, to $68,802.13 four years later. The company's success in the frozen pie field was due partly to its reputation and partly to the quick and low-cost supply, since it had a plant located in the city, while its three major competitors had to ship pies from out-of-town plants, mainly in California.

When Utah Pie entered the new field, it sold its frozen pies at $4.15 a dozen to retailers, substantially lower then $4.80 to $5.00 a dozen charged by its three major competitors. In the latter part of 1958, Pet, the nearest competitor, started to sell its pies to a supermarket chain at a price slightly lower than the $4.15 a dozen charged by Utah Pie. The three other companies followed suit.

As a result, the price structure began to deteriorate. By 1961, Pet was selling some types of its own pies at $3.56 a dozen; Carnation and Continental Baking cut their prices to $3.30 and $2.85, respectively. Utah Pie retaliated by lowering its price to $2.75.

In the suit filed in 1961, Utah Pie charged that the price cutting had held down its profit. In addition, the local price cutting by the big, nationally known, multiproduct firms constituted a serious threat to competition and to small producers.[14] The jury at the federal district court agreed to the charge and awarded the plaintiff treble damages. The defendants appealed and won a reverse verdict from a U.S. Appeals Court. The court ruled that the evidence was not sufficient to show that the price cutting had any probable injury to competi-

---

[13] The sharp decline in the market share in 1959 was the result of price cutting initiated by Pet, which raised its market share from 16.4 percent in 1958 to 35.5 percent a year later. Utah Pie's sales volume nevertheless increased, which gives some support to the argument in Chapter 2 on the validity of arguments claiming predatory competition.

[14] According to information brought out during the trial, for seven of the forty-four months Pet's prices in Salt Lake City were lower than those charged in the California markets, even though Pet had to ship frozen pies into the city from California, thus adding a freight cost of 30 to 35 cents per dozen.

tion. It held that Utah Pie was in effect asking for the privilege of keeping indefinitely the 66 percent market share the company had had in 1958. "To approve such a contention," wrote the U.S. Appeals Court, "would be to hold that Utah Pie was entitled to maintain a position which approached a monopoly."

The case was finally brought to the Supreme Court and it was settled in favor of the plaintiff. The Court ruled that "there was ample evidence to show that each (of the three big competitors) contributed to what proved to be a deteriorating price structure and each in the course of the on-going price competition sold frozen pies in the Salt Lake market at prices lower than they sold pies in other markets considerably closer to their plants."

The significance of the Supreme Court's decision in this case is that previously the Clayton Act, as amended by the Robinson-Patman Act, was applicable to cases where financially strong and nationwide companies cut prices in one locality alone, with the intention of eliminating a competitor such as in the building products case presented above. Now if a strong and large company cuts price in one area but not in all others, it may be held liable of violating section II of the Clayton Act, even though a smaller local company continues to hold the dominant position in the market. As pointed out by Justice White who wrote the majority opinion (in a 6 to 2 decision), "the (Clayton) Act reaches price discrimination that erodes competition as much as that intended to have immediate destructive impact."

Review Questions

1. What is meant by price discrimination?
2. What is the difference between price discrimination and the skimming price policy?
3. Why is price discrimination important to a firm's pricing policy?
4. What is the relation between price discrimination and the equimarginal theory?
5. What are the necessary conditions for price discrimination?
6. What is the difference between the first degree and the second degree of price discrimination?
7. How do you define the third degree of price discrimination?
8. What is the impact of the Robinson-Patman Act on price discrimination?
9. Under what conditions is price discrimination permissible by law?

Case 1. The Blue Ridge Oil Company

The Blue Ridge Oil Company, a major producer and refiner of gasoline and related products, has its main plant facilities located in northeastern Pennsylvania. It sells its products to distributors and large commercial customers in the New York metropolitan area. The normal marketing structure is sale from supplier to distributor, then to dealer and to customers.

Assume there are two major distributors, Acme Oil Company and Bulky Oil Company purchasing bulk gasoline from the supplier, who maintains two depots, in New York and New Jersey, respectively. The distributor performs the function of transporting the bulk product from the supplier's depot to its own local distribution point for delivery to retail establishments in their area. The standard procedure is for Acme Oil to pick up the product in New York, with Bulky Oil picking up bulk gasoline in New Jersey. Because of difference in transport distance, the cost of carriage from New Jersey to Bulky Oil's marshalling point is 1 cent per gallon more than the cost of transport which Acme Oil incurs. To equalize effective price between the two, the supplier has allowed a 1-cent-per-gallon discount to Bulky Oil.

The two distributors market their gasoline in two separate regions of the New York metropolitan area; however, their territory is nonexclusive. A gentlemen's agreement is in effect which limits the distributors to their respective areas. At this time, however, there are fringe areas currently developing which are not located within the area of either distributor, but whose accounts are being actively solicited by both. In addition to the activity of the distributors, the supplier sells direct to certain large commercial customers such as Aber's rental agencies and taxi companies. Under these circumstances, the supplier normally engages the distributor to supply transportation of the product from the bulk plant to the customer. As to this service, the distributors cross-deliver into their competitors' territory.

QUESTIONS

1. (a) If Bulky Oil now picks up in New York, saving 1 cent per gallon, while the supplier continues the 1-cent discount, what effect would this have on competition between the two distributors?
   (b) What effect would the Robinson-Patman Act have on this practice?
2. (a) Assuming the two distributors serviced the same area pattern, what effect would this have on competition?
   (b) What effect would the Act have on this practice?
3. (a) Assume that the supplier sells direct to a large commercial customer for its own use, at the same price as that offered to Acme Oil. In addition, the

supplier contracts with the distributor to deliver the bulk gas to the customer while absorbing the cost of delivery. What effect would this have on competition, considering that the customer lies within the service region of Acme Oil?

(b) What effect would the Act have on this practice?

Note: Case 1 was prepared by Robert E. Aber under the supervision of Francis P. Sing. Mr. Aber is a student at Georgetown University Law School.

Case 2. The Skinner Electrical and Home Supply Company

Chapter 2 has given us an insight into the effect of price discrimination on the operation of the competitive market structure. There are other closely related forms of discrimination which have the same effect. One form of discrimination and the method of dealing with it is described in section 2(e) of the Robinson-Patman Act.

This section of the Act provides:

It shall be unlawful for any person to discriminate in favor of one purchaser against another purchaser or purchasers of a commodity bought for resale, with or without processing, by contracting to furnish or furnishing, or by contributing to the furnishing of, any services or facilities connected with the processing, handling, sale or offering for sale of such commodity so purchased upon terms not accorded to all purchasers on proportionally equal terms.

With this in mind, consider the case of Skinner Electrical and Home Supply Company which brought suit against United States Steel Corporation for alleged discrimination. United States Steel controlled Union Supply Company, which operated a competing retail store in the same area. United States Steel, on direction of its employees, made a payroll deduction from their wages and paid these sums to Union Supply Company for purchases its employees made there.

Skinner Company, in its suit, maintained that (1) United States Steel had discriminated against Skinner Company by furnishing its competitor the service of withholding from employees' wages the cost of goods purchased, and refusing such service to Skinner, thereby violating section 2(e) of the Robinson-Patman Act. (2) That United States Steel and Union Supply Company conspired to discriminate against Skinner Company, thereby violating the Robinson-Patman Act.

United States Steel made direct sales to Union Supply Company. There were minimal sales between United States Steel and Skinner Company.

QUESTION

1. Was the intent of Congress, expressed in section 2(e) of the Robinson-Patman Act, to require that a manufacturer accord to all merchants that may acquire its goods, the right to extend credit to the employees of the manufacturer and have payment withheld from their wages, even though such a service was rendered to a competitor?

Note: Case 2 was prepared by Robert E. Aber under the supervision of Francis P. Sing. Mr. Aber is a student at Georgetown University Law School.

Suggested Reading

Boulding, Kenneth E.: *Economic Analysis,* 4th ed., vol. 1, Harper & Row, Publishers, Incorporated, New York, 1966.

Dean, Joel: *Managerial Economics,* Prentice-Hall, Inc., Englewood Cliffs, N.J., 1951.

Due, John F., and Robert W. Clower: *Intermediate Economic Analysis,* 5th ed., Richard D. Irwin, Inc., Homewood, Ill., 1966.

Haynes, William W.: *Managerial Economics,* rev. ed., Business Publications, Inc., Austin, Texas, 1969.

Kintner, Earl W.: *The Robinson-Patman Primer,* The Macmillan Company, New York, 1970.

Pigou, A. C.: *The Economics of Welfare,* 4th ed., Macmillan & Co., Ltd., London, 1960.

Robinson, Joan: *The Economics of Imperfect Competition,* Macmillan & Co., Ltd., London, 1933.

Spencer, Milton H.: *Managerial Economics,* 3d ed., Richard D. Irwin, Inc., Homewood, Ill., 1968.

Stigler, George J.: *The Theory of Price,* 3d ed., The Macmillan Company, New York, 1966.

Watson, Donald S.: *Price Theory and Its Uses,* 2d ed., Houghton Mifflin Company, Boston, 1968.

part 4
financial management and control

chapter 11
profit concept
and
measurement

This chapter and the one that follows take up the concept and significance of profit to a firm, and methods of measurement, planning, and control of profit. Our definition of profit follows the traditional theory of distribution of income by which we mean profit is the residual part of revenue received by a firm. From the stockholders' point of view, profit, although a residual, is the factor price for equity capital needed to induce investors, who have alternative uses for their capital, to purchase stock.

SIGNIFICANCE OF PROFIT TO A FIRM

The survival of a firm depends upon the ability of that firm to make profit. This seemingly self-evident statement needs some elaboration. It is rather easy to understand that when a firm loses money year-in and year-out, it cannot long survive. However, if the firm cannot make a sufficient amount of profit annually, it also cannot remain long in business. An insufficient amount of profit may be defined as an amount of profit expressed as a ratio to invested capital smaller than that which may be earned on a high-grade bond. Unless a company can earn, within a reasonable period of time, a rate of return on its equity greater than the prevailing high-grade bond rate, it cannot hope to compete for equity funds in the capital market. This is so because investors prefer the type of security, the yield on which is certain, to that the return on which is uncertain. If investors have reason to believe that the current return on equity which is smaller than the yield on bonds is more or less a long-run situation, they will switch from common stock to bonds, thus depressing the price of the common stock and rendering the task of financing capital expenditures through common stock issuance more difficult and more costly.[1] A firm unable to obtain equity funds at a reasonable cost probably faces the same difficulty with debt financing. Accordingly, its capital expansion program will sooner or later come to a halt and its survival may be in jeopardy.[2] Under our economic system, a firm's survival often depends upon its ability to innovate and expand.

REWARD FOR RISK BEARING

As residual share owners, common stockholders of a firm expect to receive a return on their investment depending upon the fortunes of the firm. Generally speaking, the amount of reward correlates positively with the degree of risk involved. For example, the public utility industry is a low-risk business. Because of its monopolistic power (authorized by state and/or federal governments), together with the nature of its product, a public utility is not worried about the uncertainty of getting a reasonable amount of profit. Since the risk of loss is very small, the average rate of return on invested capital for a public utility is accordingly low, and a 6 percent rate is considered typical. On the other hand, wildcat oil companies bear a very high degree of risk. When an oil company drills a hole in a piece of land where oil has not been found before, it frequently faces heavy odds against finding oil. However, when and if oil is found, the return on investment is very handsome indeed.[3]

Nowadays, we have no trouble understanding that profit is a reward for risk bearing, but economists did not explicitly expound this theory of profit until the beginning of the present century. F. B. Hawley explicitly formulated the risk-bearing theory of profit, thus anticipating Frank H. Knight's famous work, *Risk, Uncertainty and Profit* by fourteen years. However, Knight goes one step further and argues that risk which can be calculated and insured is not the cause of profit. Profit arises only when risk is unknown and cannot be insured

[1] Of course, investors buy common stocks not only on yield alone but also for capital appreciation. But capital appreciation depends upon the rate of return on invested capital and the rate of growth of earnings per share of common stock. If a company cannot earn a satisfactory rate of return for a number of years, its earnings per common share will not grow either.

[2] We assume that because the firm cannot generate sufficient funds internally, it has to raise funds from outside sources. In this connection, Joel Dean states ". . . virtually every company interviewed made realized profits a prerequisite for capital expenditures." He refers to the "Minneapolis Project," a survey concerning capital expenditures conducted in 1950. "This finding is contrary to the economist's notion that expected profits from the expenditure are the necessary condition and that past profits are irrelevant." *Capital Budgeting*, Columbia University Press, New York, 1951, p. 27.

[3] Amerada Hess, an oil firm outstanding in discovering new oil wells, earns a high rate of return on invested capital, amounting to 23.2 percent for 1969. Actually, the rate would have been higher had the firm not benefited from the depletion allowance provided in our current income tax law. What this means is that by charging gross revenue a given percentage for depletion (of exhaustible natural resources), a firm's reported income becomes lower. The current rate for depletion allowance for oil industry is 22 percent. Such allowance is taken over and above the intangible exploration expense and depreciation for oil well equipment.

against, and such risk should be properly called uncertainty.[4] Knight considers that capital is a mobile fund, and profit is not a necessity to induce investment. It tends to disappear under the condition of certainty, because the price of a product is already given and the entrepreneur knowing his demand schedule would produce at the level of output where the selling price of the product equals the lowest average and marginal cost of production.[5] The real world producer faces uncertainty as to the price level which will prevail when he ships his output to the market, nor can he tell whether or not his future cost of production and of marketing will come close to his estimates.

In a sense, profit as a reward for risk bearing poses a challenge to those businessmen with entrepreneurial spirit. One cannot help but wonder what would be the present state of our economy if it were not for profit which drove countless entrepreneurs (among the well-known ones are Andrew Carnegie and Henry Ford) to excel. There might be some other motives which prompt men of vision and courage to undertake risk in exploring minerals, building railroads, factories, and refineries, but it seems to us that none is as powerful an inducement as profit in this respect.

YARDSTICK OF SUCCESS

Profit provides the only tangible yardstick with which to measure the success or failure of a firm. For example, changes in sales volume over a period of years are not a good yardstick to compare the success of two different companies, because the one with increased sales may also have had a lower return on invested capital owing to a faster rate of increase in the cost of production and marketing. Montgomery Ward & Company, for example, reported a 31 percent decline in net profit for the fiscal year 1966, even though sales volume had set a new record, rising from $1,748 million a year earlier to $1,894 million, an increase of 8.3 percent. The company earned $16.5 million, or $1.24 per common share as compared with $24.0 million, or $1.83 a share, for the same period of years On the other hand, good will and the popularity of a firm

---

[4] In discussing John B. Clark's theory of profit (Clark contended that profit was a result of dynamic changes, such as invention and friction in the economy), Knight explains that "dynamic changes give rise to a peculiar form of income only in so far as the changes and their consequences are unpredictable in character. . . .

"It is not dynamic change, nor any change, as such, which causes profit, but the divergence of actual conditions from those which have been expected and on the basis of which business arrangements have been made. For a satisfactory explanation of profit we seem to be thrown back from the 'dynamic' theory to the Uncertainty of the Future, a condition of affairs loosely designated by the term 'risk' in ordinary language and in business parlance." *Risk, Uncertainty and Profit,* Houghton Mifflin Company, Boston, 1921, pp. 37–38.

[5] Properly speaking, the term profit as used here represents the so-called monopolistic profit, which is the excess of what is needed to induce investors to buy the common stock of a firm. Compensation for equity capital is part of the average cost of production.

cannot be subjected to quantitative measurement and comparison. How, for instance, can one compare customer's good will toward General Motors Corporation as against that toward Ford Motor Company? The only tangible way is to find out which firm has more repeat sales, and we are back to dollars and cents again.

In using profit as a yardstick to measure the success of a company, we have to consider it in terms of an absolute amount and as a ratio. When we use absolute amount of profit to gauge the success of a firm, we have to look at it in terms of its height, its breadth of base, and its trend.[6] The height of profit refers obviously to its amount. The larger the amount, the better the company is managed, other things being equal. The breadth of the profit base means the size of a firm's invested capital. If two firms earn the same rate of return on invested capital, but one has a much larger base than the other, it will naturally show a much larger amount of profit.[7] Finally, the trend of profit is important to management in that it shows where the company is heading.

Ratio analysis of profitability is preferable to that based upon absolute amount, because by reducing profit to relative terms, companies of different size (in terms of assets or sales) can be compared. Here we have measures such as the rate of return on investment and net profit margin. The former will be taken up later in this chapter. Net profit margin is widely used as a measure of the efficiency of the management. If a firm can maintain its net profit margin when sales go up, its profit in dollar terms will also rise. Generally speaking, a well-managed firm not only can maintain its net profit margin but can increase it when sales go up. Operating profit margin also reflects operating efficiency of a company. It is the difference between operating expenses and net sales. Naturally, the larger the ratio, the more efficient the firm is, because it reflects lower expenses.

FOCUS FOR OPERATION CONTROL

Profit, expressed as a rate of return on investment, is a significant tool of operation control. For control of operations, each division or subsidiary is assigned a monthly profit budget which is included in a yearly budget. The budget is prepared in conjunction with sales and production forecasts made in the preceding fiscal period. Actual results are recorded side by side with the projected figures so that the division manager is able to compare what he should have done with what he has actually accomplished. The variance is analyzed to find ways to improve the division performance if results from opera-

[6] Philip Marvin, "Some Basic Concepts Underlying Company Strategy," *Developing a Product Strategy*, American Management Association, New York, 1959, p. 15.

[7] General Motors is larger than Chrysler Corporation, not only in terms of asset value but also with respect to rate of return on investment. In 1969, the rate of return for the former was 16.7 percent, as compared to 4.2 percent for the latter.

tions turn out to be short of budget. If what is budgeted is out of line, the sales forecast and the budget are revised. Steps taken to improve the performance of the division or to revise the budget can be said to flow from the control mechanism. More on this aspect will be taken up in the next chapter.

MEASUREMENT OF PROFIT

The concept of profit has various connotations to various people. Because of the difference in their training and functions, economists and accountants measure profit differently. In the following section, we shall examine the two divergent viewpoints on this topic.

MEASURING PROFIT BY THE ACCOUNTING METHOD

Accountants define profit as the excess of income over expenses, with both of them being figured on an accrued basis. That is, income and expenses are allocated to the time period in which they are earned or incurred. Depreciation is often cited as an example of the accrued basis of measuring expenses. A $100,000 cutting machine tool with a useful life of ten years and no salvage value at the end of the period will charge $10,000 or one-tenth of the total annually as expense, if we use a straight-line depreciation method. The annual deduction of $10,000 from current revenue naturally involves no current cash outlay. Even though obsolescence is taken into consideration by the accountants in their depreciation policy, as when accelerated depreciation or faster writeoff of equipment is adopted, the fact that opportunity cost is not considered by them causes a difference in defining profit between them and economists.

Accounting procedures and practices which affect the measurement of profit include methods of depreciation, treatment of capital gains and losses, and inventory evaluation methods.

Methods of Depreciation. Depreciation in economic terms means capital consumption. From the accountants' point of view, it is an allocation of the outlay for fixed assets, an allocation of expenditures over time. What concerns us here is that reported earnings are affected by the various methods of depreciation in use today.

The present accelerated depreciation rules originate from the 1954 Revenue Act, and are applicable to any fixed assets which have at least three-year life or longer. The main purpose of the accelerated depreciation methods is to encourage capital expansion by allowing business firms to recover the major part of their investments in the early years of the useful life of the fixed assets. It is to some extent an offset to the impact of inflation on capital investments. Even though business concerns cannot reevaluate their fixed assets according to current price level as the basis for depreciation, they can now write off their plant

TABLE 11-1. STRAIGHT-LINE VERSUS ACCELERATED METHOD OF DEPRECIATION°

Year	Straight-line Annual Amount	Straight-line Cumulative Amount	Double Declining Balance† Annual Amount	Double Declining Balance† Cumulative Amount	Sum of the Year's Digits Annual Amount	Sum of the Year's Digits Cumulative Amount
1	$10.00	$ 10.00	$20.00	$20.00	$18.18	$ 18.18
2	10.00	20.00	16.00	36.00	16.36	34.54
3	10.00	30.00	12.80	48.80	14.54	49.09
4	10.00	40.00	10.24	59.04	12.73	61.81
5	10.00	50.00	8.19	67.23	10.91	72.7
6	10.00	60.00	6.55	73.78	9.09	81.81
7	10.00	70.00	5.24	79.02	7.27	89.08
8	10.00	80.00	4.20	83.22	5.45	94.54
9	10.00	90.00	3.36	86.58	3.64	98.17
10	10.00	100.00	2.68	89.26	1.82	100.00

° Figures are in thousands of dollars.
† Double declining balance is based upon a certain percentage of the preceding year's property value, and therefore, the property cannot be completely depreciated within the time limit of the useful life of the machine. Companies using such a method usually switch to straight-line depreciation about halfway through the useful life of the machine.

and equipment faster than otherwise, so as to recover their investments earlier. The following simplified case illustrates how the accelerated depreciation rules work.

Let us assume that a metal cutting machine has a useful life of ten years, and will have no salvage value whatsoever afterward. The machine costs $100,000.

As can be seen from Table 11-1, a company would show smaller reported earnings in the early years of a capital project if it adopted either of the accelerated depreciation methods. Needless to say, it would report higher earnings afterward, other things being equal.

Capital Gain or Loss. There are two aspects of the treatment of capital gain or loss which deserve discussion: one is the legal aspect, and the other, accounting procedure. According to the present tax law, property which is not held for ordinary business activity realizes a capital gain if that property is held longer than six months and its value at the time of sale has appreciated. Business firms may not deduct capital losses against ordinary income; they have to offset capital losses by capital gains.[8] If the present tax law on capital gains and losses were to be changed so that, instead of requiring a six-month period, property had to be held longer to qualify for capital gains treatment, a different amount of after-tax profit would be reported with no change in operating conditions or ef-

[8] Exceptions to this rule are accorded to commercial banks and small business investment companies. Any capital losses they suffer may be charged against current income.

ficiency. What we mean is that variations in reported profit are not necessarily the result of any vicissitude of the firm; they may be the result of a change of law.

The way capital gains or losses are handled also affects a firm's reported earnings. According to traditional accounting practice, a firm realizes profit on its investment only when the property is sold, regardless of fluctuations in property value during the period the property is held. Suppose for example, after being held for three years, securities having an initial purchase price of $1,000 are sold for $2,500, with a capital gain of $1,500. Present accounting procedure would treat the entire capital gain as having occurred in that particular year, even though the actual gain in third year's profit may be only $500. Were such an accounting procedure to be changed, so that the gain or loss from investments is recorded each year, whether or not realized, the purchaser would have reported a different amount of profit for the year when the securities were sold.

Evaluation of Inventory. Inventory adjustment is needed because of the effect of inflation or deflation and the impact of innovation or technological development on the value of inventory. To handle the first situation, accountants use two different methods of evaluation to offset, to a certain degree, the effect of price fluctuation on inventory value. These two methods are the "first-in-first-out" (FIFO) and "last-in-first-out" (LIFO) methods. During a period of rising prices, a firm which uses the LIFO method will show lower earnings than otherwise. If instead, it chooses the FIFO method, its reported earnings would be overstated, because part of the profit results from price inflation. If, on the other hand, a company adopts the FIFO method during a period of deflation, it may well show a loss in operation or its profit will be understated.

Problems in inventory adjustment also result from rapid technological change and its impact on the salability of inventory. The International Business Machines Corporation has produced several models of digital computers, the most modern one being the 370. As the new model is being manufactured, the older ones such as the 7090 become less valuable. Fortunately, IBM can sell its computers as they are produced, and so it does not have to adjust a finished goods inventory. However, some companies in other scientific product areas have to reevaluate their inventories because of technological obsolescence. American Photocopy Equipment Company, for example, lost $1,973,000 in the 1966 fiscal year, of which two-thirds was caused by a $1,218,000 writeoff of inventory.

MEASURING PROFIT ACCORDING TO THE ECONOMISTS' VIEWPOINT

The basic difference we have noted between accountants and economists in defining profit is in the recognition of opportunity cost by the latter. This concept is very important in the application of economic theory to the decision making of a firm. For example, in calculating cost of production, economists include the value of the best alternative the common stockholder's investment could earn, whether or not the company makes any profit.

Suppose the prevailing interest rate on long-term top-quality corporate bonds is 8 percent, the common stockholders should get at least that rate of return on their capital. The economist would use this rate as the opportunity cost of equity. While the common stockholders want a rate of return more than 8 percent on their investment, because of the risk in owning a business, they certainly are not willing to buy common stock if the rate of return on equity is less than 8 percent. How much more than 8 percent return the common stockholders will accept depends upon the degree of risk to which the company is subject. As a rule, the greater the degree of risk the company faces, the greater the rate of return required to attract funds from investors. The 8 percent rate is therefore considered the opportunity cost of capital and the excess is defined as profit in an economic sense.

THE PROFIT MAXIMIZATION ASSUMPTION

The question of whether or not a company tries to maximize profit has been raised over and over again in the discussion of the motives of management. To us the question should be rephrased into two separate parts: first, whether a company tries to maximize profit, and second, whether it can maximize profit.

DOES A FIRM TRY TO MAXIMIZE PROFIT?

The belief that a firm tries to maximize profit is based upon the notion that businessmen are rational and economic-minded, and that they weigh all the alternatives open to them before they commit the scarce resources at their disposal to any particular use. It follows that businessmen will attempt to choose the best among all alternatives, and profit maximization is a foregone conclusion. According to this school of thought, all activities of the firm are directed, even indirectly, toward maximizing profit. These activities include not only production and sales, but also consumer service, community aid, and other public services.

Texaco, Inc., for example, for many years has been sponsoring weekly the live broadcast of opera from the Metropolitan Opera House in New York City. To opera lovers, there is no finer public service a private corporation can offer. It would not be surprising to find that many of the listeners actually buy the company's gasoline and other oil products. Whether or not the company, by sponsoring the broadcast, has in mind profit maximization is difficult to say, but we can be sure that the company has built up a strong good will among the listeners, so that perhaps part of the annual increase in sales may be attributable to the program.

Some economists and businessmen contend that the theory of profit maximization is neither valid nor accurate as a basis for business decisions. As they see it, the basic objective of a firm and the rationale on which decisions are based is not profit maximization but the survival of the firm. Furthermore, some believe that what a company wants to earn is not maximum profit but only a satisfactory rate of return on invested capital. The following reasons have been given as to why a firm does not try to maximize profit.

Short-run Objectives. In the short run, a firm may have other goals which supersede profit maximization, such as a desire to break into a new market. It may conduct a price war to drive competitors out of a given market.

To break into a new market, the initial cash outlays are heavy. A new marketing organization may have to be set up, advertising expenditures have to increase, the cost of initial production is usually high in relation to the volume produced, and frequently new processes encounter technical difficulty in operation. The Ford Motor Company, for example, lost money for several years after acquiring Philco as a shortcut to enter the electronics business. The American Photocopy Equipment Company suffered losses in the 1965 fiscal year from the introduction of its Super-Stat, a new photocopy machine using a dry-process method, competitive to the Xerox machine.

Another factor which runs counter to the profit maximization objective is the desire to build up a business empire. To build an empire rapidly, businessmen resort to merger. In the process of buying up other companies, the empire builders are willing to sacrifice profit in the short run in order to obtain larger profits in the long run. Moreover, in the urge to become industrial magnates, they may be blind to the fundamental weaknesses of the companies they acquire, or they may feel that they are more capable and talented than the managements of the acquired firms. In any case, the empire builders are willing to pay higher prices for the acquired firms, believing that any losses, if they ever occur, will be temporary. As things turn out, some empire builders have found themselves making wrong decisions, not only for the short run but also for the long run.

Pressure for Cost Control. Because of varying conditions, a firm's desire to maximize profit will vary. During prosperity, when profits are rising, the pressure to control cost and to increase sales is reduced. On the other hand, when depression comes, management is forced by absolute and relative falling profits, to tighten cost control and to increase sales.

Satisfactory Rate of Return on Investment. Some economists contend that what management adopts as the goal of management is not profit maximization but a satisfactory rate of return on investment or a satisfactory level of profit. The "new" theory (in contrast to the classical theory of profit maximization) derives its analytical approach from psychology. According to Herbert A. Simon, the motive to act originates from drive, and once the drive is satisfied, action ceases. Furthermore, the conditions to satisfy a drive are changeable, and may be stimulated by an aspiration level which adjusts itself upward or downward depending upon experience acquired.

"If we seek to explain business behavior in the terms of this theory," Simon explains, "we must expect the firm's goals to be not maximizing profit, but attaining a certain level or rate of profit, holding a certain share of the market or a certain level of sales."[9] According to this theory, a firm would choose the best of alternatives open to it, if these alternatives are at or above its aspiration level. However, when none of the alternatives satisfies the current aspiration level, the firm will start searching for a new goal or revising the existing target of operations. In other words, a firm will adjust its aspiration level in such a manner that goals will be attainable.[10]

Sales Maximization. A variation of the satisfactory rate of return objective is sales maximization. According to Baumol, sales maximization has replaced profit maximization as a goal of a firm.[11] Under a profit constraint, sales maximization refers to maximizing total revenue. As shown in Figure 11-1, sales maximization does not require a very large physical output. Normally, there will be a well-determined production level which satisfies the sales maximization objective, and that is where elasticity of demand is unity, or what amounts to the same thing, where marginal revenue is zero, as indicated by the point, R_m.

Sales maximization, though sought after as an objective, may not enable the firm to meet the "minimum" profit level requirement if the level, as set by the competitive market condition, is higher than that obtained by sales maximization. For example, if the required profit level is OY_1, the management will be content with sales maximization and its production level will be OQ_m. However, if the required profit level is OY_3, the management has to curtail production to OQ_n in order to meet the "minimum" profit level requirement. The new

[9] Herbert A. Simon, "Theories of Decision-making in Economics and Behavioral Science," *Survey of Economic Theory*, St. Martin's Press, Inc., New York, 1967, vol. III, p. 10. Also see Richard M. Cyert and James G. March, *A Behavioral Theory of the Firm*, Prentice-Hall, Inc., Englewood Cliffs, N.J., 1963.

[10] Simon explains the process of adjusting goals in the following manner: "Psychological studies of the formation and change of aspiration levels support propositions of the following kinds. (a) When performance falls short of the level of aspirations, search behavior (particularly search for new alternatives of action) is induced. (b) At the same time, the level of aspiration begins to adjust itself downward until goals reach levels that are practically attainable. (c) If the two mechanisms just listed operate too slowly to adapt aspirations to performance, emotional behavior—apathy or aggression, for example—will replace rational adaptive behavior." *Op. cit.*, pp. 10–11.

[11] William J. Baumol, *Economic Theory and Operations Analysis*, 2d ed., Prentice-Hall, Inc. Englewood Cliffs, N.J., 1965, pp. 301–303.

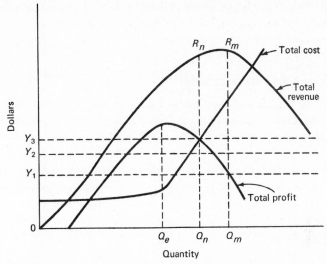

Figure 11-1. Sales maximization versus profit maximization.

output level is then below that for sales maximization but above Q_e the level for profit maximization. In other words, with a profit constraint, sales maximization objective has become, in effect, that of earning a satisfactory rate of return on investment.

Social Responsibility and Moral Principle. Social responsibility and moral principle are believed to have an important bearing on the attitude of businessmen toward profit maximization. Economists who espouse this viewpoint consider profit maximization as immoral and repugnant to businessmen's sense of fair play. They argue that businessmen maintain an equitable and balanced attitude toward labor and consumers. What businessmen try to earn is not maximum profit, but a fair rate of return on the invested capital.[12]

Pressure from Government and Labor. Antitrust laws are well known to businessmen, and the pressure put on those firms which have tried to raise prices in recent years has been great. For example, President Kennedy criticized the steel industry for its untimely action in raising steel prices in 1962. President Johnson forced oil companies to roll back part of the price hike initiated by Phillips Petroleum Company and Continental Oil Company in 1967 by threatening to lower import quotas. One way to avoid being sued for violating antitrust laws is not to maximize profit, because profit level is one of the relevant elements considered in the administration of the Sherman Antitrust Act.

[12] Robert N. Anthony, "The Trouble with Profit Maximization," *Harvard Business Review*, vol. 38, no. 6, pp. 132–133, Nov.–Dec., 1960.

Demand for higher wages by labor unions also can exert considerable pressure on firms not to maximize profit. Ability to pay is a guideline for labor contract negotiation, and to maximize profit is certainly to induce labor unions to clamor for higher wages.[13]

CAN A FIRM MAXIMIZE PROFIT?

After having discussed the tenability of the contention that a firm sets profit maximization as its goal, we come to the second question, and that is whether or not a firm can maximize profit.

Theoretical Aspect. Theoretically speaking, a firm can maximize its profit by simply equating its marginal revenue with its marginal cost. As indicated in Chapter 5, a rational consumer who seeks to obtain the maximum satisfaction from a given limited resource, say money, will not make a decision which will cause marginal cost to exceed marginal revenue or which will bring about either

[13] There are some other reasons advanced by economists concerning the untenability of profit maximization, and they include leisure enjoyed by top executives, desire to create a harmonious atmosphere conducive to healthy employee relations, and fostering of consumers' good will.

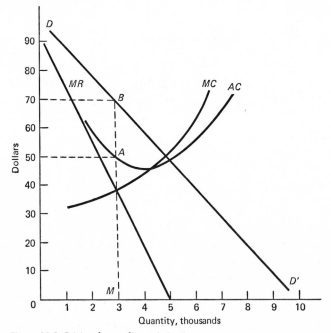

Figure 11-2. Pricing for profit maximization.

a profit reduction or an increase in loss. A businessman will therefore continue to invest so long as incremental receipts are larger than incremental outlays. When the point is reached where marginal revenue equals marginal cost, capital expansion will stop, because by then profit maximization will have been achieved. This analysis is illustrated in Figure 11-2.

In Figure 11-2, the maximum profit level of production is 3,000 units as indicated by M on the X axis. At that level, price per unit is $70; total revenue is $210,000 of which total cost (MA × OM) is $150,000 and total profit (AB × OM), $60,000. If the company produces more, it will earn less, because marginal cost will exceed marginal revenue. The gap between the two will become wider and wider as the company continues to expand output. Total revenue, however, will keep rising until the marginal revenue equals zero, as indicated by point R_m in Figure 11-1.

Practical Aspect. In theory, we know that if a firm is able to maximize profit, resources will be allocated to achieve that objective. In practice, however, because the management of a firm simply does not know when its marginal revenue and marginal cost meet, it may not be able to maximize profit. It has little idea where the curves intersect because (1) firm's records normally are not kept in marginal or incremental terms, and (2) output is normally not capable of being adjusted unit by unit.

If it were possible to use a marginal cost basis, the firm still might not be able to maximize profit, because the future is too uncertain to permit any businessman to predict successfully the outcome of his decisions. If a firm's president knew definitely that in the current fiscal year his firm could sell the 1,000 units of its product, which happened to be the optimal level of production, then he would produce exactly that amount. However, since he is not sure that his estimate of future sales will turn out to be correct, he is in no position to maximize profit.[14]

SUMMARY

In this chapter we have discussed the concept of profit, its measurement, and significance to a firm. Profit may be defined as the residual part of revenue. It is significant because (1) the survival of a firm depends upon its ability to earn profit; (2) it is a reward for risk bearing; (3) it is a yardstick of success; and (4) it provides a focus for operation control.

[14] In order to overcome the factor of uncertainty, economists have posed the idea of expected utility as a guide to decision making under uncertainty. However, the frequency distribution of the recent past may not hold true in the immediate future, and expected utility is often based on past experience.

Even though both accountants and economists have the same concept of profit, they do not agree on the measurement of profit. This is because of the economist's recognition of opportunity cost for those economic resources which have alternative uses. In this connection, we also have demonstrated that, because of the adoption of different accounting procedures, measurement of profit varies widely. Some of these procedures involve methods of depreciation, the treatment of capital gain or loss, and the methods of evaluation of inventory.

Finally, we have analyzed the profit maximization assumption, and we have concluded that, in general, a firm does not try to maximize profit because (1) in the short run, there are other objectives which require more of the management's attention; (2) pressure for cost control is not uniform throughout the entire business cycle; (3) what businessmen want to earn is a satisfactory rate of return on investment; (4) sales maximization has replaced profit maximization as a goal; (5) social responsibility has prevented many businessmen from trying to maximize profit; and (6) pressure from government and labor unions has deterred corporations from earning the optimal profit.

As a concluding remark, we have shown that, in theory, a firm can achieve profit maximization. However, it cannot do so in practice because of the difficulty in forecasting future events, together with the fact that businessmen do not keep their reocrds on a marginal concept basis.

Review Questions

1. What is profit? Why is it different from interest?
2. What is the significance of profit to a firm?
3. What is the difference between risk and uncertainty?
4. What has uncertainty to do with profit?
5. What is the basic difference in defining profit by economists and accountants?
6. What are some accounting methods which can be used to change reported profit?
7. Why is the concept of profit maximization closely related to the theory of the firm?
8. Does a firm in general adopt profit maximization as its goal in the short run?
9. Can a firm achieve profit maximization in practice?
10. What are some objections to the contention that a firm wants to maximize its profit?

Suggested Reading

Anthony, Robert N.: "The Trouble with Profit Maximization," *Harvard Business Review*, vol. 38, no. 6, pp. 26–134, Nov.–Dec., 1960.

Baumol, William J.: *Economic Theory and Operations Analysis*, 2d ed., Prentice-Hall, Inc., Englewood Cliffs, N.J., 1965.

Cohen, Kalman J., and Richard M. Cyert: *Theory of the Firm*, Prentice-Hall, Inc., Englewood Cliffs, N.J., 1965.

Cyert, Richard M., and James G. March: *A Behavioral Theory of the Firm*, Prentice-Hall, Inc., Englewood Cliffs, N.J., 1963.

Dean, Joel: *Capital Budgeting*, Columbia University Press, New York, 1951.

Knight, Frank A.: *Risk, Uncertainty and Profit*, Houghton Mifflin Company, Boston, 1921.

Machlup, Fritz: "Theories of the Firm: Marginalist, Behavioral, Managerial," *The American Economic Review*, vol. 57, no. 1, March, 1967.

Marvin, Philip: "Some Basic Concepts underlying Company Strategy," *Developing a Product Strategy*, American Management Association, New York, 1959.

Scitovsky, T.: "A Note on Profit Maximization and Its Implication," *The Review of Economic Studies*, vol. 11, 1943.

Simon, Herbert A.: "Theories of Decision-making in Economics and Behavioral Science," *Survey of Economic Theory*, St. Martin's Press, Inc., New York, 1967, vol. III.

Spencer, Milton H.: *Managerial Economics*, 3d ed., Richard D. Irwin, Homewood, Ill., 1968.

chapter 12
profit planning
and
control

In the preceding chapter, we discussed the meaning, significance, and measurement of profit and its utilization in corporate planning. Now we want to show how a firm, through profit planning and control, attempts to attain a higher level of profit.

Profit planning is no doubt one of the most important and pervasive facets of a firm's managerial operations. It takes into account the expected demand for the product and the capacity of the firm to meet the demand. It also considers measures to reduce cost, both of production and of distribution, so as to improve profit margin. In other words, profit planning consists of establishing precise objectives, prescribing ways and means to achieve them, and setting timetables to get the work done.

A firm needs profit planning and control to obtain a higher level of profit. Properly speaking, what a firm wants is the best level of profit or the optimal rate of return on its investment under the market conditions in which it operates.

Without profit planning a firm cannot tell whether or not it is able to produce enough units of product to meet the anticipated demand, even if it has some idea as to the quantity which can be sold within a given period of time.

DEVICES FOR PROFIT PLANNING AND CONTROL

In order to make sure that a given level of profit will be achieved, a firm may use one or more of the following devices to guide its operations: the profit budget, the breakeven chart, and the rate of return on investment.

USING PROFIT BUDGET AS A GUIDE

A budget is a plan. It is drawn up to show a certain result which the planner hopes to obtain. A budget can be prepared for various purposes, depending upon the type of budget one wants to use. A profit budget is a projected income statement. It shows where a firm is expected to receive income and what the firm is expected to pay out.

Construction of a Profit Budget. A profit budget is based upon the income statement of the preceding fiscal period adjusted for changes in prices, cost, and anticipated demand. In constructing a profit budget, we start with business forecasting. We have to make some estimate of the demand for the product which our firm is going to produce in the next fiscal period. In conjunction with the estimate of demand, we have to determine the price level which is expected to prevail in the immediate future. Then we should make an estimate as to the cost of operating the firm which includes all expenses incurred in the production and distribution of the product. Finally, we come to the residual item of an income statement, that is, either a profit or a loss for the fiscal period.

Function of a Profit Budget. In addition to its use in planning, a profit budget like other budgets has two other functions, coordination and control. For planning, a profit budget represents the broad outline of activities which will guide operations throughout the next fiscal period. The activities consist, among others, of those needed to produce and market a given quantity of units of output, to acquire and administer the number of workers needed for those jobs, to purchase and store the quantity of raw materials and parts required for the production, and to obtain the financial resources needed to carry out those activities.

A profit budget is usually constructed with a single set of sales and cost data for a fiscal period. Since our forecast is not perfect, in order to be more useful as a planning device a profit budget should be flexible. This means that instead of having one set of figures, which remain fixed throughout a fiscal period, a profit budget should be periodically revised if the actual result differs from the budgeted result.

The need to be flexible can be clearly illustrated by the following case. In 1968 a large, well-known machine tool manufacturer reduced its profit budget for the 1969 fiscal year below previously prepared preliminary estimates. The factors which influenced the reduction were the passage of the 10 percent surtax and the tight money policy. As the results of operations in the first quarter of 1969 were reported, the financial officer in charge of the budget realized that it was low. Economic activities in early 1969, instead of slowing down as anticipated by the majority of economists, surged ahead unabatedly.

Consequently, the 1969 profit budget was revised upward to reflect increased demand and higher operating levels.

As a corollary of planning, the coordination aspect of a budget lies in the fact that in order to draw up a budget, the officer in charge of preparing the budget has to consult with various department or division heads. From the sales or marketing department, he must determine how many units of the product can be sold in the next fiscal year, and whether or not the production department can handle that amount of output, and at what cost per unit. In subsequent consultation, the officer has to check with the personnel department as to the availability of skilled labor, and with the treasurer or financial vice-president as to the availability of funds for the operation. The required coordination enables the different division heads to plan their activities so as to ensure that there will be no gap or discontinuity in the overall operation of the firm.

If the production has to be stopped occasionally because of shortage of parts or because of lack of cash to hire additional skilled workers, even though parts or skilled workers may be available at a later date, the stop-and-start process of production may be too costly to be tolerated.[1] In addition, customers' good will may be destroyed because goods cannot be delivered on time.

The control aspect of a budget results from the fact that there are too many uncertainties in life, as well as in the economy, to allow an accurate forecast. Since we cannot forecast accurately, our budget and operating results are bound to be different, and therefore a systematic check on operations is required to bring a firm's budget in line with reality. The form shown in Figure 12-1 is for this purpose. This form is used by a major diversified manufacturing concern in controlling its operations. This table compares the actual operating result to the budget and to the forecast. As used by the company, forecast and budget mean two different things: the former refers to a plan which guides the firm in its operations, while the latter represents the profitability of the current month's activity at standard cost pricing. Any variation between the actual result and the budget, or between the actual result and the forecast, is verified and thoroughly analyzed.

The costs of production and distribution are more subject to management control than is the selling price of the product. Furthermore, the consequences of an adjustment in price are more difficult to predict than those of an adjustment in cost. A firm cannot be sure that a 10 percent increase in price will not adversely affect sales by more than 10 percent, because rivals will often react in a way not anticipated. On the other hand, cost reduction, closing a less efficient

---

[1] Before merging with the McDonnell Aircraft Company in 1967, the Douglas Aircraft Company suffered losses of $27.6 million (adjusted for tax credit) for the 1966 fiscal year, even though sales amounted to $1.05 billion. The main cause of the trouble was the interruption of production of the DC 9, because of shortage of parts.

Figure 12-1. Profit control chart.

COMPARISON OF BUDGET, FORECAST, AND OPERATING RESULTS

Description	Total Division			Total Division		
	Current Month			Year to		
	Actual	Budget	Forecast No.	Actual	Budget	Forecast No.
Gross Sales						
Less returns and allowances						
Net sales—Customer						
—Inter-divisional						
—Intra-divisional						
Total net sales						
Standard cost of net sales						
Material						
Direct labor						
Manufacturing expense						
Total standard cost						
Gross profit at standard						
Percent to sales						
Variances						
Material						
Inter-division price						
Direct labor						
Overhead—Variable						
—Volume						
Scrap						
Freight						
Royalties						
Product tooling						
Subcontracting						
Inventory adjustment						
Unexpended tooling and supplies						
Preproduction expense						
Total variances						

plant, reducing overhead staff, or furloughing workers not critically needed, will certainly produce results closer to those expected.

USING BREAKEVEN ANALYSIS AS A GUIDE

Breakeven analysis is the study of the relationship between the volume and cost of production and marketing on one hand and the revenue and profit obtained from sales of the product on the other. The name is derived from the fact that, where total cost equals total revenue, the price of the product being held constant, we have a breakeven point.

A breakeven chart is a graphic representation of a breakeven analysis.

Figure 12-1. (Cont.)

COMPARISON OF BUDGET, FORECAST, AND OPERATING RESULTS

Description	Total Division			Total Division		
	Current Month			Year to		
	Actual	Budget	Forecast No.	Actual	Budget	Forecast No.
Gross profit at actual						
Percent to sales						
Division operating expense						
Total						
Profit or (loss)—before allocations						
Percent to sales						
Staff allocations						
Corporate activities						
Net investment charge						
Total						
Division profit (loss)—before tax						
Percent to sales						
Provision for federal income tax						
Net income (loss)						
Percent to sales						

Because of its simplicity and pictorial nature, breakeven charts are usually used in place of breakeven analysis in profit planning and control.

Construction of a Breakeven Chart. There are two ways to construct a breakeven chart, the analytical approach and the statistical approach. Under the analytical approach, we use cost and revenue data of a single year and classify the cost into fixed and variable, including semivariable, costs. By plotting these data on a graph as in Figure 12-2, we have a breakeven chart. The chart in Figure 12-2 is based on the following hypothetical figures:

Total units of goods produced and sold:		100,000
Plant capacity:		120,000 units
Price per unit:	$1,000.00	
Total revenue:	$100 million	
Total cost:	$80 million	
Total fixed cost:	$30 million	
Total variable cost:	$50 million	
Total profit:	$20 million	

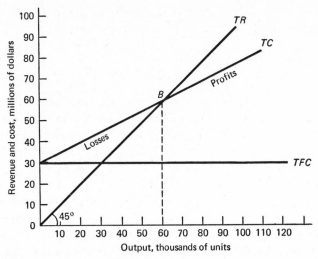

Figure 12-2. Breakeven chart.

To begin with, we plot units of goods produced along the x axis, and cost and revenue along the y axis. The total revenue line is drawn through the origin to form a 45-degree angle with the x axis, because we assume (1) there is no revenue if there is no production, (2) the price per unit of the product is $1,000, which is assumed to remain unchanged, and (3) the scale on both axes of the chart is plotted so that 10,000 units of output produced has the same value (or equal distance from the origin of the diagram) as $10 million revenue. In other words, with the price of the product being held constant, total revenue increases in the same proportion as the quantity of goods produced and sold. On the other hand, we draw the total cost line to intersect the y axis at the point 30. From that scale, we draw a line parallel to the x axis to represent total fixed cost. The distance between the total fixed cost line and the total cost line is total variable cost. The breakeven point is where the revenue line intersects the total cost line; the area to the right of the point represents profits, and the area to the left represents losses.

The breakeven production volume can be easily calculated from the data, using the formula: $PQ = F + VQ$, where P symbolizes price of the product; Q, quantity of output produced; F, total fixed cost; V, variable cost per unit of output; and Q is the breakeven quantity. Since $PQ = F + VQ$, $PQ - VQ = F$, $Q(P - V) = F$, and therefore

Using the data in our chart as an example, we have $P = 1,000$, $V = 500$, and $F = 30,000,000$, so

$$Q = \frac{30,000,000}{1,000 - 500} = 60,000$$

One can readily find out from the chart how much the company would earn if it produced more than 60,000 units of output a year, or how much it would lose if the production dropped below the breakeven point level. For example, if the output is 100,000 units, the company will make $20 million profit. If the output is to increase to 120,000 units, the company will make $30 million profit. Notice that if the output is to increase only by 20 percent, profit will rise by 50 percent. Such a phenomenon is the result of operating leverage.[2]

A modification of this method of constructing a breakeven chart, shown in Figure 12-3, is first to draw the total cost line parallel to total variable cost and above it. The space between the two lines then represents total fixed cost. The revenue line is drawn as before.

One advantage of this chart, as compared with the preceding one, is

[2] Walter Rautenstrauch and Raymond Villers, two pioneers in the study of breakeven analysis, distinguished two different types of charts: One was called a profit-and-loss chart, and the other a breakeven chart. The former was used to show the relation between sales and expenses over a period of years. For this type of chart, they plotted sales data along the x axis and expenses data along the y axis. As to the breakeven chart, Rautenstrauch and Villers plotted output along the x axis and expenses along the y axis, with the price of output being held constant. See *The Economics of Industrial Management*, Funk & Wagnalls, New York, 1949, chaps. 4 and 5.

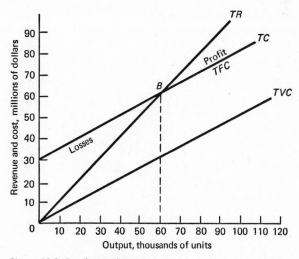

Figure 12-3. Breakeven chart.

that it shows management the contribution additional sales make toward fixed cost and profit.

Another method of constructing a breakeven chart is to use past records of production, sales, and costs. By plotting quantity of output produced along the x axis, revenue and costs against quantity produced for each year, a scatter diagram is drawn upon which a total revenue curve and a total cost curve can be fitted. The chart in Figure 12-4 has been constructed from data reported by the Inspiration Consolidated Copper Company, for the years 1950 through 1965 and given in Table 12-1.[3]

In this chart, four curves instead of two are shown. The two solid lines are constructed on the assumption that both the revenue function and the cost function are linear in nature. However, since they do not fit the data well, we may draw two more curves *TR'* and *TC'* which provide a better fit. The explanation for this is that both the price of copper and the cost of operation went up over the years. For the sixteen-year period, 1950 through 1965, copper prices fluctuated within the range of 42.0 cents per pound in 1956 and 21.5 cents in 1950. Since 1961, however, the price of copper has been higher, paralleling increases in wage rates, prices for mining equipment, and costs of plant construction.

A chart drawn by the analytical method has the benefit of bringing the most recent cost and revenue situation of the firm to top management's attention. So for short-run planning purposes, the analytical method is more appropriate. The statistical approach, on the other hand, has the advantage of giving top

[3] The Inspiration Consolidated Copper Company is chosen for the breakeven analysis because the company produces only one product. It mines, refines, and sells copper. And so, it makes our analysis much easier.

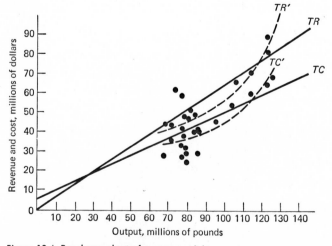

Figure 12-4. Breakeven chart of a copper mining company.

TABLE 12-1. SELECTED DATA OF THE INSPIRATION CONSOLIDATED COPPER COMPANY

	1950	1951	1952	1953	1954	1955	1956	1957	1958	1959	1960	1961	1962	1963	1964	1965
Quantity sold (millions of pounds)	77	78	85	79	68	76	74	72	84	94	81	78	105	114	123	124
Revenue (millions of dollars)	18	19	21	23	21	29	30	21	23	30	25	24	33	35	40	44
Cost of operation (millions of dollars)	13	12	14	14	13	16	17	17	20	22	20	20	26	29	32	34
Operation profit before tax (millions of dollars)	5	7	7	9	8	13	13	4	3	8	5	4	7	6	8	10
Price of copper (cents per pound)	21.5	24.4	24.4	28.9	29.8	37.5	42.0	30.2	26.3	31.0	32.3	30.3	31.0	31.0	32.4	35.4

Sources: Moody's Industrial Manual, and Standard and Poor's Industrial Survey.

management a better perspective with regard to the trends in fluctuations of cost and price. Fluctuations in cost and price are a strong reminder to the top management that the usual breakeven assumption of constant price or cost has to be made with great care.

Uses of a Breakeven Chart. Breakeven charts have two important uses. The first is that a breakeven chart acts as a thermometer to show the health of the corporation. If the chart is properly constructed and there is no significant change in the economy, the management can tell whether or not the company is covering fixed cost simply by comparing the volume of output at a particular time against the output scheduled to be sold by that date. A properly constructed chart takes into consideration all factors which may have any influence on the price and the cost of the product. For instance, if a new labor contract has been put into effect, we have to adjust the wage rate accordingly. On the other hand, when the price of the product changes, the revenue line has to be shifted accordingly. Using Figure 12-2 as an example, we see that if the firm's factory is operating at 40 percent capacity, the company is certainly losing money.

Secondly, a breakeven chart is an aid to profit planning. If we find that at present rates of output we will not break even at the end of the year, the chart will help to illustrate the effects of a cut in price as a possible tactic to increase sales. It is possible that, so long as the price will cover the variable or incremental cost and make some contribution toward fixed cost, a price reduction is warranted. As the chart will show, those companies which have a very large proportion of their capital invested in fixed assets, and consequently high fixed charges, have a high breakeven point. This implies that a price cut may be a correct action to take. Once the breakeven point is reached, the operating profit widens faster as sales go up than it would if variable costs were more important. On the other hand, an increase in the price of the product whose demand is not price-elastic will raise total revenue. The following breakeven charts are designed to illustrate the effects of price changes.

In Figure 12-5 we show the chart of a company that is losing money at a production and sales level (Q_1) of 50,000 units. Let us suppose further that the company cannot increase sales to any significant extent by promotional or other nonprice tactics. It therefore decides to cut price by 20 percent. The total revenue line is now R' instead of R. Assume the demand for this product is very elastic, so that sales go up by 60 percent, or from 50,000 units to (Q_2) 80,000 units annually. If the variable cost per unit remains constant, the firm would break even at this new level of production and achieve sales as indicated by the new breakeven sales point, B'.

Assume that, instead of cutting price, the company decides to raise prices to increase margins, in the hope of bringing its operation to a profitable posi-

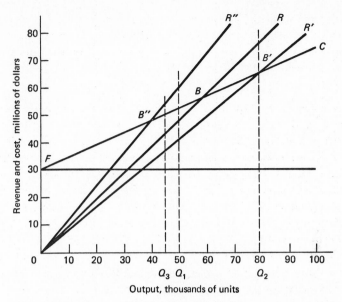

Figure 12-5. Breakeven chart: price being changed.

tion. If the company raises its price from $1,000 per unit of product to $1,200, its revenue line will shift to the left as shown by OR'' in Figure 12-5. Where previously the company had losses at Q_1 level of production, it now makes money if it can maintain the same sales level. Even allowing for a decline of sales to Q_3, the firm will still operate in the black as indicated by the spread between OR'' and FC at point Q_3.

In Figure 12-6, we consider the effect of cost cutting on the breakeven point of the company with selling prices remaining unchanged. Assume as before that the firm's production level is Q_2, and that it is losing money. Suppose the management cuts variable costs by 20 percent, from $500 per unit of output to $400, enabling the company to break even at Q_2, where the new total cost line FC' intersects the revenue line. If the cost cutting can be effectively carried out and maintained for a period during which the firm can maintain sales without lowering price, the company can then earn profits as indicated by the gap between the revenue line R and C', the new total cost line.[4]

In finding ways and means to cut costs, a company may find it desirable

[4] In early 1968, American Motors Corporation expected its new sporty car (Javelin) to sell 50,000 units. This volume would have put its 1968 model sales to 320,000 units, or 4 percent share of the market, as against 3 percent in 1967, an increase of 33 percent for the year. By drastic measures of cost cutting, the company had reduced its breakeven point below 300,000 units, the lowest level in years. American Motors had had losses in both 1966 and 1967, but managed to sell 268,000 cars, or a 3 percent share of the market, in 1968. The result was a $11,762,000 profit.

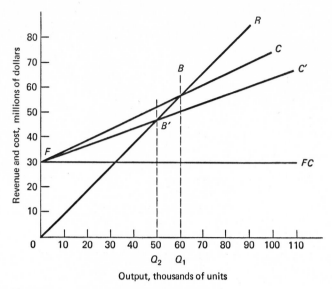

Figure 12-6. Breakeven chart: cost being lowered.

to substitute capital for labor. By using more capital, the company increases its total fixed cost but lowers its total variable cost at the same level of output. With higher total fixed cost, it may pay the firm to lower the price of the product in order to increase sales. Even though the breakeven point is now higher, once that point is crossed, profit margin widens more rapidly than before. This greater profit rate is caused by the fact that each unit of output now has a smaller amount of variable cost, and the average fixed cost drops as fast as units of output are increased. Assuming price remains stable after the reduction, the profit margin will inevitably increase, as Figure 12-7 indicates. By raising total fixed cost FC from $3 million to $5 million a year (FC'), the company moves its breakeven point from B to B', or from an annual production output of 8,000 units to 10,000 units, assuming that variable cost per unit of output declines as a result of lower labor cost. If the company lowers price to increase sales to Q'', however, the slope of the total revenue line TR is lowered to TR', and the firm will make more profit than before, as indicated by angle A' being larger than angle A. Hence, by substituting capital for labor, the firm can make more profit than before, if it can increase output by charging a lower price for the product. If the price of the product remains unchanged, total profit may possibly be even greater for the same volume.

Breakeven charts are based upon the concept of average cost pricing for the product; that is, each unit of output is assumed to contain a certain portion of fixed cost. With a constant variable cost per unit of output, fixed cost per unit declines as additional units of output are produced; at the same time, with price

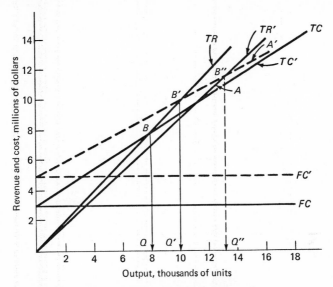

Figure 12-7. Breakeven chart: fixed cost being increased.

being held constant, profit margin per unit widens. However, when a firm uses standard cost pricing, its profit margin increases sharply once the level of output surpasses the standard volume, because additional units of output bear no fixed cost.

For example, in Figure 12-8, the firm's standard volume Q_2 is set at 80 percent of its plant capacity, its breakeven level of production Q_1 is 48 percent, while the actual level of production Q_3 is at 90 percent of capacity. Profit will increase gradually after the breakeven point is reached, but will rise sharply after the actual level of production surpasses the standard volume, as shown by the spread between *TR* and *TVC*, since total fixed cost has been covered by sales equal to 80 percent of plant capacity.

Limitations of a Breakeven Chart. Even though it is very useful for profit planning, a breakeven chart has several limitations, of which the users of the chart should be aware. First, the charts assume price and cost to be linear functions in relation to sales and production. As shown in Figure 12-2, the revenue line and the total cost line are drawn with constant slope. This is correct only if the price and the variable cost per unit of the output remain constant, regardless of how many units are sold. Constant slope may accurately reflect the demand curve if the company is a relatively small concern, so that its entire output can be sold without any noticeable effect on price, or if the demand for the product is so strong (such as the demand for automobiles after World War II) that the total output of the entire industry can be absorbed without any depressing effect on

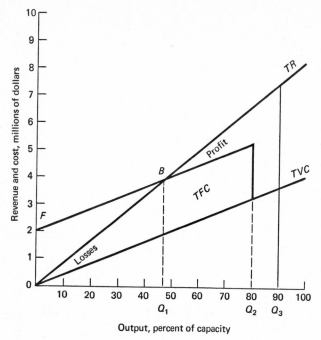

Figure 12-8. Breakeven chart based upon standard cost pricing.

price. Constant slope may give a correct cost curve if the marginal cost remains constant.

A breakeven chart may have two breakeven points formed by the same revenue line and the same total cost line if the company does not stop operation before the total cost curve intersects the revenue line for the second time. This may occur if the marginal cost rises sharply as production continues to expand beyond the plant's normal capacity, as shown in Figure 12-9.

Second, the assumption that profit is a function of output is not always tenable. This assumption is in effect a derivative of the first. If we assume total cost to increase with output, as does total revenue, then profit may be considered to be a function of quantity produced. However, a company may increase its profit without increasing its output, just by adopting a new technique or a new process of production which cuts costs. For example, steel companies in the 1950s spent billions of dollars for capital expansion, with a major portion designated for cost-saving facilities, such as sintering plants for the treatment of ores and oxygen and electric furnaces for greater and more controlled furnace heat. It was estimated that the cost of producing a ton of steel by the new method was about 10 percent lower than the old one.

Third, a major drawback of a breakeven chart is its inability to handle

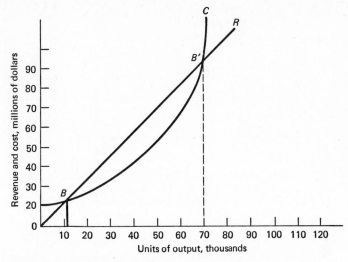

Figure 12-9. Breakeven chart with two breakeven points.

production and sales of multiple products. A single breakeven chart for a company such as General Electric, which has many products, is impossible to draw. It is feasible, however, to construct a breakeven chart for a product group such as generators of various horsepower.

One way to handle the problem of product mix in constructing a breakeven chart was advanced by Bergfeld, Early, and Knobloch, who based their approach on the idea of contribution to fixed cost and profit by one product or by a division of a company.[5] They use a P/V income (profit-volume) line instead of a revenue line to determine the breakeven point appropriate to a particular product. When different products are involved, an additional P/V income line is required for each product, as shown in Figures 12-10 and 12-11.

The P/V income represents contribution from a particular product (or a given division) to fixed cost and profit. Specific programmed cost is the cost incurred at the discretion of management specifically to increase P/V income for a particular product. The slope of the P/V income line is the ratio between the unit P/V income and unit price. What we are interested in is the amount of contribution a particular product or division makes toward the firm's overall fixed cost and profit at a given level of sales, and so it provides a basis for comparison of contribution from one product to another. A product which has a high P/V ratio is a profitable one, in the sense that a higher volume of sales for this product will ordinarily bring a larger increase in profit.

[5] A. J. Bergfeld, J. S. Early, and W. R. Knobloch, *Pricing for Profit and Growth*, McGraw-Hill Book Company, New York, 1957.

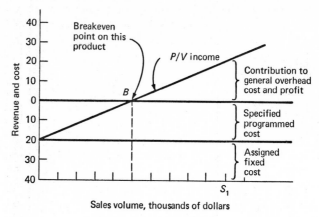

Figure 12-10. Profit chart for one product.

It is important to point out that this profit chart is different from the regular breakeven chart in two ways: First, it is drawn up for a particular product or division, or for a specific problem, such as whether it pays to accept an order for a given product. Second, the profit chart includes only specific programmed costs, and not all fixed costs, as proper offsets to revenue in measuring both breakeven point and profitability.[6]

A fourth limitation of a breakeven chart as a tool for profit planning is the difficulty of handling selling costs such as advertising and sales promotion

[6] *Ibid.*, pp. 42–43.

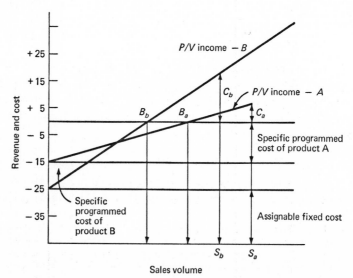

Figure 12-11. Profit chart for two products.

When an annual budget for advertising expenditures is set up, it becomes a simple matter of an addition to fixed cost. Since management anticipates an increase in sales as a result of a sales promotion campaign, the average unit cost of output will be lower with a higher level of production, thus presumably raising total profits. However, if expenditures for advertising are tied to a particular expected volume of sales, the task of project planning becomes more complicated. If sales vary from planned output for a short period of time, so that selling costs are not necessarily related to the realized production level, should the amount budgeted be cut or raised? Since the effect of advertising generally spreads over into the future, it is therefore difficult to allocate properly within a certain period of time.

Finally, in P/V analysis, it is difficult to allocate expenses for advertising accurately among different products because the effect of expenditures on behalf of one particular product spills over to other products produced by the same firm. The solution advocated under the P/V income approach is to consider advertising a management decision cost, not chargeable to any specific product.

The assumption of a static nature of business and economic activities is a well-known defect of breakeven charts. When a chart is constructed on the basis of past performance data, it is assumed that the past relationship among the variables will continue. Such an oversimplification of economic reality may overlook the possibility of shifts in the company's demand curve, altering the assumed fixed relationship between price and quantity. In addition, it is not likely that the production function or the prices of inputs will remain unchanged. In all, as the company attempts to adapt itself to the changing economic environment, the chart has to be continually updated.[7]

PROFIT CENTER CONTROL

In order to improve operation efficiency, profit centers may be set up in each division or product group within a company. The purpose is to apply profitability standards to parts of the organization which normally are not able to use these kinds of data or which do not have access to it because of their subordinate status.

RATE OF RETURN AS A CONTROL DEVICE

One way to measure profitability is through the rate of return on invested capital. The rate is the quotient of the after-tax earnings, plus interest

---

[7] Joel Dean considers breakeven analysis virtually useless for some companies: "This is particularly likely when materials that fluctuate widely in price are a predominant cost, when the product-mix varies greatly and profit margins differ among products, when advertising or sales promotion are important and highly shiftable, or when the product design of technology changes continuously over short periods." *Op. cit.,* pp. 335–336.

charges on bonds, divided by the firm's total long-term committed funds.[8] For managerial decision-making purpose, the marginal rate of return is often employed.[9]

An application to decisions concerning new product developments is termed marginal profit control. A company trying to introduce new products should at minimum be able to hold its present market share while expanding into other markets. There is, however, no point in developing and introducing a new product if the marginal rate of return is lower than the marginal cost of capital, unless we are convinced such a result is short run only and needed to break into the new market.

Examples of this sort are numerous. The RCA Corporation suffered initial losses on its investments in computer manufacturing. The company, in spite of losses, decided to continue in the computer business, believing that sooner or later it would be able to reverse the trend. Since the demand was forecast to grow faster than many other products which the company produced, with large resources both human and financial at its command, it was possible to take a long-range view of the profitability prospects of the new product.

In using rate of return as a standard for measuring the performance of subordinate divisions, it often helps to decentralize in a "federal" manner. This means that each division is separate and distinct and sells its product to the other divisions of the company at the same price as it sells to outside customers. When it buys parts from other divisions, it pays the same prices for those products as if it bought them from outside suppliers. Each division naturally has its own production schedule and profit budget.

For example, TRW, Inc., a well-managed automotive and electronic concern, has a total of twenty-four domestic divisions operating independently of one another. Each division is under the supervision of a vice-president who has the authority of a president of an individual corporation, except in financing and the overall strategy of the firm, such as the development of new products or merging with other companies. The form presented in Figure 12-12 is used by TRW, Inc., to calculate the rate of return earned by each division of the company.

The Value-added Method. When a company does not have independent divisions, it has to employ the value-added method in order to evaluate the profitability of each division. Basically, this method simulates the one discussed

---

[8] Many corporations, as well as economists, use total invested funds, both long-term and short-term, as the basis for measuring the profitability of a firm's operation. However, we consider the return on long-term funds a better yardstick, because it is the long-term funds which provide the firm with productive facilities.

[9] Several well-known and well-managed corporations interviewed have set up a 20 percent rate of return on invested capital as a yardstick for profit control. This rate is an overall rate or the average rate on all invested capital, both old and new. Marginal rate of return was used only by some.

above. For example, if a company manufactures only one product, it can set up a number of profit centers for the different stages of production. The value that each center adds to the finished product is recorded, based upon the market price. For instance, a center which produces electric motors for air conditioners would price its product as if the product were to be sold to outside customers. The difference between the two values, the one before the semifinished product enters a center and the other after the semifinished product leaves the center, is the contribution made by that center.

As we are interested here in the efficiency of productivity or profitability of labor and of capital in the form of plant and equipment, material costs are excluded. Generally speaking, each group is required not only to stand on its own feet, that is, its price should cover its own variable and assignable (incremental in terms of production sequence) fixed costs, but also to earn the target rate of return set by top management. However, this rule may be modified to fit an overall product-mix strategy.

The main difficulty involved in setting up profit centers and making them work properly is the problem posed by the need to allocate common costs. One solution is to use the profit-volume income approach discussed earlier, with the refinement that the contribution made by each product group to the unassignable overhead (or common) cost and profit is expressed as a ratio. This ratio is derived by dividing the incremental cost attributable to a given product group into the contribution made by that group, and it is used to measure the profitability of each product group. The higher the ratio, the more profitable a given product group.

Control Mechanism. Basically, any control mechanism involves setting up a standard a firm hopes to achieve, collecting and analyzing data of actual performance, comparing and measuring the actual result against the standard previously established, and revising the standard or finding remedial measures to improve actual performance.

Probably the best known profit control mechanism used by corporations is the Du Pont System of Financial Control.[10] The Du Pont system is based upon the relationship among the various factors affecting the rate of return on invested capital. These factors are classified into two groups: One is concerned with income statement items and ends up with earnings as percent of sales; while the other, balance sheet items, concludes with turnover of investment. When earnings as percent of sales are multiplied by investment turnover, the result is the rate of return on investment.

[10] This section is based primarily upon an article written by R. R. Pippin, *Executive Committee Control Charts,* Management Bulletin No. 6, American Management Association, New York, 1960. The publication was originally prepared by T. C. Davis. Both Mr. Davis and Mr. Pippin were officers of E. I. du Pont de Nemours & Company.

Figure 12-12. Rate of return chart.

STATEMENT OF RETURN ON INVESTMENT—
EXTENDED FORM

	Forecast	Actual			
		Current Month			Prior Month
	Current Month	Per Books	Allocations from (to) Other Divisions	Total Investment	
Working capital					
Current assets					
Notes & accounts receivable (net)					
Interdiv. & interco. current accounts					
Inventories (net)					
Total current assets					
Current liabilities					
Trade accounts payable					
Accrued payrolls					
Other accruals					
Interdiv. & interco. current accounts					
Total current liabilities					
Working capital (net)					
Property, plant, & equipment (net)					
Other assets					
Patents, licenses, processes, etc.					
Prepaid expenses & deferred charges					
Allocations from (to) other divisions					
Owner, equival. of leased facilities					
Division investment base					

	Forecast	Actual			Forecast
	Current Month	Current Month	Prior Month	Year to Date	Year to Date
Division total sales					
Division profit (loss)					
Division investment base *					
Turnover of investment					
Profit percent of sales					
Return on investment					

* Beginning of period.

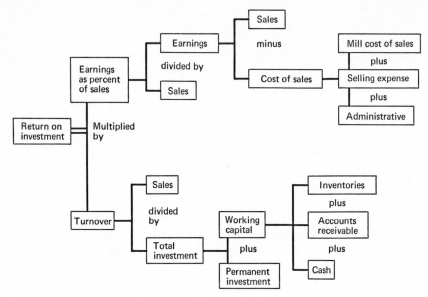

Figure 12-13. Du Pont system of financial control.

The Du Pont method focuses control on the two critical factors making up the rate of return on investment, namely, earnings as percent of sales and investment turnover. According to Pippin,

> Earnings as percent of sales reflect the success (or lack of success) in maintaining satisfactory control of costs. Turnover reflects the rapidity with which the capital committed to the operation is being worked. Thus the manager of an operating investment can improve his return by reducing costs or working existing investment harder, both of which factors are within his control.[11]

Each Du Pont department is headed by a general manager who is responsible for research, manufacturing, and sales of products assigned to his group. Each department becomes a profit center and adopts the same set of charts for profit control. As departments have a variety of products, more than one set of charts will be prepared. A "Summary Du Pont" set of charts which summarizes the operations of all twelve industrial departments also is prepared. All in all, Du Pont has some thirty separate chart series comprising over 400 individual charts. The "Summary Du Pont" set is reviewed every month, and charts for each department are reviewed once every three months. During the review of these charts, the executive committee of Du Pont discusses the past performance of departments and of the whole company. The results of the recent past are compared with the forecast made twelve months earlier. Any deviation from the forecast is traced back to determine the cause and remedial action begun.

[11] *Ibid.*, pp. 5–6.

SUMMARY

In this chapter we have discussed the employment of the profit budget as a tool in managerial planning and control. The most commonly used tool for profit planning is the breakeven chart, which portrays graphically all possible profit budget positions for a given set of prices and costs.

The chart assumes considerable importance to many firms as an instrument for internal forecasting and control, since it deals largely with factors over which the firm has control. Either dollar sales volume or physical volume can be used against which to compare costs and show the breakeven point. In the former instance, a price change is reflected in a change in revenue associated with a given expense level; in the latter case, a price change is reflected in a change in the slope of the total revenue line.

A breakeven chart may be constructed by using either the analytical or the statistical method. The former has the advantage of bringing the most recent information concerning the firm's operation to the attention of top management. The latter, on the other hand, has the benefit of giving top management the proper historical perspective as to the behavior of cost and price.

Breakeven charts illustrate the volume effect involved in standard cost pricing when the standard volume is exceeded.

Limitations of the breakeven chart include the following: first, the assumption of linear functions; second, the assumption that profit is a function of level of output; third, the difficulty of depicting multiple products satisfactorily; fourth, selling costs are difficult to handle; and fifth, the chart cannot accommodate itself to changes in the production function of the firm or to changes in demands and input prices.

The use of profit as a means of managerial control is exemplified by the twin tools of P/V analysis and profit center decentralization. In the former, separate products or departments are compared by means of their contribution to overhead and profit, while in the latter, intermediate products are priced at the market, and return on investment ratios is computed for comparison.

Review Questions

1. What is a profit budget?
2. Why is a profit budget important to a company?
3. What is a breakeven chart?
4. Why is a breakeven chart important to profit planning?
5. What are the limitations of a breakeven chart?
6. What do we mean by profit center control?
7. Why do we use rate of return as a control device?

8. What is the value-added concept?
9. Why might a division of a firm sell parts of a product to another division at the market price?

Case 1. The Mid-Atlantic Electric Company

Edward Evans, the controller of the Mid-Atlantic Electric Company, has been considering for some time setting up some profit control mechanism, on which he can rely for profit planning. The Mid-Atlantic Electric Company is a medium-sized producer of single-phase and polyphase alternating current watt-hour meters, demand meters, and related equipment. Its plants are located at Baltimore, Maryland. Sales in the latest fiscal year (1970) were $20 million, with operating profit amounting to $3 million.

After discussing his intention with the president of the firm, Frank Fischer, Mr. Evans has selected the breakeven analysis and breakeven chart as a means of profit planning and control. From the record of the latest fiscal year, he has obtained the following data:

Sales	$20,000,000
Cost of goods sold:	
Direct materials	7,300,000
Direct labor	6,500,000
Factory overhead	1,500,000
Administrative overhead	1,000,000
Selling overhead	700,000
Total operating expenses	$17,000,000
Operating profit	$3,000,000

From the conversation with the personnel manager, Mr. Evans has learned that wage rates will go up by 8 percent next fiscal year as the result of current wage negotiation with the labor union. In order to maintain a 15 percent operating profit margin, Mr. Evans is considering raising prices for all product lines. It is the company's policy to grant wage increases to its clerical employees of 80 percent of the pay hike received by the workers. Wages paid to the clerical employees in the 1970 fiscal year accounted for 30 percent of the factory overhead, 25 percent of the administrative overhead, and 3 percent of the selling overhead.

QUESTIONS

1. What do you think Mr. Evans should do with respect to the following questions:

(a) What percentage increase in price must the company decide upon in order to maintain the 15 percent operating profit margin goal?

(b) At what level of output will the company break even?

2. Construct a breakeven chart to illustrate your answers.

Case 2. Teletronics, Inc.

Teletronics, Inc., is a multifaceted company which is considering a restructuring of its component companies. To do this, it must ascertain which companies are worth keeping and which types of companies are to be acquired.

Teletronics keeps its home office on three floors of the Lone Star Building in Dallas. The rent for this space is $30,000 per month. The company is controlled by an executive staff which oversees the activities of the hierarchy of officers of each subsidiary. The staff draws an aggregate of $1,200,000 a year and requires $200,000 more for office help and materials. The cost of telephones and telegrams in the Dallas office is $1,100 a month.

The Dallas home office has managed, efficiently enough, to raise Teletronics' net income by 40 percent to a record $20,400,000 in the 1970 fiscal year. Sales experienced a similar increase to $105,000,000.

QUESTIONS

1. In order to accomplish the objective of restructuring, you are asked as a consultant to suggest a method of apportioning the cost of the Dallas office among Teletronics' divisions and subsidiaries.

2. What are the advantages and disadvantages of your proposal?

Note: Case 2 was prepared by Francis Benevento under the supervision of Francis P. Sing Mr. Benevento is a student at the University of Virginia Law School.

Suggested Reading

Bergfeld, Albert J., James S. Early, and William R. Knobloch: *Pricing for Profit and Growth*, McGraw-Hill Book Company, New York, 1957.

Carroll, P.: *How to Control Production Cost*, McGraw-Hill Book Company, New York, 1953.

Dean, Joel: *Managerial Economics.* Prentice-Hall, Inc., Englewood Cliffs, N.J., 1951.

Haynes, William W.: *Managerial Economics,* Business Publications, Inc., Austin, Texas, 1969.

Pippin, R. R.: "Executive Committee Control Charts," Management Bulletin No. 6, American Management Association, New York, 1960.

Rautenstrauch, Walter, and Raymond Villers: *The Economics of Industrial Management,* Funk & Wagnalls, New York, 1949.

Spencer, Milton H.: *Managerial Economics,* 3d ed., Richard D. Irwin, Inc., Homewood, Ill., 1968.

Tucker, Spencer A.: *The Breakeven System: A Tool for Profit Planning,* Prentice-Hall, Inc., Englewood Cliffs, N.J., 1963.

Weston, J. Fred, and Eugene F. Brigham: *Managerial Finance,* 3d ed., Holt, Rinehart and Winston, Inc., New York, 1968.

chapter 13
capital budgeting

Capital allocation is a basic business decision on which many others depend, and it is one of a firm's fundamental decisions. Given the market, the ability to produce a product competitively, and the ability to price it correctly, nothing really happens until an executive has decided it is worth an allocation or budget of financial resources.

Allocation should be determined on a rational application of the equimarginal principle, so that the firm allocates capital based upon potentrial rates of return, beginning with the highest, to the point where the marginal rate of return from one project will equal that from any of the rest. This process of determining the worthwhileness of particular projects, their anticipated rates of return, and the amounts of capital a firm can allocate is known as capital budgeting.

DEFINITION

The capital budget is a plan for the investment of funds, whose benefit will be received over a period of time. Capital budgets are organized in terms of projects, which are judged mainly by their rates of return.

A BUDGET IS A PLAN

As is true of all plans, capital budgeting requires that we first analyze the advisability of the contemplated action. Planning is fundamentally choosing, and the budgeting process requires that we formulate a basis on which to choose among competing projects. It is necessary to determine the relative benefit each capital project may bring to a firm and the relative cost each project may entail. It is for this reason that the analysis is at times referred to as a cost-benefit analysis.

REQUIRES A LONG-TERM COMMITMENT

A capital project, by its nature, often involves a long-term commitment. As it takes time to build a factory or a power-generating plant or pipeline, so it will take time before the project can begin to generate funds to pay back the investment. Furthermore, the payback period may be long, because of the relatively long useful life of many capital assets.[1]

The reason for confining our definition of capital budget to investment in fixed assets is that, in the process of creating value, capital is transformed into plant and equipment, which either replace or assist in the production process. Because of the contributions made by labor and capital, the value of inventories or of raw materials increases as a result of labor working on them with various kinds of tools and machinery. On the other hand, inventories are only a link or an adjustment mechanism between production and sales, and by their own nature do not create value. The concept of investment used here is a narrow one, of course. Not all benefits have immediate economic value. Many times definitions of capital investment encompass training of college graduates to be future executives, establishment of research and development laboratories, and the like. Investments made in these categories do not serve to enlarge production facilities, but they do lead to efficient management, the development of new products, and cost reduction.

INVOLVES A TIME PERSPECTIVE

A capital budget requires us to take account of the time perspective of future benefit. As the value of money which is to be received in the future is not the same as that of money presently on hand, when the advisability of a given capital project is under consideration, the concept of present value must be employed. The reason is that, while the benefit of a capital project will be spread over a number of years, the expenditure must be made in the present.

THE ELEMENT OF UNCERTAINTY

The size of a future flow of cash to be generated by any capital project is uncertain. A firm cannot be sure that, after a factory is built, the cash flow will be so much per year for some given term of years. Therefore, ways and means

---

[1] Investment in inventories or in accounts receivable do not constitute capital investments because their rate of turnover is relatively fast. The setting of a desirable limit between a short-term and a long-term investment, or a capital and noncapital investment, is a matter of judgment. Customarily, one follows the accountant's rule that any asset, the benefit of which is received in one year, is classified as current. It is therefore not considered a capital asset and does not fall within the capital budget. However, in figuring out the total amount of funds a given capital budget requires, we do allow additional funds for working capital needed to support a larger volume of sales.

have to be developed to meet or take into account, however imperfectly, the uncertainty the firm faces.

THE PROBLEM OF INFLATION

In view of the upward trend of the general price level we have experienced in the last twenty-five years, it is important to take inflation into account in the preparation of capital budget. Assuming inflation at an annual rate of 4 percent, a machine which is worth $1,000,000 in 1971 will cost $1,480,240 ten years hence. What this means to capital budgeting is that we have to recover during the useful life of the machine an amount of money larger than the original cost of the machine in order to compensate for the decline of the value of money. In other words, if a capital project yields only 4 percent, a firm will not be better off ten years hence by investing in such a project.

IMPORTANCE OF CAPITAL INVESTMENT

Capital budgeting is the crucial aspect of a firm's overall activity. First, the kind of capital project which a company is going to launch will determine the nature of the firm's future, for better or worse, because the type of product the firm plans to produce will determine whether it will continue to grow.

Second, capital expenditures, being generally long-term, may not easily be reversed. It takes a long time to amortize the expense of building; furthermore, some capital projects are specially built and they have, for all practical purposes, no secondary market. On the other hand, if we stock up on the wrong kind of inventory, we can get rid of it within a relatively short period of time by selling it at a discount. One may argue that we can also get rid of a factory in the same fashion, if we are willing to sell it at a loss. But there are two aspects to this problem which should be clearly understood: (1) We build a factory to manufacture products and not to sell it either at a loss or at a profit, unless we are a construction or engineering concern. (2) If we dispose of a plant, losses will be, generally speaking, much heavier than those of inventory liquidation. Because of these two important aspects of capital budgeting, adoption requires the approval of the highest levels of management.

CONCEPT OF CASH FLOW

When we measure the benefit of a capital project, we use cash flow instead of net income, because income is not an appropriate or accurate yardstick to compare costs and benefits. Cash flow refers to the flow of cash resulting from the operation of a company, that is, from sales of the firm's products. It consists of two separate components: the return *of* capital invested in the company or in a specific project and the return *on* capital used for that purpose.

Return of capital is made up of allowances for depreciation, depletion, and for the writeoff of preproduction expenses.[2] Return on capital is made up of interest on bonds or long-term notes, payments for the use of assets which have been rented, and profit before income tax. This cash flow we have derived is a gross amount because it includes rentals, interest on borrowed capital, and income tax. Net cash flow is the gross amount less rentals and taxes.

The reason for using net cash flow to measure the worthwhileness of a capital project, instead of net profit, is that we have to add the return of capital to the return on capital to compare with the amount of funds originally invested in a given project. Suppose, for example, we buy a $100,000 machine which has a useful life of ten years and no salvage value afterward. By using straight-line depreciation, we write off or charge as expense $10,000 annually from the value of the machine. If we borrow the entire amount of capital through a ten-year term loan at a cost of 8 percent per year, then we must have a net cash flow at least equal to $18,000 for the first year to meet the repayment of $10,000 principal plus $8,000 interest charges. In the second year, we must have a net cash flow of $17,200 to meet the interest payment and the annual retirement of $10,000 principal. Of this amount, $10,000 is to be derived from the depreciation process and the rest from the remainder of the firm's revenues in excess of other expenses. Of course we hope that the machine will earn us more than a net profit of $8,000, so that after paying interest charges we have some money left over for retained earnings or as dividends to our common stockholders.

Since we use the total amount of invested funds and its opportunity cost as the base to compare the worthwhileness of different capital projects, we have to use net cash flow or flow of funds as the basis for deciding which project among the alternatives should be undertaken.

NEEDS FOR CAPITAL EXPENDITURES

The development of alternative uses of money available for capital investment is sometimes termed project generation. In economic theory, capital expenditures may be classified as either capital widening or capital deepening. The former involves expansion of the scale of production, while the latter concerns changes in the technique of production. Although this distinction highlights the sources of capital projects, it does not require us to alter our method of analyzing their profitability.

REPLACEMENT OF PLANT AND EQUIPMENT

This is the most common type of capital investment. It is also the most important and most basic, because if we do not replace a worn-out part, a whole

[2] George B. Baldwin, "Discounted Cash Flow," *Finance and Development*, no. 3, The International Monetary Fund, Washington, 1969, p. 32.

machine will not work. Generally speaking, this type of investment, which involves minor capital outlay, may be a routine matter, requiring approval only from a lower-level officer. It is often termed an autonomous investment.

Replacement, as used in this context, refers to the use of the same type of part or of equipment to replace a worn-out one, and therefore we do not consider the installation of an IBM 370 to substitute for an IBM 360 as a replacement. In other words, what we group under this heading are those replacements which have the same performance capacity and efficiency as the equipment being replaced.

INCREASED DEMAND FOR THE FIRM'S PRODUCTS

When a firm experiences an increase in demand for its products and has reason to believe that the increase is not temporary, it will sooner or later need to expand its production capacity either by expanding the floor space of an existing plant or by building a new one. This type of investment is termed induced investment. The significance of induced investment is more relevant to public policy (for example, to control business cycles) than to the top management's overall operation of the firm. What concerns us here is that it involves outlays of capital, with the ramifications every capital investment decision entails. These ramifications include the advisability of a capital project in terms of cost and benefit, the means of acquiring the use of capital assets, and the methods of financing the acquisition of the capital asset.

INTRODUCTION OF NEW PRODUCTS

This type of capital expenditure is very well known. Almost every new product needs some kind of new machine or new layout of assembly line to manufacture it. Quite often a new machine has to be designed and built specifically for a particular new product, or a new type of factory has to be constructed for that purpose. For example, some highly sophisticated electronics instruments have to be assembled in a dust-free and environment-controlled room; special plant and equipment have to be built to harness atomic energy.

COST REDUCTION

The most significant cost savings come from technological improvement or innovation in production technique. The steel industry invested millions of dollars during the 1950's to replace old-model steel mills to cut costs of production. Computers are replacing bookkeepers and clerical employees in many large corporations. Another example of innovation in production technique is the introduction of completely automated assembly lines for the production of automobile engine blocks.

STRATEGIC INVESTMENT

The "type" of investment has two different connotations. One refers to those capital projects which, as Dean points out, "show no promise of profitability in themselves but shore up the rate of return in other products or markets or contribute to the general strength of the company."[3] Investments in risk-reducing and in welfare-improving activities are of this category.

The other concept of strategic investment, defined by Bierman and Smidt, comprises those investment decisions which, besides involving large sums of money, may also result in a major departure from the past.[4] We will stress the former definition.

Risk-reducing Investment. As the name implies, this form involves capital outlays for those projects which are expected to reduce the risk of failing to perform certain functions within a given period of time. For example, if we want to be sure that our customers' orders can be met on time, we had better be prepared for all eventualities, such as shortages of parts or raw materials or of skilled labor or floor space. Vertical integration is often a strategic investment to insure deliveries of raw materials or to reduce the risk of getting parts of unreliable quality. Many of the major corporations in this country are fully integrated, such as General Motors Corporation, United States Steel Corporation, and Standard Oil Company of New Jersey. Humble Oil, the domestic subsidiary of Standard Oil, markets the finished products in some states. The parent company, through its subsidiaries, also owns oil tankers, barge lines, and oil trucks for its products.

Welfare Improvement Investment. This form of investment can be illustrated by the establishment of a clean and beautiful cafeteria where employees can eat their inexpensive lunches leisurely and comfortably. This is especially important in a crowded, urban downtown area. Another good example is the provision of free parking space for employees' cars. The return on this type of investment cannot always be measured by the same standard as other capital projects.[5]

Investment in Research and Development. This type of capital expenditure, as we have seen, is essential to the survival and growth of most corporations, especially to those companies dependent upon technological advancement for product design. For example, producers of computers, electronic instruments,

---

[3] Joel Dean, op. cit., pp. 601–602.

[4] Harold Bierman, Jr., and Seymour Smidt, The Capital Budgeting Decision, 2d ed., The Macmillan Company, New York, 1966, pp. 3–4.

[5] If the alternative is a costly strike, the benefit is quite apparent.

and drugs have to spend hundreds of millions of dollars for scientific research, both pure and applied, in order to stay ahead of their competitors. Such investment may not yield any profit for a long time. Furthermore, any fruitful results from the research may not come off at regular intervals, and it is rather difficult to apply the regular cost-benefit standard to judge the desirability of this sort of capital expenditure.

THE ABILITY TO UNDERTAKE CAPITAL EXPENDITURES

The analysis of the ability of a firm to undertake capital expenditures is an integral part of capital budgeting. This ability depends upon the internal financial resources a firm may have at a given time and its willingness and ability to obtain funds from outside.

INTERNAL SOURCES OF FUNDS

Internal sources of funds refer to the availability of those funds a firm generates within itself. They consist of net income after taxes, allowances for depreciation and depletion, and other noncash charges such as writeoff of deferred charges or of goodwill. We call these internal sources of funds because they are obtained not through sale of securities, but through the production and sale of the company's products.[6] A noncash charge is a deduction against current income which reduces the reported net profit but requires no corresponding cash outlay. If a charge involves a cash outlay, a firm does not have that amount of cash available for other uses, as for example, when a company pays workers wages. The procedure is for the company to charge the wages paid against its current income and reduce its cash account by that amount. On the other hand, when a firm writes off its plant and equipment account against its current income, this charge does not involve any current cash outlay (since the firm paid for the factory and equipment some time ago), and therefore the charge provides a cash flow for the firm to use for any purpose it sees fit.

In recent years, depreciation and depletion allowances have come to surpass retained earnings (net income after income taxes and dividends) as the

---

[6] There are two ways to compute how much cash a firm may have. One is a straight cash transaction method, that is, by converting an ordinary income statement from an accrued basis to a cash basis; then adding other cash inflows, such as borrowing from banks or from the capital market, disposal of property, collection of accounts receivable, etc.; and subtracting other cash outflows, such as payments of debt, purchases of inventories, payments of dividends, and building of factory. The other method is the adjusted income statement method, that is, by finding out how much cash flow a firm can generate internally; then adding cash inflows from other sources, and finally subtracting other items of cash outflow as shown above. Reference may be made to C. I. Moore and R. K. Jaedicke, *Managerial Accounting*, South-Western Publishing Company, Incorporated, Cincinnati, Ohio, 1963, chaps. 6, 7, and 8.

major source of internally generated funds. As indicated in Chapter 11, the passing of the Revenue Act of 1954, the enactment of the 7 percent investment credit in 1962, and the 1962 revision of Schedule F (depreciation guidelines for machinery issued by the Treasury Department) gave rise to a tremendous cash inflow from these sources.[7] Of course, a larger base of property value caused by heavy investments in plant and equipment in the postwar period also contributes to the tremendous amount of cash flow from depreciation and depletion. However, this factor should also contribute to higher earnings, because earnings are a function of capital investment. Therefore, the increased importance of depreciation and depletion as the major source of funds generated internally is attributable to the changes of law. Table 13-1 shows the relative importance of net income and depreciation and depletion as internal sources of funds.

TABLE 13-1. INTERNAL SOURCES OF FUNDS°
(Billions of Dollars)

	1965	1966	1967	1968	1969
Sources, total	93.1	100.6	94.4	109.8	118.4
Internal sources†	56.6	61.2	61.5	62.5	62.5
Undistributed profits†	23.1	24.7	21.1	20.9	19.9
Corporate inventory valuation adjustment	−1.7	−1.8	−1.1	−3.3	−5.4
Capital consumption allowances†	35.2	38.2	41.5	44.9	48.0

° For nonfarm nonfinancial corporate business.
† Explanation can be found in footnote 1 *The Economic Report of the President,* February, 1971, p. 284.

The significance of larger internal cash flow is that corporations depend less and less upon external sources of funds for capital expansion, and consequently they gain more flexibility in their capital budgeting decision making. This could be quite significant in a year such as 1970, when extremely high interest rates prevailed. If a firm has more cash available from internal sources, it is generally more willing to accept capital projects which would otherwise be rejected. It also enables the firm to act more freely in its overall operations than it would if it were subject to some of the stringent provisions imposed by creditors where the funds for capital projects are borrowed.

EXTERNAL SOURCES OF FUNDS

External sources refers to money obtained from outside the firm, such as from the sale of stocks and/or bonds or bank loans.

[7] The repeal of the 7 percent investment tax credit and the reduction of depletion allowances for oil from $27\frac{1}{2}$ percent to 22 percent in 1969 are sure to have a significant adverse impact on the availability of internal source of funds, especially in the transportation and oil industries. But the effect is not as great as would be the repeal, if ever enacted, of all accelerated depreciation tax rules.

Selling Common Stock. Sales of common stock depend primarily on the potential earning power of a company and on the market conditions prevailing at the time of issuance. We should take note that it is the potential earning power and neither the past nor the present earning power which determines the relative price of common stock. Past earnings may, however, provide a clue as to the future, while present earnings are a verification of the accuracy of past projections.

As a company's potential earnings become greater, its common stock price will rise, and that rise will make the company more willing to sell common stock as a means of raising capital. The second factor which affects a firm's willingness to sell common stock is the price-earnings ratio prevailing in the current stock market. When the price-earnings ratio is high (as in a bull market), with the same amount of earnings per common share, the firm can obtain more money for the same number of shares.

The price-earnings ratio of a common stock and its price vary, depending on the degree of eagerness to buy or to sell securities in an open market. This does not mean that fluctuations in earnings have no impact on the price-earnings ratio, but that their influence normally has already been taken into consideration when the investors and speculators bid prices upward or downward. Since the relative price of a common stock is determined by the estimated earnings per share in the coming year, multiplied by the anticipated price-earnings ratio, the latter factor has as much impact on the price of the stock as the former.[8]

Selling Preferred Stock. Because of the nature of preferred stock, the factors which determine the ability of a firm to sell this type of security differ rather significantly from that needed to sell common shares. Even though the potential earning power of a firm is still the basic determinant of preferred stock price, the emphasis is now normally on stability rather than on growth potential.[9] In-

[8] For example, the price of common stock of International Business Machines Corporation reached $607 per share toward the end of 1961 but dropped to $300 per share by the middle of 1962, a decline of 49.5 percent. Meanwhile, earnings per share rose from $7.52 in 1961 to $8.72 in 1962, an increase of 15.95 percent. At the peak (within the 1961 to 1962 period), a common share of IBM was selling at a price-earnings ratio of 80.8 times the 1961 earnings or 69.6 times the 1962 earnings, and at the trough, it was selling at a ratio of 34.4 times the 1962 earnings or 28.0 times the 1963 earnings (of $10.17 per share). If IBM were short of capital for plant and equipment expenditures at that time, it would have been far better for the company (had it known) to have sold common stock at the end of 1961 than at the middle of 1962, because with the same number of shares, the company could have gotten twice as much capital as it was able to later.

[9] Even though the ability to sell a preferred or common stock does not vary as the price of the stock, for all practical purposes, what determines the price of a stock also determines the ability of a firm to market the security. If, for one reason or another, the price investors are willing to pay is so low that, after paying all costs of issuing the security, the net proceeds the company is going to receive are too low, then the ability of the company to sell stock, either preferred or common, is also practically weak. So we may say that the higher the relative price of a common stock, the greater the ability of the firm to sell that security.

vestors who buy preferred stock generally do so for fixed income purposes. That is, they want regular and dependable income from their investments. Therefore, the amount of financial risk is of primary importance. The higher the financial risk to which a company is subject, the more difficult it normally is for the firm to sell a preferred stock.

Another factor which determines the price of a preferred stock (apart from any convertible feature) is the long-term interest rate prevailing in the market. As a preferred stock is a fixed income security; that is, income does not vary with changes in company earnings, but bears rather a fixed relation to the price of the stock when issued, its attractiveness is judged by comparison with other fixed return securities.

If long-term interest rates are extremely high, as in early 1970, business firms are reluctant to sell preferred stock and be committed to a high dividend rate. This reluctance is made more pronounced by the fact that the dividend payment must be made out of after-tax profits.

Incurring Indebtedness. Using bonds to raise capital has some implications which one does not find in stock financing or short-term borrowing. Bonds are debt, and the payments of interest and principal are long-term contractual obligations. A failure to meet these obligations will endanger the very survival of the firm. In addition to the required payment of interest, there are other burdensome provisions, such as restrictions on the payment of cash dividends or a minimum equity which must be maintained. Factors which affect the ability of a firm to sell bonds are (1) the ability of a firm to generate funds internally, (2) composition of its capitalization, and (3) its accessibility to the capital market.

THE ABILITY TO GENERATE FUNDS INTERNALLY. Since investors judge a company's capability to pay interest and principal on its ability to obtain funds through depreciation and retained earnings, it follows that the greater the ability to generate funds internally, the better the chance a firm has to sell bonds.[10]

The ability to generate funds internally depends upon the degree of business risk to which each firm is subject. Public utility companies, for example, have the lowest degree of business risk because their products are daily necessities and the prices are relatively small in relation to disposable family income. On the other hand, fashion designers and producers are subject to a much

---

[10] A firm can pay interest and part of its long-term debt (sinking fund requirement) even though it has losses from operations, so long as its cash flow from other sources is large enough to meet the maturing obligations. For example, Eastern Air Lines had losses from operations for five years, 1961 through 1964, yet the company did not default on its debt. In 1964, operating losses amounted to about $10.2 million, but it was still able to pay $10.94 million interest charges on its outstanding debt, because it had a cash flow of $40.03 million from depreciation and amortization of planes and equipment.

higher degree of risk. If a dress designed for young girls does not take hold, the dressmaker can suffer heavy losses.

Another high-risk business is the electronics industry. Here, the mortality rate is high because of the potentially rapid obsolescence of its products. A company in the electronics industry requires large financial resources with which to undertake an aggressive research and development program, so as to stay ahead of its competitors in new product development. Because of rapid technological change, a small electronics concern has difficulty in prospering or even surviving, unless it has some specific products for which it is known as a quality producer.

It follows that public utility companies under most conditions have more opportunity to borrow money in the capital market than do fashion designers or small electronics companies. The smaller the degree of risk inherent in a particular line of business, the easier it is for those firms to sell bonds or other forms of indebtedness.

COMPOSITION OF CAPITAL. The ability of a firm to incur debt is partly determined by its capital structure. The larger the amount of debt in the capital account, the more difficult also will it be for that firm to sell additional debt, because the risk of failing to pay interest and principal then becomes greater.[11] The consequence of failing to meet debt service is generally bankruptcy. If a company which is subject to a great degree of business risk has no bonds outstanding, its very survival would not be immediately threatened, because it is not obligated to pay dividends on its common stock. As soon as it uses bonds to obtain capital, it has the additional risk of insolvency.

ACCESSIBILITY TO CAPITAL MARKETS. It is easy to understand that another important factor which determines the ability of a firm to raise capital for plant expansion is its accessibility to capital markets. A company which has no access to the capital market cannot sell bonds or other forms of securities.

The term "no access" requires some further explanation. Of course, every company can send a representative, its financial vice-president or controller perhaps, to Wall Street to try to persuade an investment banking house to underwrite its bond issue, but the question is whether or not that house will agree to do

---

[11] Franco Modigliani and Merton H. Miller contended, in their celebrated article, "The Cost of Capital, Corporation Finance and the Theory of Investment," *American Economic Review*, vol. 48, no. 3, pp. 261–297, June, 1958, that the cost of capital was not a function of capital structure. In other words, a company which has no long-term debt outstanding will not obtain funds from outside sources any more cheaply than another company which has one-half of its capital in the form of long-term debt. Such a viewpoint is contrary to the traditional theory which holds that within a given class of industry (of the same risk), after a certain debt-to-equity ratio is reached, the higher the percentage of debt to total capital, the higher the interest cost a firm has to pay for its bonds.

so. Generally speaking, the securities markets are accessible only to those which are large in terms of financial resources and are well known to the investors. A newly formed company or a company which has been in existence for some time but is not well known to investors will have a hard time persuading Wall Street bankers to market its securities. One of the reasons that corporations aim to have their stocks traded on the New York or American Stock Exchange is to obtain the accessibility to capital markets. By having their stocks traded on exchanges, corporations have a market ready to absorb their securities, either stocks or bonds. This does not mean that those corporations whose common stocks are traded on the New York Stock Exchange are in all cases better companies than those whose common stocks are traded over the counter. What it does mean is that the former, generally speaking, because they are better known and have a larger number of security holders, have a broader market for their securities than the latter. This is especially true when the comparison is made between corporations which have privately held common stocks and corporations whose common stocks are traded on the New York Stock Exchange.

SUMMARY

In this chapter, we have discussed the capital budget. The budget actually has two parts. The first deals with the problem of identifying worthwhile projects which will strengthen the future prospects of the firm by adding to its product line or by improving its processing or servicing effectiveness or efficiency. The second part deals with the ability of the firm to raise the necessary funds.

The measure of a firm's ability to undertake a capital project is termed net cash flow. Cash flow may be generated within the firm itself through depreciation and depletion charges, as well as by net income to be received from the capital project itself. If the firm is required to raise funds externally, both bonds and stock offerings may be used, especially by the larger firms.

chapter 14
capital expenditure
decisions

After having studied the scope and significance of capital budgeting, we come to the final aspect of the topic, and that is, whether or not a firm should undertake a given capital project. Frequently, corporations have enough resources to finance capital expenditures, yet they do not do so. The reasons for this failure include a conservative approach to business expansion, errors in estimating the future course of business, and simple inertia.[1] Conservative executives often prefer to maintain the status quo rather than to expand their corporate activities to the point where they would require more of the executives' time.

From an economic point of view, however, the willingness of a firm to undertake capital expansion is presumed to depend upon the amount of profit a given capital project will generate. A profit-maximizing firm theoretically is willing to expand its plant facilities so long as the incremental revenue is larger than the incremental cost. Actually, many corporations stop expansion long before the optimal point is reached, partly because of limited financial resources and partly because of limited executive talent.

We will begin the discussion with the calculation of incremental revenue, and then take up the calculation of incremental capital cost and methods of ranking capital investment proposals in order of desirability.

[1] One of the best examples of how a corporation, even with plenty of cash in its till, may not be willing to expand its plant and equipment is Montgomery Ward & Company, now known as Marcor, Inc. The company decided not to expand its store and plant facilities because it wanted to stay liquid to meet the economic depression which the firm was certain would come after World War II. On the other hand, its chief competitor, Sears, Roebuck & Company, rapidly expanded its physical facilities, which enabled the company to show a much better record of sales and earnings.

CALCULATION OF INCREMENTAL REVENUE

The capital budgeting decision requires that we compare two different sums of money in two different time periods and under two different risk conditions. In addition, we have to find a way to fit in cases where a given capital project yields little or no revenue, as in a strategic investment.

THE CONCEPT OF PRESENT VALUE

To calculate incremental revenue, we make use of the concept of present value. As shown in Chapter 1, revenue generated by a given project has to be discounted to the present in order to make it comparable with capital investment to be made today. A dollar of income today is worth more than the same dollar scheduled to be received in the future. This is not the problem of inflation. It is because a dollar we have today can be invested to earn income which, when added to the original amount, will result in an amount greater than one dollar. So if a dollar is to be received one year from now, it is worth only a fraction of that amount. How large that fraction is depends upon the interest rate we use to discount the future receipt.

There is nothing mysterious about the present value concept. It is derived from the compound interest formula,

$$A = P (1 + i)^n$$

where A is the amount of money to be received after a given number of years, P is the principal, i the interest rate per annum, and n the number of years the principal is to be left for interest.

By using a compound interest table such as the one presented in Appendix A to this chapter, we can easily find the value for A. The table contains values for the term $(1 + i)^n$. If i equals .05 and n is 5, we find the value for the term, 1.276,281,6, by reading down the column marked "5 percent" to the fifth row. Multiplying that amount by the principal, we have the sum of principal and interest.

Since our problem is to convert future income into present income, our procedure is the reverse of what we have just described. Mathematically, we simply transfer the time value factor $(1 + i)^n$ from the right-hand side to the left-hand side of the equation, and so we have the present value formula:

$$\frac{A}{(1 + i)^n} = P \quad \text{or} \quad P = A \frac{1}{(1 + i)^n} = A(1 + i)^{-n}$$

In connection with capital budgeting, we use V to represent present value and R to represent annual cash flow from a given project. We keep i and n as before. So the present value of a capital project which provides one lump sum of cash flow in a given future year is determined by the following equation:

$$V = \frac{R}{(1 + i)^n}$$

Assuming the current interest rate is 5 percent, the number of years we have to wait before we can receive the future income is 5 years, and the future income is $100, then its present value is $78.35. From Appendix A-2, we find $(1 + 0.05)^{-5}$ equals 0.783,527, and when we multiply that amount by $100 we will get the present value of $78.35.

From this simple present value problem, we now move to a little more complicated one. A capital project, as a rule, produces income or cash flow over a period of years. For example, electric utility companies' power plants yield benefits over a fifty-year span, and even though some airlines depreciate their aircraft over twelve years, the companies continue to derive benefits for a still longer period. Therefore, we have to develop a formula which can describe the present value of not one but a series of payments. Fortunately, mathematicians have already developed one for us and it is simply an addition of what we have already shown:

$$V = \frac{R_1}{(1 + i)^1} + \frac{R_2}{(1 + i)^2} + \frac{R_3}{(1 + i)^3} + \cdots + \frac{R_n}{(1 + i)^n}$$

$$= \sum_{j=1}^{n} \frac{R_j}{(1 + i)^j}$$

$$= \sum_{j=1}^{n} R_j \frac{1}{(1 + i)^j}$$

We go to the table of present value of an annuity, which is Appendix A-3. In that table we read down the column marked 5 percent and come to the fifth row where we find the figure 4.329. This simply means that if we are to receive $1 per year for the next five years we will have $5 in total at the end of the period. However, if we are to get the equivalent amount in a lump sum today, we would need only $4.33 to provide the same total benefit over that period. This is because $4.33 at 5 percent compound interest for 5 years yields $5.00.

From the present value formula, we notice that the farther in the future we have to wait for the income, the smaller the present value of that income will become, other things being equal. In the same manner, the larger the i becomes, the smaller the present value of a given future income will be. This means that when the current long-term interest rate is high, a given capital project is worth less, other things being equal. Hence, the changes in long-term interest rates have a great impact on the size of capital investment.

THE UNCERTAINTY FACTOR

When we start a new capital project, we cannot estimate its future cash flow with any degree of assurance. As the degree of risk inherent in a particular industry increases, the degree of accuracy of prediction as to the amount of future cash flow decreases. In preparing a capital budget, some sort of adjustment for uncertainty must be made in estimating future cash flow.

In this conjunction, we want to repeat the point we made earlier about the need to distinguish between risk and uncertainty.[2] Under risk we are able to estimate the probability of occurrence of an outcome of a decision. A good example here is the mortality table used by life insurance companies to predict the probable life span of the insured. With that table, life insurance companies are able to set up appropriate premium schedules. However, there is no known pattern of occurrence of a given event under uncertainty, so we can formulate no estimate of probability. For example, neither the probability of the next earthquake in southern California, nor the probability of snow on a given December afternoon in Washington, D.C., are known. Although there is a basic difference between risk and uncertainty, the problem is handled in the same way for both in all other respects. Except for the setting up of a probability distribution table, the procedure will be the same.

Forming a Probability Table. Let us assume that a company which produces small motors for room air conditioners and lawn mowers has decided to expand its plant facilities to accommodate increased demand. A new plant will cost $15 million to build and equip, and it will take two years to complete. The useful life of the plant is estimated at fifteen years. Based upon last year's information, the company expects to have an annual cash flow of $3 million coming from the new plant: $1 million of depreciation (based upon the straightline method) and $2 million of net income after tax, with interest on long-term bonds added back. Based upon the past ten year's experience, we can rearrange the company's earnings record into a probability distribution with which to estimate the future.

Number of Years Occurred	Net Income after Taxes plus Interest on Bonds
1	$3,000,000
1	2,600,000
4	2,000,000
3	800,000
1	0

[2] According to Karl H. Borch, such distinction is pointless because by using the Bayes-Laplace theorem, commonly known as the principle of insufficient reason, we can assign under uncertainty the same probability to each mutually exclusive event which is expected to occur if a given decision

Notice that even though $2 million net income is forecast by management as the most likely result, in four years out of the past ten the company did not earn that amount. Assuming future events will probably repeat past performance, we derive in Table 14-1 an expected monetary value for the earnings flow by using this frequency distribution of ten years as the probability table. The $1,600,000 is the expected monetary value of the after-tax net income plus interest on bonds of any future year. To this amount we add $1 million depreciation, for a total expected monetary value of cash flow of $2,600,000 from the capital investment.

TABLE 14-1. CALCULATION OF EXPECTED MONETARY VALUE

Frequency Distribution (Assumed Probability of Future Occurrence)		Net Income after Taxes plus Bond Interest		Expected Monetary Value
0.10	×	$3,000,000	=	$ 300,000
0.10	×	2,600,000	=	260,000
0.40	×	2,000,000	=	800,000
0.30	×	800,000	=	240,000
0.10	×	0	=	0
1.00				$1,600,000

An Alternative Procedure. In addition to the method we have just discussed, we may solve the problem of decision making under uncertainty, either by discounting the anticipated earnings flow once before computing the present value of the flow, or by raising the discount rate which is used to find the present value of the future cash flow.

To illustrate the first method, let us assume that even though the top management of the ABC Motors Company considers the $2 million earnings flow a most likely event, they would rather underestimate than overestimate the earnings flow. Management may in that case decide to discount the anticipated earnings flow by some arbitrary amount. Were 20 percent to be used, the result would be $1.6 million as the earnings forecast instead of $2 million. Adding the $1 million depreciation allowance, the management would then anticipate an annual cash flow of $2.6 million from the proposed project. Discounting this adjusted cash flow for present value, what we have is the present worth of the capital project.

The second method of adjusting the anticipated earnings flow for uncer-

---

is made. We therefore have a certain probability distribution table in which to work. For further information, see *The Economics of Uncertainty*, Princeton University Press, Princeton, N.J., 1968, chap. VII. See also William Fellner, *Probability and Profit*, Richard D. Irwin, Inc., Homewood, Ill., 1965, chap. 2.

tainty is to raise the discount rate used to find the present value of future cash flow. If previously we used 8 percent as the discount rate (or capitalization rate) to discount the expected monetary value of earnings flow, now we raise the rate to 10 percent to compensate for the uncertainty factor, so the additional 2 percent rate is for uncertainty.

Let us go back to the ABC Motors Company problem and sum up what we have discussed so far concerning the adjustments of future cash flow for uncertainty and for present value:

Estimated annual earnings flow (net income plus interest on bonds)	$2,000,000
Estimated annual cash flow (earnings flow plus depreciation)	$3,000,000
Adjusted for uncertainty by changing	
1. the numerator of the equation of the present value by	
a. calculating the expected monetary value, or	$1,600,000
b. discounting the earnings flow by 20 percent	1,600,000
2. the denominator of the equation by raising the discount rate from	8% to 10%

The results of the two methods are quite similar, as shown by the following examples:

1. Changing the numerator:

$$V = \sum_{j=1}^{N} \frac{1,600,000 + 1,000,000}{(1 + 0.08)^j} \quad \text{where } N = 1, 2, 3, \ldots, 15$$

$$= 2,600,000 \sum_{j=1}^{N} \frac{1}{(1 + 0.08)^j}$$

$$= 2,600,000 \times 8.559$$

$$= \$22,253,400$$

2. Changing the denominator:

$$V = \sum_{j=1}^{N} \frac{3,000,000}{(1 + 0.10)^j} \quad \text{where } N = 1, 2, 3, \ldots, 15$$

$$= 3,000,000 \sum_{j=1}^{N} \frac{1}{(1 + 0.10)^j}$$

$$= 3,000,000 \times 7.606$$

$$= \$22,818,000$$

Calculating the Expected Monetary Value under Uncertainty. If we are going to engage in a new enterprise which has no record of past performance to assist in setting up a probability table, we can assign an equal probability to each mutually exclusive event which is expected to occur. In other words if we have no a priori reason to assume one outcome any more likely than any other, we assume each is equally likely. For example, should we engage a touring ballet troupe to give an evening performance in an open-air theater in June? We have no idea as to the probability of rain on an early summer evening. Therefore, we are taking a chance in scheduling the ballet troupe to perform on a given night. In order to find out whether or not we should take that gamble, we calculate the expected monetary value for the alternatives—to perform or not to perform. Suppose we can sell 1,000 tickets at $10 each, and 3,000 tickets at $5 each, with total receipts for the evening of $25,000. Out of that amount, we will have to pay $8,000 to the ballet troupe for the performance, $1,500 for renting the theater, and $500 for ushers and box-office employees. By assuming each outcome equally likely, we can set up a payoff matrix as in Table 14-2.

TABLE 14-2. PAYOFF MATRIX FOR BALLET THEATER

	No Rain $(p = .5)$	Rain $(q = 1 - p = .5)$	Expected Monetary Value°
Perform	+$15,000	−$10,000	+$2,500
Not perform	0†	0	0†

° The $2,500 expected monetary value is calculated as follows:

No rain: 15,000 × .50 = $7,500
Rain: $10,000 × .50 = −$5,000
Expected monetary value: 7,500 − 5,000 = $2,500

† Even though the payoff is zero, we have an opportunity loss of $15,000 or an expected monetary value of the opportunity loss of $7,500. The opportunity loss represents what we could have made if we had engaged the ballet troupe to perform that evening.

Actually business executives have some idea (they may be right) as to the probable outcome of each premeditated decision. The businessman who contracts with the ballet troupe to perform in the open-air theater must believe that the odds are more than 50:50 in his favor as to the probability of rain that very evening. We do not know what odds he has in mind, but let us assume he believes the chances to be 3 to 1 that it will not rain in the early part of that evening. If so, his payoff matrix will look like this:

TABLE 14-3. PAYOFF MATRIX FOR BALLET THEATER

	No Rain $(p = .75)$	Rain $(q = 1 - p = .25)$	Expected Monetary Value
Perform	+$15,000	−$10,000	+$8,750
Not perform	0	0	0

From the two matrices presented, we naturally come to the conclusion that we should engage the ballet troupe to perform. However, one word of caution is warranted. When an action taken under condition of uncertainty involves monetary losses and not merely less profit, the expected monetary value is not a valid or an appropriate guide for decision making.

In the first matrix, for example, a 50:50 chance of making $15,000 or of losing $10,000 has an expected monetary value of $2,500, but for many businessmen this is not a bargain. Instead, they might prefer not to engage the troupe to perform in an open-air theater. This decision, even though it has a zero expected monetary value, will not entail any out-of-pocket losses either. In such a situation, we have to use expected utility (personal preference and aversion to risk) as the criterion for our decision making.[3]

CALCULATION OF INCREMENTAL CAPITAL COST

Having estimated the potential revenue for a capital project, we now consider the possible cost. There are four different components in a capital account, and it is necessary to analyze each one of them to get an accurate estimate of the cost of capital. The cost of capital refers to the price a firm has to pay in order to have the use of capital. It normally depends on the required level of interest for borrowed money or the dividend rate which has to be paid on equity capital. Even though a firm frequently uses only one type of security to finance a new project, the impact of that financing spreads over the whole spectrum of the capital structure.

COST OF BONDS

There are two different kinds of bond cost: explicit and implicit. The explicit cost is the coupon rate on bonds, plus any discount the company may have to pay or minus any premium the company may receive in issuing the securities, plus the flotation cost of the bond issue. For an issue of bonds sold at par, the cost of the bonds is the coupon rate the bonds carry plus the flotation cost. When an issue of bonds is sold at par, there is nothing for which to adjust. However, when bonds are sold below par or at a discount, the company has to amortize the whole amount of discount over the entire life of the bonds.

Because interest payments are deductible for income tax purposes and dividend payments to stockholders are not deductible, a firm that pays out 8 percent interest annually actually pays an after-tax rate of only 4.16 percent, assuming the tax rate is 48 percent. If we compare bonds with preferred stock

[3] The concept and significance of expected utility will be taken up in Appendix B to this chapter. Reference may also be made to Neil E. Harlan, Charles J. Christenson, and Richard F. Vancil, *Managerial Economics*, Richard D. Irwin, Inc., Homewood, Ill., 1962, sect III; and to Robert Schlaifer, *Analysis of Decisions under Uncertainty*, McGraw-Hill Book Company, New York, 1969, chaps. 4 and 5.

solely on the basis of the explicit cost to the firm of using each type, it pays to obtain capital funds by selling bonds.

The implicit cost of bonds to a firm arises out of the restrictive provisions imposed upon the firm by the lenders. These restrictions take the form of requirements, such as that the firm may not pay cash dividends over a given portion of current income, must maintain a net working capital (total current assets minus total current liabilities) above a certain amount, may not dispose of its plant unless an equal amount of bonds is retired, and may not incur any long-term obligation which is senior to the current issue.

How much weight will the management of a firm attach to such restrictive provisions? A clear-cut answer is difficult to give, because there are several factors involved.

Many firms, for example, especially in growth industries, do not pay a dividend on common stock. For them, the restriction on dividend payment would have no practical meaning. Similarly, to a corporation with no long-term debt outstanding, the limit on the amount of consolidated outstanding funded debt does not constitute a real obstacle to its bond-selling ability. Nevertheless, these restrictive provisions are generally considered to limit flexibility in decision making.

One way to measure the implicit cost of these restrictions is to use a linear programming model to evaluate proposed changes in the restrictive provisions through sensitivity analysis and thereby determine the opportunity costs of these restrictions.[4] In the construction of a linear programming model, the assignment of a numerical value to each parameter depends upon the financial resources of a firm, the type of industry the firm is in, and the temperament of management. For our purposes, it is enough to know that it may be better to pay a higher explicit cost to compensate for a lower implicit cost, if the result is to minimize the overall cost of borrowing.

COST OF PREFERRED STOCK

The cost of preferred stock also may be divided into the two classes: explicit and implicit. The explicit cost of preferred stock is of course the dividend rate a share of preferred stock carries, plus the flotation cost. Any premium or discount on selling preferred stock is difficult to handle, because preferred stock has no maturity date and therefore we have no way to compute an effective dividend rate by amortizing any discount that occurs. True, most preferred stocks outstanding have call dates attached, but the majority of the companies do not choose to call their preferred stocks. Also, many preferred stocks today have no

---

[4] James Van Horne, "A Linear-programming Approach to Evaluating Restrictions under a Bond Indenture of Loan Agreement," *Journal of Financial and Quantitative Analysis*, vol. 1, pp. 68–83, June, 1966. For a brief discussion of sensitivity analysis, see Chapter 16.

par value, and it is difficult to tell whether or not there is any discount or premium on the initial sales of preferred stocks.

The implicit cost of preferred stock arises from the same kind of restrictive provisions as those imposed by bond indentures, except that they are not as strict nor as cumbersome.

Basically, the restrictive provisions aim to protect the preferred stockholders against any weakening of protection to preferred dividend payments.[5]

COST OF COMMON STOCK

The cost of common stock is the required rate of return investors hope to obtain, plus the flotation cost of the security. The required rate of return, or capitalization rate, is derived by dividing the expected earnings per share by the price per share. Mathematically, the rate *r* is obtained from

$$r = \frac{E}{P}$$

where *E* is the expected earnings per share, and *P*, the price per share of common stock. The capitalization rate is an opportunity cost of capital, because if the estimated rate of return on a given stock proves to be lower than investors can obtain elsewhere, the stock will not be bought by a rational investor. This is another way of saying that the cost of common stock is the expected required earnings per share, and the capitalization rate becomes merely the earnings-to-price ratio.

It is important to point out that earnings per share (or properly speaking, expected earnings per share) and not dividends per share are considered to be the cost of common stock, because a dividend is only a form of distributing the earnings. Furthermore, investors nowadays buy common stock mainly for potential price appreciation or capital gains and only secondarily for income purposes, as an examination of the relatively lower yield on common stocks in comparison to the higher yield on bonds of the same firm or rating will confirm.

Because capital gains depend upon a firm's earnings potential, the stronger the potential becomes, the greater the appreciation in price. The earnings rate affects share prices through the mechanism of the price-earnings ratio, or conversely, the capitalization rate. When investors think that the future earnings per share of a particular firm will grow rapidly in years to come, they are willing to adjust upward its price-earnings ratio. Larger actual present

---

[5] Curtis Publishing Company, which was badly in need of cash in early 1963, was unable to incur any additional long-term debt because of a negative vote from the majority of its prior preferred stockholders. This power of the preferred stockholders stemmed from a provision in its charter which read "that the consent of the holders of two-thirds of the prior preferred stock be obtained prior to the issuance of mortgage, secured or long-term debt."

earnings per share, plus a price-earnings ratio made higher by anticipation, will increase the price of a common share considerably.[6]

The capitalization rate actually is written as the reciprocal of the price-earnings ratio. Hence, if a company's earnings per share is $2 and the price of its common stock is $20, the price-earnings ratio is 10 times, and the capitalization rate or the earnings-to-price ratio is the inverse or 10 percent. With given earnings per share, the price of a common share is determined automatically by the capitalization rate currently demanded by investors.

Earlier models for evaluating common stock prices used dividends instead of earnings as the numerator, because dividend payment was formerly considered a basis for the purchase of common stock.[7] However, since the middle 1950s, capital gain has been considered much more important. True, corporate earnings will sooner or later be paid out as dividends, but we may have to hold a stock for a long time in order to get any reasonable yield from a growth stock. For example, an investor who bought a share of Xerox common stock in 1958 and held it through 1968 received negligible returns in the form of dividends. However, the rate of return in terms of capital gains was phenomenal. Using the peak price in 1958 and in 1968, Xerox common stock rose from $1.67 per share to $109.50, an increase of 65.6 times or a rise of about 52 percent compounded annually. Therefore, the cost of common stock, after taking into consideration the dividend yield as well as price appreciation, is as follows:

$$r = \frac{D}{P} + g$$

where r is the expected rate of return or capitalization rate; D, the dividend payment; P, the price of common stock; and g, the anticipated growth rate in price or capital gain rate.

Suppose a common stock is selling at $20 a share and earnings per share amount to $2. The firm pays $1 dividend a year, which gives the stock an annual yield of 5 percent. Assume that an investor expects to double his money in eight years through capital appreciation, an increase in value of 9.1 percent compounded annually. Altogether, the investor anticipates having an annual rate of return of 14.1 percent on his investment. We get the result by substituting the values into the equation given above and solving for r as shown:

$$r = \frac{1}{20} + 9.1\%$$
$$= 14.10\%$$

[6] Anticipations of future growth in Xerox Corporation, for example, based on its growth rate of earnings per share for 1957 to 1961 of 32.8 percent compounded annually, by December, 1961, caused its common stock to sell at a price-earnings ratio of 122.4 times.

[7] For example, John B. Williams' model is of this type, as explained in his book, *The Theory of Investment Value*, Harvard University Press, Cambridge, Mass., 1938.

COST OF RETAINED EARNINGS

We have now come to the most elusive part of the problem of how to calculate the cost of capital, that is, the calculation of the cost of retained earnings. The idea that a common stock which pays no dividend has any cost to a firm is difficult enough to grasp, but the idea of a cost associated with retained earnings seems incomprehensible. The cost, upon reflection, will be seen to be an opportunity cost.

Retained earnings is normally considered as part of the net worth of the firm and therefore belongs to the common stockholders. If the firm does not use this resource for the benefit of the common stockholders, then theoretically it should be paid out as dividends, so that the stockholders can use it as they see fit. Hence, we can say that the opportunity cost of retained earnings is the return in the best alternative use of the funds available to the stockholders. If stockholders may invest in Aaa bonds which currently yield approximately $7\frac{1}{2}$ percent annually, then retained earnings have a cost at least equal to $7\frac{1}{2}$ percent a year.

We can also explain the cost of retained earnings in terms of a fully subscribed rights offer, which has tax advantages for the stockholders. Suppose, for example, a firm distributes all of its net income to common stockholders, then sells enough shares of common stock to the same stockholders to restore net worth to its former level. By doing this, the firm, from the viewpoint of common stockholders, incurs two types of cost which could be avoided: First, common stockholders have to pay income taxes on the dividends received, and second, the firm has to pay flotation cost for the new issue of stock.

Mathematically, the cost of retained earnings can be expressed as follows:

$$C = \frac{(1 - t - f) E}{P}$$

where C is the cost of retained earnings; t, the marginal income tax rate of stockholders; f, the flotation cost; E, the anticipated earnings; and P, the price of a common share. Assuming then that it costs a firm 10 percent of the issue price to float a new issue of common stock and its stockholders' marginal tax rate is around 40 percent, the cost of retained earnings may be calculated as

$$C = \frac{(1 - 0.40 - 0.10)\, 2.00}{20.00} = 5.0\%$$

Normally, the higher the stockholders' marginal income tax rate, the better off they will be if the firm retains more earnings for investment purposes. This reasoning assumes that the firm can earn a higher rate of return on investments than its stockholders can. For fast-growing companies, such as those in the newer technologies, therefore, it is far better to plow back all earnings for capital expansion than to pay them out as dividends.

WEIGHTED AVERAGE COST OF CAPITAL

Weighted average cost of capital refers to the overall cost of capital, computed with due regard to the proportional importance of the cost of each component in relation to the total cost of capital. What this means is that, if a firm has 60 percent of its capital in bonds and 10 percent in preferred stock, a given change in the long-term interest rate will have more impact on the overall cost of capital than would an equivalent change in common stock prices. This is because 70 percent of the capital is in fixed income obligations directly affected by long-term interest rate fluctuation.

TABLE 14-4. CALCULATION OF WEIGHTED AVERAGE COST
(AMOUNT IN MILLIONS OF DOLLARS)

Component	Amount Outstanding (millions of dollars)	Percent Distribution	After-tax Cost	Weighted Average Cost
(1)	(2)	(3)	(4)	(5)
Bonds	35	35.0	4.16%	0.0146
Preferred stock	15	15.0	5.00	0.0075
Common stock	30	30.0	10.00	0.0300
Retained earnings	20	20.0	5.00	0.0100
	100	100.0		0.0621

From that definition we may proceed, as in Table 14-4, to construct a weighted average cost of capital. First, we set up a table showing each component of the capital account and calculate the proportion each of the components bears to the total. Second, we find the after-tax cost of each component by the appropriate percentage weight and sum them up to arrive at the weighted average cost.

Let us assume that the capital structure of Company XYZ is as shown in columns 1–3 of Table 14-4. We assume further that the company sold the bonds at par with a coupon rate of 8 percent, the preferred stock bearing a dividend rate of 5 percent, while the common stock is currently selling around 10 times estimated earnings. Most of the common stock, we will assume, is held by persons whose marginal income tax rate is approximately 40 percent, and the current corporate income tax rate is 48 percent. With these data, we can now compute the weighted average cost of capital by multiplying the items in column 3 by the after-tax cost shown in column 4 and summing the result to obtain a weighted average cost of capital of 6.21 percent.

CHOOSING AMONG CAPITAL EXPENDITURE PROPOSALS

Assuming that a firm is willing to expand its plant facilities so long as the anticipated revenue exceeds projected cost, a decision must be made concerning what
to do if all proposed capital projects meet that requirement. One way to solve
the problem is to rank the projects in a descending order according to
their estimated benefit and then to choose projects, beginning with the most
profitable, until the available funds are exhausted.[8] This method assumes that
we have no other reason for preferring one to another.

There are three basic methods for choosing among projects. They are (1)
the payback period criterion, (2) the present value method, and (3) the internal
rate of return method. In discussing these procedures, we will introduce formulas
which are refinements of the basic three.

THE PAYBACK PERIOD CRITERION

This criterion refers to the time it will take to get our money back after we
have made an investment. Mathematically, payback period is the quotient of the
cost of investment, divided by the after-tax net cash flow:

$$X = \frac{C}{R}$$

We would then choose that project having the shortest payback.

This method is easy to calculate, easy to understand, and easy to use,
and because of that, it is the most widely used formula for determining the desirability of a given capital project.

The payback period method, however, has the following shortcomings:
(1) It does not take into consideration the importance of the present value concept, since all after-tax cash flows are the same, whether currently received or
not. (2) It does not take into consideration possible fluctuations in earnings flow,
so that next year's earnings are assumed to be the same as this year's. (3) It does
not accurately discriminate between some kinds of investment proposals.

For example, if we are presented with two separate investment proposals, one with an initial investment of $1 million, an annual anticipated after-tax
cash flow of $250,000, and a useful life of six years, and the other with an ini-
tial investment of $1.2 million, an annual anticipated after-tax cash flow of
$300,000, and a useful life of nine years, we would not be able to make an in-
telligent choice, because both projects will have the same payback period of
four years.

[8] For large and reputable corporations, the limitation on the ability to accept profitable investment proposals comes not so much from the lack of funds but more from the shortage of capable
managerial personnel.

Refinements of the payback period method have been made by Gordon.[9] The reciprocal of the payback period formula,

$$r = \frac{R}{C} - \frac{R}{C}\left[\frac{1}{(1+r)^n}\right]$$

which is derived from the internal rate of return formula presented on page 358, is a good estimate of the project's rate of profit if the useful life of the project is relatively long and the discount rate is relatively high. As both n and r are getting very large, the last term of the equation may be disregarded, and what we have left is the simple annual rate of return of the project.

THE PRESENT VALUE METHOD

The concept of present value can be used to select among proposed capital projects. Suppose there are three capital expenditure proposals, and the task is to allocate $25 million which is available for capital investment at a given period. The salient data for the proposed capital projects are as follows:

	Cost of the Project (to be paid out in year zero)		
	Project #1: $10 million	Project #2: $15 million	Project #3: $25 million
Estimated annual cash flow (adjusted for uncertainty and income tax)	$2 million	$4 million	$6 million
Number of years of useful life	10	7	8
Salvage value	0	0	0
Weighted average cost of capital (rounded)	6.00%	6.00%	6.00%

$$V_1 = \sum_{j=1}^{N} \frac{2,000,000}{(1+.06)^n} \quad \text{where } n = 1, 2, 3, \ldots, 10$$
$$= 14,720,000$$
$$V_2 = \sum_{j=1}^{N} \frac{4,000,000}{(1+.06)^n} \quad \text{where } n = 1, 2, 3, \ldots, 7$$
$$= 22,328,000$$
$$V_3 = \sum_{j=1}^{N} \frac{6,000,000}{(1+.06)^n} \quad \text{where } n = 1, 2, 3, \ldots, 8$$
$$= 37,260,000$$

[9] Myron J. Gordon, "The Payoff Period and the Rate of Profit," *Journal of Business,* vol. 28, pp. 253–260, Oct., 1955.

From these results, we are still unable to decide which of the three projects or which of the two projects (if we combine projects 1 and 2) we should select, because the cost of each project is not the same. Furthermore, the useful life of each project varies, and that variation makes direct comparison difficult. For example, project 2 has a life of seven years, while project 1 has ten years, and the question is, what to do with our money after project 2 has been completely written off? Can we then invest the capital at a rate of return of 6 percent per year? Finally, we have to consider whether or not the 6 percent weighted average cost of capital is an appropriate discount rate to use.

Since the initial investment for each of the three projects is not the same, we cannot use the present value of the future cash flow from each project as the basis for comparison. We have to use either the net present value and/or the benefit-to-cost ratio (also known as the profitability index) as the yardstick to select the best of the alternatives. The first yardstick is an absolute value, while the second is a ratio. To make a comparison, we should convert to a ratio where possible.

Net Present Value. Net present value is the present value of the future cash flow, minus the cost of investment. It is therefore the future net income, discounted for the time value factor. The net present values for the three proposed projects of our illustration then appear as follows:

	Project #1	Project #2	Project #3
Present value of future cash flow	$ 14,720,000	$ 22,328,000	$ 37,260,000
Cost of investment	−10,000,000	−15,000,000	−25,000,000
Net present value	$ 4,720,000	$ 7,328,000	$ 12,260,000

From the net present values shown above, we notice that even if we add projects 1 and 2 together, the net present value of the two combined is $12,048,000, which is still smaller than the net present value of project 3. Since the initial investments in projects 1 and 2 are equal to that in project 3, the two results are then comparable, bearing in mind of course that the useful lives of the three projects will differ.

Benefit-to-cost Ratio. Instead of using the absolute amount as the basis for comparison, we can convert those absolute values into benefit-to-cost ratios and use them as a selection basis. The benefit-to-cost ratio is derived by dividing the present value of future cash flow by the cost of investment as shown:

$$B = \frac{V}{C}$$

Substituting the values from the three projects, we have

$$B_1 = \frac{14,720,000}{10,000,000} = 1.47$$

$$B_2 = \frac{22,328,000}{15,000,000} = 1.49$$

$$B_3 = \frac{37,260,000}{25,000,000} = 1.49$$

This shows that projects 2 and 3 are better than project 1. If we combine projects 1 and 2, our choice is still project 3.

All three proposed projects are profitable, because each of them has a benefit-to-cost ratio greater than 1; that is, the present value of future cash flow from each of the three proposed projects is larger than the cost of investment. If the ratio turns out to be 1, it then makes no difference to a firm whether or not it invests in that proposed project, because the rate of return from that project will just match the weighted average cost of capital, nonmonetary factors aside.

Annualized Profit. The choice we made in the preceding paragraph is not, strictly speaking, a valid one, because each proposed project has a different useful life. One way to correct this defect is to use a 280-year cycle of investment. What this means is that for project 1, we presume we will build a sequence of twenty-eight factories each having a useful life of ten years. For project 2, we will build forty factories, and for project 3, thirty-five factories. If we expand our plant facilities in a 280-year cycle, assuming that the rate of return remains unchanged, the present value method will be useful. For a firm actually to decide what capital projects should be undertaken using the method we have just described is out of the question, but the annualized profit method may provide the same answer.

Annualized profit is an adjusted annual cash flow. It is derived by subtracting the annual opportunity cost of an investment from its annual cash flow.[10] In order to understand how annualized profit works, we must first know how to compute the annual opportunity cost of investment. The annual opportunity cost of investment is the amount of cash flow a given capital project should generate in each year of its life to recover the capital invested in that project and to provide a given rate of return on the unrecovered balance of the capital. We calculate the annual opportunity cost of investment by simply dividing a given present value factor into the amount of capital invested in a particular project. Assuming that the amount of capital invested in a given project is paid out in one lump sum, the annual opportunity cost of project 1 in our example is derived

---

[10] Neil R. Harlan, Charles J. Christenson, and Richard F. Vancil, op. cit., pp. 256–257.

in the following manner:

$$C_i = \frac{10,000,000}{7.360} = \$1,358,696$$

where 7.360 is the present value factor of 6 percent for 10 years.

In the same manner, we calculate the annual opportunity cost of investment for projects 2 and 3 as $2,667,503 and $4,025,765, respectively. After we have obtained these values, we can calculate the annualized profit for each proposed project:

	Project #1	Project #2	Project #3
Annual cash flow	$2,000,000	$4,000,000	$6,000,000
Annual cost of investment	1,358,696	2,667,503	4,025,765
Annualized profit	$ 641,304	$1,332,497	$1,974,235

Since the initial investment in project 3 is as large as those in projects 1 and 2 combined, we will compare them on that basis. The annualized profits for projects 1 and 2 total $1,973,801, which is about the same as that for project 3. So, after three different testings, we may finally be convinced that project 3 is the best choice of the three proposed projects.

The Discount Rate. The last item in the present value method which deserves some further analysis is the discount rate used to convert future cash flow into the present value of that flow. In our example, we used the weighted average cost of capital as the discount rate. This is only one of several possible alternatives. Two other rates which may be used are the opportunity cost of capital and the "cutoff" rate. The latter should be, in an economic sense, the same as the former; however, as a general practice, the cutoff rate has become a target rate of return on investment which a firm strives to achieve. It may not, therefore, bear any close relationship to the opportunity cost of capital.[11]

The rationale for using weighted average cost as the discount rate is that a firm should recover what it has to pay for capital. In our example, we did just that. The 6 percent is the weighted average cost of capital to be recovered, and is, at the same time, the discount rate. Notwithstanding its obvious reasonableness as a discount rate, the weighted average cost method suffers defects

[11] More discussion on the discount rate problem will be taken up in Appendix C. Reference may be made, however, to William J. Baumol and Richard E. Quandt, "Investment and Discount Rates Under Capital Rationing—A Programming Approach," Economic Journal, vol. 75, no. 298, pp. 317–329, June, 1965; J. Hershleifer, "On the Theory of Optimal Investment Decision," The Journal of Political Economy, vol. 66, no. 4, pp. 329–352, Aug., 1958; and James H. Lorie and Leonard J. Savage, "Three Problems in Rationing Capital," Journal of Business, vol. 28, pp. 229–239, Oct., 1955.

inherent in any historically based accounting method of determining cost which does not include opportunity costs.

The opportunity cost of capital is another yardstick which can be used as the discount rate in the present value formula. The rationale for this is that the weighted average cost of capital may be out of line with the time horizon of the decision. For example, the 5 percent rate which we assigned to the preferred stock in our case is not the current cost of preferred stock, and therefore it is not a relevant cost for decision making. Furthermore, suppose the company has some excess funds which are primarily obtained from depreciation and retained earnings. Would we use the weighted average cost of those funds?

One may argue that the funds derived from depreciation might represent the recovery of bond proceeds which were originally used to build the plant. Would we then say that if we cannot get a rate of return larger than the weighted average cost of capital, we are not going to use the funds at all? The answer is evidently no.

If we really have no better alternative for the funds, we might possibly use them to retire bonds and thus save annual interest expense. Another alternative is to use the excess funds to purchase bonds of highest quality of another company, thus assuring ourselves a steady and reliable income every year. The return on either of these alternatives is the opportunity cost of the funds which can be employed as the discount rate in the present value formula.

In using the weighted average cost of capital or the opportunity cost of capital, management implicitly has established a floor for the discount rate. This means that, if the present value of the future cash flow from a given project, discounted by the lower of either the weighted average cost or the opportunity cost of capital, is smaller than the amount of funds invested in that project, the proposed project will not be undertaken. The lower of the two rates is the floor for the discount rate, because one rate may be higher than the other for one firm at a given time, and the situation may be the other way around for another firm. The opportunity cost coincides with the weighted average cost of capital at the time a firm is raising capital for a proposed capital project, because at that time the firm has the option of postponing the raising of funds if the weighted average cost is higher than the opportunity cost of capital. Here, the discussion leads us to the use of the cutoff rate as the discount rate.

The cutoff rate is not entirely an opportunity cost of capital. It is the rate set up by management as the target rate of return a firm hopes to obtain from capital investment. Theoretically, the cutoff rate is an opportunity cost of capital, the highest alternative return a firm is able to get under present market conditions. However, in an actual situation, the cutoff rate may become an a priori rate of return which may not be achievable under current economic conditions.

For example, one of the authors once interviewed management personnel of major corporations concerning their established cutoff rates. An after-tax rate of return of 20 percent on invested capital was most commonly cited. It is doubtful, however, that some major corporations could have achieved that goal more than half the time.

INTERNAL RATE OF RETURN METHOD

The last, but not the least important, of the three methods for selecting capital projects is the internal rate of return method. The internal rate of return may be defined as the discount rate which brings the present value of future cash flow from a capital project equal to the cost of investment. In other words, the internal rate of return is the interest rate which sums the net present value of a capital project to zero.[12] The formula for internal rate of return is as follows:

$$C = \frac{R_1}{(1 + r)^1} + \frac{R_2}{(1 + r)^2} + \frac{R_3}{(1 + r)^3} + \cdots + \frac{R_n}{(1 + r)^n}$$
$$= R \sum_{i=1}^{N} \left[\frac{1}{(1 + r)^i} \right]$$

where C is the amount of capital to be invested in a new project; R, the amount of cash flow from the project; and r, the internal rate of return.

What the equality of cash outflow and cash inflow means is that a firm is able to recover the entire amount of capital invested in a particular project, while earning a certain rate of return on the unrecovered balance during the life of the project. For example, the proposed project 1 of our example has an estimated annual cash inflow of $2 million for ten years, while the cost of investment is $10 million. Now the question is, what rate of return will equate those two amounts? Following the internal rate of return model presented above, we locate that present value factor of an annuity of $1 for ten years, which, when multiplied by the annual cash inflow, will equal the amount of cash outflow. In this instance we find it to be $5.0188. Multiplying that factor by $2,000,000 yields a present value of $10,037,600. The rate, therefore, at which the investment equals the present value of the future cash flow turns out to be around $15\frac{1}{8}$ percent. The internal rate of return is larger than the weighted cost of capital, and therefore, the company should accept project 1, assuming that it has enough cash on hand to undertake all three projects at the same time and that it needs all of them at the same time.

Leaving detailed discussion on internal rate of return method of se-

[12] The internal rate of return is what John M. Keynes called the marginal efficiency of capital which he defined as being equal to "that rate of discount which would make the present value of the series of annuities given by the returns expected from the capital-asset during its life just equal to its supply price." *The General Theory of Employment Interest and Money,* Harcourt, Brace and Company, Inc., New York, 1936, p. 135.

lecting capital project to Appendix C, we can now make a summary comparison between the present value method and the internal rate of return method as a means of choosing one or more capital expenditure proposals among many. We start by comparing their similarities.

First of all, both of them have taken into consideration the time value of money, and therefore they make comparable the costs and the benefits of a capital project incurred in two different time periods. Second, if the anticipated cash flow fluctuates greatly year to year, both methods can handle this problem. (Of course, this situation will give us more work, because we cannot sum the anticipated cash flows into one figure as we have in the above-mentioned examples.) Third, these two methods allow for the differences in the useful lives of two or more capital projects.

As the yardstick to measure the acceptability of a capital project (in simple cases), both methods give us the same answer. If a project has a positive net present value, its internal rate of return is higher than the weighted average cost of capital. In both cases, then, we will accept the proposed project.

There are two differences between the two methods. First, in the present value model, V (the present value of the future cash flow) is unknown, and a proposed project will be accepted if V is larger than C (the cost of investment or the amount of cash outflow). On the other hand, in the internal rate of return model, r is unknown, and a proposed project will be accepted if r is larger than i (the weighted cost of capital). Second, the discount rate used in the present value model may take one of the three forms indicated above, while the discount rate used in the internal rate of return model takes only one form; that is, its value is determined by the values assumed by other variables. In other words, we cannot assign the cutoff rate (fixed by the top management) to r, because if we do that, the model ceases to be one of internal rate of return. It may happen, of course, that the anticipated cash flow from a given capital project when discounted by the fixed cutoff rate is just equal to the cost of investment. But this will be a rare occurrence indeed.

CAPITAL RATIONING

In the preceding discussion of capital budgeting, we assumed that a firm could obtain funds from both internal and external sources without any limitation. So long as a firm can get a rate of return from invested capital higher than its weighted average cost of capital it can and should continue to expand its plant and equipment facilities until the incremental cost and the incremental revenue arising from the investment are equal.

In Figure 14-1, we depict the marginal rate of return on investment (or in the Keynesian terminology, the marginal efficiency of capital) as r, a curve of negative slope, on the theory that a firm will first undertake those capital proj-

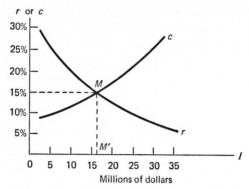

Figure 14-1. Determination of rejection rate.

ects which will yield very high rates of return. As more profitable investment opportunities are exhausted, the firm reaches out to less profitable projects, and therefore, as the amount of investment increases, the marginal rate of return decreases.

Let us take copper mining as an example. A firm will start by mining those ores which have the highest copper content. As ores of highest copper content are exhausted, the firm will mine those with lower copper content. It will follow this procedure until the grade of ores is so poor that is will not be worthwhile to mine any more. For simplicity's sake, let us assume that all deposits are located in the western region of the United States and that the mining cost, including labor wages, is about the same for all deposits. We can easily construct an investment schedule showing, on a declining scale, the grade of ores a given mine possesses and the priority of investment in each mine. Since the higher the grade of ore, the better the return on investment will be, we therefore have a curve of negative slope representing the marginal efficiency of capital.

On the other hand, the marginal cost curve c is one of positive slope, because the more funds a firm wants to raise, the higher the cost of additional funds will be.

The plausibility of this assumption lies with the fact that, as a firm uses up its funds derived from internal sources, it has to go to the capital market for additional funds. These additional funds may be obtained by selling common stock and/or bonds (or preferred stock, for that matter). If the firm sells more common stock, per share earnings will be diluted in the short run, and that effect tends to depress the price of stock more than proportionally, so the cost of common stock will rise. Unless the effect is offset by a drop in debt cost, the weighted average cost of capital will increase.

If, however, the firm sells bonds to finance the proposed capital projects, the additional debt will tend to increase the risk of default and that will make debt financing more costly.[13] Increased risk of default will depress the prices of both preferred and common stocks, and therefore the weighted average cost will also go up. Hence, the curve is one of positive slope. The point M where the two curves c and r intersect in Figure 14-1 represents the cutoff point or rejection rate. Proposed projects yielding less income than M' will be rejected.

A situation such as the one depicted will prevail only if there are plenty of alternative investment possibilities which will produce attractive yields, and a firm has almost unlimited financial and human resources to undertake these profitable projects. But obtaining additional amounts of funds from external sources may raise the weighted average cost of capital. Also, in practice, unlimited funds are not available, and therefore what is available must be rationed

When a firm rations capital, it does so by setting the rejection rate higher than the previously illustrated optimal levels. For example, instead of setting the rejection rate at the point of intersection which happens to be 15 percent in Figure 14-1, management may adopt a cutoff rate of 20 percent. Though valid to meet the conditions of capital rationing and possible executive scarcity, this rate prevents the firm from achieving its optimal investment, since it has not used up all profitable investment opportunities which yield less than 20 percent but more than 15 percent. In other words, the firm is not expanding its plant and equipment to the point where marginal revenue equals marginal cost.

In addition to setting a cutoff rate higher than the one determined by the optimal investment theory, capital rationing raises the problem of the effect of current year's investment on the firm's ability to take advantage of investment opportunities in years ahead. For example, if a proposed capital project, to be built three years hence, will be a very profitable one, the firm should choose a prior project which is expected to give the fastest payback, so that the funds released can be utilized for the next project.

Capital rationing normally is not a serious problem to financially large corporations, such as General Motors and General Electric, in their capital budgeting, but it is really a handicap to financially small companies in their planning for capital expenditure programs.

SUMMARY

In this chapter, we have discussed methods of calculating incremental returns and costs from a capital investment. We have also covered methods of choosing among capital expenditure proposals and of calculating the cutoff rates.

Incremental revenue calculation requires that we determine the net worth today of an expected flow of income in the future. The calculation takes

---

[13] Chances are the cost of debt will not rise at all if the amount of bonds outstanding is not out of proportion to equity. In other words, within a given range of debt-to-equity ratio, debt financing will not raise the weighted average cost of capital.

both the interest rate and the probability of occurrence of the income stream into account. When we have no other basis for prediction, we may extrapolate from past earnings experience and then compute an expected monetary value, or we may assume all probabilities are equally likely.

Incremental cost calculation has four components to consider. They are: (1) the explicit and implicit cost of bonds, (2) the cost of using preferred stock (almost always higher because dividends paid are not deductible from taxes), (3) the cost of common stock in terms of the price-to-earnings ratio investors will demand to support the price that management would like to get per share, and (4) the cost of retained earnings. The last element is actually the cost of paying the earnings out as dividends and then attempting to restore the lost net worth by a new stock issue. All components of cost may be combined in a weighted average, in which the weights are the proportions of total capital.

Choosing projects is seen to be somewhat more complicated than mere ranking in order of prospective benefit. We may choose that project which minimizes the period within which our investment is returned, that which has the greatest discounted present value of net benefit, or that whose prospective internal rate of return exceeds the weighted average cost of capital by the largest amount. The discussion ended with a presentation of methods of capital rationing.

Appendix A-1. Amount of 1 at Compound Interest $(1 + i)^n$

Year	1.0%	1.5%	2.0%	2.5%	3.0%	3.5%	4.0%	4.5%	5.0%	5.5%
1	1.01000	1.01500	1.02000	1.02500	1.03000	1.03500	1.04000	1.04500	1.05000	1.05500
2	1.02010	1.03022	1.04040	1.05062	1.06090	1.07122	1.08160	1.09202	1.10250	1.11302
3	1.03030	1.04567	1.06120	1.07689	1.09272	1.10871	1.12486	1.14116	1.15762	1.17424
4	1.04060	1.06136	1.08243	1.10381	1.12550	1.14752	1.16985	1.19251	1.21550	1.23882
5	1.05101	1.07728	1.10408	1.13140	1.15927	1.18768	1.21665	1.24618	1.27628	1.30695
6	1.06152	1.09344	1.12616	1.15969	1.19405	1.22925	1.26531	1.30225	1.34009	1.37884
7	1.07213	1.10984	1.14868	1.18868	1.22987	1.27227	1.31593	1.36086	1.40709	1.45467
8	1.08285	1.12649	1.17165	1.21840	1.26676	1.31680	1.36856	1.42209	1.47745	1.53468
9	1.09368	1.14338	1.19509	1.24886	1.30477	1.36289	1.42330	1.48609	1.55132	1.61909
10	1.10462	1.16053	1.21899	1.28008	1.34391	1.41059	1.48024	1.55296	1.62889	1.70814
11	1.11566	1.17794	1.24337	1.31208	1.38423	1.45996	1.53945	1.62284	1.71033	1.80208
12	1.12682	1.19561	1.26823	1.34488	1.42575	1.51106	1.60102	1.69587	1.79585	1.90120
13	1.13809	1.21354	1.29360	1.37850	1.46852	1.56394	1.66506	1.77219	1.88564	2.00576
14	1.14947	1.23175	1.31947	1.41297	1.51258	1.61868	1.73167	1.85193	1.97992	2.11608
15	1.16096	1.25022	1.34586	1.44829	1.55796	1.67534	1.80093	1.93527	2.07892	2.23246
16	1.17257	1.26898	1.37277	1.48450	1.60409	1.73397	1.87297	2.02236	2.18286	2.35525
17	1.18429	1.28801	1.40023	1.52161	1.65283	1.79466	1.94789	2.11336	2.29201	2.48479
18	1.19614	1.30733	1.42823	1.55965	1.70242	1.85747	2.02580	2.20847	2.40661	2.62145
19	1.20810	1.32694	1.45680	1.59864	1.75349	1.92249	2.10683	2.30785	2.52694	2.76563
20	1.22018	1.34684	1.48593	1.63861	1.80610	1.98977	2.19111	2.41170	2.65328	2.91774

APPENDIX A-1 (CONTINUED)

Year	6.0%	6.5%	7.0%	7.5%	8.0%	8.5%	9.0%	9.5%	10.0%
1	1.06000	1.06500	1.07000	1.07500	1.08000	1.08500	1.09000	1.09500	1.10000
2	1.12360	1.13422	1.14490	1.15562	1.16640	1.17722	1.18810	1.19902	1.21000
3	1.19101	1.22161	1.22504	1.24229	1.25971	1.27728	1.29502	1.31293	1.33100
4	1.26247	1.28646	1.31079	1.33546	1.36048	1.38585	1.41158	1.43766	1.46410
5	1.33822	1.37008	1.40255	1.43562	1.46932	1.50365	1.53862	1.57423	1.61051
6	1.41851	1.45914	1.50072	1.54330	1.58687	1.63146	1.67709	1.72378	1.77156
7	1.50362	1.55398	1.60578	1.65904	1.71382	1.77013	1.82803	1.88754	1.94871
8	1.59384	1.65499	1.71818	1.78347	1.85092	1.92060	1.99256	2.06686	2.14358
9	1.68947	1.76256	1.83845	1.91723	1.99900	2.08385	2.17189	2.26321	2.35794
10	1.79084	1.87713	1.96714	2.06102	2.15892	2.26097	2.36736	2.47822	2.59374
11	1.89829	1.99914	2.10484	2.21560	2.33163	2.45316	2.58042	2.71365	2.85311
12	2.01219	2.12908	2.25218	2.38177	2.51816	2.66167	2.81265	2.97145	3.13842
13	2.13292	2.26747	2.40983	2.56040	2.71961	2.88792	3.06579	3.25373	3.45226
14	2.26089	2.41486	2.57852	2.75243	2.93718	3.13339	3.34171	3.56284	3.79749
15	2.39654	2.57183	2.75902	2.95886	3.17216	3.39973	3.64247	3.90131	4.17724
16	2.54034	2.73900	2.95215	3.18078	3.42593	3.68870	3.97029	4.27193	4.59496
17	2.69276	2.91703	3.15880	3.41934	3.70000	4.00224	4.32762	4.67776	5.05446
18	2.85432	3.10664	3.37992	3.67579	3.99600	4.34244	4.71710	5.12215	5.55990
19	3.02558	3.30857	3.61651	3.95147	4.31568	4.71154	5.14164	5.60875	6.11589
20	3.20712	3.52363	3.86966	4.24783	4.66094	5.11202	5.60439	6.14159	6.72748

Year	11.0%	12.0%	13.0%	14.0%	15.0%	16.0%	17%	18%	19%	20%
1	1.11000	1.12000	1.13000	1.14000	1.15000	1.16000	1.17000	1.18000	1.19000	1.20000
2	1.23210	1.25440	1.27690	1.29960	1.32250	1.34560	1.36890	1.39240	1.41610	1.44000
3	1.36763	1.40492	1.44289	1.48154	1.52087	1.56089	1.60161	1.64303	1.68515	1.72800
4	1.51807	1.57351	1.63047	1.68896	1.74900	1.81063	1.87388	1.93877	2.00533	2.07360
5	1.68505	1.76234	1.84243	1.92541	2.01135	2.10034	2.19244	2.28775	2.38635	2.48832
6	1.87041	1.97382	2.08195	2.19497	2.31305	2.43639	2.56516	2.69955	2.83976	2.98598
7	2.07615	2.21067	2.35260	2.50226	2.66001	2.82621	3.00123	3.18547	3.37931	3.58318
8	2.30453	2.47596	2.65844	2.85258	3.05901	3.27841	3.51144	3.75885	4.02138	4.29981
9	2.55803	2.77307	3.00403	3.25194	3.51787	3.80295	4.10839	4.43544	4.78544	5.15977
10	2.83941	3.10584	3.39456	3.70721	4.04555	4.41143	4.80682	5.23382	5.69467	6.19173
11	3.15175	3.47854	3.83585	4.22622	4.65238	5.11725	5.62398	6.17591	6.77666	7.43008
12	3.49844	3.89597	4.33451	4.81789	5.35024	5.93601	6.58005	7.28758	8.06423	8.91609
13	3.88327	4.36348	4.89800	5.49240	6.15277	6.88578	7.69866	8.59934	9.59643	10.6993
14	4.31043	4.88710	5.53474	6.26133	7.07569	7.98750	9.00743	10.1472	11.4197	12.8391
15	4.78457	5.47355	6.25425	7.13792	8.13704	9.26550	10.5387	11.9737	13.5895	15.4070
16	5.31088	6.13038	7.06731	8.13723	9.35760	10.7479	12.3302	14.1289	16.1715	18.4884
17	5.89507	6.86602	7.98606	9.27644	10.7612	12.4676	14.4264	16.6721	19.2440	22.1860
18	6.54353	7.68995	9.02425	10.5751	12.3754	14.4624	16.8788	19.6731	22.9004	26.6232
19	7.26332	8.61274	10.1974	12.0556	14.2317	16.7764	19.7483	23.2143	27.2515	31.9479
20	8.06228	9.64627	11.5230	13.7434	16.3664	19.4606	23.1005	27.3929	32.4293	38.3375

SOURCE: Compound Interest Tables for Determining Growth, Union Carbide Corp., New York, 1960.

Appendix A-2. Present Value of $1.00 $P = \dfrac{1}{(1+r)^n}$

Year	1%	2%	3%	4%	5%	6%	7%	8%	9%	10%
1	0.990099	0.980392	0.970874	0.961538	0.952381	0.943396	0.934580	0.925926	0.917431	0.909090
2	0.980297	0.961169	0.942596	0.924556	0.907030	0.889996	0.873439	0.857339	0.841680	0.826446
3	0.970591	0.942322	0.915143	0.888997	0.863838	0.839619	0.816298	0.793832	0.772184	0.751314
4	0.960981	0.923846	0.888488	0.854804	0.822703	0.792093	0.762896	0.735029	0.708425	0.683013
5	0.951467	0.905731	0.862610	0.821927	0.783527	0.747258	0.712987	0.680583	0.649931	0.620921
6	0.942047	0.887972	0.837486	0.790314	0.746216	0.704960	0.666343	0.630169	0.596268	0.564473
7	0.932720	0.870560	0.813093	0.759917	0.710682	0.665057	0.622750	0.583490	0.547034	0.513158
8	0.923485	0.853491	0.789411	0.730690	0.676841	0.627412	0.582010	0.540268	0.501866	0.466507
9	0.914342	0.836755	0.766418	0.702587	0.644610	0.591898	0.543934	0.500249	0.460429	0.424098
10	0.905289	0.820348	0.744096	0.675564	0.613914	0.558394	0.508350	0.463194	0.422412	0.385543
11	0.896326	0.804263	0.722423	0.649581	0.584680	0.526787	0.475094	0.428883	0.387534	0.350494
12	0.887452	0.788493	0.701382	0.624597	0.556838	0.496969	0.444013	0.397114	0.355535	0.318631
13	0.878666	0.773033	0.680953	0.600574	0.530322	0.468839	0.414965	0.367698	0.326179	0.289664
14	0.869966	0.757875	0.661120	0.577474	0.505069	0.442301	0.387818	0.340461	0.299247	0.263331
15	0.861353	0.743015	0.641864	0.555264	0.481019	0.417265	0.362447	0.315241	0.274539	0.239392
16	0.852825	0.728446	0.623169	0.533908	0.458113	0.393646	0.338735	0.291890	0.251870	0.217629
17	0.844381	0.714163	0.605019	0.513373	0.436299	0.371364	0.316576	0.270269	0.231074	0.197845
18	0.836021	0.700160	0.587397	0.493629	0.415523	0.350344	0.295865	0.250249	0.211995	0.179859
19	0.827744	0.686431	0.570289	0.474643	0.395736	0.330513	0.276509	0.231712	0.194490	0.163508
20	0.819549	0.672971	0.553678	0.456387	0.376891	0.311805	0.258420	0.214548	0.178432	0.148643

Year	11%	12%	13%	14%	15%	16%	17%	18%	19%	20%
1	0.900901	0.892857	0.884956	0.877193	0.869565	0.862069	0.854701	0.847458	0.840336	0.833333
2	0.811623	0.797194	0.783147	0.769468	0.756144	0.743163	0.730514	0.718184	0.706165	0.694444
3	0.731191	0.711780	0.693050	0.674971	0.657516	0.640658	0.624371	0.608631	0.593416	0.578704
4	0.658731	0.635518	0.613319	0.592080	0.571753	0.552291	0.533650	0.515788	0.498669	0.482254
5	0.593451	0.567426	0.542760	0.519368	0.497178	0.476113	0.456112	0.437109	0.419050	0.401878
6	0.534641	0.506631	0.480319	0.455587	0.432328	0.410442	0.389839	0.370431	0.352143	0.334898
7	0.481659	0.452349	0.425061	0.399638	0.375938	0.353830	0.333196	0.313925	0.295918	0.279082
8	0.433927	0.403883	0.376160	0.350559	0.326902	0.305026	0.284783	0.266038	0.248671	0.232568
9	0.390926	0.360610	0.332885	0.307508	0.284263	0.262953	0.243404	0.225456	0.208967	0.193807
10	0.352185	0.321973	0.294589	0.269744	0.247185	0.226684	0.208038	0.191065	0.175603	0.161506
11	0.317284	0.287476	0.260698	0.236618	0.214944	0.195417	0.177810	0.161919	0.147565	0.134588
12	0.285841	0.256675	0.230707	0.207559	0.186908	0.168463	0.151974	0.137219	0.124005	0.112157
13	0.257515	0.229174	0.204165	0.182070	0.162528	0.145227	0.129893	0.116288	0.104205	0.093464
14	0.231996	0.204620	0.180677	0.159710	0.141329	0.125195	0.111019	0.098549	0.087567	0.077886
15	0.209005	0.182696	0.159891	0.140096	0.122895	0.107927	0.094888	0.083516	0.073586	0.064905
16	0.188293	0.163121	0.141496	0.122892	0.106865	0.093040	0.081101	0.070776	0.061837	0.054088
17	0.169633	0.145644	0.125218	0.107800	0.092926	0.080207	0.069317	0.059980	0.051964	0.045073
18	0.152823	0.130039	0.110813	0.094561	0.080805	0.069144	0.059245	0.050830	0.043667	0.037561
19	0.137678	0.116107	0.098064	0.082948	0.070265	0.059607	0.050637	0.043076	0.036695	0.031301
20	0.124034	0.103667	0.086782	0.072762	0.061100	0.051385	0.043279	0.036505	0.030836	0.026084

SOURCE: From Ward S. Curran, Principles of Financial Management, McGraw-Hill Book Company, New York, 1970, pp. 593–596.

Appendix A-3. Present Value of an Annuity of $1.00 per Year $P = \dfrac{1-(1+r)^{-n}}{r}$

Year	1%	2%	3%	4%	5%	6%	7%	8%	9%	10%
1	0.990057	0.980401	0.970872	0.961542	0.952377	0.943398	0.934574	0.925922	0.917429	0.909090
2	1.97029	1.94153	1.91345	1.88609	1.85939	1.83339	.80801	1.78326	1.75910	1.73554
3	2.94089	2.88386	2.82858	2.77508	2.72323	2.67301	2.62430	2.57709	2.53129	2.48685
4	3.90186	3.80771	3.71705	3.62990	3.54593	3.46510	3.38720	3.31212	3.23972	3.16987
5	4.85330	4.71346	4.57965	4.45182	4.32946	4.21236	4.10018	3.99270	3.88965	3.79078
6	5.79529	5.60140	5.41714	5.24213	5.07567	4.91733	4.76652	4.62288	4.48591	4.35526
7	6.72798	6.47199	6.23024	6.00205	5.78635	5.58238	5.38928	5.20637	5.03295	4.86842
8	7.65147	7.32546	7.01963	6.73274	6.46318	6.20979	5.97129	5.74664	5.53482	5.33492
9	8.56576	8.16221	7.78605	7.43533	7.10780	6.80170	6.51522	6.24689	5.99523	5.75901
10	9.47104	8.98259	8.53014	8.11089	7.72171	7.36010	7.02357	6.71007	6.41764	6.14456
11	10.3673	9.78684	9.25255	8.76048	8.30639	7.88688	7.49864	7.13896	6.80518	6.49505
12	11.2547	10.5753	9.95393	9.38508	8.86323	8.38384	7.94266	7.53607	7.16071	6.81369
13	12.1334	11.3483	10.6348	9.98565	9.39355	8.85267	8.35763	7.90377	7.48689	7.10335
14	13.0034	12.1062	11.2960	10.5631	9.89861	9.29497	8.74545	8.24424	7.78614	7.36668
15	13.8647	12.8492	11.9378	11.1183	10.3796	9.71224	9.10789	8.55948	8.06068	7.60607
16	14.7174	13.5776	12.5610	11.6523	10.8377	10.1058	9.44663	8.85137	8.31255	7.82370
17	15.5618	14.2918	13.1660	12.1656	11.2740	10.4772	9.76320	9.12164	8.54362	8.02155
18	16.3978	14.9920	13.7534	12.6592	11.6895	10.8276	10.0590	9.37189	8.75561	8.20141
19	17.2256	15.6784	14.3237	13.1339	12.0852	11.1581	10.3355	9.60359	8.95010	8.36492
20	18.0451	16.3514	14.8773	13.5903	12.4621	11.4699	10.5939	9.81814	9.12853	8.51356

Year	11%	12%	13%	14%	15%	16%	17%	18%	19%	20%
1	0.900897	0.892858	0.884955	0.877193	0.869563	0.862068	0.854700	0.847456	0.840335	0.833333
2	1.71252	1.69005	1.66810	1.64665	1.62570	1.60523	1.58521	1.56564	1.54650	1.52777
3	2.44371	2.40183	2.36115	2.32163	2.28322	2.24588	2.20958	2.17427	2.13991	2.10648
4	3.10244	3.03735	2.97447	2.91371	2.85498	2.79818	2.74323	2.69006	2.63857	2.58873
5	3.69589	3.60477	3.51723	3.43308	3.35214	3.27429	3.19934	3.12716	3.05763	2.99060
6	4.23054	4.11141	3.99754	3.88866	3.78447	3.68473	3.58918	3.49760	3.40977	3.32550
7	4.71218	4.56375	4.42260	4.28830	4.16041	4.03856	3.92237	3.81152	3.70569	3.60459
8	5.14611	4.96763	4.79876	4.63886	4.48732	4.34359	4.20716	4.07756	3.95435	3.83715
9	5.53704	5.32824	5.13164	4.94637	4.77158	4.60654	4.45056	4.30302	4.16332	4.03096
10	5.88922	5.65022	5.42623	5.21611	5.01876	4.83322	4.65860	4.49408	4.33893	4.19247
11	6.20651	5.93770	5.68693	5.45272	5.23370	5.02864	4.83641	4.65600	4.48649	4.32705
12	6.49235	6.19437	5.91763	5.66028	5.42061	5.19710	4.98838	4.79322	4.61050	4.43921
13	6.74986	6.42354	6.12180	5.84235	5.58314	5.34233	5.11827	4.90951	4.71470	4.53268
14	6.98185	6.62816	6.30248	6.00207	5.72447	5.46753	5.22929	5.00806	4.80227	4.61056
15	7.19085	6.81086	6.46237	6.14216	5.84736	5.57545	5.32418	5.09157	4.87586	4.67547
16	7.37915	6.97398	6.60387	6.26505	5.95423	5.66849	5.40528	5.16235	4.93769	4.72955
17	7.54878	7.11963	6.72909	6.37285	6.04716	5.74870	5.47460	5.22233	4.98966	4.77463
18	7.70161	7.24966	6.83990	6.46741	6.12796	5.81784	5.53385	5.27316	5.03332	4.81219
19	7.83928	7.36577	6.93796	6.55036	6.19822	5.87745	5.58448	5.31624	5.07002	4.84349
20	7.96332	7.46944	7.02475	6.62313	6.25933	5.92884	5.62776	5.35274	5.10086	4.86958

SOURCE: From Ward S. Curran, *Principles of Financial Management*, McGraw-Hill Book Company, New York, 1970, pp. 601–604.

Appendix B. Expected Utility and the Factor of Risk

As indicated in the text of this chapter, the management of a firm will change its attitude toward a capital expenditure decision if that decision involves risk of losing money. In other words, when a capital project may bring losses and not just a smaller amount of profit, the expected monetary value is not a valid guide for decision making. Instead, the management of the firm has to use expected utility as a criterion to judge the desirability of a capital project. The reason for this is that utility of money does not remain constant, as indicated by the well-known Bernoullian utility theory. According to Bernoulli, utility of money is a decreasing function of the amount of money possessed. In other words, the marginal utility of money declines in a certain manner as additional amounts of money are received. Mathematically, this theorem can be stated as

$$\frac{dy}{dx} = \frac{b}{x}$$

where y represents utility; x, money; and b, some positive constant, or

$$y = b \log \frac{x}{\alpha}$$

where α is another positive constant.[14]

Since the marginal utility of money declines in a given proportion to the amount of money a person already possesses, it follows that the more money he has, the more he is willing to take risk. In other words, if two teams of management face an identical capital expenditure decision which is highly risky yet may be very profitable, the two teams will decide differently if one has much more financial resources than the other, other things being equal.

In addition to the amount of financial resources possessed, the other factor which accounts for the variation in attitude toward risk is a person's propensity to gamble. "Some people were born gamblers," is a common statement.

The understanding of these two factors is essential to the analysis of expected utility as a criterion for capital investment decision. In the following example, we endeavor to show how utility value is assigned to a given consequence of an act (an investment decision) and the derivation of the expected utility for the act.

Suppose the management of ABC Motors Company decides to branch out

[14] For further discussion, reference may be made to Daniel Bernoulli's article, "Exposition of a New Theory on the Measurement of Risk," published in the *Papers of the Imperial Academy of Science in Petersburg,* vol. V, 1738. Translation from Latin into English was done by Louis Sommer and published in *Econometrica,* vol. 22, no. 1, pp. 23–36, Jan., 1954.

into new business such as manufacturing plastic toys. After some detailed study, management concludes that the probability of making a profit or losing money and the amount of anticipated profit or loss are:

Consequence of Act	Probability of Occurrence
$ 500,000	0.10
300,000	0.14
150,000	0.16
0	0.25
−150,000	0.13
−200,000	0.12
−400,000	0.10
	1.00

The information presented above does not look attractive enough for most businessmen, because only four times out of ten will the company expect to make money from the deal. However, we may assume that somehow someone is willing to undertake such a new enterprise. Now the question is how we can assign utility value to those consequences and to the act itself. One way to do this is by means of inference. If a person is indifferent to consequences of two acts, we may say that both have the same utility to him.

Following the same reasoning, we may utilize a calibrating urn to assign utility value to a given consequence of an act.[15] Suppose someone offers you a chance to draw a ball from an urn which contains 100 balls of identical quality, one-half of them white and the other half red. If the ball you draw (one at a time) is white, you win $5,000; if the ball is red, you lose $4,000. The game is a fair one and also in your favor, since it has a payoff of $500. However, you are probably not willing to play it, because the potential loss of $4,000 is too much for you to bear.

How much is this game worth to you? We can find this out by means of comparison. Suppose you are asked to pick one of two alternatives: a 50:50 chance of making $5,000 or losing $4,000, or a 100 percent assurance of making no profit or incurring no loss, that is, all balls in the other urn are marked $0.00. If you choose the later, it means that the consequence of an act with a zero monetary value has a utility value higher than .5. What utility value does that act have then? Well, it all depends upon your personal preference toward risk, and we can find that out by changing the makeup of the balls in the calibrating urn. By substituting white balls for red balls, we finally have fifty-five white balls and forty-five red balls. If you are now indifferent to the

---

[15] This section is based upon the work of Neil E. Harlan, Charles J. Christenson, and Richard F. C. Vancil, *op. cit.*, sect. III, which may be consulted for detailed information.

two alternatives, then we may say an act with zero monetary value has a utility value of .55. The utility value of an act can be as high as 1.00, which means all 100 balls in the urn are white; and it can be as low as 0.00, which means that all the balls are red.

By the process of substitution, the makeup of the balls in the calibrating urn changes, and so does the utility value the urn represents. The utility value for each consequence of an act, shown below, is derived in such a manner:

Consequence of Act	Utility Value
$ 5,000	1.00
3,000	0.75
1,500	0.65
0	0.55
−1,500	0.35
−2,000	0.20
−4,000	0.00

The assignment of a utility value of .20 to the consequence of losing $2,000 needs some explanation. We assume that you are indifferent to a 20:80 chance of making $5,000 or losing $4,000 on one hand, and losing $2,000 for sure on the other hand. Of course you may argue that no one is willing to pick the alternative whereby he is certain to lose $2,000. Instead of losing money for sure, why not take a chance and pick the other alternative, since there is still a 20 percent chance of making $5,000? (Do not forget that there is also an 80 percent chance of losing $4,000.) To answer the question satisfactorily, we have to go back to the two factors which determine a person's attitude toward risk.

After we have established a utility value for each consequence of an act, we can calculate the expected utility of the act.

Consequence	Utility Value	Probability	Expected Utility
$ 5,000	1.00	0.10	0.1000
3,000	0.75	0.14	0.1050
1,500	0.65	0.16	0.1040
0	0.55	0.25	0.1375
−1,500	0.35	0.13	0.0455
−2,000	0.20	0.12	0.0240
−4,000	0.00	0.10	0
		1.00	0.5160

Needless to say, the larger the expected utility an act has, the more the act is worth to the firm. In other words, if the management of a firm faces two alternatives, one having a larger expected utility than the other, the management should choose the former.

Appendix C. Present Value Method Versus Internal Rate of Return

In the text we have already discussed the similarity and difference between the present value and the internal rate of return methods for choosing alternatives among capital investment proposals. There are partisans who defend the usefulness of each of the methods as the more appropriate means of selecting a correct investment decision. The present value criterion is advocated because of its simplicity and consistency of application.[16] Furthermore, it takes into consideration the difference between lending and borrowing rates (the point being emphasized so much by Jack Herschleifer), since we can use either rate as a discount factor.[17] In other words, we may use either the opportunity cost (lending rate) or the weighted average cost of capital (borrowing rate) as the discount rate. On the other hand, the internal rate of return has received stout defense for its theoretical refinement, especially since its adoption by John M. Keynes in his analysis of capital investment.[18] (As indicated before, Keynes called the internal rate of return the marginal efficiency of capital.) In this appendix, we try to give a summary of some limitations of the applicability of each method under some specific conditions.

In discussing capital expenditure decisions, we tend to assume, and with good reason, that a capital project, once started, will provide a stream of positive cash flow. When this assumption is true (ignoring other complications), either method will give a correct decision as to which project to undertake. However, when a capital project involves a terminal negative cash flow, such as the closing down of a mine after the ore has been exhausted, the internal rate of return method does not give a clear and unambiguous answer. Here we have the so-called dual-rate problem in capital budgeting.[19] The following example

[16] James H. Lorie and Leonard J. Savage, *loc. cit.*, Harry V. Roberts, "Current Problems in the Economics of Capital Budgeting," *Journal of Business*, vol. 30, pp. 12–16, Jan., 1957. Paul A. Samuelson, "Some Aspects of the Pure Theory of Capital," *Quarterly Journal of Economics*, vol. 51, pp. 469–496, 1937.

[17] J. Herschleifer, "On the Theory of Optimal Investment Decision," *The Journal of Political Economy*, vol. 66, no. 4 (August, 1958), pp. 329–352.

[18] Kenneth E. Boulding, "The Theory of Single Investment," *Quarterly Journal of Economics*, vol. 49, pp. 475–494, May, 1935; Joel Dean, *Capital Budgeting*, Columbia University Press, New York, 1951; Ezra Solomon, "The Arithmetic of Capital-budgeting Decisions," *Journal of Business*, vol. 29, pp. 124–129, April, 1956.

[19] James H. Lorie and Leonard J. Savage, *op. cit.*, p. 237.

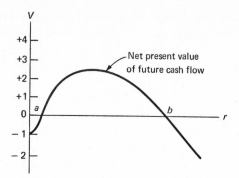

Figure 14-2 Capital project with dual internal rate of return.

illustrates the difficulty involved in using internal rate of return as a criterion for capital investment decision.

The curve representing the net present value of future cash flow intersects the horizontal axis twice. This means that there are two internal rates of return which render the net present value zero. Therefore, a problem exists as to which of the two rates is the right one to use. On the other hand, the present value method, with the cost of capital as the discount rate, will give a clear-cut answer.

In some situations, the present value and the internal rate of return criteria give contradictory answers to the capital investment decision. For example, from Figure 14-3 presented below, we see that AA' has a higher present value if

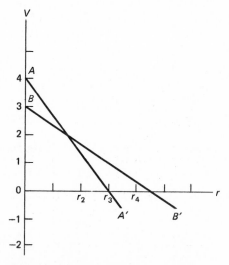

Figure 14-3. Two options for capital projects.

the discount rate is lower than r_2, while the BB' curve has a higher internal rate of return and also a higher present value when the discount rate is higher than r_2. In such a situation, neither method can give a clear-cut and unambiguous answer as to which investment is a better choice, because the answer depends upon what discount rate one wants to use.

Under capital rationing, neither method can provide the correct answer to capital expenditure decisions. For example, from the two capital projects presented in the following chart, we cannot make a right choice as to the desirability of a project unless we have an indifference map superimposed upon the chart. The reason is that, since we cannot raise an unlimited amount of capital with the interest cost we can afford to pay, we have to weigh the benefit from additional investment against the sacrifice we have to bear because of the curtailment of current consumption. In other words, we have to balance the utility of present-day consumption versus future consumption. The indifference map is, as we know, a series of indifference curves, each of which represents utility function to the firm. The curves VAB and VDE represent two investment opportunities, with the latter representing a more modest project.[20] The VDE curve touches the indifference curve UU' at the point D. The slope of the line YDY', which is tangent to VDE and intersects VAB at point A, is the rate of return for the project VDE. By discounting the future cash flow with that rate, the larger project, VAB, has a

[20] Martin J. Bailey, "Formal Criteria for Investment Decisions," *Journal of Political Economy*, vol. 67, pp. 476–488, Oct., 1959.

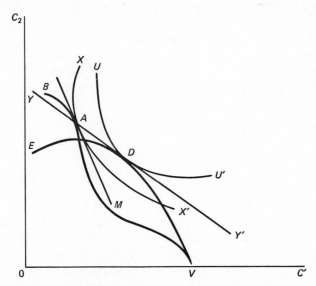

Figure 14-4. Selection of capital project under capital rationing.

higher present value at any point above A. On the other hand, the curve VAB touches an indifference curve XX', which is lower than the UU' curve. When the future cash flow from the larger project is discounted by the rate of return represented by the slope of the line AM, which is drawn in the same manner as the line YDY', VAB has a present value smaller than does VDE. What we have here is an example which shows that the present value criterion does not work. Therefore, we have to take into consideration the utility value of present consumption versus future consumption, and the capital project the present value of which touches the highest indifference curve is the right one to select.

Review Questions

1. Why is capital budgeting important to a firm?
2. What is the basic distinction between an investment in inventory and one in capital assets?
3. What are the uses of a capital budget?
4. What are the major internal sources of funds?
5. What are the major external sources of funds?
6. What are some factors which determine the ability of a firm to undertake debt financing?
7. What is a weighted average cost of capital?
8. What are three main methods which are used to select alternative investment projects?
9. What are the defects of the payback period method?
10. What are the differences between the present value method and the internal rate of return method as a means of selecting a capital project?
11. How do you calculate the expected monetary value of a given act?
12. When losses may occur, why is the expected monetary value no longer a valid criterion for choosing a capital project?

Case 1. Sal-Jeans Corporation

Sal-Jeans Corporation manufactures and sells a wide range of casual slacks and outerwear for men and women. It owns four major factory-office complexes, which are located in the Northwest. From its head offices in Eugene, Oregon, it directs the operations and sales of its products. Most of its customers are relatively small retail shops on the West Coast, which specialize in contemporary clothing for the youth market.

Most of the company's growth has been internal; however, in 1968, it speeded its expansion through the acquisition of Sal, Inc., a maker of sportswear, which was acquired through a new issue of common stock. Capital for the firm's plant expansion was obtained through a combination of debt, equity, and internal cash flows. An issue of twenty-year, 6 percent debentures was sold in 1965 at par with flotation cost amounting to 1 percent of the entire proceeds. Its common stock was issued in 1965 and in 1968. It pays no dividends. Sal-Jeans also has an issue of 5 percent cumulative preferred stock outstanding, which was sold recently with a 1 percent flotation cost.

Mr. Richard Archie, president of Sal-Jeans, discussed the firm's progress at its most recent board of directors' meeting. Sales were expected to exceed last year's by at least 20 percent. Furthermore, he noted, because of the efficiency of the relatively new plants and a high-volume sales force, profit margins were widening. This, he concluded, would mean a continuation of Sal-Jeans' steady earnings growth.

He noted, however, that competition in the field had grown substantially in the past few years. "Sal-Jeans' success has been its knack for beating its competitors to the market with popular, low-priced, 'gimmick items' which will appeal to the college set," he said. "This year we believe our fashion department has come up with a future trend-setter for that market. It is the 'Blue Sal-Jean.' Our initial market surveys of this new style jean indicate that it can be a big revenue producer for us within a year. However, at the moment, our established lines are doing so well that all of our factories are working near capacity. The only alternative is to expand our facilities, not only for this new item, but also for future product-line expansion. Our estimates indicate that making an addition to one of our present plants would adequately serve our purposes at the lowest cost. We estimate that a total of $5 million will be required for the plant expansion and equipment."

Mr. Joseph McDonit, the company's treasurer, then presented his plans to obtain this capital. For a variety of reasons, he ruled out using internal sources of funds. Moreover, he objected to issuing more preferred stock since the firm got no tax break, because dividends are paid from after-tax income. This left a choice of offering either a new issue of debentures or one of common stock. His discussion with the investment banking firm of R. J. Freeham and Company indicated that a new issue of twenty-year bonds would probably be sold at around $98. The current long-term interest rate was 7 percent. Flotation cost would be 2 percent of the total par value of the issue.

"On the other hand," he reported, "Sal-Jeans' stock continues to show good market strength. In fact, it is approaching a new high for this year. **Currently out stock is selling at 17 times 1970 earnings. We expect that the P/E ratio should hit at least 24 this coming year, since our projected earnings are for about $2 a share, a 25 percent increase over this year's estimated earnings." Flotation cost for a new issue would be 2 percent. "If we are to float a new issue, we would continue our policy of paying no dividends on our common stock. It seems that most of our stockholders are in the 25 percent tax bracket, so they would rather we plow the earnings back into the company."**

EXHIBIT 1. SAL-JEANS CORPORATION BALANCE SHEET, DECEMBER 31,1970 (DOLLAR FIGURES IN MILLIONS)

Assets		Liabilities	
Cash	$ 5.0	Accounts payable	$ 15.9
Marketable securities	4.2	Accrued liabilities	4.1
Accounts receivable	13.5	Accrued taxes	3.7
Inventories	48.2	Other current liabilities	6.9
Total current assets	$ 70.9	Total current liabilities	$ 30.6
Other investments	1.5	5% debentures due 1985	15.0
Net fixed assets	61.4		$ 45.6
Prepaid expenses	.8	Capital stock:	
Total assets	$134.6	5% cumulative preferred*	14.0
		Common†	30.0
		Earned surplus	45.0
			$134.6

* Par $100.00, 140,000 shares outstanding.
† No par, 5,000,000 shares outstanding.

EXHIBIT 2. INCOME STATEMENT (DOLLAR FIGURES IN MILLIONS)

Net sales		$114.3
Cost of goods sold:		
Material, labor expense		84.3
		$ 30.0
Other expenses:		
Depreciation	$6.0	
Administration and selling expense	5.0	
Interest	.9	
Rent	1.6	
Total other expense		13.5
Net profit before income tax		16.5
Income tax		7.8
Net income		$ 8.7

QUESTION

1. For many years, the company has used a weighted average to determine its cost of capital. By this method, should Sal-Jean issue the stock or the debentures to have the lower cost of capital?

Note: Case 1 was prepared by Christian J. Hoffmann, III, under the supervision of Francis P. Sing. Mr. Hoffmann is the Assistant Dean of the School of Business Administration, Georgetown University.

Case 2. Herd, Inc.

Herd, Inc., is a service-oriented firm which provides marketing services for small- to medium-sized companies. The company was founded in New Hampshire fifteen years ago by P. J. Sully and J. P. Calls. Since they were primarily selling service, very little capital was required. As a result of the founders' hard work, the business has grown so much that they now have ten assistants working for them and have expanded their operations into several surrounding states. Through their wide range of business contacts, they recently discovered a possible new venture for Herd, Inc.

At a recent meeting, Mr. Sully, who is the president, outlined his proposal to the treasurer, Mr. J. P. Currey. "Over the past few years the problem of security protection for one's home or business establishment has grown considerably," he said. "In fact, people are becoming so concerned with protecting themselves from burglary that I believe there is a good market to be tapped here. My good friend, Mark Tempolo, has invented a new type of alarm which should revolutionize the concept of alarms. He has invented two basic types, one for home and the other for business. Since they are quite different, we would need two different kinds of manufacturing facilities."

Mr. Currey then presented the following figures for the alternative projects:

	Alarms for Business	Alarms for Home
Cost of investment (to be paid out in the first year)	$8,000,000	$5,000,000
Estimated annual cash flow (adjusted for uncertainty and taxes)	$2,400,000	$2,100,000
Useful life (no salvage value afterward)	9 years	8 years
Weighted average cost of capital	7%	7%

"As the table shows," reported Mr. Currey, "the business alarm will cost more, but the return per year will also be greater."

"Well, in order to determine which project to pursue, I suggest that we use the payback period method; it has always worked well for us in the past," said Mr. Calls.

Mr. Sully, however, suggested that more accurate means should be used to determine the acceptability of the projects. He proposed the net present value or internal rate of return method. Also, he maintained that the firm's weighted average cost of capital should be used as the discount rate since that would be the cost of capital for any project to be undertaken.

QUESTIONS

1. Will the three methods lead to the same decision on which project to choose?
2. Which of the three methods would you use to make the decision? Why?
3. What do you think about using the firm's weighted average cost of capital as its discount rate?

Note: Case 2 was prepared by Christian J. Hoffmann, III, under the supervision of Francis P. Sing. Mr. Hoffmann is the Assistant Dean of the School of Business Administration, Georgetown University.

Case 3. URT Polyfiber Company

URT Polyfiber is a small German foam and plastics producer. Despite its size, URT has broad patents on processes with enormous profit potential. The company produces a plastic which is superior to any other building insulator in the world, in terms of resistance to heat and shrinkage. Additionally, the material drives away rodents. It consequently has far-reaching implications for low-cost housing. Significantly, Teletronics broad marketing base could be easily adapted for the promotion of URT's products.

The Teletronics management in Dallas feels that URT is an ideal acquisition candidate. However, Teletronics is already heavily laden with debt, and an increase in the number of its outstanding shares of common stock would have an adverse effect on its earnings per share. This figure is the crucial factor of the future growth of a conglomerate. Funds can be obtained in Europe, but only at the high rate of 12 percent. URT management has mentioned $20 million as a target figure.

QUESTIONS

1. Can you suggest several plans for the acquisition of URT? Which one would you implement?

2. In your opinion, what return must be expected from URT to justify the implementation of each of your plans?

Note: Case 3 was prepared by Francis Benevento under the supervision of Francis P. Sing. Mr. Benevento is a student at the University of Virginia Law School.

Suggested Reading

Baumol, William J.: *Economic Theory and Operations Anslysis,* 2d ed., Prentice-Hall, Inc., Englewood Cliffs, N.J., 1965.

Bierman, Harold, Jr., and Seymour Smidt: *The Capital Budgeting Decision,* 2d ed., The Macmillan Company, New York, 1966.

Dean, Joel: *Managerial Economics,* Prentice-Hall, Inc., Englewood Cliffs, N.J., 1951.

_____, *Capital Budgeting,* Columbia University Press, New York, 1951.

Haynes, William W.: *Managerial Economics,* rev. ed., Business Publications, Inc., Austin, Texas, 1969.

Nemmers, Erwin E.: *Managerial Economics,* John Wiley & Sons, Inc., New York, 1962.

Quinn, G. David: *The Capital Expenditure Decision,* Richard D. Irwin, Inc., Homewood, Ill., 1967.

Spencer, Milton H.: *Managerial Economics,* 3d ed., Richard D. Irwin, Inc., Homewood, Ill., 1968.

Weston, J. Fred, and Eugene F. Brigham: *Managerial Finance,* 3d ed., Holt, Rinehart and Winston, Inc., New York, 1969.

part 5

expansion
and other
decisions

chapter 15
expanding and
locating
new
facilities

The expansion of existing plant facilities, or the building of a new facility, is the consequence of a capital budgeting decision. Some amount of money is invested or "sunk" in a fixed asset, in the expectation that it will provide a return over a number of years. The amount of the return is chiefly dependent upon the potential sales revenue of the facility and the corresponding expense. In turn, these are functions of the probable demand and cost schedules. It is at this point that the element of location intrudes.

The demand schedule assumes a certain distribution of customers and competitors over geographic space. The cost schedule assumes a certain distribution of suppliers over the same or similar space. But our economic analysis thus far has assumed buyers and sellers to be in the same place.

The question of location does not arise in most capital budgeting decisions, because the decisions generally concern investments in equipment, where the element of location is not a factor. For small items, location is a technical or an architectural question within the present production coefficient. Location for large items, however, involves other variables, such as the prices of inputs and outputs, and the probable impact on the competitive environment of substantial additions to productive capacity. What is more, the larger the increase in productive capacity, the longer and more significant the commitment horizon. Because the purchase of new equipment and the building of new plant will commit capital for a relatively long period of time and commit the firm to a particular location or manufacturing process which may be changed only with some difficulty, a good manager will always explore the various alternatives which may exist.

In some industries, the location decision can be crucial, as Dale has indicated in his reference to the production of mobile homes. "Since it costs $1 a mile to transport a single home, a plant that produces a home at a cost of $500 below that of a competitor 500 miles away, will be barely able to meet the latter's prices in his home city."[1] Since increases in operating efficiency can easily be offset by the added costs of transportation made necessary by poor location choice, the size of plant and its location are intimately connected.

In this chapter, we will examine something of the economic theory of location, beginning with the various attempts to explain the effects of expansion on the economic characteristics of the firm, considered from a spatial point of view. We will take up the relation of expansion to pricing policy and cost behavior. Next, we will examine the problems posed in locating new facilities, including the relative role played by material sources, markets, and transportation forms. Next, we will look at methods of regional analysis. In an appendix, we will give a simple transportation model showing how to minimize the cost of supplying a number of facilities from a number of sources.

ALTERNATIVES TO EXPANSION

Many capital investments simply do not return planned payouts over much of their lives. The longer the time interval, the more likely it is that estimates will fall short of their mark or that changes in technology and markets will occur that were not foreseen. Consequently, managements are justifiably cautious where changes in the production or distribution structure that are in any way fundamental are involved.[2]

A decision to expand or alter the location of facilities involves estimates of production, distribution, and transportation costs, and there is little likelihood that these costs will remain at their present levels. Furthermore, it is difficult to forecast the direction and amount of change. For these reasons, managements prefer, if possible, to solve their problems with the least possible commitment of resources over time and with the greatest possible certainty of payback.

USE OF WAREHOUSE STOCKS

The first alternative to establishing new plant, in order to widen geographic distribution or serve existing areas more intensively, might be to establish field warehouse stocks. In theory, optimum inventory investment is calculated using the same marginal calculation procedure as for any other investment or expenditure. That is to say, using the equimarginal principle, one

[1] Ernest Dale, *Management Theory and Practice*, 2d ed., McGraw-Hill Book Company, New York, 1969, p. 118.
[2] For an excellent discussion of the problems and hazards involved, see Dean S. Ammer, *Manufacturing Management and Control*, Appleton-Century-Crofts, New York, 1968, pp. 68–78.

ought to invest in inventory to the point where it provides the same return per dollar invested as any other form of expenditure.[3]

The firm with large inventories is slower to react to changes in demand, although more able to place inventory or ship new inventory where it will do the most good. It is therefore able to use its resources better from a geographic point of view. It is using inventory instead of new plant and giving up economic flexibility to obtain geographic flexibility, because reliance on inventory places a great burden on the managerial ability of the firm to coordinate inventory levels with changes in economic activity.

ACQUIRING ADDITIONAL PLANTS

Where markets are very large, and it is desired to penetrate new market areas, multiple plant operation is often resorted to instead of dispersed inventories. This course is often taken where freight costs are higher on finished goods than on raw materials, or where expanding the present plant would involve more of a security problem to the firm than the building or acquiring of more plants.

Where transport costs are high relative to the value of the product, as for example for cement, fertilizer, and bread, or where raw material sources or inputs are widely dispersed, as in fruits, vegetables, and meat, multiple plant operation in scattered locations is often practiced.[4]

Where scale of plant is a limiting factor, expansion will bring about increases in numbers of plants, but not necessarily in various locations, especially if there are other reasons to centralize. On the other hand, input-output weight ratios are also important. If the raw materials weigh significantly more than the finished product, plants tend to be decentralized at sources of materials in order to reduce freight costs. This is especially true where the output tends to have a relatively high value compared to the input, and the transport costs can more easily be absorbed in the final price of the output. If, however, the final product is more fragile, heavier, or larger, then it may be more expensive to ship, and production will take place at or near the place at which it is consumed. So, for example, wine and alcoholic beverages will be made near the source of materials, because of the material shrinkages involved and the wide divergence in value between input and output. A conventionally built house would be more difficult to ship than the raw materials of which it is made, and it is therefore assembled where it will be used.[5]

---

[3] See, for example, Ammer's illustration of inventory substituting in a simple man-machine system for both labor and equipment. Conclusion: if the inventory is worth less than the value of the machine time and labor, invest in inventory; otherwise in machines. Ammer, *ibid.*, p. 94.

[4] Ralph L. Nelson, *Concentration in the Manufacturing Industries of the United States,* Yale University Press, New Haven, Conn., 1963, pp. 70–75.

[5] Dale, *loc. cit.*

Where locally available materials are extensively used, and the final product does not have a particularly great value, it is likely that it will be produced nearer to the market in order to reduce transportation costs. Thus, soft drinks and, current advertising notwithstanding, beer are produced as close to consumption points as possible, not to keep them fresh, but to reduce their cost.[6]

It is not very surprising, then, that a recent decision by the General Foods Corporation to build a new food processing plant for the Jell-O Division should result in the consolidation of the operations of four older plants. The plants had been acquired in the process of growth of the corporation and were considered obsolete and inadequate for present and projected company growth. The products involved were gelatin, puddings, cornstarch, tapioca, processed rice, syrups, chocolate, and coconut products. Sugar consumption was about 500,000 pounds per day, and nearly all inputs were imported. The factors of material shrinkage, relatively high value of output compared with input, and the reliance on imports made it no surprise that the facility ultimately was located primarily with reference to sources rather than to markets. Since there were considerable economies of scale possible, one plant was built to replace the previous four.[7]

RELEVANT FACTORS IN THE DECISION

Often it may appear advisable to increase the capacity of an existing plant, either because there are definite economies of scale and long-run marginal production costs are falling or, as we have seen, because consolidating previously separate facilities allows us to reduce managerial overhead costs. But even though increasing plant capacity may make it possible to reduce total production costs, it may result in increases in distribution and transportation costs, a not entirely looked-for result. Hence, the decision whether or not to centralize new capacity cannot depend only on an analysis of production costs, but must consider all relevant costs in delivering a finished product to the consumer.

Choosing a location implies a process of cost substitution whose objective is to find the point at which the combination of production and transportation costs is a minimum. Once again, the equimarginal principle is involved. As markets expand, the scale of output rises in an attempt to service them. With increases in output, raw materials and other inputs may be drawn from more distant sources, and the additional transportation costs will serve to increase average total cost of output. Production cost changes result from changes in the scale of output (or in its level), or from changes in labor or fuel or in other costs

[6] See more extensive treatments in Alfred Weber, *Theory of the Location of Industries,* trans. C. J. Friedrich, The University of Chicago Press, Chicago, 1929; Edgar M. Hoover, *The Location of Economic Activity,* McGraw-Hill Book Company, New York, 1948; and Ralph L. Nelson, op. cit., p. 75. For an exceptionally lucid exposition, Hugh O. Nourse, *Regional Economics,* McGraw-Hill Book Company, New York, 1968, pp. 74–76.

[7] Edmund S. Whitman and W. James Schmidt, *Plant Relocation,* American Management Association, New York, 1966.

which may be peculiar to an industry. Other inputs are sensitive to changes in location; hence, we should offset distribution cost increases with production cost decreases, so that the marginal physical productivities are proportional in each use.

Depending on the structure of freight rates, a distant source of raw materials may be preferred to a closer one. Or, a decision to operate at an increasing scale may imply the use of larger-scale transport media, with savings in both directions allowing a centralization not otherwise possible, assuming the market is large enough.

Isard and Schooler point out that major considerations in the location of a natural-gas based, petrochemical complex were regional differences in total transportation cost as compared with economies of scale of production. Given two means of transportation, rail and barge, the site offering a net advantage for barge transport was selected because it allowed a larger plant to be built and enabled the company to achieve substantial economies of scale. Having access to barge transportation meant that larger shipments were possible, which in turn meant that a larger market could be served, making it possible to operate at increased scale.[8]

Where finished goods distribution costs are high in relation to price, plants will be built in market areas rather than at sources of materials, and technology and the scale of output will determine the degree to which plant size will be a factor in deciding how many plants will be built. Where cost reductions are possible through increases in plant size, needed inputs are available, and transportation costs of inputs or outputs are not high in relation to price, then existing plants will ordinarily be expanded before additional plants are built.

If, as was true in the General Foods case, the present plant cannot be expanded economically, and new construction allows the use of entirely new or seriously modified processes, new locations will be sought for the new capacity. Where the new location will allow production to take place closer to sources of supply, or to markets, multiple plant operation will result. If there are inhibiting factors, such as high freight costs on finished goods, plants may be located closer to markets. This is especially true where, in addition, the process employs stages of production that are closer to the consumer, and, the products being in a more highly finished form, they bear higher distribution charges. Dispersion to market areas for these reasons happens in industries such as printing and publishing, lumber, apparel, and fabricated metal products.

If technology limits the effective size of plant, and it is not advantageous to build additional capacity, but sources of supply are a critical factor, or if the manufacturing process is a complex one and the value of the end product is

---

[8] Reported in Walter Isard, *Methods of Regional Analysis: An Introduction to Regional Science*, The M.I.T. Press, Cambridge, Mass., 1960, pp. 235–240.

relatively high as compared with the raw materials or inputs, then, although multiple plant operation is indicated, all plants appear to cluster in the same general region. An apt illustration is the photographic equipment industry.[9]

If we assume uniform freight rates, the selection of the lowest-cost location implies, all other things being equal, an ability to penetrate the widest geographic market. The better the choice of a location, the larger the market area which can be served because f.o.b. factory costs are lower, outbound freight costs are lower, or their sum is less than costs of rivals, and therefore the firm can compete on a price basis over a wider area than can rivals.

But all freight charges are not uniformly proportional to distance, so the choice of location often depends on the peculiarities of freight rate structure. Also firms tend to reduce transportation costs by locating near other firms which are either supply sources or customers. This tendency has become more and more important as products become more complex and as more producers become willing to make "make or buy" decisions at various points in the production cycle. In recent years, the desire to achieve geographic flexibility and market domination has become increasingly important in the decision to locate, especially where increasing volumes of output have imposed limits to the cost reduction possibilities of further centralization. The result has been the dispersion of plants near centers of population where market control has come to be emphasized in corporate strategy, and price competition is deemphasized.

[9] Hoover, op. cit., p. 89. See also statement by Dr. John Blair, *Hearings before the Senate Subcommittee on Antitrust and Monopoly of the Committee on the Judiciary,* pursuant to S.R. 26, pt. 6, 90th Cong., 1st Sess., U.S. Government Printing Office, 1968, pp. 2968–2970.

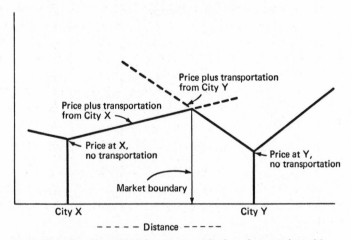

Figure 15-1. The effect of freight rates on market boundaries. (Adapted from Guy Black, *The Application of Systems Analysis to Government Operations,* Frederick A. Praeger, Inc., New York, 1968, p. 110, by permission.)

Increases in production needed to serve increasingly wider market areas may bring about changes in marginal costs, which result from changes in both production cost and distribution cost. These marginal costs should be related to the marginal revenue arising from the wider market. Unless transportation and production costs can be lowered through changing the form of the product or the way in which it is shipped, total marginal costs (production and distribution) may rise more rapidly than production marginal cost alone. Sales increases may be unprofitable from a distribution cost standpoint, costing more to acquire than they contribute in revenue. On the other hand, if marginal costs are not an increasing function of the level of production, or following the conventional profit-maximizing model, if the firm is to the left of the point at which marginal revenue equals marginal cost, then any increase in the level of production, even if out-of-pocket distribution costs are not covered, may be worthwhile.

THE IMPLICATIONS OF EXPANSION

A normal demand curve or schedule depicts the relationship between a schedule of prices and the amounts that will be taken at each price. On the assumption that a market or selling price exists at a given point, there is a given amount that will be taken. The conventional economic construction imposes no further condition, because the model assumes perfect mobility of resources and factors and instant communication. If, however, we introduce the more realistic notion that goods must be shipped and freight costs must be paid, then as consumers are positioned out from the center or source of the goods, the price they pay must be the price at the center, plus the added freight costs. Addition of freight costs will increase the total price of the goods to the consumer. But, if we add to the price, assuming the same demand curve facing the producer, there will be a reduction in the amount demanded, varying as the distance from the producer. The sloping demand curve of conventional economics is seen to have not one but two determinants: price and location.

In this section, we will explore the interrelationship between this spatially considered demand function and the cost implications of serving an enlarged market.

ON THE DEMAND CURVE

Price times quantity represents the volume of demand and is represented by a cone, rather than an area, because distance occurs over a 360-degree arc about the source, rather than in the linear fashion depicted by the usual demand curve.

If we calculate the volume of the demand cone for a list of prices, we can draw a new demand curve representing the relationship between price plus transport costs and amount demanded, independent of the demand at the

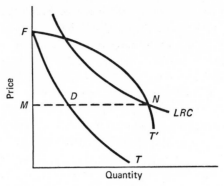

Figure 15-2. The spatial demand curve.

source. In Figure 15-2, *FT* represents the demand *D* at price *M*, in the conventional sense, at the place of origin. *LRC* is the long-run average cost curve. The shipping distance is *MF*, which represents the cost addition to the cost of production (cost equals price) at the limit of the demand curve. Beyond price *F*, no further demand exists in a spatial and quantitative sense. The new total demand curve is *FNT'*, and since any net price below *M* is below current cost of production, the amount that will be sold is *MN*.

The market radius is different for different goods. In his characteristically homely way, Lösch states:

> This we know from daily experience. Suppose one is to have a cake baked near home. Nobody would carry the heavy pan of batter across the whole town, even to the best baker. But no one would mind a long trip to leave a watch for repair with a skillful watchmaker, and one would go even outside the town to a medical specialist.[10]

Markets can be described as geographic regions, whose characteristics depend for the most part on the structure of distribution costs and the assumptions one makes about the behavior of competitors. The appropriate economic model is that of the monopolistic competitor with sloping demand curve, who maximizes profit by equating marginal cost with marginal revenue. We cannot use the purely competitive model, because each seller monopolizes his own region, and his customers cannot patronize another seller, except by paying a price which rises as the distance increases.

Lösch uses as a model a farmer who tries to sell the excess of his homemade beer to others. Although he must pay freight costs, a larger scale of operations and specialization manages to offset these costs, and he is able to sell in a circular area where the demand exists. Where demand does not

[10] August Lösch, *The Economics of Location*, trans. from 2d rev. ed. by William H. Woglam, Yale University Press, New Haven, Conn., 1954, pp. 106–110.

provide a price sufficient to cover cost, he cannot sell. With the entry of competitors, the demand curve shifts to the left, and the circular area becomes smaller. Although Lösch believed that the circular area would give way to a hexagonal pattern which would cover all unclaimed space, under most conditions of monopolistic competition, the circular form persists.[11]

Demand varies with price, and delivered price varies as the distance from the source or plant. It follows, then, that price changes will alter the shape of market regions, and one may not determine an optimum location based on a simple calculation of costs of production at different sites. Even a high-cost location may turn out to be most profitable if there are other compensating features. The market space is a grouping of consumers, not simply geographic space. It may be expanded by introducing a cheap or convenient route. It may be altered by price discrimination where freight charges are concerned, as we have already seen in Chapter 10.

When setting geographic pricing policy, a producer has three distinct possibilities:

1. Adapt to the individual situation
2. Enter into collusion with other producers so that all agree to the same f.o.b. plant price
3. Collusion regarding uniform delivered prices

Since the selling price and the freight rate on the manufactured product determine the cost (f.o.b. purchaser's plant), any reduction in either variable serves to widen the region within which the consumer may advantageously buy. Two sellers will then divide a market area, depending on their location, evenly between them. The boundary will, of course, bend backward toward the plant having higher costs or paying higher freight rates. The actual boundary cannot be generalized, since it depends on freight costs, production costs, and the kind of competition and pricing policies which may prevail.

In Figure 15-3, let d_0 be the demand curve at delivered prices, and d_1 the demand curve at f.o.b. plant prices. The vertical distance between them is the unit freight cost, which is similar to the shipping distance MF noted in Figure 15-2. Let a vertical UT intersect d_0 at the level $U'U$, indicating a uniform delivered price similar to a basing point price. UT cuts d_1 at A, the f.o.b. plant price for the quantity T, extended to H on the vertical price and cost axis. AH can then be extended to the right to meet the delivered price-demand curve d_0 at J.

If customers must pay freight of HU', then at price H, only T will be demanded instead of S'. Net revenue to the firm, however, will be equal to the area $HATO$, plus that part of the freight charges collected but not incurred. If

[11] E. S. Mills and Michael R. Lav, "A Model of Market Areas with Free Entry," *Journal of Political Economy*, vol. 72, no. 3, pp. 278–288, June, 1964.

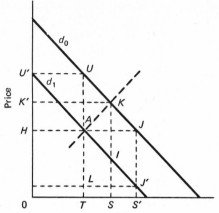

Figure 15-3. Setting geographic pricing policy.

we assume customers to be randomly distributed, the firm might retain half the freight charge, and this would be equal to AUU' or, since our demand curves are 45 degrees, AHU'.

Suppose our firm establishes a uniform delivered price as before, but this time at a price of OH. Then OS' will be sold, and the freight retained will be equal to ALJ'. This result assumes total freight of $ALJ'J$ and, once more, a random distribution of buyers.

Finally, the seller may simply offer to prepay freight as incurred, the actual charge depending on the customer's location. Prices would then be quoted as f.o.b. plant, freight inclusive, or what is sometimes referred to as cost and freight. To illustrate this effect, we draw a bisector of d_0 at K which goes through A, and from K extend lines to the vertical axis at K' and to the quantity axis at S. On the assumption once more that buyers are uniformly distributed, the quantity OS will be sold at an average delivered price of OK', which includes freight as incurred. Incremental revenue will then be $AIST$.

Note that in the first example, the firm produces quantity T; in the second, where it sells at a delivered price equal to its former f.o.b. plant price, it produces S'; while if it merely pays freight as actually incurred, it has a production level of S. Which output level maximizes net profit depends naturally on the shape of the marginal cost function. If we assume that there is available capacity and that the firm is actively seeking business, hence making excursions into distant markets, it may also be likely that it is operating in the declining portion of its marginal cost curve. Then any increase in output would serve to increase revenues more than it would increase cost, or it might even decrease marginal cost. If we assume the typical industrial standard costing method of pricing, then marginal cost is constant over a wide range of output, and the added sales would be evaluated in terms of their profit contribution.

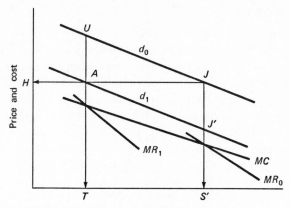

Figure 15-4. The significance of falling marginal costs.

The significance of falling marginal costs is shown in Figure 15-4. As in the preceding illustration, demand curve d_1 assumes f.o.b. plant pricing without freight absorption, while demand curve d_0 assumes that a certain maximum freight charge has been added. T is the quantity sold without freight absorption at price H, while S' is the amount sold at the same price, the seller absorbing freight charges. MR_1 intersects MC so as to make quantity T and price H equilibrium quantities, and refers to demand curve d_1. MR_0 refers to demand curve d_0 and intersects MC similarly at the equilibrium position for quantity S'. Now, should the marginal cost be rising, it is evident that the firm will not stand to gain by inducing distant buyers to trade with it, since it expands output only at the expense of rising marginal costs. In fact, the steeper the upward slope of the marginal cost curve, the less distant trading appears advantageous; the general rule would seem to be that the slope of the marginal cost curve should approximate that of the demand curve for spatial expansion to be rewarding.

The absorption of freight costs may, as Greenhut indicates, create uncertainty as to the potential size of a competitor's reach and therefore induce concentration, because "The less certain an entrepreneur is concerning the location policies of his rivals, the less willing he will be to chance a location away from the center of the market area."[12] In any case, before we can understand the interrelationship between the spatial monopolist's marginal cost and demand functions, the relation between his freight cost and his demand functions needs exploration. Since demanders are geographically dispersed, for all price variation caused by the passing on of freight costs, the greater the price change the greater the distance with which it is associated. The demand schedule is not independent of location, because the spatial distribution of demanders helps govern the shape of the curve.

[12] Melvin L. Greenhut, *Plant Location in Theory and Practice*, University of North Carolina Press, Chapel Hill, 1956, p. 40.

ON THE COST CURVE

Changes in cost which arise from expansion and relocation (apart from those which result from the employment of a new production process) stem from increases in the volume of production, changes in the prices of inputs, and changes in the cost of distribution. Input prices may also be affected by changes in the scale of output, if, to obtain increased amounts, the firm must draw from wider sources and pay higher freight costs per unit of input or higher wages.

To find a least-cost solution, we must compare the price ratios of the inputs to their marginal productivities for various output levels in the same way that we make any production level decision, except that now the price ratios of the inputs may vary with different locations. Consequently, our price ratios will have as many kinks or changes in slope as there are locations to be considered.

Figure 15-5 depicts isocost lines for labor man-hours and for material inputs (considered in total) on the x and y axis, respectively, and shows isoquants for the production process at each of two sites. At site A, labor is cheaper than at site B, while the reverse is true with regard to materials. Notice that the slope of the isocost line in Figure 15-5(a) is lower because a unit of money will buy more labor at A than under the conditions shown in Figure 15-5(b), while it will buy less materials than at B. At each site, the line connecting the points of tangency represents the path of production expansion.

By combining the two illustrations, we see in Figure 15-6 that for outputs in excess of 600 units per day, location A is preferred to location B, because the isoquants are tangent to the isocost line where the slope is less, and the lesser slope is derived from the price ratios which are obtainable by locating at A.[13] Note that the path of production expansion *EE'* rises to isoquant 400, then is interrupted, and begins at a point lower and to the right at isoquant 600.

[13] This analysis is taken from Leon Moses, "Location and the Theory of Production," *Quarterly Journal of Economics*, vol. 73, pp. 259–272. May, 1958. See also Nourse, *op. cit.*, pp. 25–28.

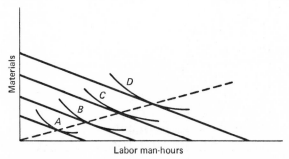

Figure 15-5(a). The effect of input prices on scale of output at site A.

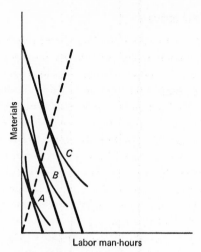

Figure 15-5(*b*). The effect of input prices on scale of output at site B.

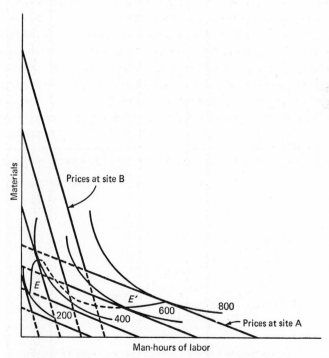

Figure 15-6. The effect of input prices on choice of location.

INVENTORY MANAGEMENT ASPECTS

We noted earlier that inventory is a substitute for other productive assets. The art of management consists of selecting the proper inventory–fixed asset mix for a range of levels of production. The amount and mix of fixed assets depends on the production function and on the technical possibilities of substitution among the items in that function. By item substitution in a production function, we refer to the method employed to obtain internal balance among different stages in the production process. Since inventory may be used at any stage, balancing involves the use of inventory, whose costs in turn depend on freight rate structures and the interrelationship between marginal production cost and marginal distribution cost.

For any given production function, the larger the volume of fixed assets employed, the larger the requirements for inventory. Under normal conditions, the level of inventory varies as the square root of total sales volume.[14] At any stage of the production cycle, and hence under various configurations of plant, it is always possible to use inventory instead of production assets, and the relationship is not necessarily predictable. Nor is the asset-labor mix predictable, since much depends on the capacities of equipment and on adjustments needed to balance production lines. In turn, the decisions made in balancing production assignments will have an effect on the amounts of inventory which are carried.

Line production frequently is operated at that level at which unit production costs are a minimum, even though the capacity is far greater than the demand for the output. Inventories then follow the typical sawtooth pattern, being built up rapidly and then worked down while the line is being devoted to the output of other items. The larger the area being served by a single production facility, the greater the need to accumulate inventories in this manner. This extra inventory requires added investment which, of course, has an opportunity cost. One balances the cost saving possible by high-level production against the costs incurred through inventory accumulation, as indicated in footnote 14.

Where investment in new plant is contemplated in order to reduce operating costs, payback calculations must take into account associated inven-

---

[14] Assuming total annual costs of inventory are the sum of carrying costs and ordering costs generally written as

$$C = a + \frac{bs}{Q} + \frac{iPQ}{2}$$

in which a is the fixed cost of ordering, b the variable costs of ordering, S annual unit sales volume, i the opportunity cost of capital, P the unit purchase price for inventory, and Q the optimum order size calculated from usage or the actual order size. The first derivative of C with respect to Q set equal to 0, provides

$$Q = \sqrt{\frac{2bS}{iP}}$$

tory carrying costs, because any machine or plant which increases production capacity will also require the carrying of added inventory. The additional inventory may arise from balances produced in short-term runs, to be used up as outlined above, or balances of purchased items needed for assembly with manufactured items. Which items will be purchased and which manufactured once more depends on the nature of the resources available to the firm as well as on economic matters such as the structure of freight rates and the availability of inputs at competitive prices. What the optimal distribution ought to be, among assets, inventory, and labor, is beyond the scope of this chapter.

FINDING THE BEST SITE

Where a firm is actually located, and where rationally it ought to be located, are, as Lösch indicates, two different matters.[15] But to Lösch, a rational location is another way of referring to a low-cost location. It can also mean a location which results in maximizing profit. On the other hand, a desire to dominate a market may overshadow short-run profit considerations. A decision as to location may be based on personal preference and may not be predictable by an economic model at all. We can only discuss here the factors which are normally part of an economically rational choice, as we have defined it.

CONSIDERING THE STAGE OF PRODUCTION

Where a particular economic activity is to be found is often dependent upon the relationship between the form of production and distance from the market. This is especially true where products may be shipped partly assembled or disassembled. It may prove advantageous to ship a large machine to a nearby purchaser in fully assembled form, taking advantage of the specialized tools and personnel of the producing plant. As the distance from the plant increases, the additional cost of shipping and handling may well offset the economies of plant assembly, so that beyond some point, depending on the form of transportation available and its tariff structure, machines will be shipped unassembled.

The particular form in which an item is shipped or produced will thus vary, depending on distance from the point of consumption. The important criterion is total cost with respect to the unit of consumption. The higher the value of the consumption item, the better it can absorb transportation charges.[16] It is commonplace that one can purchase "good" citrus everywhere except in the locality

[15] Op. cit., p. 4.

[16] Transportation overhead, except for trucking lines, tends to be high. The need to allocate this overhead to shippers plays an important part in setting freight rates, as does the awareness that items which are relatively unimportant as an input cost tend to be price inelastic with respect to demand. The consequence is a structure of freight rates which discriminates against high-value shipments, unless there are substitute transportation facilities available.

in which it is grown. By good citrus one might mean "eating oranges," for example, as compared with "juice oranges." Similarly, most wines shipped from France are of the expensive chateau or regional bottlings, which are not the kind usually consumed at point of origin. Rich and poor ores may be mined at the same place, but the better ores are available below the surface at higher cost. The poorer ore will be used locally, and the better ore will be shipped. The criterion applicable is final cost per Btu of heating, because the consumer purchases Btu's.

Stages of production which are closest to the final consumer are also closest in a locational sense. Early stages tend to be bulky, and goods need to be preserved or they require grading or standardizing, or there is a need for heavy fuel consumption to reduce them to easily transportable form. Final stages involve more value or more size with respect to weight and subdivision into smaller shipping lots, hence they are more valuable per pound as freight than are raw materials. Often they have greater perishability in style or in a physical sense, and for that reason are more costly to ship than are the materials which go to make them.

THE ROLE OF SOURCES

Production may gravitate to one place because it is tied technically to some important source of raw materials, as in coal mines or wineries, or because it is tied to the availability of certain kinds of labor skills or merchants. If, as we have pointed out, raw materials weigh significantly more than the finished product, plants will be located nearer to sources in order to reduce freight costs. Closeness to sources of materials has become less important than it was because of the lengthening of the processing chain associated with modern outputs. Hence, closeness to sources of supply has come to mean, not so much closeness to raw materials, but closeness to other producers. Unless the plants of other producers are particularly few in number or large, there is in many instances no real "source" restriction on location.

Historically, the construction of canals and railroads brought about the large-scale reorganization of industry with concomitant manufacturing economies of scale. Money was saved by cost reductions in manufacturing and by location near raw material sources. Chinitz and Vernon point out that the transportation cost reductions were actually responsible for the rise of big steel, meat-packing centers, and the like.[17] As it became increasingly hard to obtain further economies from centralization, pressure was put on transportation firms to lower rates, and producers looked for lower-cost distribution media. Nearness to raw materials, transport economies, and an evolving technology argued, they

[17] Benjamin Chinitz and Raymond Vernon, "Changing Forces in Industrial Location," *Harvard Business Review*, vol. 38, no. 1, pp. 126–136, Jan.–Feb., 1960.

say, for concentration, especially where outputs weighed less than inputs, and it was possible to obtain reductions in marginal cost which were greater than reductions in freight charges. Now that manufacturing cost reductions are not so easy to obtain, there is, they say, pressure on transportation cost to allow dispersal to markets and away from sources. The pressure against centralization came first in the form of reduced cost of short hauls and second from lowered terminal and packing costs.

THE PULL OF THE MARKET

Markets take various forms for various reasons. They may be found to be unique points, clusters, belts, and networks. An example of the unique point or *punctiform* market is Gloversville, New York, since the eighteenth century a particular source of gloves; another would be Troy, New York, a source of collars and shirts. Clusters are often dictated by the availability of raw materials in a given region, as for example coal mines or the wineries on the West Coast and in the Lake Region of New York. The location of cotton gins or grain elevators is an example of the existence of a belt. Grain and cotton may not be transported long distances without processing, and grain elevators have no economies of scale and are therefore limited as to their size. Both elevators and cotton gins would tend to disperse over a region where the raw material is available. A network is typified by bakeries, whose need is to distribute themselves as their customers because, unless artificial preservatives are used, closeness to the market is essential.[18]

Graduated, discriminatory transportation tariffs tend to group industry about input centers or markets. Tariffs were constructed in order to bring about concentrations or agglomerations which would benefit particular transportation media and lines. Transport costs tend to be lower at established material sources or at markets because lines of communication are well established and because these points generally also have a history as junctions.[19] The growth of trucking has served to reduce the impact of the differentiated rail tariff and of the junction point on industrial location.

To compare the relative advantage of locating at the market, the source, or some intermediate location, we must compare the total transportation cost per unit of output for the range of possible sites. In order to simplify the analysis, we will assume that transportation costs are proportionate to distance and that the procurement cost of input materials per unit of output rises uniformly the farther

---

[18] Lösch, op. cit., p. 411.

[19] Location near a rail junction allows the firm to avoid transshipping costs and handling charges and allows it to ship from the beginning point of a tariff, thereby obtaining the full benefit of reductions available to distant rail shipments. If it were located somewhere between, it would incur relatively higher rates on one line, handling charges at a junction point, and higher rates for a short haul on the connecting carrier.

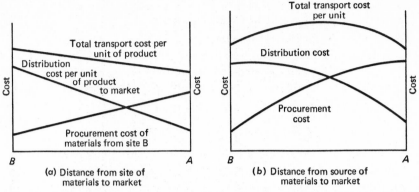

Figure 15-7. The effect of transportation costs on choice of location. (From Hugh O. Nourse, *Regional Economics,* McGraw-Hill Book Company, New York, 1968, pp. 77, 78. Used with permission of the McGraw-Hill Book Company.)

we are from its source, while the distribution cost per unit of product decreases the closer we are to the market. The total transportation cost per unit of product will then be the sum of these divergent variables, as shown in Figure 15-7(a). Allowing transportation costs to increase at a decreasing rate, as they in fact do, results in a total transportation cost per unit of output which is a minimum either at source or at market, but as indicated in Figure 15-7(b), higher at any intermediate point.[20]

The effect of locating a transshipping point between the material source and the market can be shown by locating a point X on the horizontal scale at which transportation costs take a sharp rise. Note in Figure 15-8 that in order to ship raw materials through point X, costs equal to CD must be paid, while in order to ship finished goods back through that point, costs equal to EF must be paid. The assumption here is that the firm is locating at some point between X and A, the market. In Figure 15-8 it is seen that the curves are now not smooth but stepped. The steps come about because rates are quoted in zones or brackets. Depending on the way in which the combined tariffs add up, it is possible for total transport costs to vary quite inconsistently, as the diagram shows.

There are many forms of transportation rate structure in use which alter the application of a theoretically correct analysis. For example, many times less is charged for freight moving between two terminals where there is competition between railways than for movement between one of these terminals and an intermediate point, or between two intermediate points on an alternative route where the distance is smaller.

[20] These diagrams are taken from Nourse, *op. cit.,* pp. 77, 78.

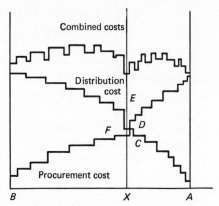

Figure 15-8. The effect of transportation zones on location decisions. (From Edgar M. Hoover, *The Location of Economic Activity*, McGraw-Hill Book Company, New York, 1948, p. 39. [Paperback edition.] Used with permission of the McGraw-Hill Book Company.)

For the most part, however, the structure of rates follows some systematic relationship to distance, and it is possible to predict the variation in these costs over geographic space. Needless to say, a complete analysis includes many other features, such as business expenses for labor, power, water, taxes, insurance, and the like, which are not uniformly variable as to distance. In addition, we must also consider that location is affected by economies of scale and other agglomeration economies.

Industrial agglomeration takes place because people are attracted to a common center. Firms find it profitable to locate close to one another, population begins to group, consumer demands begin to be satisfied more and more within a local area, and some business firms discover that they can begin to enlarge. Because junction points on rail lines are advantageous for industrial location, industrial agglomeration often occurs there. The concentration brings about other savings in transportation cost, as internal movement makes it advantageous to create road systems and public transportation.

Hoover refers to the agglomerating tendencies in retail markets which are caused by the nature of the goods. Shopping goods affords one such example. Shopping goods are defined as those which are purchased only after review of similar goods. The amount of concentration or agglomeration which can provide several sources of similar goods is limited to the distance buyers will travel. The more competitors there are in a given place, the greater the power of the place to attract potential buyers. The more buyers there are, the greater the attractiveness of the place to sellers as a place in which to locate, and the process becomes self-reinforcing beyond a certain point, depending on the average size of transaction.[21]

Industrial agglomeration results in what have been termed external economies of scale or sometimes urbanization economies. These include the improved internal transportation system referred to, but more important the growth of a trained labor supply, the presence of skilled specialists to advise firms which are unable to use such services full time, educational opportunities for employees, banks and utilities, municipal services such as fire and police protection, and so on. The development of the electronics industry during the 1950s is an apt illustration. Many firms chose to locate in the region of Massachusetts State Highway 128, the beltway around Boston. It is interesting to note, however, that these agglomerating tendencies are balanced against the cost savings which are possible by locating in other regions, and this calculation takes place at all stages of the development of a product, or line, or technology. The agglomeration in Boston was associated with the early development of electronics technology. When the technology became more or less stabilized and competitive pressures mounted, some firms found it useful to move northward into Maine communities anxious to attract industry by offering cost incentives.

EVALUATING AREA POTENTIAL

Locating a new plant requires that we price out the probable consequences of location at alternate sites. But a plant is a long-term commitment, so we are more concerned with future costs than with present costs. If we cannot be sure of future costs, then we elect those locations which promise the fastest payback, and this may explain what might otherwise appear to be unsound locational decisions.[22] The only other approach is to develop some means of detecting the forces which affect the location of industry, so that we can estimate the direction which costs are likely to take in the future. In this type of analysis there are several methods which may be of assistance. The next two sections of this chapter are concerned with two general kinds of analysis: the use of analytical coefficients and the use of input-output and flow analysis. We begin with the use of analytical coefficients.

[21] Hoover, op. cit., p. 61.

[22] The decision by General Foods in the Jell-O plant move referred to earlier in this chapter, while defensible on other grounds, apparently was based on payback considerations. ". . . the task force studies point to . . . one new Eastern plant combining all four old Eastern plants, with Calumet as it was — as the only justifiable plan. Estimated annual savings for this plan were near the top of the range for all alternatives; payback time was estimated at less than ten years; and the estimated effect on division profits at the end of 15 years was the best of all alternatives." Whitman and Schmidt, op. cit., pp. 17, 18.

ANALYTICAL COEFFICIENTS[23]

Net Shift. This coefficient is used to measure regional changes by comparing the actual proportion of some characteristic with the expected proportion if the region had varied as the entire country. For example, suppose that United States per capita income had increased by 10 percent over a period, then one might assume that the change in regional per capita income ought to be the same.

If the regional change is 8 percent, then we have a downward shift represented by the ratio 8/10, or less than unity. If the region expanded by more than 10 percent, then the net shift coefficient would be greater than 1. Such shift ratios or coefficients can be used to evaluate changes in economic characteristics such as employment, income, manufacturing value added, payrolls, or population.

Another method of depicting the distribution of regional changes is to calculate the amount presumed to result from national activity and deduct it from the reported shift, in order to highlight changes peculiar to a region. Table 15-1 shows the growth in personal income in the United States as compared with estimates.

TABLE 15-1. CALCULATION OF NET SHIFT IN PERSONAL INCOME (MILLIONS OF DOLLARS)

Item	United States	New England	Pacific
1960–1965 average	454,542	29,091	65,454
1957–1960 average	371,010	23,745	49,344
Difference	83,532	5,346	16,110
Percent change	22.5	22.5	32.0
Expected difference at U.S. rate		5,346	11,102
Net shift (actual difference less calculated)		0	5,018

Had personal income in New England grown at the rate at which the Pacific states' personal income grew, it would have reported a positive shift of $2,253 million or an increase of 42 percent. Its failure to obtain anything like the share of growth being experienced by the Pacific states is seen quite plainly.

[23] Material in this section is based on:

Walter Isard, *Methods of Regional Analysis: An Introduction to Regional Science*, The M.I.T. Press, Cambridge, Mass., 1960. See in particular chap. 7, written with Eugene Schooler.

Harvey S. Perloff, Edgard S. Dunn, Eric E. Lampard, and Richard F. Muth, *Regions, Resources and Economic Growth*, The Johns Hopkins Press, Baltimore, 1960.

Lowell Ashby, "The Geographic Redistribution of Employment: An Examination of the Elements of Change," *Survey of Current Business*, vol. 44, no. 10, pp. 13–20, Oct., 1964.

See also Hugh O. Nourse, *op. cit.*, and James A. Constantin, *Principles of Logistics Management*, Appleton-Century-Crofts, New York, 1966, pp. 491-516, for comprehensive treatments.

Location Quotient. This index compares an activity rate with the national activity rate, i.e., the ratio of a region's percentage share of a particular activity to its percentage share of some relevant base. Thus we might compare the percent that Maine fishermen are of total fishermen with the percent of total employment in extractive industries for the nation as a whole, or with the percent of employment. An index of more than 1 suggests that more than the usual concentration is to be found in that region and that the region is a net exporter. Of course, such data must take into account local or regional demands. It is entirely possible that more-than-normal output may not be exported except at penalty rates or that the industry has surplus capacity. People in the different regions may not have the same tastes or expenditure patterns, or the statistical aggregation process may introduce error into the results.

An example of the location quotient computation would be:

$$\frac{\text{Number of fishermen in Maine}}{\text{Number of fishermen in the United States}}$$

divided by

$$\frac{\text{Number of extractive workers in Maine}}{\text{Number of extractive workers in the United States}}$$

The result equals the percent of fishermen in Maine divided by the percent of workers in extractive industries in Maine, or the location quotient.

If the location quotient were, for instance, more than 1, then it would suggest that, as compared with extractive industries as a whole, there are relatively more fishermen in Maine than one might expect—a not unlikely conclusion.

Isard and Schooler also refer to a coefficient of localization which compares the distribution of employment in a given industry over various regions with the distribution of all manufacturing employment. The coefficient is calculated by summing the arithmetic deviations of the industry percentage distribution from the total manufacturing percentage distribution and dividing by 100. The coefficient varies from 0 to 1, with the greater value indicating greater concentration and hence greater exports. As we have indicated, however, the presence of a particular coefficient only presumes that exports of given lines of goods will take place. The procedure is at best diagnostic, and care must be taken to ensure that there are no extenuating or disqualifying conditions hidden by the data.

Labor Coefficient. This is Alfred Weber's ratio of labor cost per ton of output to the total weight of locally purchased raw materials and inputs per ton of output. Thus, if the labor cost per ton of output is $1,000 while the output needs 500 pounds of local materials, then the coefficient is $1,000/500 or 2. The ratio is meaningless, of course, unless it is compared with another industry or the same industry in another region, where the comparison will indicate the relative importance of labor to the industry. For another industry in the same region, the coefficient might be 5, which would mean that, all other things being equal, it is more of a labor user than is the first industry. We might also, however, use the labor cost per dollar of output.[24] The larger the cost, the greater the incentive to move the plant or industry to a low labor-cost region.

COMMODITY FLOW ANALYSIS

Commodity flow analysis is used to make preliminary distribution system designs and to define sales territories and markets. It amounts to a procedure for determining the geographic location of customers, tabulating the amount of freight each has received over some time period, and computing the weighted average ton-mile center. It is primarily a method of finding production and consumption centers by tabulating sources and destinations of freight in various classifications. Such a market pattern analysis also enables one to see the extent and form of regional interdependence.

INPUT-OUTPUT TABLES

Regional interrelationships also are analyzed with the help of input-output tables. Isard, Schooler, and Vietoriez present a hypothetical case illustrating how a three-region model might be designed.[25] Since they are presenting a case study analyzing the potential of Puerto Rico as a site for refinery-petrochemical-synthetic fiber complexes, the input-output table considers Puerto Rico and its impact on the two key regions on the mainland with which the island deals, namely, the Gulf Coast and the New York–Philadelphia–Baltimore urban industrial area. The table could be expanded to include other regions such as the Pacific Coast and the remainder of the United States. It differentiates heavy manufacturing from light manufacturing and export activities and identifies eight other sectors assumed to be local, such as power and communications, trade, transportation, insurance and rental activities, business and personal services, education, construction, and households. These simplified economies are linked through export activities. The coefficients are derived from a Bureau of Labor Statistics interindustry study for 1947, although as we have seen earlier, more recent coefficients are now available.[26]

[24] Constantin, op. cit., p. 553.
[25] The technique is the same as discussed in Chapter 3. See Walter Isard, Eugene Schooler, and Thomas Vietoriez, *Industrial Complex Analysis and Regional Development*, John Wiley & Sons, Inc., New York, 1959.
[26] An input-output grid for the electronics industry is reported in *Business Week*, Jan. 25, 1969, p. 62. The inputs are in terms of components and equipment detail not before available.

Each item in the stub, which also appears quite naturally as a column heading, is an aggregate of more specific commodity flows. For example, light manufacturing consists of food and kindred products, tobacco manufactures, textile mill products, printing and publishing, chemicals, rubber products, and leather and leather products.

The table is used to illustrate the probable effect of a given increase in a particular industry in one region upon all other regions and industrial sectors.

The critical aspect of the procedure occurs when, after accounting for the initial establishment and recording initial changes in trade flows, it is necessary to account for the secondary and subsequent flows. These subsequent flows depend on the size of the Keynesian multiplier and must of course be estimated. It is, nonetheless, a good technique for a community or region desiring to assess the impact of a new or additional industry. A firm desiring to determine whether or not to locate in a given area may find such tables useful as clues to potential volumes of business and regional sources of presently used inputs.

SUMMARY

Location analysis is an often ignored, yet important, aspect of applied economics. We began by dropping the earlier assumption that buyers and sellers were in the same place and went on to examine some of the economic characteristics of the firm that would be affected by location. Location economies affect the degree of production centralization which may be desirable as we balance distribution cost increases against decreases attainable through economies of scale. The impact of location on pricing policy and cost behavior was next discussed, as was the problem of locating new facilities. We considered the stage of production of the item produced, and its form, with respect to its distance from the market, observing that, in general, final goods are often processed closest to the customer. Conclusions depend also on the exact structure of freight rates, input prices, and the presence of all forms of economies of scale.

We next presented various methods which are available for evaluating the potential of an area as a possible plant location. Two such methods are input-output analysis and the use of analytical coefficients.

In the appendix we illustrate an application of linear programming methods to a location problem involving three plants and four markets.

Appendix. A Transportation Cost Problem

The number of locations from which to serve markets depends upon many variables, among which are the desired level of customer service. Timeliness of delivery often means as much as cost savings. It has already been pointed out that decisions as to location should be made from a total cost standpoint. Hence, all relevant forms of cost are involved. Sometimes, for example, adding to transportation cost will allow reductions in manufacturing cost. Sometimes inventory-holding cost reductions are possible, as for instance where slow-moving items are involved. The reduction from 40 sales branches to 7 distribution centers, stocking 20 percent of the items found to be relatively fast-moving, enabled Xerox Corporation to send the remaining 80 percent slow-selling items by air as needed. The unit transportation cost was increased considerably; the overall saving in expense, however, added profits of $9 million over a three-year period.[27]

Where, however, the form of transportation may not be changed, and it is desired simply to minimize the overall cost of transportation, there is a simple linear programming technique, called a transportation model, which will suffice. Essentially, the model operates to minimize the opportunity costs in the allocation process.

One way to find a good allocation is by using the Vogel approximation method of solution.[28] This procedure makes allocation decisions based on the difference between the lowest and the next-lowest transportation cost for each material source and destination.

We will assume that we have three factories and four markets, with indicated capacities and demands, and transport costs as given in Table 15-2. The problem is to arrive at an output allocation that will minimize transportation costs.

[27] "New Strategies to Move Goods," *Business Week*, Sept. 24, 1966, pp. 112–136.
[28] For additional information, see N. V. Reinfeld, "VAM: Shortcut to Mathematical Programming," *Tooling and Production*, vol. 23, no. 1, pp. 94–99, Apr., 1957, or N. V. Reinfeld and W. R. Vogel, *Mathematical Programming*, Prentice-Hall, Inc., Englewood Cliffs, N.J., 1958. The method also may be found illustrated in Thomas R. Hoffman, *Production Management and Manufacturing Systems*, Wadsworth Publishing Company, Inc., Belmont, Calif., 1967, pp. 179–180.

TABLE 15-2. TRANSPORTATION COST MATRIX

	Transportation Costs (¢ per 100 lb)				
	To Markets				Daily Factory Capacity (100 lb)
From Factories	A	B	C	D	
I	16	30	31	34	2,950
II	6	8	8	10	1,800
III	24	14	10	23	750
Market daily demand (100 lb)	2,000	1,400	700	1,400	5,500

The procedure is as follows:

1. Find the difference between the lowest and the next-lowest cost for each row and for each column.

   Answer: Rows   I   14   Columns A   10
                 II   2   B   6
                 III   4   C   2
                                       D   13

2. Select the row or column difference which is largest and allocate as much output as possible to the lowest cost cell responsible for the difference.

   Answer: **a.** Largest difference is in row I.
            b. Minimum transportation cost cell is 16 cents per 100 pounds.
            c. Allocate 2,000 (hundredweight) from factory I output to market A, leaving 950 for future allocation.
            d. Cross out column A.

3. Recalculate differences as before, but without cells in column A.

   Answer: **a.** Rows   I   1   Columns B   6
                    II   2   C   2
                    III   4   D   13
            b. Allocate 1,400 from factory II to market D, leaving 400 for future allocation.
            c. Cross out column D.

4. Recalculate differences as before, but without cells in columns A and D.

   Answer: **a.** Rows   I   1   Columns B   6
                    II   0   C   2
                    III   4
            b. Allocate 400 from factory II to market B and cross out factory II.

5. Recalculate differences, but without columns A and D and row II.

   Answer: **a.** Rows   I   1   Columns B   16
                    III   4   C   21
            b. Allocate 700 from factory III to market C and cross out column C. Leave 50 for future allocation.

6. The 950-hundredweight pounds remaining of factory I capacity and the 50 of factory III will satisfy market B and the process is over.

Note: The total transportation cost for 5,500,000 pounds by this method is $854 per day. No freight was sent from factory II to market A, even though the cost of 6 cents per 100 pounds is a minimum, since to do so would have required us to ship from factory I to market D at the prohibitive rate of 34 cents. The total cost of one such allocation, because of the opportunity costs involved, would have been $1,098.

Review Questions

1. Which costs might be relevant to the selection of a new warehouse site for a wholesale liquor distributor? How would you go about computing those costs? What predictions for the future would be relevant?

2. Evaluate the statement: "There is no unique plant location which is optimal. A number of possible orientations can occur."

3. The location histories of individual industries often appear to follow a pattern of initial concentration followed by later dispersion. Why? Under what conditions would recentralization occur? What do you suppose will be the effect of the computer on plant location?

4. It has been said that the availability of electricity would decentralize industries formerly centralized in order to use nontransportable forms of energy. What reasons would you advance to explain the fact that this prediction has apparently not come true in the United States?

5. What is the effect of basing point pricing on the location of plants?

6. What modern interpretation might you give to Adam Smith's statement that the division of labor is limited by the extent of the market?

7. Under what conditions would you recommend dispersed inventories instead of decentralized operations?

8. Rank the following in the order of importance they would assume in locating a new plant for (a) animal feed, (b) fine chemicals for the pharmaceutical industry, (c) typewriters, (d) beer, and (e) gasoline refining.

   (1) Markets
   (2) Materials and services
   (3) Labor
   (4) Transportation
   (5) Financing

   (6) Water and waste disposal
   (7) Power and fuel
   (8) Community characteristics
   (9) Individual site orientation

9. Based on the material presented in this chapter, can you formulate what might be termed principles of "good" plant location?

10. Why is accurate forecasting essential to a location decision?

11. Prepare a list of reasons why (a) cement manufacture is a market-decentralized industry, and (b) until recently, electronics was centralized.

12. What does the equimarginal principle have to do with the location decision?

13. In what way, and why, does the spatial demand curve differ from the customary demand curve (as in Chapter 5)?

14. In what way is inventory a factor in location decisions?

15. Evaluate the significance and validity of "carrying coals to Newcastle," which implies that it is futile to import a product into a region where it is produced.

16. How important is it to be close to material sources?
17. Describe the effects of discriminatory transportation tariffs in industrial location decisions.
18. Describe the various ways in which population and income data can be used in connection with the evaluation of prospective locations.
19. Redraw Figure 15-6 to take into account (a) an increase in wages of 25 percent, or (b) an increase in material costs of the same percentage. What are the location conclusions likely in each case?

Case 1. The Checkers Milling Company

Traditionally, the Checkers Milling Company had been in the animal feed business. Between World Wars I and II, it had developed a string of fifty-five mills spread across the country and an extensive dealer network. In the early 1960s, rival, but centralized, shippers of special animal feeds found that rising freight costs made it necessary to decentralize. By this time, however, the capital investment required was uneconomical compared to potential returns from other products, so they dropped animal feeds from their line, leaving Checkers as the dominant concern in an industry of about 12,000 small mills and plants.

In a reorganization from a functional (production, marketing, research, etc.) form of centralized operation, to a form of federal decentralization (such as General Motors), a consumer products division was formed around a line of dog foods as a nucleus.

Currently under study in the new consumer products division is the development of a line of desserts and foods whose principal customers would be chain retail stores and wholesale grocers. Its appeal would be largely in urban areas, contrary to the major thrust of Checkers' activities heretofore. This followed the pattern of the dog food, for which the major customer was urban rather than rural.

Large quantities of raw material inputs would come from overseas, contrary to Checkers' purely domestically oriented history in the feed business. There was some indication, however, that in the future the company would be interested in foreign feed plants. For the present, the raw material inputs would be sugar, coffee and cocoa beans, coconut, and tapioca. While sugar consumption would be expected to be fairly sizable in the future, demands would be modest until the new line really became accepted. An eventual sugar consumption rate of 250,000 pounds per day was visualized.

The sugar industry had no way of estimating whether available refinery capacity near urban centers would be adequate in the future. A new refinery, if needed, would mean that deep-water frontage would be involved. The reliance on foreign inputs also seemed to dictate a waterfront location.

The company had followed a policy of quoting f.o.b. mill prices, using its closest mill in each case as the basing point. There was some feeling that this policy would not be suitable for the new line, however.

The new plant might require about 500 people to start, with ultimate employment in the neighborhood of 1,500. Wages and salaries would follow local patterns.

QUESTIONS

1. Which factors appear most important to Checkers Milling Company in making its plant location decision?
2. To what extent are required data likely to be influenced by future events or directions?
3. Is there any basis for assuming that multiple plant operation might be preferable?
4. What appear to be the characteristics of a good location?
5. If the United States employed a directly proportionate or uniform rail tariff, would the final recommendation be different?
6. What pricing policy would be advantageous for the new consumer products line? Why?
7. How important ought payback calculations to be in making the final decision as to location?
8. Assuming the company decides to build a plant near the Gulf Coast to serve the Eastern half of the United States, could further expansion mean a change in the consumer division production policy?

Suggested Reading

Alonso, William: *Location and Land Use,* Harvard University Press, Cambridge, Mass., 1964.

Borts, George H., and Jerome L. Stein: *Economic Growth in a Free Market,* Columbia University Press, New York, 1964.

Chenery, Hollis B., and Paul G. Clark: *Interindustry Economics,* John Wiley & Sons, Inc., New York, 1962.

Fuchs, Victor R.: *Changes in the Location of Manufacturing in the United States since 1929,* Yale University Press, New Haven, Conn., 1962.

Miernyk, William: *The Elements of Input-Output Analysis,* Random House, Inc., New York, 1965.

Nourse, Hugh O.: *Regional Economics,* McGraw-Hill Book Company, New York, 1968.

Weiner, Jack B.: "Myth of the National Market," *Dun's Review and Modern Industry,* vol. 83, no. 5, May, 1964.

chapter 16
the business
decision

Somewhere in a book about economics for business decisions, there ought to be a discussion of the decision process itself. Economists have not always been concerned with the way in which decisions are made, because they presumed that it was not an interesting question. With profit maximization as a goal, entrepreneurs would naturally and simply select that course of action which produced the largest short-run return. There was never any question about sacrificing long-run interests for short-run gain since, in the usual short-run model, there were no long-run interests. Businesses operated from year to year, without assets, but with costs which arose from the operation of the firm. We do not mean that businesses had no assets, but that the factors which economists said had to be taken into account in making an operating decision did not include assets. Decisions between alternatives were to be made on the basis of the greater of the marginal returns which were possible in the short run. When the marginal returns from one course of action exceeded those from another, resources would begin to flow in that direction. When the resources moved into a particular kind of revenue-producing activity, diminishing returns would see to it that revenue began to decrease as costs rose, so that at some point it no longer was as profitable as some other course of action. At that point, the principle of opportunity cost became operative, and this indicated, as a factor in decision making, that unless another and more profitable action was taken, the differential returns forgone would have to be considered as a net cost of operation. And so our economic model decision maker set his level of output at that point at which his average cost per unit was a minimum. The only output point at which that could occur was where marginal cost equaled average cost, and opportunity costs were covered by the current line of activity. Later, the model became somewhat more complex, and we assumed that the decision maker set that price which established his output at a level at which his marginal costs were just balanced by his marginal revenue, regardless of the level of average cost for the short run. Opportunity costs naturally still had to be met, if there was to be profit maximization.

Economic analysis of the firm customarily is segmented into separate process areas dealing with consumer demand, competitive environment, and the internal environment of the firm. The analysis does not question the relevance of the economic models to the kinds of decisions which the entrepreneur must make, nor the availability of data on which he must operate. It presumes that economic information is available without cost and that it can be used as presented for making decisions. The models presume a certain world in which the estimates the entrepreneur formulates to guide future operations are outside the competitive model, as is the exact process by which he makes decisions.

Economists were, after all, not really concerned with how businesses made decisions, but how the economy operated. The flow of national income went through the business firm and made it a key sector of the economy. The firm was important because its decisions governed the amount and kind of output, and it distributed its share of national income in the form of payments for services and factor inputs, helping to set the prices at which the factors became inputs. The method by which these prices were set and the processes of allocation of resources put into motion were the focal points of inquiry, not the entrepreneurial decision-making procedure.

To deal with the problem of decision making in an uncertain environment, there has arisen a body of applied mathematics called *decision theory*, which tries to formulate analytical frameworks which take account of uncertainty. Decision theory tries to present the best way in which to make a decision under (1) conditions of risk, where the probabilities are known, and (2) uncertainty, where they are not. It presents procedures for calculating the possible arrays of outcomes, variously termed payoff tables or game payoff matrices. We used this technique in our discussion of capital budgeting. Sometimes the outcome of alternatives is depicted in the form of a branching diagram, termed a decision tree.

Decision theory is really not one theory but a method of applying a number of theories about the way in which a person might go about deciding among a number of alternatives, each having given outcomes and probabilities of success. It is, as Dale has aptly pointed out, ". . . an organized way of subdividing a complex problem into small problems of manageable size and of taking into account the decision-maker's judgment of odds and the extent to which he is willing to take a risk."[1]

[1] Ernest Dale, *Management: Theory and Practice*, 2d ed., McGraw-Hill Book Company, New York, 1969, p. 556.

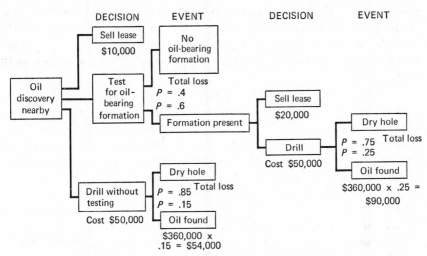

Figure 16-1. A decision tree showing the possible alternatives which might follow from the discovery of oil on nearby land. (Adapted from Chester R. Wasson, *The Economics of Managerial Decision*, Appleton-Century-Crofts, New York, 1965, p. 187.)

But decision theory is applied mathematics, and since it was developed by mathematicians, it contains procedures which are quite naturally of interest to the mathematically inclined. While it may assist managers in arriving at a decision, it does not deal with problems of organizing information so that decision theory techniques will apply. We still have to cope with the problems of (1) securing accurate information, (2) formulating the respective probabilities, and (3) interpreting the data.

In this chapter, we want to continue a line of thought first brought up in Chapters 3, 4, and 5, namely, that the difficulty in securing accurate information arises from delays, distortions, and the inherent interrelationship of much business and economic data. We want to explore the way in which the usefulness of probabilities depends on the worth of the expectations and of the available information on which they are based. Expectations, because they bias data, also affect recognition of a need for decision.

We will begin with a description of the dimensions of the decision process. We will then discuss it in terms of the data environment, the system environment to which the decision applies, and the expectations on which the need for decision was based and on which the results will be judged. Last, we will review measures of decision evaluation, taking up the concept of the effective decision.

THE DECISION PROCESS

Behind every managerial decision or action are assumptions about the accuracy and reliability of data and of system behavior, to paraphrase Douglas Mc-

Gregor, a well-known writer in the field of behavioral theory of management. From the calculation of a need for funds to expand plant, through the arrival of assets and their installation and the beginning of production and the implementation of the sales plan, activities rest on data purporting to represent the functioning of the elements and on a descriptive model of the behavior of the system.

The essence of managerial control is action to adjust operations to standard, but its basis is information. The information is a representation of underlying reality. Decisions are made on the basis of internal communication and estimates having varying degrees of accuracy, reliability, and representativeness. Biases and distortions occur because (1) top management uses a system of interpretation which is incongruent with the system on which the data are produced, (2) the data represent forecasts about the future and therefore contain errors in extrapolation, or (3) the data contain the incomplete results of prior decisions which will become fully effective at some later date, or they contain other simple errors in observation, measurement, or judgment.

In addition to the data environment, the decision process must be considered in connection with the system environment to which the decision applies. Economic activities in a firm constitute a system of decisions and processes which refer to inputs, the production function, and outputs over time. Decisions have a life cycle which is reflected in the system behavior in the form of increasing costs and declining benefits. Some of these systematic structures are cybernetic. That is to say, there is a feedback control system in which the environment causes a decision to be made, which alters some rates of activity, which in turn affects the environment. Growth, variations in operating rates, and decline are determined by flows of materials and other inputs, all having certain operating characteristics over time. When decisions are made, it is with respect to these rates and levels of activity. All flows interact with other flows, hence no decision stands alone.

Since decisions are largely concerned with changes in future activity, predictions regarding the future are needed. Predictions are involved, because the need for change is seen against a backdrop of expectations concerning the future and because the amount of change desired must be measured against future expectations. At this point we should inquire as to the bases for the formation of expectations. The environment must be perceived and interpreted. What bases are used, and with what effect?

Decision making involves selecting among alternatives often based on estimates of future costs. The alternatives generally represent different configurations or structures designed under various assumptions. Since so many elements are uncertain, it may be more significant to compute the possible range over which costs may vary, rather than particular estimates, especially as some of the alternatives may not cause significant changes in the estimates.

The last element of the decision process is that of evaluation. On what basis can we judge the merit of a decision? What is a bad decision? Is there such a thing as a good decision? How much assistance can mathematical or economic models render? Classical theories stress rationality, and in most instances this suffices. But a decision may be technically valid and still not be desirable as a course of action. For one thing, really important decisions generally include judgments of value. Second, decisions are never as precise as the figures might lead one to conclude, and the frames of reference and the standards by which one might judge change as we approach the effective date of the decision.

Ordinarily, decisions are based on a relatively small number of alternatives. Is a decision correct because it represents a choice of one of a number of possibilities which have been developed? Or is there some objective basis which relates to the problem and the effectiveness of the solution in meeting the problem, as systems analysts suggest.

To continue, is it possible for a decision to be correct as an answer to a problem, yet be incorrect in that it failed to prevent the occurrence of similar problems?

To some of the questions raised, there may well be no definite answer. For others, it may be possible to define a region within which an answer may be found.

THE DECISION ENVIRONMENT

The data and the system are the two components of the decision environment. The data represent reality and substitute for face-to-face contact. The system refers to the various forms of behavior of the elements which will be affected by the decision.

THE DATA ENVIRONMENT

The data are subject to a number of failings which effectively interfere with the job of representing what is happening. Apart from the well-known fact that data are often late, they also incorporate what are known as distributed lags. Other failings include distortion because of "noise" or random disturbances in related variables or in the data themselves, instability in the system, amplification resulting from feedbacks in the system, and human factors arising from errors in judgment and procedure. Data arising from economic life are generally interrelated, and available tools for analysis are less than satisfactory for dealing with the problem of intercorrelated information.

The Problem of Lags. Distributed lags occur when an effect on a dependent variable is not instantaneous, but is spread or distributed over a number of subsequent periods. Failure to account for lags is responsible for many serious errors in forecasting and decision making.

In the late 1960s, the failure to see that prices and interest rates were related resulted from the failure to observe that the two were in a lagged relationship. There is a lapse of time between the beginning of a sustained price rise and the commencement of a strong upward movement in interest rates. "High interest rates, in short, reflect not only inflation itself, but also the expectation that it will continue. . . . interest rates began (in 1969) to rise strongly only after inflation had continued for about 18 months."[2] Current theories of interest, on the other hand, regard the interest rate as the price of loanable funds, with no relationship to the price levels of other commodities.

A classical example of lags is given by the well-known cobweb phenomenon or theorem of economics. Here, the problem might be attributed to the farmer's reliance on stale information.[3] But it might also be attributed to the fact that crops take time to grow, and the growing process is not capable of instantaneous response. Hence, as Figure 16-2 indicates, output in year 2 is a response to price in year 1, and so on.

The best information the farmer has refers to the price P_1 last quoted in the market. He must therefore use this price, or something based on it, in making his production plans for the coming year. As often happens, all farmers responded to the lure of the high price and grew an amount q_2, represented by the point on the supply curve related to price P_1. Quite naturally, such an inflated supply forced the price down to P_2. At that price in the succeeding year, amount q_3 was produced, which in turn brought price P_3, higher than the previous year, but lower than the year before that.

[2] "A Classical Look at the 'Real' Cost of Money," *Business Week*, June 28, 1969, p. 131.
[3] Donald S. Watson, *Price Theory and Its Uses*, 2d ed., Houghton Mifflin Company, Boston, 1968, p. 370.

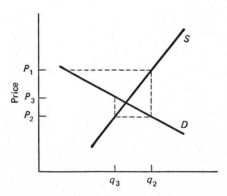

Figure 16-2. Cobweb theorem in which sequences are damped and converge because the slope of the demand curve is less in numerical value than the slope of the supply curve.

The cobweb model has been applied to the production of hogs for slaughter and shows a four-year cycle, based on reactions to past prices and partly to the use of annual data.[4]

It is possible, to cite another illustration, for factory workloads to be at a peak when retail sales are at a minimum. Eight- to ten-week delays in response are not unknown in very simple situations in which one assumes a frequency of change of retail sales of thirty-eight weeks or less. Lengthening the cycle of retail sales change in levels to fifty-five weeks results in factory orders varying at the same time as retail sales, and when the retail cycle is extended to two years, factory orders can lead retail sales by ten weeks.[5] Small variations in the rate of change of some system variables can cause the lag to be converted to a leading relationship in other economic sectors.

A well-known lagging relationship is that of the output of producers' goods with respect to consumer goods or to gross national product. The relationship is generally known as the "acceleration principle" and refers to the accelerated effect on producers' goods output of small changes in consumer

[4] Arthur A. Harlow, "The Hog Cycle and the Cobweb Theorem," *Journal of Farm Economics,* vol. 42 no. 4, p. 842, Nov., 1960.
[5] Jay W. Forrester, *Industrial Dynamics,* The M.I.T. Press, Cambridge, Mass., 1961, pp. 423–425

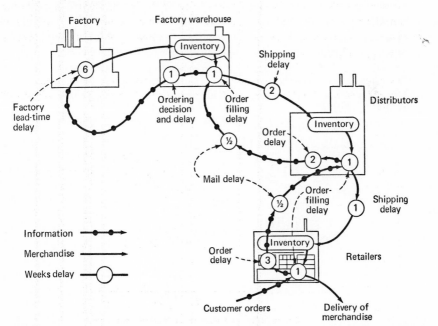

Figure 16-3. Possible lags in production-distribution system. (Adapted from *Industrial Dynamics* by Jay W. Forrester, by permission of The M.I.T. Press, Cambridge, Mass. Copyright 1961 by the Massachusetts Institute of Technology. pp. 22, 139.)

goods output. It comes about because past levels of producers' goods output were just sufficient to replace the capital goods used up each year in producing the normal level of consumer goods. Any increase in consumer goods output must then be met by increasing the capital stock or producing assets, and this demand, coming on top of the annual demand for replacement, has an amplified effect.

Inventory systems are notable for including lags simply because of cycles in review of stocks and time delays in ordering. There are many illustrations of inventory systems having this kind of structure. Typically, items in retail stock are supplied on demand. Retailers review inventory levels several times per month, perhaps every ten days, and order restocks from wholesalers. This process takes several days. The distributor takes several days to process the order and several more days to ship it to the retailer. The retailer cycle is then perhaps twenty days. The distributor's cycle is perhaps twice that, and so on back to the factory. Hence, we get the kind of lagged system to which Forrester refers in his work in industrial dynamics and which is essentially not much different from the acceleration effect. A small change in retail demand causes a response many days later in commercial channels, and the response is wavelike motion resulting from a disturbance. The more removed the basic source of inventory is from the point of consumer demand, the wider is the fluctuation in size for given fluctuations in demand. Hence, most writers conclude that improvements in the distribution-communication structure will yield better results than will be obtained by simply improving efficiency by working harder or faster. The fact that some economic variables lag and others lead is used to advantage in forecasting cycle trends.

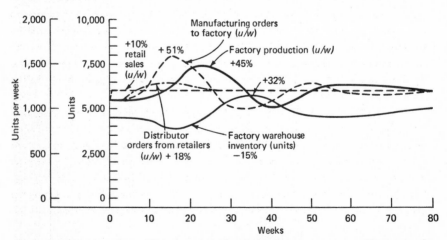

Figure 16-4. Response of some elements in a production-distribution system to a sudden 10 percent increase in retail sales. (Adapted from *Industrial Dynamics* by Jay W. Forrester, by permission of The M.I.T. Press, Cambridge, Mass. Copyright by the Massachusetts Institute of Technology. p. 24.)

Distortions. By this term we mean an out-of-proportion response to a stimulus of some kind. It may be out of proportion because noise or random disturbances enter during the communication process, because the system is unstable, because of what is termed amplification of the response, or because the management system has a built-in bias which distorts information.

By noise or random disturbance we mean unexpected variations in a system variable. Rumor of an impending price increase may cause consumers to stock up on some goods. Fear of material shortages may cause a similar run on stocks. Of less consequence might be the unexpected appeal of some style or model. Naturally, there are random "shocks" caused by political events as well.

Difficulties attributed to external independent causes on closer examination often appear to be self-generated within the business system. Forrester illustrates this point with a model in which consumer purchases are randomly distributed over time on a weekly basis. The system tends to amplify these retail sales changes so that factory output begins to rise and fall with periodicity. After a simulated four-year study, during which serious amplitudes were built up in the first year, it was found that factory production tended to cyclic behavior, which was reinforced by swings in sales volume, so that a casual observer might believe a seasonal sales pattern was natural to factory production, even though retail sales retained random fluctuations only.[6]

The usual justification for inventories is that they help to decouple successive phases of a production-distribution process. This decoupling is necessary in order to allow the production process to operate smoothly, rather than respond to every little change in retail demand. Raw material inventories are accumulated to allow buying to take place smoothly and in a planned manner. Yet many times it can be shown that inventory contributes to peaks and valleys in production. In some instances production takes place only when inventory is insufficient to meet consumer demand. Production then fluctuates more than do sales, because it is scheduled when stocks are low and is used to meet customer demand and to fill inventory at the same time. Normally, inventory should fall at times of sales peaks, rather than rise.[7]

Amplification is tied closely with what has been covered in the above sections. The acceleration effect is basically an amplification, as is the scheduling of production in response to inventory shortage. Some other kinds of systems which cause amplification are termed "threshold" systems, because a stress or need of some kind must reach a certain minimum level before corrective action takes place. When the action does occur, however, the cumulative action may far exceed the amount of action needed. Also, because of lags in the system, if the

---

[6] Forrester, op. cit., Appendix N, pp. 443–449. See also his "Industrial Dynamics— A Major Breakthrough for Decision Makers," *Harvard Business Review*, July–Aug., 1958, p. 52.

[7] Forrester, *Industrial Dynamics*, p. 209.

structure is complex, those parts of the system having the lowest resistance to change may change first.[8]

Amplification, in practice, may take place because orders are increased for purposes of speculation, or to counter slowdowns in deliveries, or when there is overordering of factory capacity because of optimistic views of the future. Ordering may be delayed, on the other hand, when it is believed that prices in the future may be lower than at present.

Distortion in decisions from information distortion is another related problem. In a sense, one who has an optimistic view of the future and who therefore orders more than he ought is acting on distorted information if, in retrospect, it seems the decision was in error. But the kind of distorted information intended is rather that which comes about when averages are substituted for actual data, or descriptive terminology is used instead of scalars.

One source of information distortion in decision making arises from the need to express uncertainty or to quantify it in order to communicate it. For example, how does one go about interpreting the statement that "There is a good chance that sales will exceed $2 million," or "There is a reasonable chance that a certain problem will be solved next year"? A well-known system for project control, PERT, requires in its original formulation the expression of an optimistic and a pessimistic time for phase completion. Unless some standard definition can be rigorously enforced, the error introduced through the use of such terms greatly impairs the usefulness of the procedure.

One manager might, when asked to evaluate the sales volume possibilities of a project, offer the opinion that the difference between an optimistic and a pessimistic estimate is a range of $500,000, while another manager might be thinking of a range of $800,000, based on an optimistic maximum of $200,000 more and a minimum of $100,000 less than the first manager. What then were the chances of achieving the higher volume of sales? The first manager had applied the term optimistic to mean a 10 percent probability of success, while the second thought it meant, at minimum, a 5 percent probability.[9]

Many firms reward subordinates who exceed budget forecasts and penalize those who fail to achieve them. A subordinate who exceeds his forecast by too wide a margin is also many times criticized for having estimated too low. A subordinate who meets his budget usually generates no comment. There would appear to be little incentive to submit an accurate assessment to top management under these conditions.

Perhaps data derived from a control system ought not be used to provide

[8] Kenneth E. Boulding, *Economic Analysis*, Harper & Row, Publishers, Incorporated, New York, 1966, vol. II, p. 201.

[9] Donald H. Woods, "Improving Estimates that Involve Uncertainty," *Harvard Business Review*, July-Aug., 1966, p. 92.

objective information for decision making, unless it is treated in a way similar to labor standard data when it is modified for effectiveness or efficiency. A decision requiring an estimate of sales might be as much as 20 percent in error unless it was corrected for the bias introduced, because the source of data was an incentive system. A district manager reporting sales volume estimates of $1 million may actually believe that sales will go 20 percent higher, but if management does not specify what it wants to do with the information, there will be control-system-induced bias.

Autocorrelation. Successive observations of economic and business data are rarely independent, but are generally highly and positively correlated with each other. Let us consider prices as an example. The current price of an item does not stand alone, but has reference to the price at which the item sold in the preceding time period and the expectation of the price that will be posted in the next time period. The demand curve, as we have already seen, is based not only on today's situation, but on the extent to which demands were satisfied yesterday, expected usages tomorrow, expected supplies, and so on.

Any price series, then, contains data which are intercorrelated, i.e., they are correlated with each other from one period to the next, because of the expectations link with adjoining time periods. By autocorrelation we mean, then, that an ordered series may be correlated with itself when the beginning point of the series is changed. A lagged series is of this kind. Since the price at time period 1 has an effect on the price in time period 2, we may establish another series based on the original, but lagged by one time period and correlate that series with the first.

A time series connected with a secular trend such as population growth of national income can be viewed in this manner, since the value in time period 2 depends on the value that obtained in time period 1. Similarly, economic time series are affected by nonsecular trends, such as cycles or seasonal effects or the general level of prices, and the latter, in turn, may be affected by the general level of income.

There are, of course, a number of ways in which the methods of statistical analysis can be used to "remove" the effect of trend or cycle. They vary from the elementary, which we have described, to the more complex given in advanced works in econometrics.[10]

If we are not so much interested in tracing the cause of the direction of the variability as the reason for its amplitude or fluctuation, then we will want to

[10] See for example, Norman N. Barish, *Economic Analysis for Engineering and Managerial Decision-making*, McGraw-Hill Book Company, New York, 1962, chap. 30, for an elementary treatment; a more complete discussion is in Edward E. Lewis, *Methods of Statistical Analysis in Economics and Business*, 2d ed., Houghton Mifflin Company, Boston, 1963, chaps. 10 and 11; or a more advanced treatment in Gerhard Tintner, *Econometrics*, John Wiley & Sons, Inc., New York, 1952, pt. 3.

relate the period-to-period changes in one variable to the changes for the same period in another variable. Since economic time series are generally auto-correlated, the straightforward correlation of two time series will not produce the intended result of demonstrating a particular kind of relationship. But relating the *differences* from period to period will succeed in demonstrating the interaction of changes in one variable on the second. If, in addition, we have distributed lags, then it may be that the changes in one variable will have to be related to subsequent changes in a second variable.

The acceleration effect in producers' goods production referred to earlier is an example of this kind of correlation analysis. If we relate the year-to-year changes in the production of producers' goods of some kind to changes in consumer goods production, we will probably not succeed in showing that any kind of relationship exists. If, however, we recall that the change in producers' goods is dependent on whether or not an increase in consumer demand is maintained as a rate, then we will want to correlate changes in producers' goods to the second differences in consumer goods output. Table 16-1 illustrates this phenomenon, with hypothetical data.[11]

TABLE 16-1. HYPOTHETICAL DATA SHOWING POSSIBLE RELATIONSHIP BETWEEN CONSUMER GOODS DEMAND AND SALES OF A PRODUCERS GOOD

Year	Consumer Goods Demand	First Difference	Second Difference	Producers Good Demand	First Difference
1	518				
2	516	− 2		33.3	
3	570	+54	+56	41.1	+7.8
4	658	+88	+34	45.0	+3.9
5	694	+36	−52	39.7	−6.3
6	735	+41	+ 5	42.1	+2.4
7	726	− 9	−50	36.5	−6.6
8	794	+68	+77	46.4	+9.9
9	838	+44	−24	43.7	−2.7

Note: Comparison of signs of the first difference columns shows disagreement in two years, while second differences of consumer goods demand relates to the first differences each year in the same direction. The initial series show virtually no statistical relationship.

THE SYSTEM ENVIRONMENT

All decisions refer to one system or another. One of the reasons why data exhibit autocorrelation resulting from lags and other distortions is that the systems are not mechanically inert, but dynamic. An often-used analogy is a

[11] The Durbin-Watson statistic is the usual test for the presence of autocorrelated errors. It is found by dividing the sum of the squares of the first differences of residuals from least-squares regression by the sum of squares of residuals. It cannot be used if the equation contains a lagged dependent variable, however.

comparison with the difference between dynamic systems and the solar system. One might also refer to plumbing or electrical systems, which are open ended, in that a source of power is applied to one end and it traverses the entire system to operate its parts, but with no other effect. The fact that they operate does not make them dynamic.

Economic systems have feedback characteristics. Decisions constantly are made based on information drawn from the operation of the system, and these decisions operate to alter the level or rate of operation, either to stabilize it or to aggravate present disturbance. An external "shock" or disturbance to the system will set in motion decisions which attempt to restore the equilibrium of the system, with varying degrees of success.

The systems have the following characteristics:[12]

1. *Continuous variation and flows.* While decisions may be separately identified, they act in a manner best characterized by a process of continuous change. Business and economic data are not discrete but continuous variables.
2. *Change as a progressive rather than an abrupt phenomenon.* Decision functions are not discrete, and even if a decision depends upon some threshold being reached, the reaction within the organizational system is gradual.
3. *Essentially nonlinear behavior.* Attained levels are reached by gradually increasing rates of activity. The forces set in motion create the acceleration which provides a velocity from which a particular position is reached.

Nonlinearity takes several forms. One form assumes that the effect on a decision is not proportional to the amount of the factor. This is a typical threshold situation in which deliveries of merchandise will take place until such time as inventories drop below a given point, when a small order will result in an out-of-stock condition and the cessation of deliveries. Alterations in the level of inventory will not affect deliveries, provided the level is more than the threshold figure.

A second form of nonlinearity involves a decision which is responsive, not to one or more variables, but to a multiple of some kind. In the foregoing illustration, the delivery of goods is not independently a function of the inventory level and of unfilled orders. If there are orders, but no inventory, there will be no deliveries. If there is inventory but no orders, there will be no deliveries. Only if there are orders and there is an inventory above a certain level will there be deliveries.

A third type has to do with various measures of operating efficiency, such as might be typified by the much-maligned U-shaped average cost function. As the maximum capacity of production equipment is approached, marginal

[12] Taken from Forrester, *op. cit.*, pp. 102, 105, 106, 453–456.

physical productivity of labor decreases up to the point of maximum physical output. Beyond this point, further doses of labor are superfluous. Hence, for some of the labor-output relationship, we have a nonlinear response which, depends on the level of capacity at which the plant is operating.

4. *Amplification caused by feedback loops.* Feedback loops operate on flows of information, orders, materials, money, personnel, and equipment, which interlock, cause change, and fluctuate. Any independent decision may change the behavior of the system, but the pattern of system interconnection, the amplification coefficients, the delays in action, and the distortion in information flows jointly determine the net result. We are dealing basically with what has been defined as the individually motivated, aspiration-governed actions of a number of participants in a dispersed environment, responding to information of doubtful reliability transmitted over a communication system having qualified clarity. Every action generates information that may form the basis of decisions at widely dispersed places having varying coefficients of amplification, depending upon behavioral and other factors.

5. *Overt and implicit decisions.* Here we refer to the distinction between conscious and unavoidable decisions. Overt decisions include many of the kinds usually defined by classical decision theory and constitute the usual management process of selecting from a known set of alternatives in accordance with some rational decision rule. The decision may be postponed at the option of the manager. An implicit decision is one which is an unavoidable consequence of a set of conditions. There may be a desire to effect a change, but the actual form the decision takes will depend on conditions beyond the control of the decision maker, hence the decision that is implicit may govern. Overt decisions normally may be implemented without significant limitations by the other elements of the system.

6. *Interconnected subsystems having a capability for internal readjustment.* Changes in stocks help to offset changes in purchasing decisions, while leaving the relationship between changes in the rate of purchasing and other system variables in a firm unchanged. A repayment rate of accounts receivable which is slow would cause the level of accounts to increase, but the rate of setting up of new accounts will not be changed because it is based on the rate at which consumers incur new obligations. Once the level of accounts receivable is adjusted for the alteration in the repayment rate, the system will operate as before.

THE DECISION PROCESS

Decisions are made with the help of expectations and from available information, acting on a closed loop in which any independent decision alters system behavior. Ordinarily, decisions are based on a relatively small number of alternatives. The organization reacts to feedback rather than attempting to forecast the environment, learning from past experience to find satisfactory answers.[13]

"Rational" decision making is supposed to contain the following six elements common to all decisions:

1. The state of nature or environment of the decision, including competition, economic conditions, and so forth.
2. The decision maker, who is influenced by the environment and by the total set of social, political, and economic forces around him.
3. The goals or ends desired. These may of course be consequences of past decisions which are not yet available because of the long planning lead time.
4. The relevant alternatives and the ability to develop alternatives.
5. The structure or ordering of the alternatives.
6. The actual choice.

In the usual closed-end classical model, the individual is faced with a number of choices and possible alternatives and must choose one. Each alternative is understood to have a unique consequence or group of possible consequences which are related. The individual is supposed to consider the possible consequences, consider his preferences as to outcomes and their contribution to his utility, and select that outcome which will maximize his total utility.

This classical closed-end model has been shown by Simon, March, and Cyert and others to be inappropriate for the modern business organization. They have advanced a model which is termed "open ended," in which the maximizing assumption is not used. This view, first advanced by Simon, holds that decisions are made when the system indicates a need, and that instead of maximizing utility or some other objective function, the decision maker "satisfices," which means he settles for that consequence which meets his level of aspiration. If no alternative appears, he reduces his aspiration level to meet attainable goals. Search activity is limited to uncovering reasonably satisfactory goals (the principle of bounded rationality), rather than a complete set of all possible alternatives as assumed by the classical closed-end model.[14]

Any number of reasons might be offered for satisficing behavior, beginning with the marginal analysis which asserts that one ought to stop looking for alternatives when the marginal benefit from revealing an alternative is less than the marginal cost of developing it. In this connection, the principle of bounded

---

[13] See Richard M. Cyert and James G. March, *A Behavioral Theory of the Firm*, Prentice-Hall, Inc. Englewood Cliffs, N.J., 1963, p. 35.
[14] See, for example, Herbert A. Simon, "A Behavioral Model of Rational Choice," *The Quarterly Journal of Economics*, vol. 69, no. 1, pp. 99–118, Feb., 1955; *Administrative Behavior: A Study of Decision-making Processes in Administrative Organizations*, 2d ed., The Macmillan Company, New York, 1957; with James G. March, *Organizations*, John Wiley & Sons, Inc., New York, 1958, p. 48; and Cyert and March, *op. cit.*

rationality asserts that the typical decision problem is, after all, so complex that one can act in a rational manner only within limits and not really in an objective sense. One simply cannot discover all alternatives or select an objectively optimal solution, only a satisfactory one. On the other hand, one might assert that in reality one is interested only in solving a problem with minimum effort.[15]

While decisions have economic characteristics, if important, they have also policy and organizational goal implications. Decisions having economic characteristics are generally simpler to defend and easier to quantify, so that the consequences are capable of being decided in an objective fashion. Decisions having ethical or goal-identified overtones are much more complex. One reason for their complexity is that judgments about their correctness and effectiveness depend on expectations of the future. The business environment is unstable, with very complex economic and interpersonal forces and distortions which are introduced by differences in the ways in which these forces are seen by the parties concerned. Under these circumstances, the organization employs expectations of the future to bring about certainty in its environment and to protect it from the unexpected in the real world. One substitutes assumptions or patterns which one believes are likely as approximations of essentially unknown future behavior.

THE FORMATION OF EXPECTATIONS

In this section, we will take up the ways in which one formulates expectations in connection with decision making. We have discussed elsewhere formal methods of forecasting the level of demand of the product. Expectations play a large part, not only here but also in many other areas in which estimates must be calculated. The ways in which people react to economic alternatives or adapt to external economic forces depend largely on the way in which they perceive the future.

EXTRAPOLATION FROM THE PRESENT

In classical decision theory, expectations are incorporated in the procedure by the decision maker's estimating the probability of some alternative occurring in the future. The decision then will maximize expected utility or profit by multiplying the profit, if the event is considered to be certain, by the probability of it really coming to pass. But this procedure begs the question, since it does not explain how expectations (probabilities) are formulated.

---

[15] Therefore, a decision maker in an organization will advance those decisions which are easiest to implement, which least concern other functional areas or decision points, and which minimize the commitment per unit of time, so that the initial area affected by the decision is kept as small as possible, but if need be can be expanded at a later date. See Paul Diesing, "Noneconomic Decision-making", *Ethics*, vol. 66, no. 1, pt. I, pp. 18–35, Oct., 1955.

Simon refers to three "naive" models of expectation formulation. The simplest assumes that the next period will be identical with the present period. The second assumes that the change that has taken place from the immediate past period to the present will operate on the present period to produce the future position. The third is somewhat more general and asserts that the future is a weighted average of recent periods. One form of this model is the so-called exponential smoothing procedure in which weights are assigned, so that the closer the period is to the present, the more heavily it is weighted as part of the overall estimate.[16]

ADAPTIVE EXPECTATIONS

P. D. Cagan has formulated a method which utilizes past experience in expectation formation to arrive at a new expectation. He employed this adaptive expectations hypothesis to explain price behavior over time. The method is to estimate the expected value of a variable for a future time period from the expected value of the previous period, by using the difference between the actual result for that period and the relevant estimate. Thus, where x_{t-1} is the expected value of x_t in time period $t-1$, and $\hat{x}_t$ is the expected value for the future time period now being calculated, the expected value $\hat{x}_t$ becomes the weighted average of past observations in accordance with the expression

$$\hat{x}_t - \hat{x}_{t-1} = (1 - \gamma)(x_t - \hat{x}_{t-1})$$

or

$$\hat{x}_t = \gamma x_{t-1} + (1 - \gamma)x_t$$

where $0 \leq \gamma < 1$

The closer γ comes to unity, the more prices from the more distant period enter the present expectations and current information is discounted.[17]

Simple substitution will allow us to compare the estimate, using the adaptive expectations hypothesis, with the three naive models given by Simon. Let us assume that the actual value in time period $t-1$ is 20, that the expectation arrived at in time period $t-1$ is 30; or one assumes prices will increase, that in reality prices increase to 23, which is not as great an increase as had been expected, and that, finally, the estimate for the future is to be calculated.

Under the first model, the future is to be exactly the same as the actual present, regardless of the relationship between the present and the past, so the expectation is 23. Under the second model, the rate of change from the past to

[16] Herbert A. Simon, "Theories of Decision-making in Economics and Behavioral Science," *The American Economic Review*, vol. 49, no. 3, pp. 253–293, June, 1959.
[17] Philip D. Cagan, "The Monetary Dynamics of Hyperinflation," in Milton Friedman (ed.), *Studies in the Quantity Theory of Money*, The University of Chicago Press, Chicago, 1956.

⁺he present is to govern the change to the future. Since the past was 20 and the present is 23, the future will be estimated at 26, or as a 15 percent increase. Under the third of the naive models, some weighting of past and present must be employed. Using the assumption that the present is weighted 70 percent and the past 30 percent, the expectation is

$$.7(23) + .3(20) = 16 + 6 = 22$$

Using adaptive expectations, prior forecasting success enters. With an a priori estimate of γ of .287, and substituting in the equation above, we have

$$30(.287) + 23(1 - .287) = 8.61 + 16.399 = 25$$

To use the method for decision-making purposes, one must of course formulate some estimate of γ in advance. Normally, this value can be estimated by analysis of past successes in estimation. Were the estimate and the actual to be available for both $t - 1$ and t periods, then the equation

$$\hat{x}_t - \hat{x}_{t-1} = (1 - \gamma)(x_t - \hat{x}_{t-1})$$

could be solved for γ and used for future estimation.

Another procedure used by Cagan is to substitute different values of γ and see which explains most readily the divergence between expectations and actual prices in a regression formula. If γ is allowed to equal unity, in which case data are accurately forecast, then the model approaches Simon's first naive model, in which the forecast is equal to the actual. The difference is of course that adaptive expectation requires proof from actual results before accepting the estimate.

The adaptive expectations hypothesis has apparently been able to describe the formation of expectations with regard to the general price level, consumer real income, and relative prices of farm products, and a method by John F. Muth has been advanced to predict simple forecasts where there are problems of autocorrelation.[18]

Common to the three naive models is the practice of adjusting the data for out-of-the-ordinary fluctuations and attempting by some kind of smoothing procedure to arrive at a trend which may be extrapolated into the future. If, however, the data are basically cyclical, extrapolation of a past trend may serve to introduce an unstabilizing influence, bringing about a system which is more likely to fluctuate erratically and become more vulnerable to random shock.[19] Needless to say, the further into the future extrapolation is attempted by these means, the more unstable the system tends to become.

[18] See "Optimal Properties of Exponentially Weighted Forecasts," *Journal of the American Statistical Association*, vol. 55, pp. 299–306, 1960, and by J. F. Muth, "The Demand for Non-Farm Housing," in A. C. Harberger (ed.), *The Demand for Durable Goods*, The University of Chicago Press, Chicago, 1960.

[19] Forrester, *op. cit.*, p. 439

An interesting comparison of the relative degree of success one might obtain with each method can be made by applying each to the prices predicted by the cobweb model. In the cobweb model, the predicted price is the actual price for the preceding period, while the actual alternates between being first below then above the estimate. The system might operate quite differently also if one started from an initial steady-state condition rather than from an assumption which did not include a prior equilibrium price.

DECISION EFFECTIVENESS

Decisions in which economics plays a part are those which involve marginal analysis or the concepts of opportunity cost. Since decision making involves the three steps of (1) recognizing a problem, (2) developing alternative solutions and (3) making a choice, we are required first to recognize the need to improve profitability, then to select some solution that can be implemented and which improves profitability. An effective decision, we will note, must properly distinguish the short run from the long, and the particular from the general. These are not areas with which economics has been concerned, yet there are economic points of view. What must be considered in order to make an effective decision from an economic standpoint? How do you distinguish an effective from a noneffective economic decision?

DRUCKER'S EFFECTIVE DECISION

Peter Drucker, who undoubtedly has done more writing and thinking in this area than most, has stated that an effective decision is one which gets down to the underlying basic situation, to distinguish the generic from what is only unique. All events, he says, except the truly unique, call for a generic solution. A generic solution is the formulation of a rule or a policy so that all future instances of the same phenomenon can be settled in the same way. The executive who treats each case on its merits and does not try to organize the unstructured situations which he sees to learn the implications of their organization is not operating effectively. He is dealing with symptoms, not underlying processes.[20]

Policy is what is sometimes referred to in the literature as a decision rule. It is a formal statement giving the relationship between information sources and resultant decisions and is therefore the key to system behavior.[21]

But policies cost money. They imply objectives, whose means are commitments of resources that ought to yield a return. Adherence to policies that have outlived their usefulness may compel the sacrifice of other more profitable opportunities, or cause a disaster. The local power failure on the New York–Ontario border that snowballed into a blackout of the whole northeastern part of

[20] Peter F. Drucker, "The Effective Decision," *Harvard Business Review*, p. 92, Jan.–Feb., 1967. See also David G. Moore, "What Decision-Makers Need," *Nation's Business*, Nov., 1960, p. 92.
[21] Forrester, *op. cit.*, pp. 96–97.

the United States in November, 1965, is cited as an example of a new event that was treated as though it was an example of an old problem to which old rules should be applied.

> The power engineers, especially in New York City, applied the right rule for a normal overload. Yet their own instruments had signaled that something quite extraordinary was going on which called for exceptional, rather than standard, countermeasures.[22]

To develop a policy, it is necessary to find a pattern or to form a concept of system behavior from information about the environment and system operation. Economic models provide a good approximation if the relevant variables are economic and the system is responsive to changes in those variables. There are areas in which economic models are not initially appropriate, in which, for example, there is noneconomic motivation behind much human behavior. Even for these, however, there are ultimate economic consequences. We are not concerned, therefore, so much with the method by which policy is determined, as with the economic consequences of that policy and the limitations of the available economic information on which the determination procedure may rely.

SENSITIVITY ANALYSIS

In order to arrive at the basis for problem solving, in order to determine what is generic and what is simply unique, one must abstract from the information that is presented and find underlying patterns of behavior. A common means of determining patterns of behavior in data is the so-called "smoothing" process. Sometimes this process is accomplished by the method of moving averages. Its purpose is to remove the random fluctuation, or noise, from a data series by averaging present data with past data. Our three naive models, and to some extent the adaptive expectations model, are essentially methods of smoothing.

Another method of determining what is important is termed sensitivity analysis. Sensitivity analysis often is undertaken in conjunction with, or arises out of, systems analysis, and so we will discuss that first.

By systems analysis, we mean a rational process of selecting one from several decision alternatives. Alternative courses of action are compared with knowledge of possible or probable consequences, on the basis of specific assumptions and with objectives and criteria carefully defined. The method assumes the use of quantitative measures, but only in order to allow the efficient use of expert intuition and judgment. Because these normally qualitative bases for decision making are quantified, the assumptions and probabilities may be examined by others, and reviewed and modified if need be, in the light of addi-

[22] Drucker, op. cit., p. 94.

tional information or later events. Basically, the method consists of the following steps.[23]

1. Formulate the problem.
2. Select the objectives.
3. Design the alternatives.
4. Collect the data.
5. Build the models.
6. Weigh cost against performance.
7. Test for sensitivity.
8. Question assumptions and data.
9. Reexamine the objectives.
10. Open new alternatives.
11. Build better models . . . and so on.

By sensitivity analysis (see step 7 above), we mean a process of experimentally determining how sensitive the attainment of a particular objective might be to changes in the amounts or kinds of resources which are available or which might be procured. By sensitivity analysis, we also infer a process of answering "what-if" questions. The method is the customary scientific one of allowing one thing to vary at a time. The aim is to determine which variables or factors are really critical or strategic to a decision. By analyzing the allocation of resources among various uses to determine how resource consumption responds to the elimination of uses, taken one at a time, we get a good idea of the incremental nature of the costs involved.

An example in opportunity costing is provided by considering a proposed product whose variable costs are $5, and which requires an increment to fixed cost of $100,000 to undertake production. If, instead, we decided to produce more of an existing product, we would obtain an increase in profit of $200,000. How can we decide which alternative to choose?[24]

Our first question is, "What profit volume is the new product likely to yield?" and our second, "How much of the new product is needed to match the profit volume of the alternative?"

Naturally, we do not know what price to charge, nor what the amount demanded will be at all possible prices. But we can estimate how many of the contemplated product must be sold to equal the profitability of the existing product at the greater volume. Since the profit we must cover is $200,000, the fixed

[23] E. S. Quade, *Systems Analysis Techniques for Planning–Programming–Budgeting,* The Rand Corporation, P-3322, Santa Monica, Calif., March, 1966.
[24] Based on material from Robert K. Jaedicke, "Analytical Techniques Useful in All Decisions," vol. 34, no. 2, of the Stanford Graduate School of Business *Bulletin.* Copyright 1965 by the Board of Trustees of Leland Stanford Junior University. All rights reserved.

cost is $100,000, and the contribution to overhead and profit (termed the profit contribution) per unit is calculated at anything in excess of the $5 variable cost, we can begin with any likely price and produce a corresponding list of volumes which would be needed.

At a hypothetical price of $10, the profit contribution is $10 less $5 (variable cost), and it will take 60,000 units to cover fixed cost and the required opportunity cost.

$$\frac{\$100,000 + \$200,000}{\$10 - \$5} = 60,000 \text{ units}$$

A table of what might be termed "breakeven demand" is constructed having the following values:

Quantity	Price	Quantity	Price
60,000	$10.00	35,000	$13.57
50,000	11.00	30,000	15.00
40,000	12.50	25,000	17.00

Now we are in a position to begin asking "what-if" questions, such as: If we charge $12, can we sell more than 40,000 units?, or at $10, could we sell 60,000 units?, and so forth. The next step might be to examine the other variables to see how much error the system can tolerate. In other words, we want to know how wrong our analysis might be and still lead to the same conclusion. Hence the term sensitivity analysis. What we want to know is how sensitive the variables are to changes in parameter values.

Take the variable cost figure for example. Notice that we have assumed a linear function. Variable cost is $5 per item. Suppose, however, that, variable costs tend to fall as output increases above minimum quantities, and then rise at higher volumes. In other words, what if variable costs were not linear, but were shaped as the economist predicts. We can test this assumption by letting out $5 cost decrease by 20¢ for every 10,000-unit increase in volume in excess of 20,000, and then increase by the same amount for volumes over 40,000. Our breakeven demand curve might then be calculated from the formula:

$$\frac{100,000 + 200,000}{x - 5 + v} = \text{specified volume}$$

where v is the cost increment or decrement associated with the selected or specified volume, and x is the calculated price or unknown in the equation.

For a supposed volume of 30,000, then, we presume that variable costs will be $5 less 20¢, or $4.80, and we solve for x, finding a new price of $14.80. At the old cost, the 30,000 units would be associated with a price of $15. The new and old price lists are as follows:

Quantity	Old Price	New Price
30,000	$15.00	$14.80
40,000	12.50	12.10
50,000	11.00	10.80
60,000	10.00	10.00
70,000	9.30	9.50
80,000	8.75	9.15

Obviously at quantities of 60,000 or less, the change in variable cost works to our benefit. At volumes above 60,000, prices will have to be higher in order to compensate for increases in marginal cost.

Suppose we look at the maximum deviation in price which occurs at 40,000 units. Suppose we decide to use the lower price on the assumption that the cost function is indeed curved and it in fact turns out to be linear. We will have lost 40¢ per item, and on a volume of 40,000, our loss will be $16,000. But our sales volume at the lower price will be $484,000, and against this volume our error will be 4 percent. What assurance do we have that our sales estimate is within that degree of accuracy? If, in fact, our estimate of probable sales has an error of plus or minus 10 percent, then probable sales volume at $12.10 would vary between 36,000 and 44,000. At the lower volume, our costs are rising so that they are 8¢ more than at 40,000 (if costs are curved), while at the greater volume they are 8¢ less.

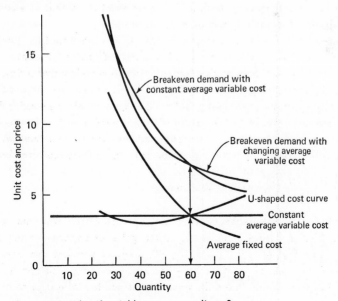

Figure 16-5. What if variable costs are not linear?

At this point, a decision tree will be of assistance. We will presume that although the sales estimate is 40,000, it might equally be likely to be as high as 44,000, or as low as 36,000. Also we will assume that although we are pricing at breakeven price (for purposes of calculation) of $12.10 on the assumption that costs are curvilinear, they may in fact be linear. We have, in other words, six combinations at which to look.

We Estimate Sales at 40,000, but They May Be	Costs May Be	Bringing Total Costs to	Against Sales of
44,000	$5.00	$542,000	$532,400
	4.52	498,880	
40,000	5.00	500,000	484,400
	4.60	484,000	
36,000	5.00	480,000	435,600
	4.68	468,480	

The worst that can happen is that we will sell 36,000 and find out that costs are linear after all. How much do we have to add to our price in order to insure that we are protected against this kind of error? The dollar loss is $480,000 less $435,600 or $44,400. At a volume of 36,000, this means we must add $1.24 to the price. At this point the question becomes, How sure can we be of selling 36,000 at a price of $13.34?

Somewhat similar are questions concerning the effect on production cost size calculations of varying the assumptions as to the amount of delay the system can tolerate in placing the order. The less the lead time allowed before beginning production, the more likely the firm is to receive an order and be unable to fill it. The more the lead time, the higher the inventory carrying costs, because it is more likely to be carrying larger amounts at any one time. Hence, we would ask questions like: If we allow eight days lead time, what would be the economic lot size? For each size we consider the tradeoff between carrying cost and stockout cost and select that lead time which minimizes total cost.

DANGERS OF SUBOPTIMIZATION

An optimum solution would mean that all possible alternatives had been considered and all possible allocations among them, taking into account all possible external factors bearing on the problem. Also it would involve complete knowledge of the preferences of the individuals concerned. Needless to say, optimums are rare.

Most decisions are made under conditions of incomplete optimization. Sometimes they are incomplete because, while they involve alternatives, they are not really likely or probable, and the calculation is not worth the effort. Sometimes they are incomplete because worthwhile alternatives were overlooked or not considered for some reason, such as:

1. If adopted, the effects, while beneficial, would be too drastic at this time
2. All possible assumptions cannot always be known.
3. All possible effects of particular alternatives cannot be significant, or the parts of the organization affected are not sensitive to changes in the variables under consideration.

When we say, then, that some decision is best, we usually write it with quotation marks as "best," because the term is relative.

Suboptimization is in a sense also incomplete, but for quite another reason. Suboptimization refers to the kind of objective that is being sought, and infers that it is a lower level in some way, that higher level objectives exist, and their consideration is within the capability of the decision maker. Suboptimization does not mean that someone deliberately avoided consulting a higher echelon, but that any organization having system characteristics must avoid emphasizing any one part more than is needed, given the end purposes of the organization. If one pursues too far the objectives of a functionally subordinate element of an organization, the results, while efficient from the point of view of the element, are not necessarily effective for the organization as a whole. The sales department, for example, is interested in maximizing sales, and the credit department is interested in minimizing credit losses. If each pursued its objective without regard for the other, the end could scarcely be effective for the entire organization.

Failure to consider the opportunity costs involved in the decisions of functionally separate departments is one important consequence of suboptimal decision making. The present value of a machine in a process department, for instance, may be its salvage value or worth in trade on a new one. The machine may have a use in a maintenance department which far exceeds the former. A decision to sell at salvage cost, then, would be suboptimal.

If we are interested in operating the entire production process at minimum cost, then we will, if possible, expand output until marginal cost is equal to average cost, at which point average cost is a minimum. If we are interested in operating the firm at maximum profit, we will probably not produce quite that much. Of course, the exact amount we will produce will depend on the nature of the demand curve. If we follow the usual marginalist assumptions, we will turn out only that quantity determined by the quantity corresponding to the equality of marginal cost and marginal revenue. Under these conditions, the production manager who tried to operate at minimum cost would be doing his company a disservice. Similarly the production manager who ignored the fact that inventory would have to be stored if not sold would reduce production cost at the price of additional inventory carrying costs and deterioration.

Suboptimization may come about simply because of wrong standards. Standards are generally thought of as being in some way optimal. In the minds of most people, there is a connection between the notion of optimum perform-ance and the attainment of a standard. But no standard can really be optimal except in regard to some particular framework or environment, and this fact is often forgotten in decision making. Standards and measures of performance must relate to the goals of the organization. If not, unless we are careful, the organization will achieve what is being measured, but it will not be consistent with proper organizational objectives.

Suboptimization often occurs also because most organizations are unbelievably complex, and in order to use modern analytical techniques, a simpler problem which can be solved is often substituted for the more complex real-life situation. Decision makers rarely solve problems without going through some process of abstraction in order to present issues in as simple a manner as possible. Unfortunately, the process often results in adopting some questionable assumptions or omitting certain features because they cannot be adequately measured or encompassed within a conceptually simple framework. Once, for example, we assume that most business data are linear, we can produce some very elegant analyses, but often without an accompanying statement of the error, which is introduced by reason of the fact that the true, underlying rela-tionship is not linear.

Where the effects are within the present operating limits, the error in-troduced by suboptimization may well be accepted as within chance error or errors in the data. Another reason for accepting error is that the sensitivity being sought is of such magnitude that errors in the data, if not self-canceling, are not significant. A 2 percent difference in the quality of an estimate is of no impor-tance if a 15 percent sensitivity is being sought. The important test is whether or not the model provides accurate prediction. Does the organization or the system react to specific decisions in the manner predicted by the model? How much faith can one have in a recommended course of action which is based on the behavior of a model?

A model purports to predict the way in which reality will change if the variable changes occur in real life as they do in the model. The model behavior, in other words, predicts real-life behavior. If we adopt a model which assumes an 80 percent correlation coefficient between a dependent and an independent variable, the quality of prediction will be quite useful for many applications in the social sciences. If, however, we are interested in forecasting the manpower needs of a facility, or the cost implications of a particular decision, and we rely on the predictive power of a relationship having the same coefficient, we ma be correct only ⅔ of the time.[25] How accurate ought a good model to be?

There are some systems in which a knowledge of what will occur in the future will have a feedback effect on the operation of the system so as to invalidate the predictive powers of the model. Usually these effects result from the fact that the model did not incorporate feedback within the system. The knowledge that a model of the economy predicts a downturn in gross national product may actually result in the downturn becoming more severe or occurring sooner than one might expect. The feedback would consist of businessmen and consumers withholding expenditures in the expectation that prices would soon fall. Naturally, this action is guaranteed to bring about the anticipated reaction all the sooner.[26]

THE SHORT RUN AND THE LONG

Sometimes distinctions are made between short-run and long-run decisions, as though they were independent. Decisions, whether described as short run or as long, always involve a commitment of resources which have opportunity costs and hence possible consequences over some period of time. All decisions, then, have implications beyond the present. One measure of an effective decision might be the extent to which the decision maker has taken account of the long-run effects of what appears to be a short-run decision.

We have seen that by far most of the products that appear in retail stores today were not available ten to twenty years ago. However, unless decisions are made concerning the outputs of today's firm, the products ten to twenty years hence will not be very different from those of today. Decisions as to plant location and characteristics today might well determine the kind of company we will have for he next five years. Decisions as to what kind of product we ought to manufacture might well determine the characteristics of the company for the next ten years. Decisions as to what kind of research and development we ought to conduct would possibly determine the kind of company we will have for the next twenty years. Long-run decisions are constantly being made, and what appear as short-run decisions must be fitted into this complex.

A century or so ago, the consequences of short-run decisions were fairly straightforward because they had few long-run implications, and it was relatively easy to see that they were closely related to the criterion of short-run profit maximization. The time interval in those days between the commitment of

---

[25] The amount of explained variation in the dependent variable would be the square of the correlation coefficient, or 64 percent.

[26] "Why Nixon's Advisers Listen Less to Models," *Business Week*, Nov. 15, 1969, p. 128, contains an interesting sidelight in the operation of feedback. Any change in monetary policy, it is stated, will be interpreted as a sign that the boom has once more begun, and the applicable models may not be able to ascertain the development of inflationary expectations. How does one incorporate expectations in a model?

resources and the evolution of results was relatively short. But with the subsequent development of more roundabout methods of production, the time interval has been steadily lengthening. As a result, the relationship between short-run decisions and possible consequences has tended to become obscure. The increasing involvement of the long run has meant that the decisional criteria also have been changing. If today we uncritically elect to employ profit maximization as an objective criterion for judging the worth of a business decision, we run the risk of neglecting its long-run implications. If the gross present worth of a course of action may be measured by the capitalized value of the flow of future expected benefits, and its profitability is calculated by subtracting from that figure the required capital investment, then profit maximization actually becomes net present worth maximization.[27]

There is reason to believe, furthermore, that one ought to distinguish between managerial objectives, which include profit maximization, or net present worth maximization, and organizational objectives, which, because they are concerned with the "what" rather than the "how," are quite something else. Within the hierarchy of managerial objectives, profit maximization tends to become overriding as an objective criterion by which we judge the ultimate success of the devices used by management to direct and to control. Organizational objectives, however, are met by judging such attainments as share of the market, growth of sales, capital asset ranking, and the like.

Lastly, where management was once conceived as simple resource commitment, it is now extended to the management of resource flows over time, and its decisions many times concern the success of alternative methods of carrying on continuing operations rather than the success of some single isolated decision. Success in management depends more and more on the degree to which we intermesh flows of information, materials, manpower, and capital assets, with inputs of new orders and financing, so that the "how" we operate is efficient. "The way these . . . systems interlock to amplify one another and to cause change and fluctuation will form a basis for anticipating the effects of decisions, policies, organizational forms and investment choices."[28]

THE IMPACT OF A PROBABILISTIC ENVIRONMENT

Even if the data with which we work represent a reality, effective decisions often depend on our ability to interpret the significance of what has taken place, simply because the environment is not a certain one. We can never be sure that what has happened will again rise from the same circumstances. "Unintended consequences and unexpected results comprise much of the history

[27] Ezra Solomon, *The Theory of Financial Management*, Columbia University Press, New York, 1963, p. 20.
[28] Forrester, *op. cit.*, pp. 8, 9

of any business."[29] We may make the same decision twice, but that does not insure that the same consequences will follow because, among other reasons, the organizational response may differ. Some random input may be present in critical quantity, and the system in attempting to respond to the decision may move in some other direction. Lags in resource availability may cause the effective date of the decision to coincide with other random occurrences which are not favorable.

It is not only that decisions have a time lag, but that the assumptions that were made about the conditions under which the decision is to be implemented, may, in the process of implementation, become altered. One of Forrester's dynamic models presumes for instance that it is not unexpected or unusual to have a nine-month delay between production planning decisions and customer reaction to advertising.[30] During that time, business conditions may change, as may factors such as income expectations which influence consumer behavior.

It is not so much that we would now want to stress the imperfection of our

[29] David G. Moore, "What Decision-makers Need," *Nation's Business*, Nov., 1960, p. 92.
[30] Forrester, *op. cit.*, p. 37.

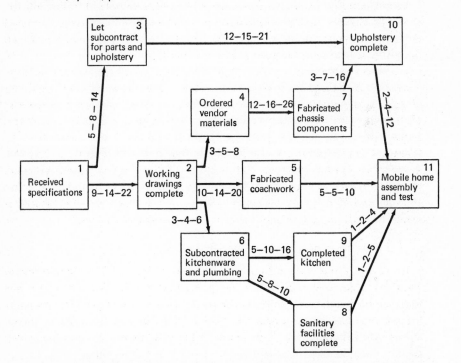

Figure 16-6. When will the mobile home be completed for certain? A hypothetical PERT diagram showing the steps which might be needed to construct a mobile home to order. Numbers above arrows refer to optimistic time, average, and pessimistic time estimated for each step, respectively

ability to foresee the future. This point has already been made. In these last pages, we want to stress the fact that once a decision has been made, we normally contemplate a certain reaction and flow of events which stem from the decision, and we assume that reaction and flow will follow some pattern we have seen before under similar circumstances. But the interaction of a decision and a business system rarely recurs. In other words, the manner in which a decision is implemented is itself a probabilistic thing, arising from the dynamics of the system, events over which no businessman has control, and pure chance.

DECISIONS CANNOT BE PRECISE

It follows from what has thus far been said that no important decision can really be precise, because of the inherent complexity of the system and the environment and the interaction of the elements over time. It is more likely that difficulties in estimation which arise from the environment will affect all decisions, rather than only some. Hence it would appear more important to be consistent in estimating, or in developing the data used on which to make decisions, than to try to look for some absolute standard of accuracy.

Where organizational goals are assessed, moreover, decisions will involve value judgments. Where there are no value elements, decisions are generally routine and can be reduced to a formula. Deciding among alternatives based on systems of values can rarely be neatly packaged, nor become routine. They are not therefore likely to be amenable to precise solution or implementation. Models, then, are classified as normative or prescriptive, because they try to describe what ought to be. Under such circumstances, whether or not a decision which has been made was an effective decision can only be determined subjectively. In any case, the future is not known and the usefulness of alternatives increases, the farther out in time one must project. As a consequence, the effective decision often turns out to be the one which delays irrevocable commitment as long as possible. In terms of the present, the effective decision may well be the imprecise decision, which offers a range of future possibilities.

SUMMARY

We have discussed the problems encountered in securing accurate information on which to make business decisions. These problems arise largely because of delays and distortions characteristic of complex human systems. Purely economic models, because they presume a certain world, have in recent years been augmented by the use of subjective probability and models of decision theory. Nevertheless, one generally pays little attention to the extent to which system instability, delays, lags, and feedbacks impair the ability of the data to represent reality. Because of the presence of these factors, data production systems are rarely improved by speeding them up. What are regarded as business and economic system characteristics, attributable to exogenous causes, may on closer examination be found to be self-generated. Economic data often suffer from autocorrelation problems, because basically all series arise from one large economic system and are more or less interdependent:

Change is a continuous process and is nonlinear, involving thresholds and feedback loops. Decisions normally feed back to alter system behavior. Because decisions are complex, often a more simplified model is substituted for reality, and in these, expectations of the future play a strong part. Distortion often arises from our failure to keep sufficient variety in our systems of control, through averaging, for instance, so that data become biased. In forming expectations, we take the past into account in varying ways, depending on how successful we have been in predicting the past.

Decisions based on economic models are generally those in which opportunity cost or marginalism play a part. These have generally been applied to short-run phenomena. Since the effective decision is one which deals with the direction of underlying processes or policies, it implies a commitment of resources to objectives that should yield a return. Sensitivity analysis and smoothing of data are two means of attempting to identify the general rule from the particular incident. Management involves the organization of resource flows in a dynamic system over time, and the older static analysis must be reevaluated to determine its limitations and usefulness.

Decisions ought rarely be considered as optimal because, first, the ultimate effects of decisions cannot be known at the time the decision is made. Second, the decision maker cannot take a truly objective view, because the standards by which he judges system efficiency are not relevant to the larger system of which he is a part, but whose dimensions he may only dimly perceive.

Review Questions

1. What part does the concept of opportunity cost play in decision making?
2. What interest does the economist really have in business decision making?
3. Lags are one of a family of factors which interfere with data in its job of representing reality. What are some of the others? What is the interrelationship among lag, amplification, and threshold?

4. There are several forms of nonlinear behavior described in this chapter. What is meant by nonlinear behavior? Why is the word "linear" significant?
5. Explain the distinction between an overt and an implicit decision with respect to the concept of nonlinearity referred to in question 4.
6. Define a "rational" decision. On what grounds has rational decision making been criticized?
7. In what way does "adaptive expectations" differ from other data-smoothing devices?
8. Apply each of the smoothing models referred to in the text to prices predicted by the cobweb model, using hypothetical data. Does "adaptive expectations" give better results?
9. In January, 1971, the Federal Communications Commission allowed the American Telephone and Telegraph Company a temporary average increase of 4 percent in rates in response to the company's request for a 6 percent average increase. The company had estimated the increased revenue to be obtained would be $250 million, instead of the $760 million hoped for. Other important factors with which it was concerned were the earnings per share of common stock and the rate of return on long-distance plant investment.

   The FCC, on the other hand, believes estimates are imprecise because of uncertainty over the exact price elasticity of demand for person-to-person and operator-dialed calls, as well as the effect on total expense of the possible reduction in the more costly operator-assisted calls.

   Set up a problem for sensitivity analysis whose results might be useful in filing for a reconsideration.
10. In connection with what kinds of decisions would you expect operations research (decision theory) to be of value and why?

Suggested Reading

Drucker, Peter F.: *The Effective Executive*, Harper & Row, Publishers, Incorporated, New York, 1967.

Evarts, Harry F.: *Introduction to PERT*, Allyn and Bacon, Inc., Boston, 1964.

Hitch, Charles J., and Roland N. McKean: *The Economics of Defense in the Nuclear Age*, Harvard University Press, Cambridge, Mass., 1960, chap. 7.

Kurnow, Ernest, Gerald J. Glasser, and Frederick R. Ottman: *Statistics for Business Decisions*, Richard D. Irwin, Inc., Homewood, Ill., 1959.

Luce, R. Duncan, and Howard Raiffa: *Games and Decisions,* John Wiley & Sons, Inc., New York, 1957.

Magee, John F.: "Decision Trees for Decision Making," *Harvard Business Review,* July–Aug., 1964, pp. 126–138.

McGregor, Douglas: *The Human Side of Enterprise,* McGraw-Hill Book Company, New York, 1960, p. 17.

Simon, Herbert A.: *Administrative Behavior,* 2d ed., The Free Press of Glencoe, Inc., New York, 1957.

index